SLAVERY ON TRIAL

STUDIES IN
LEGAL HISTORY

*Published by the
University of North
Carolina Press in
association with the
American Society for
Legal History*

Thomas A. Green,
Hendrik Hartog, and
Daniel Ernst, editors

SLAVERY
ON TRIAL

Law,
Abolitionism,
and Print
Culture

Jeannine Marie
DeLombard

The University of
North Carolina Press
Chapel Hill

Designed by Kimberly Bryant
Set in Quadraat and Quadraat Sans by Tseng Information Systems, Inc.

This book was published with the assistance of the Z. Smith Reynolds Fund
of the University of North Carolina Press.

Parts of this book have been reprinted with permission in revised form from Jeannine
DeLombard, " 'Eye-Witness to the Cruelty': Southern Violence and Northern Testimony
in Frederick Douglass's 1845 Narrative," American Literature 73:2 (2001): 245–75, © 2001
Duke University Press, all rights reserved, used by permission of the publisher; "Advocacy
'in the Name of Charity'? Or Barratry, Champerty, and Maintenance? Legal Rhetoric and
the Debate over Slavery in Antebellum Print Culture," REAL: Yearbook of Research in English
and American Literature 18 (2002): 259–87; and "Representing the Slave: White Advocacy
and Black Testimony in Harriet Beecher Stowe's Dred," New England Quarterly 75:1
(March 2002): 80–106.

Library of Congress Cataloging-in-Publication Data
DeLombard, Jeannine Marie.
Slavery on trial : law, abolitionism, and print culture / Jeannine Marie DeLombard.
p. cm. — (Studies in legal history)
Includes bibliographical references and index.
ISBN 978-0-8078-3086-4 (cloth : alk. paper) — ISBN 978-0-8078-5812-7 (pbk. : alk.
paper)
1. Slavery—Law and legislation—United States—History—Sources. 2. Slavery—United
States—History—Sources. 3. Slavery in literature. I. Title.
KF4545.S5D45 2007
342.7308'7—dc22   2006036296

cloth   11 10 09 08 07   5 4 3 2 1
paper   11 10 09 08 07   5 4 3 2 1

For MY FATHER, who read to me then
and reads with me now

CONTENTS

ILLUSTRATIONS

ACKNOWLEDGMENTS

With its rigorous yet caring faculty and its collegial graduate community, the University of Pennsylvania English Department offered a valuable model of scholarly commitment. It is typical of Penn that I now think of my dissertation readers, Houston Baker and Nancy Bentley, as good friends as well as mentors. I am also thankful to Evelyn Brooks Higginbotham, Chris Looby, Herman Beavers, Wendy Steiner, Farah Griffin, Charlotte Pierce Baker, Peter Stallybrass, and Jim English. Penn alums Teresa Goddu, Stephen Best, Stephanie Camp, Marc Stein, Kendall Johnson, Giselle Anatol, Tony Viego, Rhonda Frederick, Crystal Lucky, Melissa Homestead, Leigh Edwards, Jeremy Braddock, Hester Blum, and Martha Schoolman have become valued colleagues and fellow travelers. On my path to Penn and this book, I benefited immeasurably from the guidance of my undergraduate and master's thesis advisors: to this day, I hear the voice of G. Moses Nkondo whenever I read Frederick Douglass's *Narrative*; through his writing, his teaching, and his personal example, Ngũgĩ wa Thiong'o taught me the power of documentary literature.

Philadelphia will always be home. Not surprisingly, then, it was at the Library Company of Philadelphia that this book first began to take shape. Thanks to Phil Lapsansky (for sharing his own research, his support, and his Reese's Pieces); to Jim Green (for his good-natured friendship); and to Connie King (for tracking down lost sources). I will always find a way back to the LCP, but a Mellon Fellowship in American History and Culture and a Faculty Research Fellowship from the University of Puget Sound made it much easier to do so.

Worcester may not be home, but it's a surprisingly nice place to visit, thanks to the wonderful people one always finds at the American Antiquarian Society. John Hench will be sorely missed, but I look forward to tea and conversation with Caroline Sloat and lovely evenings in the garden with Joanne and Gary Chaison. Through its Northeast Modern Language Association Fellowship and William J. Gilmore-Lehne Stipend, the AAS supported not only research on this project but its methodological development as well in the form of two summer seminars in book history. Among the great people I met at AAS, I must single out Scott Casper, Jeff Groves, Dan Cohen, Lloyd Pratt, Ann Baker, François Furstenberg, Ethan Robey, and Patricia Cline Cohen—special appreciation to the latter two for directing me to chapter 1's indispensable James Hamlet illustrations. Farther east, the Massachusetts Historical Society, thanks to the African American Studies Fellowship I held there, yielded some of the book's richest archival nuggets.

Out west, in San Marino, I owe a huge debt of gratitude to Susi Krasnoo for helping me find a new home not once but twice while I held the W. M. Keck Foundation and Fletcher Jones Foundation Fellowship at the Huntington Library. My time at the Huntington was so productive that much of this book was drafted, as well as researched, in the old reading room. For airing me out on evenings and weekends, I thank Susi, Mary Helen McMurran, Nicole Pohl, Mona Shulman, Judith Jackson Fossett, and Dian Kriz.

It is impossible to imagine a more congenial intellectual home than the English Department at the University of Toronto. Here one finds brilliant interlocutors who—rarer still—are always up for dinner or a drink. Because the department is so large (and so consistently friendly and supportive), collective thanks will have to suffice. Special appreciation, though, goes to Jill Matus, Linda Hutcheon, and Brian Corman for their mentorship and, for their friendship, Heather Jackson, Robin Jackson, Michael Cobb, Paul Stevens, Lynne Magnusson, and Chris Warley (with Roseanne Currarino). One reason why we're all so good-humored, of course, is the generous funding U of T faculty receive; I am tremendously grateful for a Social Sciences and Humanities Research Council of Canada Standard Research Grant, several SSHRC Institutional Grants, a Connaught New Staff Matching Grant, a Connaught Start-Up Grant, and the Dean's Travel Grant. I'm also grateful to my research assistants, especially Andrea Stone.

My own tendency toward isolated introspection notwithstanding, several people have informed this study with their incisive questions and ideas. For such productive collaborative moments, I want to thank Gregg Crane, Al Brophy, Dana Nelson, and Priscilla Wald (to whom I will be eternally in debt for introducing me to Seattle's Green Lake). My participation in the Interdisciplinary Law and Humanities Junior Scholars Workshop was, simply put, a conversion experience in which this book was born again. Thanks to all of those who made the 2003 and 2004 workshops so productive but especially Katherine Franke, Nan Goodman, Clyde Spillenger, Naomi Mezey, Nomi Stolzenberg, Austin Sarat, Cheryl Harris, Robert Weisberg, Robert Post, Ariela Gross, Hilary Schor, Walter Johnson, and Jon-Christian Suggs. In addition to offering insightful feedback, Sally Gordon helped this book find a good home at the University of North Carolina Press. This study's conclusion, on John Brown, is virtually a transcription of the rich Q & A session following my talk at the Princeton University English Department's Americanist Colloquium: thanks, then, to Bill Gleason and Briallen Hopper. At the University of North Carolina Press, I am deeply grateful to Chuck Grench for his patience, guidance, and commitment to this project. Special thanks to Paula Wald and Mary Lou Kowaleski for their generous, thoughtful treatment of the manuscript and its author. I am indebted to Dan Ernst, who helped formulate more clearly the book's key legal historical concepts. It is daunting to discover that one's anonymous readers are two of the scholars one most respects; I cannot thank Brook Thomas and William Andrews enough for providing two full sets of the most sensitive, thought-provoking feedback a writer could ask for. The carefully considered readers' reports I received from Duke University Press also strengthened this project in the final stages.

This book is dedicated to my father for so many reasons; I will have to trust that he knows most of them. One, though, is that, back in 1969, he thought it completely appropriate to commence any bedtime story session with a full reading of the title and copyright pages—"because they're part of the book, too." To this day, the intersections of law, literature, and book history continue to fascinate. I have so much to thank Tina Gilbert for, from investing in this wayward teenager's education to providing such a warm, loving home for me to return to, year after year. As the three of us know too well, from houses to books, "Perfection takes time." Thanks for helping me to remember that however elusive perfection may be, it's the time spent getting there that matters.

My mother read to me, too, and her Eeyore voice remains unsurpassed. Thanks, Mom, for passing on to me the love of books and the sense of family history that Grandma Potter instilled in you. Perhaps I would have become a nineteenth-century Americanist even if I hadn't grown up immersed in stories and artifacts from that world, but I know that, without your love and support, especially during our joint return to Philadelphia, this book simply could not have been written.

Finally, my greatest thanks go to Dan White, who said, "You know, for most runners two miles is just a warm-up"—and who, three years later, was there to run the twenty-sixth mile with me. As you've read countless drafts of this book over the past ten years, you have taught me to find the exquisite pleasure of endurance—in running, in work, and in love. We've crossed so many finish lines together. Here is another one.

INTRODUCTION

During the three decades leading up to the Civil War, slavery was on trial in the United States. The legal status of the South's peculiar institution was placed on trial every time slave cases appeared on federal and state dockets, as lawyers, judges, and juries worked out the technicalities of American slave law. From the imprisonment of abolitionist editor William Lloyd Garrison for libel and the execution of slave revolutionary Nat Turner for insurrection in the early 1830s to the trials of John Brown and his Harpers Ferry co-conspirators for treason in late 1859, numerous cases involving slavery became causes célèbres in the antebellum United States. Throughout the period, throngs of men and women crowded courtrooms, overflowing into the hallways and the streets outside. Countless others followed the most minute details of famous cases through lengthy trial transcripts published in newspapers and pamphlets. Still others read portrayals of notorious cases in poetry and fiction.

Outside the nation's jammed courthouses, slavery was on trial in another sense, as a new interracial cadre of abolitionists redirected the legal tactics of earlier reformers into the mass medium of print, converting antebellum print culture itself into an alternative tribunal. In this legally saturated climate, those who wished to capture their audiences' attention resorted to the language of criminal litigation, depicting the slavery controversy as a vast, ongoing trial. But unlike actual court cases, in which enslaved people, Southern slaveholders, and Northern abolitionists tumbled about in a constantly shifting kaleidoscope of legal positions, each of the participants in this imagined trial occupied a fixed role. Figuring slavery as a crime, those who conjured this tribunal consistently portrayed slaveholders as perpetrators and defendants, slaves as victims and witnesses, white abolitionists as advocates for the slave, and the American reading public as a court of public opinion.[1]

Adopting this juridical rhetoric, former slaves like Frederick Douglass and Harriet Jacobs portrayed themselves as "eye-witness[es] to the cruelty" of slavery and their narratives as "testimony" to "what Slavery really is," while white reformers such as Theodore Dwight Weld vowed to "put slaveholders . . . through a course of cross-questioning" in an effort to "draw their condemnation out of their own mouths."[2] And even when those whom Douglass identified as "perpetrators of slaveholding villainy" refused to incriminate themselves, they obligingly assumed a defensive posture when addressing the popular tribunal.[3] "I can put my hand upon my Bible," Douglass's former master Thomas Auld declared in an effort to refute the famous fugitive's *Narrative* (1845), "and with a clear conscience swear that I never struck him in my life."[4] Following the adversarial model, both sides submitted their arguments and evidence to "the judgment of an impartial public."[5]

The purpose of this book is to demonstrate that thinking about the slavery controversy in such legal terms had far-reaching implications for the abolitionist movement, its visions of African American citizenship, and its contribution to American literature. Evoked by a variety of commentators (from abolitionist to apologist to fence-sitter) in a range of venues (from lecture stage to newspaper column to popular novel), this view of the print debate as a trial was most thoroughly elaborated — and interrogated — in the stories antebellum Americans told about slavery. Reading the autobiographies of Douglass, the sentimental fiction of Harriet Beecher Stowe, and a proslavery novel by Southerner William MacCreary Burwell alongside coverage of famous trials involving Garrison, Sojourner Truth, and Brown, I suggest that antebellum American literature cannot be fully understood without an appreciation for the popular legal consciousness that permeated both the slavery controversy and the print culture in which it was conducted. For if the trope of the trial initially helped abolitionists to direct Americans' passion for legal spectatorship into support for their cause, it eventually came to dictate the terms by which authors of different sectional and racial affiliations negotiated their print relationships. Moreover, it was precisely through such narrative appropriations of legal language and imagery that antebellum writers debated not only the status of Southern slavery but the place of African Americans in the national polity.

Laying the historical and theoretical groundwork for the remainder of this study, this introduction demonstrates why abolitionist appeals to the court of public opinion cannot be dismissed as clichés any more than Jacksonian legal spectatorship can be reduced to voyeurism. From its very beginnings, the debate over slavery occurred in "the shadow of the law," as a brief survey of representations of slaves and slavery in colonial America and eighteenth-century Britain illustrates.[6] This legally inflected Anglo-American print culture would become in the new republic an important alternative to law as a forum for black political speech. In antebellum America, the publishing strategies of the new national antislavery movement dovetailed with the avid cultivation of legal spectatorship in the cheap press, making the era's many legal crises over slavery central to the abolitionist print campaign. Viewing that campaign against the backdrop of changes in early American religion and jurisprudence (especially with respect to crime) helps us to appreciate the range of moral and political meanings that antebellum audiences could have attached to abolitionist appropriations of legal language. Read through the critical lens of cultural legal studies, abolitionists' juridical rhetoric offers a revealing nineteenth-century case study of the transformative political potential of popular legal consciousness. Yet, even as the projective capacities of narrative and metaphor allowed abolitionists to envision alternatives to African American legal exclusion, the trope of the trial also served to reinforce black discursive subordination within the movement. This introduction concludes, therefore, by addressing the impact of the adversarial model on the racial politics of antebellum abolitionism, contending that the debate's legal rhetoric could prove constraining as well as liberating, especially for African American activists and writers.

Negromantick Summons

Colonial America's earliest print colloquy over slavery was inspired by— and mired in—legal disputes. "Having been long much dissatisfied with the Trade of fetching Negros from Guinea," Salem witch-trial judge Samuel Sewall finally published his pamphlet *The Selling of Joseph* (1700) when prompted by a local slave case and proposed legislation involving slavery.[7] The debate began when John Saffin, Sewall's colleague on the bench, responded with his own pamphlet, to which he appended "A True and Particular Narrative by Way of Vindication of the Author's Dealing with and Prosecution of his Negro Man Servant for his Vile and Exorbitant Behaviour towards His Master" (1701).[8] Like Sewall, Saffin was motivated by a particular legal crisis, one that has become known as *Adam Negro's Tryall*.[9] In 1694, Saffin had written an instrument promising to manumit his slave Adam after a term of seven years, pending good behavior; when the time expired and Saffin reneged on his promise, Adam refused to labor further for Saffin and arranged for Sewall to intervene on his behalf. Obeying what he called Adam's "Negromantick Summons" to report to the influential judge's house, Saffin met with Sewall in a testy exchange that ultimately led to Saffin's print rejoinder, as well as a series of court cases in which Saffin instituted criminal proceedings against

Adam "for his turbulent, outragious and insolent Carriage towards him" and in which Adam countersued for his freedom.[10]

Adam's ultimately successful attempt to claim "all benefits of Law as an English man" may have seemed to Saffin as a kind of black magic, or necromancy, but seventy years later, a landmark English case made it harder for Anglo-American slaveholders to dismiss blacks' legal appeals for freedom as mere "Negromantick Summons."[11] In *Somerset v. Stewart* (1772), William Murray, Lord Chief Justice Mansfield, found that slavery "is so odious that nothing can be suffered to support it but positive law."[12] The Mansfield decision capped the tireless print and legal activism of British reformer Granville Sharp, whose abolitionism had originated with his participation in a series of cases involving slaves recaptured in England.[13] In a treatise that would serve as a sort of brief for the *Somerset* case, *A Representation of the Injustice and Dangerous Tendency of Tolerating Slavery; or of Admitting the Least Claim of Private Property in the Persons of Men, in England* (1769), Sharp had argued that slaveholding in England (if not the colonies) was contrary to the British constitution, common law, and equity. After submitting the manuscript version for comment to Sir William Blackstone, who was then completing his *Commentaries on the Laws of England* (1765–69), Sharp revised his polemic and circulated it in London's legal community.[14] Two years later, Sharp's American counterpart, Quaker Anthony Benezet, appended an excerpt of *Representation* to his most recent antislavery tract.[15] During the Revolutionary period, Americans' thinking about slavery was heavily influenced by the ongoing pamphlet debate over *Somerset*, much of which was reproduced in colonial periodicals.[16] In such an atmosphere, it seemed only natural for two graduating Harvard students to hold—and subsequently to publish—*A Forensic Dispute on the Legality of Enslaving Africans* (1773).

The founding of the British Society for the Abolition of the Slave Trade in 1787 placed slavery on the Anglo-American legislative agenda, largely through extralegal tactics that would resurface in the antebellum American antislavery movement.[17] Along with national petition campaigns and boycotts of West Indian sugar and rum, the society's London Committee solicited and published eyewitness accounts of the slave trade from doctors, mariners, and other Englishmen involved in the Middle Passage. Collected by Thomas Clarkson and presented to the House of Commons in hearings before the Privy Council's Committee on Trade and Plantations, this testimony was published in two abridgments.[18] Often incorporating hearsay evidence from Africans given in sign language or through interpreters, the published testimony was nonetheless exclusively that of white witnesses.[19] Compensating for this deficiency were the narratives that Afro-Briton abolitionists Quobna Ottobah Cugoano and Olaudah Equiano published respectively in 1787 and 1789.[20] Like the contemporaneous firsthand accounts published by Clarkson's two star witnesses, the Reverend John Newton (former slave-ship captain and composer of "Amazing Grace") and the surgeon Alexander Falconbridge, these works were intended to corroborate the Parliamentary testimony in favor of legislative abolition of the slave trade.[21]

At the same time that slave trade legislation was being debated in England and the jurisprudence of slavery itself was being canvassed in the former colonies, the encounters of individual blacks with the legal system figured prominently in popular American gallows literature. From Cotton Mather's pamphlet sermon for Joseph Hanno, A Miserable African, Just Going to Be Executed for a Most Inhumane and Uncommon Murder (1721), to Henry Channing's Sermon . . . Occasioned by the Execution of Hannah Ocuish, a Mulatto Girl, Aged 12 Years and 9 Months (1786) and The Life and Confession of Cato, A Slave of Elijah Mount (1803), early American crime literature disproportionately featured malefactors of color.[22] Advertised in newspapers and sold at public executions, these widely circulated broadsides and pamphlets reached the height of their popularity in the eighteenth century. At the close of the early national period, the commercialization and secularization of this crime literature coincided with broader literary trends toward Romanticism and the gothic, resulting in a shift in focus from the exemplary sin and penitence of the condemned to a highly individualized portrait of the criminal and an equally detailed account of his or her crime.[23] By the time executions had moved from crowded public fields to enclosed prison yards in the 1830s, the Puritan gallows literature tradition had yielded to a national print culture obsessed with legal spectatorship. No longer permitted direct access to the dying speeches and suspended bodies of condemned criminals, curious Americans turned to the new penny press and other cheap publications for accounts of everything from the low comedy of the local police court to the melodrama of the era's most closely watched trials.[24]

These developments in antebellum print culture were crucial to what historian Richard S. Newman has called the "transformation of American abolitionism."[25] For, just as the elite early national conjunction of legal and literary aesthetics described by Robert A. Ferguson was giving way to a more plebian amalgam of law and literature, the gradualist republican legal tactics employed by a coterie of white legal professionals were being replaced by more democratic print appeals for immediatism by a racially diverse group of male and female activists led by Garrison.[26] Following the American Revolution, antislavery organizations such as the Pennsylvania Abolition Society and the New York Manumission Society had broken with the religious and philosophical approaches of previous reformers, choosing instead to use legal strategies to achieve practical antislavery ends.[27] Boasting "an impressive group of legal minds" supported by "a second tier of legal workers who were not formally trained in the law," these organizations had sought gradual abolition through petitioning and precedent-setting antislavery litigation on both the federal and state levels.[28] In the antebellum period, the new generation of abolitionists represented by the recently formed American Anti-Slavery Society (AASS) agreed with these earlier organizations that "slavery had to be removed from the realms of private interest and long-standing custom and put on the scales of justice"; where they differed was in seeking a verdict on slavery from the American reading public rather than the bench.[29] Whereas the older organizations tried through their "legal work . . . to put the slavery issue before the nation's judicial leaders for learned and favorable decisions," the AASS placed the matter before the public by employing the extralegal print tactics of British abolitionists like Sharp and Clarkson as well as of such black pamphleteers as Richard Allen, Absalom Jones, Prince Hall, James Forten, Maria Stewart, and David Walker.[30]

While their white counterparts were depicting blacks in relation to law primarily as objects of property or as condemned criminals, these African American writers—much like their Afro-British predecessors, Cugoano and Equiano—turned to print as an alternative forum in which to speak and be heard. Excluded from professional training and legal careers in the early republic and "told by white reformers that they could not perform many of the essential duties of early abolitionism—in particular, arguing legal cases before judge and jury—African Americans were forced to fight slavery in the public realm," through pamphleteering, journalism, and other publishing activities.[31] On 16 March 1827 in the nation's first black newspaper, *Freedom's Journal*, Samuel Cornish and John Russwurm articulated this redirection of African American political energies. "We wish to plead our own cause," the editors asserted in their inaugural issue, explaining, "[T]oo long have others spoken for us."[32] Subsequent African American newspapers such as the *Weekly Advocate* and the *Northern Star and Freeman's Advocate* endorsed this extralegal strategy in their titles.[33]

Combining the print and legal tactics of earlier black and white activists both at home and abroad, immediatist abolitionists introduced a distinct form of antislavery propaganda that exploited the public's enthusiasm for legal spectatorship even as it appropriated the language and imagery of the courtroom to bring the "crime" of slavery before the court of public opinion. So doing, they participated in a legally inflected mass print culture that throve on the era's sensational court cases, such as the trials of the Reverend Ephraim Avery for the death of New England mill girl Sarah Cornell and of clerk Richard P. Robinson for the arson-murder of New York prostitute Helen Jewett.[34] At a time when "Robinsonian Juntos" sported cloaks and hats in the style of the Jewett murder suspect, and crowds vied for a splintered "relic" of the murdered prostitute's charred footboard, tantalizing legal crises involving slavery did not go unnoticed.[35] Quite the contrary: the defendants in the Amistad murder trials were featured in phrenological profiles; the Anthony Burns fugitive slave case became the basis for a patent-medicine advertising slogan; and nearly five hundred visitors flocked to Pennsylvania's Moyamensing Prison to see abolitionist martyr Passmore Williamson.[36] And just as the murder of "beautiful cigar girl" Mary Rogers inspired Edgar Allan Poe's "The Mystery of Marie Rogêt" (1842–43), the legal crises of slavery generated fiction of their own, from classics like Douglass's "The Heroic Slave" (1853), Herman Melville's "Benito Cereno" (1856), and Harriet Beecher Stowe's best-selling *Uncle Tom's Cabin* (1852) and *Dred* (1856) to now-forgotten antislavery novels like F. C. Adams's *Manuel Pereira; or, The Sovereign Rule of South Carolina. With Views of Southern Laws, Life, and Hospitality* (1853), Hattia M'Keehan's *Liberty or Death; Or, Heaven's Infraction of the Fugitive Slave Law* (1858), John Jolliffe's *Belle Scott* (1856) and *Chattanooga* (1858), and William O'Connor's *Harrington* (1860).[37]

Slavery's Legal Scandals

By the antebellum period, the court of public opinion had become, in the words of legal historian Michael Grossberg, "a second major legal arena vying with courts of law for the power to give meaning to a legal experience" by enabling the lay public to gain "social knowledge about critical issues" through the process of reaching a popular verdict on well-publicized cases.[38] Examples abound of nineteenth-century Americans shuttling strategically between the two venues, from West Point superintendent Captain Alden Partridge's newspaper challenges to the court-martial proceedings against him, to the wealthy D'Hautevilles' protracted print and legal custody battle over their son Frederick.[39] But perhaps the greatest occasions for legal spectatorship in the years before the Civil War were those involving the South's peculiar institution.

In addition to the learned print debates over the constitutional status of slavery and the gladiatorial legislative battles over the Missouri Compromise (1820), the status of slavery in Virginia (1831), the Gag Rule (1836–44), the Compromise of 1850, and the Kansas-Nebraska Act (1854), the era was marked by a series of gripping court cases involving slaves, slaveholders, and abolitionists.[40] Some, important for the precedents they set regarding slavery, interstate comity, states' rights, and constitutional law, found their way into the nation's new legal journals and law reports.[41] Other cases became what Grossberg has termed "precedents of legal experience," as crowds packed into courthouses, journalists filed daily reports, ministers thundered from their pulpits, abolitionists organized protest meetings, and printers issued an endless stream of periodicals, pamphlets, and broadsides recounting all these activities in copious detail.[42]

As Robert M. Cover noted in his classic study, *Justice Accused: Antislavery and the Judicial Process*, such litigation provided the antislavery movement with "a dramatic forum for ideology."[43] The era's longest running and most influential abolitionist newspaper, the *Liberator*, edited by Garrison and supported by a core of black subscribers who had long appreciated the importance of print as means for extralegal activism, commenced publication on 1 January 1831 with a lead story devoted to the editor's libel case. By September of the same year, the *Liberator* joined newspapers across the nation in breathless coverage of the Southampton rebellion and the subsequent trials of Nat Turner and his fellow conspirators. As with Garrison's own trial, print coverage of the cases extended into cheap pamphlets, most notably the hastily published *Confessions of Nat Turner*.[44] The controversial case of Connecticut schoolmistress Prudence Crandall received similar treatment in 1833, prompting the founding of a local antislavery newspaper, the *Unionist*.[45] In 1839 and 1841 two maritime cases, involving slave uprisings on the *Amistad* and the *Creole*, respectively, illustrated, in Cover's words, "the interaction of the antislavery movement with the courtroom and the continued search for dramatic enactment of the injustice of 'law.'"[46]

During the early antebellum period three landmark cases presaged the legal crises that would follow the passage of the Fugitive Slave Act in 1850. In *Commonwealth v. Aves* (1836), a case instigated by the Boston Female Anti-Slavery Society on behalf of Med, a six-year-old girl accompanying her New Orleans mistress on a visit to Massachusetts, Chief Justice Lemuel Shaw found that "all persons within the jurisdiction of Massachusetts were free, except fugitive slaves, because their status was controlled by the U.S. Constitution," thereby setting the precedent for Northern state courts' treatment of issues of comity and slave transit.[47] Six years later, the U.S. Supreme Court case of *Prigg v. Pennsylvania* (1842) explicitly placed the responsibility for enforcement of the 1793 Fugitive Slave Act in federal, rather than state, hands.[48] The Boston arrest of fugitive slave George Latimer in 1842 galvanized Northern resistance to the act and, combined with *Prigg*, led to the passage of personal liberty laws throughout the free states.[49] Although each of these pivotal cases prompted an outpouring of print, *Latimer*, "the Somerset case of Massachusetts," is especially noteworthy in that it led Boston abolitionists to publish a newspaper devoted to the case, the *Latimer Journal and North Star*.[50] That such a case could spark interest among diverse legal, religious, and literary readerships is suggested by the virtually simultaneous treatment of *Latimer* in a *Law Reporter* article by Peleg W. Chandler, a sermon by Unitarian minister John Pierpont, and a poem by "Mr. Latimer's Brother"—all of which appeared in pamphlet form.[51] Just as the case itself was understood to set a precedent for Northern noninvolvement in the South's peculiar institution, the tremendous print treatment it received anticipated that to be garnered by subsequent well-known cases.

Already extensive before the Compromise of 1850, print coverage of the legal crises of slavery became exhaustive after passage of the controversial new Fugitive Slave Act. Some of the most celebrated cases were those that never took place: in 1851, the same year that African American abolitionists freed suspected fugitive Shadrach Minkins from the Boston courthouse, an antislavery mob accomplished the successful "Jerry Rescue" in Syracuse, New York.[52] In the Oberlin-Wellington Rescue (1859) alleged Kentucky fugitive "John" was liberated by members of Ohio's free black community, who became martyrs to the abolitionist cause during their subsequent imprisonment.[53] Attempts to capture other fugitives produced thrilling and often violent confrontations that in turn led to carefully scrutinized trials. The Christiana, Pennsylvania, uprising of 11 September 1851, in which Maryland fugitives and free black Pennsylvanians killed slaveholder Edward Gorsuch and wounded members of his posse, led to "the largest mass indictment for treason" in U.S. history when federal prosecutors charged "thirty-eight men on 117 separate counts of 'levying war' against the government."[54] The arrest and imprisonment of Thomas Sims in 1851 and Anthony Burns in 1854 produced a siegelike atmosphere in Boston when chains and militia companies encircled the courthouse.[55] In 1856, the cases arising from fugitive Kentucky slave Margaret Garner's tragic decision to kill her children rather than see them reenslaved inspired novelists well before Toni Morrison, including Garner's own abolitionist lawyer, John Jolliffe.[56] The legal scandals of the 1850s culminated in the era's two most infamous cases, those of Dred Scott in 1857 and John Brown in 1859, each of which served in its own way as a prelude to the Civil War.[57]

Slavery's legislative and judicial crises attracted attention that was consistent with the era's other legal scandals. Registering the scrutiny the Christiana treason trials received, the beleaguered prosecutor complained, "The outside pressure is all with the prisoners," as "crowds of women and negroes openly applaud the favourable points or the wit of . . . counsel."[58] Awareness of such legal spectatorship produced its own spectacles: reporting on the trials, the *North American* noted that the "object that first struck the eye on entering the court room . . . was a row of colored men . . . alleged to have been engaged in the treason at Christiana," all twenty-four of whom were "similarly attired, wearing around their necks 'red, white, and blue' scarfs" chosen and purchased for the occasion by a local antislavery society.[59] Held in Philadelphia's Independence Hall, where additional seating and "new gas fixtures and state-of-the-art ventilating devices had been installed specially for the event," the Christiana trials, like others in the period, provided abolitionists a welcome opportunity to satisfy the nation's appetite for legal scandal while at the same time questioning African Americans' unequal status under United States law.[60]

Abolitionist propagandists worked hard to ensure that the era's exciting court cases provided Americans with both entertaining spectacles and object lessons in the jurisprudence of slavery and freedom. As Cover put it, "The story of abolitionist legal theory by no means stops in the courtroom or with the speculations of established lawyers"; quite the contrary, "after 1840 a significant part of all antislavery writing was devoted to analysis of the legal system of the United States and to its bearing on problems of slavery," indicating "the pervasive concerns of the leaders of the antislavery movement with the legal structures of slavery."[61] Whether physically present in the courtroom or vicariously present through the medium of print, spectators were well prepared to "applaud the favorable points" in the proceedings by a wide array of publications fostering popular legal knowledge of slavery.

Much of the print ephemera on slavery and law assumed readers' familiarity with due process even as it sought to sharpen their legal literacy. For example, in *The Old "Habeas Corpus,"* a song sheet published in response to the Fugitive Slave Law (1850), George W. F. Mellen, author of *An Argument on the Unconstitutionality of Slavery* (1841), put the following to the catchy, patriotic tune of "Yankee Doodle":

If that old Habeas Corpus clause
Was not so dead a letter,
Then none but criminals would be
Compelled to wear a fetter. . . .

Our social and religious rights,
As also all our civil
By this can only be preserved
From present, future cavil. . . .

Let every man and woman, then,
And every child be taught, sir,
To know the object of this law,
And then our battle[']s fought, sir.[62]

As the last stanza suggests, an important goal of such ephemera was to educate the American public about the specific points of law at issue in slavery's legal controversies. It is only through this kind of awareness, Mellen explained in a note at the bottom of the sheet, that "a true sense of what constitutes a free American citizen, shall be well understood, and what secures to every one their civil and religious privileges."[63] Such awareness, in turn, would demonstrate that "there need be no doubt, as regards the legality of slavery, in any state in this Union."[64] That this inclusive appeal for activist knowledge of law was not inhibited by separate-spheres ideology is suggested by the injunction to "let every man and woman . . . / and every child be taught" the writ's purpose.

Commensurate with this call for universal legal literacy, even potentially abstruse legal treatises targeted a diverse audience of both professional and lay readers. Part of the broader nineteenth-century explosion in legal publishing, numerous legal tomes devoted to slavery appeared between 1827 and 1862, from the abolitionist tracts of George M. Stroud and William Goodell, to a proslavery volume by Thomas R. R. Cobb, to the seemingly neutral works by Jacob D. Wheeler and John Codman Hurd.[65] Stroud's widely circulated *Sketch of the Laws Relating to Slavery in the Several States of the United States of America* (1827; revised and expanded in 1856) became even more accessible when it was published in a German translation in Philadelphia, abridged in pamphlets by other abolitionists, and excerpted in a handbill by the author himself.[66] An advertisement tipped into Harriet Beecher Stowe's popular antislavery factbook promotes attorney Goodell's *American Slave Code in Theory and Practice* (1853) as a "Companion Volume to the Key to Uncle Tom's Cabin."[67] Wheeler's *Practical Treatise on the Law of Slavery* (1837) featured prefatory "Recommendations" by both Judge H. Hitchcock of Alabama and the *New York Star*; the judge anticipated the book's usefulness for "the members, particularly of the Southern Bar of the United States," while the newspaper predicted the book's "great circulation in the Southern States, as well as those States in which the question is agitating."[68] Noting "the number and variety of the existing works on [the] subject," latecomer Hurd felt the need to emphasize that his own two-volume work on *The Law of Freedom and Bondage in the United States* (1858–62) was "designed and published as a legal or juristical treatise, or one which, if not technical, may still with strictness be called a 'law book' " —this despite Hurd's concession that "the questions considered . . . are not frequently matters of controversy in courts of law, and derive their principal interest from their connection with objects of more political and public importance."[69] In other words, its professional pretensions notwithstanding, Hurd's "juristical treatise" pertained more to the court of public opinion than the court of law. (Similarly, in his earlier *Topics of Jurisprudence Connected with Conditions of Freedom and Bondage* [1856], Hurd had acknowledged that although readers interested in "the metaphysics of jurisprudence . . . are not numerous even in the ranks of the professors and practitioners of legal science," he was sure his book would appeal to that "certainly far more numerous" group of readers "who wish to examine those legal questions, arising out of the existence of domestic slavery.")[70] Abolitionists extended the reach of these legal treatises by incorporating them into their antislavery lectures, pamphlets, and books: for example, lengthy citations from Stroud, Wheeler, or Goodell crop up in Lydia Maria Child's *Appeal in Favor of That Class of Americans Called Africans* (1833), Douglass's post-1845 speeches, the autobiographical *Narrative of William Wells Brown, A Fugitive Slave* (1847), and Stowe's *Key to Uncle Tom's Cabin* and *Dred*.[71]

Man-Stealers

Spearheaded by a print campaign that devoted countless pages to legal crises involving slavery, the new national abolitionist movement also encouraged Americans to imagine the slavery debate *itself* as a vast, ongoing trial by pitting testifying slave victims and their abolitionist advocates against Southern "perpetrators of slaveholding villainy" and "their slaveholding abettors" in the North.[72] But when the AASS charged in its Declaration of Sentiments "that every American citizen, who retains a human being in involuntary bondage is a MAN-STEALER," and that "because SLAVERY IS A CRIME," "the slaves ought instantly to be set free, and brought under the protection of law," the organization did more than simply play to the popular fascination with legal drama.[73] It also reactivated the powerful religious connotations that had attended the concept of crime since the colonial period.

In accordance with their commitment to establishing an exemplary community of visible saints, early Puritan legal reformers had revised English criminal law to bring it more closely in line with scripture. Most notably, they did so by reducing the number of property crimes considered as capital offenses, replacing them with crimes against morality specified in the Bible, such as man-stealing, rape, and adultery.[74] In the early eighteenth century, however, colonial law, like the rest of New England culture, underwent a process of Anglicization, characterized by a nascent professionalization of the bar and a corresponding attentiveness to the procedures of common law and rules of evidence.[75] Accordingly, the target of early American criminal law shifted from moral and religious transgressions to those involving property.[76] Despite these legislative changes, earlier definitions of crime continued to shape popular understandings of criminality: "While failing to build a new Christian order," legal historian Edgar J. McManus has observed, "Puritan law remained a powerful force in New England well into the eighteenth century. Crime continued to be regarded as sinful; the criminal, as fundamentally a sinner; and the criminal law, as the earthly instrument of God. The courts continued to function . . . as the custodians of public morality."[77]

The disestablishment that followed the founding of the new republic would appear to have decisively separated religion from law. But as Mark DeWolfe Howe's classic analysis of the First Amendment demonstrates, the policy of separation of church and state resulted in "a *de facto* establishment of religion" under which American Protestantism "is maintained and activated by forces not kindled directly by government"; put differently, "the ultimate strength of our religious establishment is derived . . . not from the favoring acts of government, but, in largest measure, from the continuing force of the evangelical principle of separation."[78] Far from weakening religion or separating it from law, politics, and economics, disestablishment diffused it throughout nineteenth-century American culture in the form of a pervasive, powerful Christian morality.[79]

With its emphasis on both individual and collective conversion, perfectionism, and benevolence, evangelical Protestantism would impel a host of antebellum reform movements, including abolitionism.[80] Led by charismatic attorney-turned-preacher Charles Grandison Finney—who asserted that in his sermons "a minister ought to do as a lawyer does when he wants to make a jury understand him perfectly"—the Great Revival directed the advocate's trademark skill, persuasion, to the monumental project of national moral reform.[81] Using moral suasion to call for the immediate abolition of slavery, evangelical activists invoked higher-law reasoning in their efforts to prevail upon the consciences of Southerners and other Christians in the slaveholding republic.[82] Influenced by Scottish moral-sense philosophy and Protestant revivalism, abolitionists engaged in highly visual, emotional, and often sensational storytelling to provoke activist sympathy in their audiences. In the process, they refined rhetorical strategies introduced by earlier Quaker pamphleteers such as John Woolman and Anthony Benezet, who had enlivened their antislavery polemics with searing kidnapping scenes, urgent calls for readerly sympathy, and vivid firsthand accounts of the slave trade.[83] If, during the Enlightenment, such rhetorical strategies had jibed with the empiricist stress on experience, in the nineteenth-century United States, historian Elizabeth B. Clark has argued, the movement's emphasis on personal testimony simultaneously "avoided hearsay and fulfilled the evangelical desire to hear of things close to the heart."[84] Given that for many antebellum Americans "the measure of authenticity lay in the feelings, not the intellect[,] the most striking oral and written testimony was the eyewitness account, which put the reader as close as possible to the slave's pain."[85]

By using evocative terms like "crime," "witness," and "testimony," abolitionists—who alternated between churches and courthouses for their meetings and lectures—developed an antislavery rhetoric that while adopting the culturally current grammar of the courtroom, nevertheless retained stirring religious overtones.[86] Thus, in *American Slavery as It Is: Testimony of a Thousand Witnesses* (1839), the subtitle of which implicitly grounds its appeal in a combined moral and legal authority, Finneyite Theodore Dwight Weld applied the Lockean concept of possessive individualism in order to allege that slaveholders "not only rob [slaves] of all they get, and as fast as they get it, but rob them of *themselves*, also; their very hands and feet, all their muscles, and limbs, and senses, their bodies and minds, their time and liberty and earnings, their free speech and rights of conscience, their right to acquire knowledge, and property, and reputation."[87] Cataloguing such invasions of African Americans' natural rights, Weld's best-selling factbook depicted slaveholders as "Plunderers" and "Robbers" who are "guilty" of "filching all [slaves'] time" and "stealing the use of their muscles."[88] A decade later, when Weld's anonymous tracts were being supplemented by the firsthand accounts of former slaves, abolitionist J. C. Hathaway concluded his preface to William Wells Brown's *Narrative* by insisting that slaveholders "must be treated as 'MEN-STEALERS—guilty of the highest kind of theft, and sinners of the first rank,'" adding, "Honest men must be made to look upon their crimes with the same abhorrence and loathing with which they regard the less guilty robber and assassin," for only "when a just estimate is placed upon the crime of slaveholding, the work will have been accomplished."[89] Such indictments echo

Judge Samuel Sewall's characterization of Exodus 21:16 as a "Law . . . of Everlasting Equity, wherein Man Stealing is ranked amongst the most atrocious of Capital Crimes" and the Quaker pamphleteers' insistence that the slave's purchaser was as guilty of manstealing as the trader.[90] Charging slaveholders with being "sinners" and "man-stealers" as well as "plunderers" and "robbers," nineteenth-century activists summoned the vestigial Puritan understanding of crime as a sin, the early national reformulation of crime as an invasion of property (including property in oneself), and the sentimental evangelical appeal to higher law.[91] In this way, abolitionists couched their radical calls for legal and political reform in more conventional appeals to Christian morality.

The Crime of Slaveholding

If the moral power of abolitionists' juridical rhetoric accrued from the changing meaning of crime in early American religious thought, the political significance of that rhetoric was augmented by developments in Anglo-American criminal procedure. From a legal standpoint, antebellum commentators' propensity to depict the case in front of the popular tribunal as a criminal rather than a civil proceeding was essential. Unlike Mansfield's England, where slavery had questionable legal standing at best, in the United States both the Constitution and Southern state laws protected slavery. Under such a legal regime, calling slaveholding a crime was a highly charged rhetorical gesture. An 1847 law dictionary, addressing "the distinction between a *crime* and a civil injury," explained that "the former is a breach and violation of the *public rights* and duties due to the whole community, considered as such, in its social aggregate capacity; whereas the latter is merely an infringement or privation of the civil rights which belong to individuals considered merely in their individual capacity."[92] This was because, as early national legal theorist James Wilson had explained in a paraphrase of Locke's *Second Treatise on Government*, "In the social contract, the party injured transfers to the publick his right of punishment, and . . . by the publick, the party injuring agrees to be judged," concluding, "In criminal prosecutions, the state or society is always a party," and "from the necessity of the case, it is also always a judge."[93] By contrast, he noted, in civil cases "the juridical balance . . . hangs in perfect equipoise between" the two sides.[94] Figured as a criminal rather than a civil injury, involuntary servitude involved more than a dispute over the right of individual slaveholders to hold human property versus the right of individual blacks to property in themselves; it was an offense against the entire society, and thus one that required adjudication by that society.[95] Offering much more than a challenge to "the Dangerous Tendency . . . of Admitting the Least Claim of Private Property in the Persons of Men," this construction of slavery as a crime distinguished the extralegal tactics of the antebellum abolitionist movement from those of its British antecedents.[96]

The suitability of the trial trope for the slavery controversy was further enhanced by the recent restructuring of criminal procedure. As legal historian John H. Langbein has documented, a century of incremental procedural change led to the emergence of the Anglo-American adversarial criminal trial in the 1780s.[97] Whereas earlier English criminal trials tended to be speedy affairs in which the defendant, and usually the plaintiff, represented him- or herself before the judge and jury, who frequently worked together to reach a decision, from the mid- to the late eighteenth century, the "lawyer-conducted criminal trial" gradually became the norm.[98] In America, James D. Rice concurs, the professionalization of the bar gave rise to " 'complex' criminal trials which were marked by closer cross-examinations, increasingly well-defined extra-statutory rules of evidence, multiple counsel, large numbers of witnesses, extended addresses to the jury, and a more thoroughly adversarial spirit than in 'traditional' trials," which were more of "a collaborative enterprise."[99] As they grew longer in duration and more complex in format, American criminal trials also became increasingly contingent, largely as a result of the elimination of highly technical common-law pleading. The capaciousness of the new complex trial accorded well with the protracted debate over slavery, with its arguments and counterarguments, testimonial and documentary proofs, numerous participants, and persistent appeals to an adjudicative reading public. And although daunting for actual litigants, the variability and uncertainty that had been introduced into criminal trials in the early republic correlated easily with the unpredictable and fluid nature of the free-floating antebellum debate over slavery, in which multiple participants simultaneously addressed a wide range of issues through a variety of arguments drawn from a continuous accumulation of evidence.

Indeed, this cumulative impulse is one of the most striking characteristics of the abolitionist print campaign. The AASS, for example, presented American Slavery as It Is, compiled from over twenty-thousand newspaper clippings, as the beginning, rather than the end, of a massive documentary project. In its prefatory note the society's executive committee invited "all who have had personal knowledge of the condition of slaves in any of the states of this Union, to forward their testimony," exhorting, "let no one withhold his testimony because others have already testified to similar facts."[100] They were careful to explain that "the value of testimony is by no means to be measured by the *novelty* of the horrors which it describes," stressing that "*corroborative testimony,* —facts, similar to those established by the testimony of others, — is highly valuable."[101] A similar urge to contribute additional "facts" to the case against slavery inspired Douglass to revise and expand his *Narrative* as *My Bondage and My Freedom* (1855); moved Stowe to supplement *Uncle Tom's Cabin* with her nonfiction *Key to Uncle Tom's Cabin; Presenting the Original Facts and Documents upon Which the Story is Founded. Together with Corroborative Statements Verifying the Truth of the Work*; and prompted Solomon Northup to present his own narrative, *Twelve Years a Slave* (1853), as "Another Key to Uncle Tom's Cabin."[102] In a period when "newly discovered evidence became . . . 'the most common cause for granting new trials,'" the adversarial criminal trial was the ideal metaphor for the slavery controversy as it continually unfolded in the decades before the Civil War.[103]

As their enthusiastic gathering of antislavery evidence suggests (and as Finney's motto underscores), abolitionists' strategic deployment of legal language and imagery was consistent with the Garrisonian commitment to moral suasion. Under the adversary system, the collection and presentation of evidence are highly partisan undertakings. Persuasion thus stands at the heart of the criminal trial. In his *Rationale of Judicial Evidence* (1827), Jeremy Bentham defined "evidence" as "any matter of fact, the effect, tendency, or design of which, when presented to the mind, is to produce a persuasion concerning the existence of some other matter of fact."[104] However problematic it may have been in the courtroom, it was this emphasis on the discovery process that made the criminal trial such an attractive model for the highly rhetorical print debate over slavery.[105]

Consistent with the legalization of nineteenth-century American culture, the figure of the trial was ultimately less important as a symbol of dispute resolution than as a paradigm of adversarial procedure.[106] Commenting on those "major controversial trials that immediately grow into public or political 'affairs,'" critic Shoshana Felman has observed that such cases' "symbolic impact is immediately perceived in the intensity with which they tend at once to *focus* public discourse and to *polarize* public opinion."[107] If Felman's observation helps to clarify the American compulsion toward legal spectatorship, it also bears on the antebellum disposition to imagine the slavery debate as a trial. Abolitionists used legal language primarily as an effective rhetorical strategy for focusing public discourse over slavery and consolidating popular sentiment against the South's peculiar institution; thus, they emphasized "charges" against or "indictments" of slaveholders, with the ultimate goal of a unanimous guilty verdict in the court of public opinion. Seldom did they specify the sentence appropriate to such a verdict. Garrison himself was inconsistent: in his first antislavery speech he sought only "to obtain the liberation" of slaves, whereas in an early editorial, he stridently demanded that those complicit in the crime of slavery be sentenced to lifetime solitary confinement.[108] Garrison's call for incarceration was anomalous; on those occasions when abolitionists projected punishment for slaveholders and their accomplices, they tended to do so in religious rather than legal terms. Moral suasionist references to the Day of Judgment and jeremiads prophesying divine vengeance for the national sin of slavery had long been staples of antislavery rhetoric. But, like the Puritan sermons from which they were in part derived, such appeals sought to reinforce, not supplant, Earthly justice by invoking the divine tribunal.[109] Crucially, the verdict pursued was a profoundly secular one. It was not to God that antebellum abolitionists directed their arguments and evidence—after all, divine judgment was both omniscient and inevitable. Instead, they sought censure for the crime of slaveholding from the American reading public. As radical, black pamphleteer David Walker proclaimed in 1829, "I shall give the world a development of facts, which are already witnessed in the courts of heaven."[110]

Atrocious Judges

But if the new criminal trial seemed perfectly designed to accommodate the print controversy over slavery, it, along with other changes in antebellum jurisprudence, also heightened Jacksonian concerns about the judiciary as a potential threat to popular sovereignty. After all, one of the hallmarks of the adversarial process was the increased involvement of legal professionals and the diminished participation of lay people, from individual litigants to the jury itself.[111] Thus, even as they laid claim to the rhetoric of the criminal courtroom, abolitionists effected a change of venue, from the court of law to the court of public opinion, symbolically restoring lay participation to the legal process. As noted earlier, British abolitionists had amassed "evidence" about the slave trade to influence legislative proceedings—hence the carefully orchestrated distribution of abolitionist testimony to members of Parliament. If the very fact of publication ensured that previous antislavery literature was "Submitted to Serious Consideration of All," such works were "More Especially" directed at "Those in Power," notably legislators, planters, and legal professionals.[112] Along with their greater emphasis on the criminality of slaveholding, antebellum reformers differed from their predecessors in directing their appeals primarily to an adjudicative lay public. The opening lines of *American Slavery as It Is* exemplify this new tactic: "READER, you are empannelled as a juror to try a plain case and bring in an honest verdict."[113]

By investing critical authority in the reader, antislavery propagandists drew on the ancient tradition of popular constitutionalism while exploiting contemporary concerns about judicial supremacy and the status of the jury. Derived from English traditions of fundamental law and shared by the lay public and legal officials alike, popular constitutionalism, as legal historian Larry D. Kramer has argued, understood the community to have a simultaneously political and legal responsibility to protect liberty from the encroachments of government power. In a reversal of ordinary positive law, fundamental law was "law created by the people to regulate and restrain the government"; at popular constitutionalism's core, then, stood an "inversion of interpretive authority," which authorized the people to supervise and, when necessary, correct government officials through enforcement mechanisms ranging from voting and petitioning to assembly in the form of disciplined crowds.[114] Within this framework, judges played an important role by enforcing fundamental law, thereby obviating the need for the people to resort to such extralegal means; in this view, the courts represented an alternative to (rather than a check on) public opinion.[115] Beginning with the Federalist expansion of the judiciary's powers in the late 1780s and culminating with the *Dred Scott* decision in 1857, however, Kramer documents a gradual shift toward judicial supremacy that would ultimately vest the courts with final authority on constitutional issues and the corollary responsibility of safeguarding the Constitution from popular opinion.[116]

Kramer's account of popular constitutionalism helps to explain why the abolitionist cultivation of legal spectatorship and the movement's invocation of juridical rhetoric struck such a powerful chord in antebellum American print culture. At the very moment when the public's critical prerogative over political-legal issues was coming under attack and increasing pressure was placed on the judiciary to align itself with the legislative and the executive branches against public opinion, abolitionists maintained Americans' duty (and thus power) to supervise and correct government actions through strategies that went beyond voting to include petitioning, assembly, and print protest.[117] (Garrisonians shunned the former altogether in preference for the latter.) By appealing to the people as an authoritative alternative tribunal, abolitionists were making use of what had long been understood to be "a very real, very available legal remedy, albeit one not to be called upon lightly."[118]

Of course, "the people" (or, more accurately, adult white males) could also participate directly in the judicial process through the jury. Significantly, then, roughly the same period that saw the waxing of judicial supremacy also witnessed the waning of the jury's power. Initially, the jury, widely viewed as the personification of the community, seemed the one legacy of English jurisprudence most clearly destined to attain fulfillment in American law. Seen as a "jury of the country—an abstract . . . of the citizens at large," the American jury trial represented not only the palladium of liberty, as it long had in England, but also "the sublimity" of the republican experiment."[119]

It would not be long, however, before the combined pressures resulting from a newly organized legal profession, the ascent of legal instrumentalism, and the emergence of increasingly powerful commercial interests would make "uniformity in adjudication . . . more important than unrelieved democratic sentiment," weakening considerably the power of the jury to inject communal equity considerations into verdicts.[120] At issue in what legal historian Kermit Hall has termed the "antebellum debate over the criminal jury" were the respective powers of judges and juries, specifically whether juries were triers of law as well as fact.[121] Writing in the early 1790s, Wilson had acknowledged that the judge's primary responsibility was to decide questions of law, whereas the jury's task was to ascertain the truth of the facts, or the evidence, presented to them—with the caveat that the interconnectedness of fact and law in many criminal cases required juries to try both.[122] But a century later, the Supreme Court ruling in *Sparf and Hansen v. United States* (1895) effectively put an end to the debate in the United States by holding that in both criminal and civil cases, the jury must follow judicial instruction on legal matters.[123] Historians disagree as to the exact distribution of power between judges and juries in early American trials.[124] Nevertheless, it is certain that *Sparf and Hansen* epitomized the effort to sharpen the distinction between law and fact on the one hand and the corresponding duties of judge and jury on the other—in short, to standardize legal practice by circumscribing the jury's power.

Although this shift in American jurisprudence occurred gradually, it did not occur quietly. Those who sought to restrict juries to adjudicating facts depicted jury members as ignorant, easily misled, and necessarily dependent upon guidance from the bench. In the April 1829 issue of a new professional journal, the *American Jurist*, the anonymous reviewer of a *Treatise on the Law and Practice of Juries* (1826) referred to "a complicated commercial case" in which a Boston jury "comprehended no more . . . than if the whole [testimony] had been read in Sanscrit."[125] A quarter-century later, novelist James Fenimore Cooper would follow his highly successful Leatherstocking Tales (which chronicle frontier hero Natty Bumppo's ongoing struggle with law) with *The*

Ways of the Hour (1850), a fictional exposé of jury corruption and ineptitude that garnered considerable public interest.[126]

But unlike the wealthy (and litigious) Cooper and the *American Jurist* writer, many Americans perceived juries as crucial safeguards of democratic rights against the despotic tendencies of a corrupt judiciary.[127] In a government in which the people, not king and parliament, were sovereign, judicial independence risked making the judge's cloak of immunity resemble a "shield of utter irresponsibility."[128] A filler item in the *New York Evening Post* gave a humorous nod to this view: "A witness lately examined before a judge in a case of slander, was requested to repeat the precise words spoken," the squib began. "The witness hesitated until he had rivetted the attention of the whole court upon him, then, fixing his eyes earnestly on the judge, he began—'May it please your honor, *you* lie, and *steal*, and get your living by *thieving*.' The face of the judge reddened and he immediately exclaimed, '*Turn to the Jury, Sir!*' "[129]

Articulated at the same time that the new wave of immediatist abolitionists were developing popular constitutionalist strategies to expose American slave law to the scrutiny of the people, this growing distrust for the judiciary, such reformers quickly came to appreciate, could potentially attract public support to their fringe movement. Given that shared suspicion of the judge as an "arbitrary" and "corrupt" "judicial despot" offered a rare spot of common ground to Conscience Whigs and Jacksonian Democrats, it is not surprising to find abolitionists injecting antijudicialism into their print propaganda.[130] In 1852, the same year that John P. Jewett published *Uncle Tom's Cabin*, the firm also brought out antislavery lawyer Lysander Spooner's flank attack on the Fugitive Slave Law, his lengthy *Essay on the Trial by Jury*. Four years later, when Stowe published her second antislavery novel, *Dred*, Spooner's fellow abolitionist attorney Richard Hildreth weighed in on a particularly infamous slave case by publishing an American edition of *Atrocious Judges: Lives of Judges Infamous as Tools of Tyrants and Instruments of Oppression* (1856)—"With an Appendix Containing the Case of Passmore Williamson," imprisoned abolitionist. As the timing of these two volumes suggests (and as chapter 1 explores in more detail), it was upon the passage of the Fugitive Slave Act of 1850—which dispensed with jury trials for suspected fugitives, replacing them with summary hearings in which federal commissioners received ten dollars for finding in favor of the claimant but only half that amount if the person in question was liberated—that antijudicial sentiment and the slavery controversy most powerfully converged in antebellum America.

Affirming the public's interpretive authority over both facts and law in the case in front of the popular tribunal, the frequently invoked metaphor of the adversarial criminal trial offered a powerful model of lay involvement in the legal process. Those who addressed readers as jurors—explicitly or implicitly, in pamphlet polemics or sentimental novels—understood the act of reading as a practice that was not restricted to edification or entertainment (although these could also be important objectives); they valued reading as a political act with the potential for social, political, and legal transformation.[131]

The Language of the Law as a Vulgar Tongue

The transformative potential of the slavery debate's legally inflected print propaganda lay in those two key elements of the adversarial criminal trial, narrative and rhetoric.[132] As theoretical legal studies by Cover and Steven L. Winter suggest, storytelling and rhetorical devices like metaphor are intrinsic to the ways in which we assign cultural meaning to law. In his influential essay, "Nomos and Narrative," Cover reminds us that "we constantly create and maintain a world of right and wrong, of lawful and unlawful, of valid and void"; law and narrative are intertwined in this normative universe because "no set of legal institutions or prescriptions exists apart from the narratives that locate it and give it meaning."[133] As a result, Cover maintains, most societies are characterized by "a radical dichotomy between the social organization of law as power and the organization of law as meaning"; in liberal societies like the United States in which government and other authorities do not claim the right to control the stories that endow law with its meanings, such meaning-making narratives have the potential to destabilize law's power.[134] For Cover, this dynamic manifested itself most vividly in the antebellum United States, where slavery stood as the "fault line in the normative topography" of the nation's law.[135] Focusing on antislavery constitutionalism in particular, Cover presents the slavery debate as one moment when the "is" and the "ought" of American law confronted the "what might be" made legible through narrative, enabling a radical abolitionist like Frederick Douglass to embrace "a vision of an alternative world in which the entire order of American slavery would be without foundation in law."[136]

Like narrative, metaphor is one of the primary practices through which the discourses of law and culture acquire and produce their interdependent meanings, as Winter's study of metaphor in legal reasoning suggests.[137] And, also like narrative, metaphor is key to the cognitive processes that enable us to imagine political, social, and legal change. By modeling unfamiliar ideas on established notions, metaphor enables us to expand our conceptual repertoire.[138] Winter's work is grounded in the insights of linguist George

Lakoff and philosopher Mark Johnson, who reject the prevalent assumption that metaphor is merely "a device of the poetic imagination and the rhetorical flourish—a matter of extraordinary rather than ordinary language"; approaching metaphor as a cognitive process, Lakoff and Johnson emphasize that "what we perceive" and "how we relate to other people . . . is very much a matter of metaphor."[139] Thinking of metaphor in this fashion, we can begin to see that rather than just relying on hackneyed turns of phrase, abolitionists, through their figurative use of legal language, deployed the projective capacities of both metaphor and narrative to envision an alternative regime of race and citizenship in the United States.

It is in this sense that the antislavery movement appealed to popular legal consciousness in order to adjudicate the issue of slavery in what Alexis de Tocqueville called "the shadow of the law." (In antebellum America, Tocqueville explained, "The authority which is awarded to the intervention of a court of justice by the general opinion of mankind is so surprisingly great that it clings to the mere formalities of justice, and gives a bodily influence to the shadow of the law.")[140] Analyzing displays of popular legal consciousness in late-twentieth-century New Jersey, sociologists Patricia Ewick and Susan S. Silbey discovered that people often invoke law in situations that neither receive nor require approval or even recognition from official legal institutions and actors; such popular appeals to legality, they conclude, provide "both an interpretative framework and a set of resources" through which we construct our social reality—including law itself.[141] In other words, it is often by resorting to the "language, authority, and procedures" of law that we structure both our own individual lives and our social relationships.[142] Tocqueville found such popular legal consciousness pervasive in the antebellum United States: "All parties are obliged to borrow the ideas, and even the language, usual in judicial proceedings in their daily controversies," he observed, noting that "the language of the law thus becomes, in some measure, a vulgar tongue."[143]

Although scholarship on popular legal consciousness has tended to focus on rights consciousness, Tocqueville's insight suggests how central a legal institution such as the criminal court could be to popular thought and politics.[144] In the slavery controversy, references to the practices, power, and logic of the adversarial criminal trial served to order, authorize, and give meaning to both individual and collective interventions in the print debate. For example, when Douglass characterized masters as "perpetrators of slaveholding villainy" or his enslaved former self as "an eye-witness to the cruelty" of slavery, he moved well beyond simply contrasting Southern guilt with African American innocence.[145] Instead, invoking legality to replace the relationship of master and slave with that of perpetrator and victim, or defendant and witness, Douglass provided a means to reconceptualize contemporary race relations in an alternative legal framework, one not based on black subjugation. On another level, Douglass's appropriation of legal language effectively authorized his *Narrative*: striking the testimonial posture of the witness, Douglass implicitly confirmed his competency and veracity and thus his right to be heard by the public tribunal. Finally, Douglass's allusion to one juridical role introduced into his writing the entire interpretive apparatus of law: the trial metaphor's internal coherence ensures that one does not have a perpetrator or an eyewitness without a crime, a victim, evidence, and a verdict. The invocation of legality thus called into question the actual status of slavery under American law by drawing on the authority of legal language to construct human bondage as a crime. Inserting legal logic into the abolitionist text, the trope of the trial also offered a pointed corrective to contemporary American legal practice. By figuratively rejecting the actual legal status of both African Americans and slavery—by imagining slavery as illegal and African Americans as possessing procedural rights—antislavery writers like Douglass presented the American public with a benchmark for legal reform. Speaking of slavery as a crime when it wasn't and portraying slaves as witnesses when they often couldn't be, abolitionists envisioned a nation in which human bondage would be illegal and blacks' constitutional right to due process (at the very least) would be recognized.[146]

Such appeals to popular legal consciousness indicate abolitionists' awareness that law was not the only discursive field in which black subjectivity was established and maintained in nineteenth-century America. Throughout the antebellum period, print culture became the venue in which African Americans' legally mandated civic identity could be reassessed and reformulated, a process that gained cultural legitimacy through abolitionists' extralegal appropriation of legal discourse. Figuratively taking the witness stand against slavery, African Americans went beyond authorizing their entry into the print debate over the legal status of race in America; they rejected widespread imputations of their legal and cultural outsidership to assert their civic belonging in the nation as a whole.

Collaboration and Constraint

Depicting the slavery debate as a vast, ongoing trial enabled abolitionists to promote popular interest in their cause, to marshal both divine and legal authority in their attack on slavery, and to offer an alternative vision of race under American law. Closer to home, this approach also offered a convenient way around some of the internal challenges facing the antislavery movement. For at the same time that the evidentiary practices of the courtroom imposed a juridical order on the voluminous and unruly print debate, the familiar personae of the criminal trial offered a ready-made set of roles on which to pattern interracial political collaboration. As commentators since Sewall had acknowledged, it was impossible to address the problem of slavery without simultaneously taking into account the status of free people of color in the American polity. Anticipating Jefferson's query on "Laws" in *Notes of the State of Virginia* (1787), Sewall maintained in 1700 that due to the "disparity in their Conditions, Colour & Hair," blacks "can never embody with us, and grow up into orderly Families, to the Peopling of the Land: but still remain in our Body Politick as a kind of extravasat Blood"; eighty-one years later, Jefferson asked the slaves' "advocates" simply, "What further is to be done with them?"[147]

The question was particularly pressing for immediatist abolitionism, which by rejecting the emigrationist and colonizationist agendas of previous antislavery efforts inevitably raised larger questions about the place of African Americans — slave and free — in the United States. And, because theirs was the first large-scale national reform movement in which blacks and whites collaborated closely for political and social change, antebellum antislavery activists faced the daunting task of putting theory into practice. Such collaboration required a series of complex, and often unspoken, negotiations of shared public space, from hotel rooms, dinner tables, and steamship decks to lecture stages, newspaper columns, and book pages. The racial division of this discursive space intensified in the late 1830s and the 1840s with the increasing public involvement of African American agents on the antislavery lecture circuit and the emergence of the slave narrative as a popular genre of literary abolitionism. In a movement that devoted a disproportionate amount of its resources to print, collaboration could easily become competition — for readers and sales as well as for authority and recognition.[148] Adopting the model of the criminal trial appeared to reduce the need to negotiate the slavery debate's discursive spaces.

White abolitionists had the most to gain from that model: it authorized their interventions into the slavery debate as "advocates" for the slave, even as it ordered potentially awkward interracial relationships within the movement. Proslavery Southerners who participated in the slavery debate's legal language (and many did) had less incentive, as doing so forced them to address the public tribunal from a rhetorically disadvantageous defensive posture. More subtly, however, those with the greatest stake in immediate abolition and future legal reform — African American activists — also stood to lose the most from imagining the slavery controversy as a criminal trial. Granted, by striking the testimonial pose of eyewitness, formerly enslaved African Americans gained the hearing otherwise denied them, rhetorically laying claim to the fundamental legal rights of American citizens. But in the newly adversarial criminal trial on which the slavery debate was structured, the laymen and laywomen who served as witnesses were by no means considered the equals of the increasingly professional class of almost exclusively white men who represented them. (Tocqueville found that lawyers occupied "a separate station" in American society, constituting as they did "a sort of privileged body in the scale of intelligence.")[149] Further, distinguishing between the roles of black and white abolitionists in this manner contributed to the larger process in which white activists endorsed ideas of racial equality and racial difference simultaneously, a phenomenon that critic Dickson D. Bruce Jr. has called the "reinscription of race within abolitionism."[150] For, despite the occasional passing reference to Charles Remond, James McCune Smith, or even Douglass as "advocates" by whites within the movement, the rudimentary trial model seemed to have little room for the figure of the free black abolitionist—one who, perhaps, had never been enslaved and, therefore, could not depict himself or herself as either victim of or witness to the crime of slavery.[151] Thus, even as the call for former slaves' testimonial contributions to the slavery debate provided a platform for extralegal black political participation on a national scale, such calls, combined with the persistently embattled status of the black press, also had a tendency to limit African American abolitionists to the confined, newly racialized space of the "witness stand" in mainstream American print culture.[152] As Douglass would point out after well over a decade in the movement (and as chapter 4 considers in more detail), such demands tacitly restricted African Americans' discursive authority to their experience of racial oppression while identifying their white colleagues with the weightier task of antislavery argumentation. Appearing to create a workable model for both interracial collaboration and black civic agency, the widespread habit of patterning the slavery controversy on the criminal trial also constrained that collaboration and circumscribed that agency by subordinating the public contributions of African American "witnesses" to that of their white "advocates."

In the thirty years that separated William Lloyd Garrison's first antislavery speech from John Brown's attack on Harpers Ferry, former slaves, white abolitionists, and apologists for slavery all drew heavily on the language and imagery of the courtroom to frame their contributions to the national debate over the South's peculiar institution. But in some of the era's most sustained literary portrayals of slavery (and, implicitly, of the larger controversy), representatives of each of these groups—Frederick Douglass, Harriet Beecher Stowe, and William MacCreary Burwell—registered profound discomfort with the very legal rhetoric that ensured them a hearing at the bar of public opinion. Tellingly, though, none of these authors rejected outright the comparison of the slavery debate to the trial; instead, in their writing, all three imaginatively revised the relationships among slave witnesses, abolitionist advocates, and slaveholding defendants. These modifications, as the following chapters will reveal, offered competing visions of American citizenship by imagining different forms of legal inclusion—or exclusion—for African Americans.

Part 1 tells the story of how early abolitionists deployed print tactics to decriminalize both the antislavery movement and enslaved African Americans in the eyes of the Northern reading public. Centering on two pivotal moments in the antislavery campaign, the early 1830s and the early 1850s, chapter 1 examines how, by aligning their movement with those core civil liberties of freedom of speech and trial by jury, abolitionists effected a radical transformation in public perception regarding the correct relationship among print, law, and antislavery agitation. Chapter 2 revisits Sojourner Truth's role in one of the nation's first penny-press scandals to demonstrate how such abolitionist appeals to the popular tribunal meshed with the transformation of the black subject in early antebellum print culture from guilty confessing criminal to righteous testifying witness.

Focusing on literary interventions in the slavery debate, part 2 examines how a former slave, a Northern abolitionist, and a proslavery Southerner negotiated their respective roles in the court of public opinion. Douglass, abolitionism's most exemplary (and ambivalent) eyewitness, entered the print fray over slavery just as the nation's first black lawyers were admitted to the bar. Emphasizing this synchrony, chapters 3 and 4 read Douglass's personal narratives and oratory of the 1840s and 1850s to suggest that his revised self-fashioning—from witness to advocate—represents his growing appreciation that independent black advocacy was indispensable to the struggle for African American citizenship.

Together, Douglass and Stowe, the era's most influential literary abolitionists, offered what were at once the most fully elaborated narrative renderings of the slavery debate as criminal trial *and* the most thoroughly considered explorations of that trope's confining implications for black political speech and African American citizenship. Much like Douglass after the success of his *Narrative*, Stowe in the wake of *Uncle Tom's Cabin* became aware that well-meaning white advocacy frequently worked to contain and curtail black testimony. Yet, as chapter 5 argues, *Dred*, Stowe's legally themed second antislavery novel, registers the restriction of black discursive autonomy only to reinscribe that restriction through its conclusion, in which a paternalist slave-holding lawyer effectively suppresses insurgent African American speech and political action.

By the late antebellum period, ubiquitous abolitionist appeals to the court of public opinion had become ripe for satire, as evidenced by Burwell's comic proslavery allegory, *White Acre vs. Black Acre. A Case at Law* (1856). Burwell, who would later edit the South's venerable *DeBow's Review*, never attained the fame of fellow proslavery ideologues John C. Calhoun, James Henry Hammond, or George Fitzhugh, nor did his novel attract the readership of popular anti-Tom fictions like Mary Eastman's *Aunt Phillis's Cabin* (1852) or Caroline Hentz's *Planter's Northern Bride* (1854). But as chapter 6 demonstrates, Burwell's "admirable burlesque" merits consideration for its deft reversal of abolitionists' favorite trope: imagining the sectional dispute as a civil rather than a criminal suit, the novel rejects the South's assigned defensive posture while reasserting sectional claims that slavery was a matter not of black natural rights but of white property rights.[153]

Ultimately, the slavery debate would be resolved through neither popular print consensus, nor legislative compromise, nor a judicial decision but by the bloodiest war in American history. The conclusion, therefore, briefly analyzes coverage of John Brown's 1859 treason trial in *Frank Leslie's Illustrated Newspaper*. In lavish engravings that literally illustrate the continuing national obsession with legal spectatorship, *Frank Leslie's* also documents how at the close of the antebellum period the American judiciary's apparent failure to dispense justice demonstrated the inevitability of a military (rather than a legal or a print) response to the slavery question. The last and most sensational of the era's legal crises over slavery, Harpers Ferry marked the end of three decades of abolitionist efforts—however troubled—to construct antebellum print culture as a forum for interracial collaboration and black civic agency in America.

Law, Print, and the Slavery Controversy

It should be clear by now that this book intends to offer more than an exploration of the role of law in the print debate over slavery or the influence of literature on the law of race and slavery in America. This study seeks to contribute to the growing body of book-history scholarship that considers how, rather than simply serving as a medium for the slavery controversy, print played an important role in advancing the project of African American civic inclusion.[154] This goal is consistent with the study's theoretical investment in cultural legal studies, a field of inquiry that, instead of treating law as exterior to an everyday life and culture that is somehow anterior to law, understands law and culture as mutually constitutive (rather than separate, contiguous, or even overlapping) domains.[155] By combining these methodologies—by attending, in other words, to the ways in which "the language of the law" became "a vulgar tongue" in the print debate over slavery—we can move away from the elite and official perspectives offered by the nation's founding documents, legal treatises, statute books, judicial decisions, and congressional reports in order to view the intersection of slavery and law from the lay perspective of popular print culture through pamphlet trial transcripts, newspaper articles, slave narratives, sentimental fiction, and the plantation novel.[156]

What sets this study apart from the few other works that have begun to address slavery and law in nineteenth-century American culture is its focus on the criminal trial, as opposed to constitutional or property law.[157] Prompted by the rhetorical power of abolitionist invocations of the trial trope as a model for the slavery controversy, this focus on criminal law also serves as a reminder that both white abolitionists and African Americans had to shake off their own identification with criminality before they could persuasively indict slaveholders in the court of public opinion.[158] More to the methodological point, following nineteenth-century Americans in approaching the problem of slavery through the conceptual frame of criminal litigation requires that we attune ourselves to corresponding procedural and substantive concerns. As we have seen, the roles and procedures of the recently developed adversarial criminal trial provided a structure for the slavery debate while distinguishing the extralegal tactics of American abolitionists from those of their British counterparts. As the remainder of this study demonstrates, the figure of the trial, which foregrounds crime and punishment, focuses attention on substantive questions of agency and civic belonging—questions that have been fundamental to Anglo-American articulations of race and law throughout modernity.

Briefly, in keeping with Western legal thought's foundational opposition of the rational, secular nations and individuals posited by Enlightenment philosophy to the lawless racial other imagined by European imperialism, African Americans (among others) have been denied full citizenship in the United States on the basis of what political scientist Rogers M. Smith calls inegalitarian ascriptive Americanism—the idea that "'true' Americans are 'chosen' by God, history, or nature to possess superior moral and intellectual traits associated with their race, ethnicity, religion, gender, and sexual orientation," whereas others are (or should be) excluded to varying degrees from national belonging by "involuntarily acquired traits that differentiate people."[159] Defining citizenship as a form of group inclusion that entails not only suffrage and other participation in governance (such as jury duty) but also majoritarian recognition of one's belonging to the civic community, legal historian Mark S. Weiner has charted African Americans' struggle since the colonial era to overcome the enduring "perception of their legal incapacity" in order to gain civic inclusion through recognition as "people of law": imperative to the achievement of full citizenship, to be a people of law is to have an inherent capacity to honor the nation's founding legal principles, to be worthy of legal protection, and to evince a demonstrable commitment to law.[160] Thus, even as we are careful not to idealize citizenship—even viewing it, in literary critic Russ Castronovo's terms, as "an impoverishment of subjectivity"—we, too, must acknowledge that "ignoring the positive significance that formal legal status had for former slaves seems dangerously glib."[161] Hence the importance of the trial trope as a model for the slavery debate. If pervasive assumptions about black legal incapacity complicated the antislavery movement's project not only to emancipate but to enfranchise African Americans, the abolitionist strategy of rhetorically criminalizing slavery entailed nothing less than a radical reevaluation of the perceived relationships among race, nation, and citizenship in Jacksonian America.

Along with these larger procedural and substantive insights, the nineteenth-century criminal trial, when approached from the dual perspective of book history and cultural legal studies, offers a practical solution to that persistent dilemma of Americanist literary scholarship—namely, the question as to whether early America is best understood as a print or an oral culture.[162] Even the briefest glance at the everyday components of the antebellum adversarial trial confirms the correctness of book historians' growing appreciation for the complex interpenetration and inextricability of oral and written forms.[163] In nineteenth-century America, the adversarial process typically involved initial contacts among the various parties (which could be conducted by written correspondence or face-to-face interviews); the filing of the necessary legal paperwork (including handwritten completion of preprinted blank forms); manuscript briefs prepared by lawyers (often based on published treatises, commentaries, statutes, and court reports); the oral performances of lawyers, their clients, and the judge (which could be spontaneous or rehearsed); the response of the assembled courtroom audience (the note-taking of judges, jurors, and journalists as well as the verbal outbursts, laughter, and applause of the spectators); the formal decisions of the judge and jury (rendered in oral, manuscript, and print forms); and, finally, the accounts published in newspapers, trial transcripts, and eventually court reports. And we need only shift our gaze from the courtroom to the careers of orator-writers like Garrison and Douglass—not to mention that of the illiterate author Sojourner Truth—to affirm that such an imbrication of oral and written forms similarly characterized the slavery debate. Far from excluding oral performance through its focus on print culture, this study assumes that the artifacts on which the analysis tends to center are suffused with and responsive to "oral" texts delivered from stumps, pulpits, and platforms (texts, of course, that could never have been purely oral, in that they were themselves influenced by various written forms from notes and diary entries to newspapers and pamphlets). Of more interest than asserting the primacy of one textual form over another will be the endeavor to discern how the slavery debate as it was conducted in print (among other media) revealed changing American attitudes about the proper relationship of such cultural forms to law.

PART I   BANDITTI AND DESPERADOES,
          INCENDIARIES AND TRAITORS

THE TYPOGRAPHICAL TRIBUNAL

Although the story of abolitionist appeals to the court of public opinion begins in the early 1830s, jumping ahead to autumn 1850 can help us to appreciate the profound change in Northern attitudes toward slavery, print, and law that took place over the course of the antebellum period. On 26 September 1850, just after the passage of the nation's controversial new Fugitive Slave Act, James Hamlet was arrested in New York City.[1] A "man of a dark complexion, who followed the honest vocation of a laborer," Hamlet "was seized whilst in pursuit of his lawful business" and "dragged before one of the tools of tyranny," the New York Atlas reported in eye-catching front-page coverage of the case.[2] Marshaling both words and images to depict the alleged fugitive's odyssey through New York's "Halls of Justice," the Sunday paper assured its readers the following week that "Hamlet, in the engraving before us, is placed in the position he was reputed to be in, when he was taken before the Commissioner of the United States"—emphasizing that the "scene is taken from real life."[3] It is safe to assume, however, that James Hamlet, a porter for the Tilton and Maloney firm, did not walk the streets of New York dressed only in a loincloth, as he is portrayed in the Atlas engravings (figs. 1 and 2).

The Atlas's repeated claims to verisimilitude and the illustrations themselves begin to make sense, however, when viewed from the perspective of the paper's readers—and particularly if we take into account those readers' attitudes about African Americans, slavery, and law. For even if the portrait of the kneeling, half-naked black man looked nothing like the real James Hamlet, it would have matched many Northerners' mental image of "The Slave." That image had its material origins in the seal that British pottery manufacturer and reformer Josiah Wedgwood had begun producing for the Society for the Abolition of the Slave Trade in the winter of 1787–88 (fig. 3).[4] Like the first Atlas engraving, versions of the Wedgwood seal bore the slogan, "Am I Not a Man and a Brother?" Reproduced on everything from sugar bowls, snuff

35

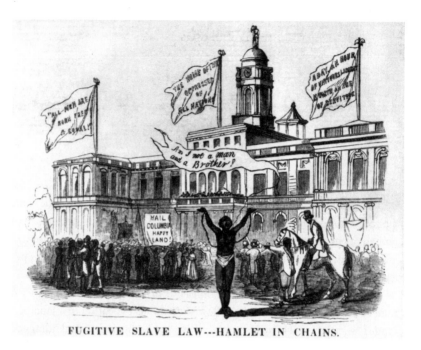

FUGITIVE SLAVE LAW---HAMLET IN CHAINS.

Figure 1. "Fugitive Slave Law—Hamlet in Chains," *New York Atlas*, 13 October 1850. (Courtesy Rare Books Division, The New York Public Library, Astor, Lenox and Tilden Foundations)

boxes, and figurines to handkerchiefs, brooches, and hairpins, Wedgwood's image had become on both sides of the Atlantic a familiar sentimental icon of the innocent, suffering slave.[5]

Why, then, didn't the *Atlas* pair the modified Wedgwood icon with an equally stylized image of Justice, as a blindfolded woman holding scales? After all, the second illustration's incongruity lies in the contrast between the iconic Slave and the comparatively lifelike depiction of the hearing's principal white actors. Again, we must imagine ourselves as part of the newspaper's burgeoning middle-class audience that, along with the North's bustling cities and booming market economy, had grown out of the industrial revolution.[6] Tied to the slaveholding South by economic interests and racial ideology, the *Atlas*'s readership likely joined the newspaper's editors—self-identified "State Rights men"—in their Union-preserving tolerance for "slavery in the States, in which it exists by law and by the voice of the people."[7]

Whatever their feelings about the South's peculiar institution, *Atlas* readers were assumed to share the frequently voiced Jacksonian fear that a despotic

FUGITIVE SLAVE LAW---HAMLET IN COURT.

Figure 2. "Fugitive Slave Law—Hamlet in Court," *New York Atlas*, 20 October 1850. (Courtesy Rare Books Division, The New York Public Library, Astor, Lenox and Tilden Foundations)

judiciary sought to usurp the democratic powers of American juries.[8] Hence the paper's allusion to the federal commissioner as "one of the tools of tyranny." What made the "infamous and bloody" Fugitive Slave Law "so utterly odious and abhorrent to anything that is manly, honorable or just" for the *Atlas* was that the act intolerably extended the powers of the judiciary while curtailing the rights of Northern citizens, albeit "of a dark complexion."[9] For, in addition to issuing warrants and appointing deputies and posse comitatus, the law's newly created federal commissioners (who were not necessarily judges) could also conduct the summary hearings in which alleged fugitives were denied jury trials and prohibited from testifying; anyone found guilty of interference or noncompliance with the law was liable to stiff fines and imprisonment.[10] Thanks to the new Fugitive Slave Law, the *Atlas* explained, a mere court clerk like New York's Alexander Gardiner suddenly " 'under the law' held, in one hand, the '*Habeas Corpus*,' the 'trial by Jury'—the prerogatives of the Judiciary—and was, at once, Court, Jury, and Executioner."[11] Denigrating Gardiner as "this tool, this pimp, this pander, this petty engine of power," the *Atlas* made it clear that the Fugitive Slave Law's greatest threat was its elimination of crucial checks on the tyrannical tendencies of an ex-

Figure 3. "Am I Not a Man and a Brother," in Erasmus Darwin, *The Botanic Garden* (New York, 1798). (Courtesy American Antiquarian Society)

panded judiciary.[12] As the visual tension between the formulaic rendering of the slave and the more precise delineation of the representatives of bench and bar suggests, what was at stake was not so much the liberty of an individual African American, James Hamlet, but the civil liberties of white Northern citizens. "We do not know to what extent it may not be attempted to carry this infamous Fugitive Slave Law," the *Atlas* cautioned, intimating ominously, "it may take the white man as well as the black."[13]

Two years later, an engraving in the first English edition of Harriet Beecher Stowe's Fugitive Slave Law–inspired novel, *Uncle Tom's Cabin*, inverted the *Atlas*'s representational strategy while retaining its message. George Cruikshank's illustration depicts Stowe's tragic quadroon Emmeline being auctioned off in front of allegorical statues of Justice, Liberty, and Faith (fig. 4).[14] While Liberty and Faith look sadly down from their niches, Justice stands blindfolded and indifferent, her scales aloft. In keeping with antebellum abolitionists' efforts to humanize enslaved African Americans for their white readers, here it is Justice, not the slave, that is reduced to an icon, whereas the slave girl, although sentimentalized, is nonetheless portrayed as an individualized human being, denied her rights by America's legally sanctioned system of bondage. Differing in emphasis, the illustrations in both the *Atlas* and *Uncle Tom's Cabin* view the plight of the slave in light of the Fugitive Slave Law's broader threat to American civil liberties.

Like the *Atlas*'s lavish coverage of the Hamlet case, the unprecedented success of Stowe's novel suggests the seismic shift that had occurred in Northern public opinion over the previous two decades. In the early 1830s, both abo-

EMMELINE ABOUT TO BE SOLD TO THE HIGHEST BIDDER.

Figure 4. George Cruikshank, "Emmeline about to Be Sold to the Highest Bidder," in *Uncle Tom's Cabin. With Twenty-Seven Illustrations on Wood by George Cruikshank* (London, 1852). (Courtesy American Antiquarian Society)

litionists and African Americans were widely perceived as dangerous, even criminal, elements who threatened to disrupt the young republic's fragile law and order with seditious publications and insurgent violence. In 1850, as the *Atlas*'s editorial disclaimers attest, most white Northerners were almost as reluctant to identify themselves as abolitionists as to embrace African Americans as their social and political equals. What *had* changed after twenty years of antislavery agitation, capped by passage of the Fugitive Slave Act, were Northern understandings of the appropriate relationship among print, law, and slavery. For rather than opposing law to the antislavery print tactics of organized abolitionism as they had in the early 1830s, by the 1850s many in the North had come to appreciate the extent to which their own civil liberties—most notably, freedom of speech and due process—were imperiled by slavery and the legal institutions that protected it.

Historians have long pointed to the free-speech controversy of the 1830s as a watershed in the antislavery movement's relationship to public opinion outside the South, just as they have marked the fugitive slave crisis of the 1850s as a turning point in Northern views of slavery.[15] Focusing on these two key moments, this chapter examines how abolitionists used extralegal print strategies to decriminalize antislavery agitation in the court of public opinion, enabling them to indict their slaveholding opponents before the popular tribunal, which they presented as an alternative to the nation's corrupt courts of law. Print, it bears emphasizing, was not merely a medium for reformers to circulate and promote their antislavery principles. Because print itself represented a hard-won civil liberty in the early republic, it held tremendous symbolic significance when opposed to oppressive—and repressive—governmental power and institutions. When the Fugitive Slave Law of 1850 endangered that other fundamental civil liberty, due process, print became an important alternative to law, the judiciary in particular. Print provided a forum in which Americans could adjudicate the question of slavery in the shadow of courtrooms seemingly corrupted by the Slave Power.[16] Thus, whereas in the 1830s it was precisely their use of print that made abolitionists vulnerable to criminal libel indictments, extradition, and incendiary-publications legislation, in the 1850s, the antislavery movement threatened to undermine judicial power through its appeals to what one editor called the "Typographical Tribunal."[17] As slaves' unjust encounters with law filled the printed page throughout the 1850s, such visual and verbal images encouraged the Northern reading public to respond to encroachments on due process by using print to convene a true "trial *per patriam*," a trial by the country.[18]

In the national antislavery movement's first decade, from William Lloyd Garrison's highly political imprisonment for libel in 1830 to the unpunished murder of antislavery editor Elijah P. Lovejoy in 1837, abolitionist print activism was often treated as criminal behavior by both government authorities and violent mobs. Focusing on the oratory, journalism, and pamphleteering of Garrison, Benjamin Lundy, and William Jay, the first part of this chapter argues that these early abolitionists repositioned themselves vis-à-vis American public opinion by identifying the Slave Power with a corrupt judiciary and the suppression of free speech and, at the same time, cultivating the association of their movement with cherished civil liberties. Exploiting recent changes in American print culture, they accomplished this turnabout by borrowing from the new penny dailies' trademark crime coverage while at the same time reinvigorating republican assumptions about the supervisory function of the press and the adjudicative role of the reader.[19]

Another twenty years would pass before abolitionists met real success in their attempts to braid their antislavery principles together with both strands of Jacksonian democracy, freedom of the press and trial by jury. Turning to Boston during the fugitive slave crisis of the 1850s, the remainder of the chapter analyzes the movement's persistent efforts to construct print as an alternative to the nation's increasingly compromised courts of law. As the illustrations in the New York Atlas and Uncle Tom's Cabin indicate, distrust of the judiciary surfaced most vividly and powerfully in images of enslaved African Americans encountering American "justice." In the aftermath of the Fugitive Slave Law, a range of print and legal sources, from newspaper engravings and trial testimony to sentimental fiction and Henry David Thoreau's "Slavery in Massachusetts," depicted the American courthouse as no longer the temple of justice it had once been but rather as a forceful symbol of the Slave Power. Transforming the courthouse into a barracoon, a slave auction block, or a fortress, images of slavery and the judiciary reveal how thoroughly interconnected concerns about black civic exclusion and white citizenship had become by the 1850s, when the authority of the court of public opinion finally threatened to supersede that of the court of law in the popular imagination.

Opening the "Case"

Early in his career as abolitionist editor, William Lloyd Garrison reported in the Genius of Universal Emancipation that the ship Francis, owned by Francis Todd and captained by Nicholas Brown, had recently sailed from Maryland laden with human cargo destined for sale in New Orleans. "Men who have the wickedness to participate" in such "domestic piracy," the young reformer railed, "should be SENTENCED TO SOLITARY CONFINEMENT FOR LIFE" as "*highway robbers and murderers.*"[20]

But in 1829, when Garrison published his inflammatory article, few would have been inclined to impeach an upstanding merchant like Todd or a respected mariner like Brown for his involvement in the domestic slave trade. Quite the contrary, as the coming months would show, Americans were far more likely to inculpate those who dared to criticize slavery in print. In December, for example, Georgia would respond to African American abolitionist David Walker's recently published *Appeal . . . to the Coloured Citizens of the World* (1829) by introducing legislation to punish those who circulated seditious literature and to detain black seamen (who potentially served as conduits for such dangerous material).[21] At the dawn of the antebellum period, it was abolitionists and African Americans, not slaveholders and their associates, who appeared to pose the greatest danger to law and order in the young nation. Cast as "banditti" and "desperadoes," abolitionists were accused throughout the 1830s of "writing, printing and publishing exhortations to rob, ravish, burn, and murder."[22] The challenge facing Garrison and his colleagues in the coming decade was to reverse this widespread public perception, for only then would they be able to gain a hearing as advocates for the slave.

The prosecutorial stance Garrison affected as the new coeditor of Quaker Lundy's Baltimore antislavery newspaper recalled the oratorical posture he had struck the previous summer in his first antislavery speech, delivered on Independence Day at Boston's Congregationalist Park Street Church. Then, knowing that to convey his abolitionist message successfully he would have to overcome his own relative obscurity and his audience's discomfort with his subject, the novice lecturer sought to capitalize on the popular passion for legal drama.[23] "Last week this city was made breathless by a trial of considerable magnitude," he reminded his listeners, recalling how the "court chamber was inundated, for hours, day after day, with a dense and living tide, which swept along like the rush of a mountain torrent."[24] Jumbling his metaphors, the inexperienced speaker remembered how "tiers of human bodies were piled up to the walls, with almost miraculous condensation and ingenuity. It seemed as if men abhorred a vacuum equally with Nature: they would suspend themselves, as it were, by a nail, and stand upon air with the aid of a peg."[25] Despite its "barren, ineloquent subject," the recent civil suit of *Farnum, Executor of Tuttle Hubbard v. Brooks* had attracted attention largely because it allowed the city to watch two of the era's most celebrated legal orators in action: Massachusetts's own Senator Daniel Webster and former U.S. attorney general and Virginian William Wirt.[26] As Garrison put it, the "excitement was natural," given that the trial featured "a struggle for mastery between two giants—a test of strength in tossing mountains of law."[27]

Warming to his subject, Garrison declared to his Park Street audience, "I stand up here in a more solemn court, to assist in a far greater cause."[28] Contrasting the recent lawsuit with his own "cause" and implicitly identifying himself with those two legal "giants," Webster and Wirt, Garrison extended the juridical metaphor, asserting that his task was "not to impeach the character of one man, but of a whole people—not to recover the sum of a hundred thousand dollars, but to obtain the liberation of two millions of wretched, degraded beings, who are pining in hopeless bondage—over whose sufferings scarcely an eye weeps, or a heart melts, or a tongue pleads either to God or man."[29] Modestly expressing his "regret that a better advocate had not been found, to enchain your attention and to warm your blood," the earnest twenty-three-year-old nevertheless displayed remarkable conviction. "Whatever fallacy . . . may appear in the argument, there is no flaw in the indictment," he insisted, affirming, "what the speaker lacks, the cause will supply."[30]

Six months later, however, it was the abolitionist advocate who found himself under indictment. In early 1830, Francis Todd, owner of the ship that had figured so centrally in Garrison's print diatribe on the domestic slave trade, filed a libel suit against Garrison and Lundy; soon afterward, the Maryland Grand Jury handed down an indictment against the *Genius*'s editors for "a gross and malicious libel" against Todd and Captain Brown.[31] Although Lundy's absence from Baltimore at the time of publication ultimately shielded him from prosecution, Garrison was convicted and imprisoned on the criminal charge.[32]

Early in the proceedings, reporting the withdrawal of the suit against him, Lundy gleefully indulged in an apt pun: "The 'case' is not to be disposed of so readily," he crowed, "[Judge Nicholas] Brice has dismissed it—but I *have not*, just yet. He presides over one 'Court of Justice'—I over *another*! He conducts business with the aid of musty folios, pettifoggers, and 'Swiss' bailiffs —I with bristling types, and iron screws, and levers!"[33] Playing on the syllepsis—"case" as both a legal action and the receptacle for printer's types—Lundy (who had learned the printer's trade in order to promote his antislavery beliefs) accepted the dismissal of the libel suit against him only to insist that the (printer's) "'case' is not to be disposed of so readily." Expanding the trope, Lundy asserted that editor/printer's "business," like that of the judge, is to "preside over" a "Court of Justice"—one characterized not by an Old World assemblage of arcana, obfuscation, and mercenariness but by a distinctly American combination of literacy, technology, and labor. In the United States, Lundy suggested, the press, not "the ermine of Judicial power," was the true dispenser of justice.[34]

It was former printer's apprentice Garrison, however, who most successfully used "bristling types, and iron screws, and levers" to challenge Judge Brice's dubious justice. Unwilling to rest content with ongoing coverage in the *Genius* and the "more than an hundred periodical works" that Lundy claimed had joined him in denouncing "this attack" on "our proper editorial privileges," Garrison published his own pamphlet on the criminal case, *A Brief Sketch of the Trial of William Lloyd Garrison, for an Alleged Libel on Francis Todd, of Massachusetts* (1830).[35] He continued his print campaign over the following years, reporting on the civil case in the *Liberator* and publishing an enlarged edition of his pamphlet in 1834. Like his first pamphlet, these print treatments of the proceedings issued an "appeal to the people for a change of the verdict."[36]

By his own account, Garrison's appeal to the court of public opinion was successful. Although "stigmatized as '*a convicted felon*'" in some circles, Garrison claimed in the second pamphlet to have received countless "consolatory letters" from individuals and "periodicals of all kinds, from every section of the Union, (not even excepting the south,) all uniting to give me a triumphant acquittal—all severely reprehending the conduct of Mr. Todd—and all regarding my trial as a mockery of justice."[37] Indeed, Garrison could assert that, at the urging of friends, he was expanding and republishing his pamphlet on the libel case "in order to rebut the defamation of my enemies."[38] The popular tribunal, it seems, had reversed the Baltimore court: not only could Garrison proclaim that the "verdict of the nation" had been "given in my favor," but he could portray his proslavery "enemies" as themselves guilty of "defamation."[39]

Yet, Garrison's *Brief Sketch* is no fiery antislavery polemic. Given his subsequent career as abolitionist gadfly and that his manifestly unjust trial turned on the pivot of slavery politics rather than libel law, it may seem surprising that Garrison did not seize the pamphlet's publication to present the kind of sustained attack on slavery that had been impossible in his lectures and journalism.[40] Not once in his prefatory comments—the first quarter of the pamphlet—does the abolitionist editor mention or even allude to the topic of slavery. Instead, the tract's preamble implicitly links Garrison's antislavery agitation to the two hallmarks of republican self-government, trial by jury and freedom of the press.

Playing to his audience's nationalism, Garrison favorably contrasts the status of the press in the United States with that in Europe, crediting "the republican nature of our government" and the First Amendment in particular for the nation's comparatively limited number of libel prosecutions.[41] But it is precisely these vaunted liberties that are endangered by what the pamphlet presents as a corrupt judiciary's self-serving attack on the press. Noting a pattern of "bias" in the few known American libel cases, Garrison cautions against "a growing tendency in many of the courts, to stifle free inquiry; to dishearten every effort of reform, and to intimidate the conductors of newspapers."[42] Speculating that judicial "hostility" to the press "arises from a prudent selfishness," Garrison suggests that by limiting freedom of the press, a potentially corrupt judiciary seeks to protect itself from public scrutiny: "By denying our right to investigate public measures, or to interrogate men in their official or private capacity," judges "hope to raise themselves above responsibility and suspicion"—as a result, "it is almost impossible to impeach any one of their number, though his guilt be as obvious as the sun in heaven."[43]

Seventeen years after Garrison first published his pamphlet and thirteen years after its republication, Baltimore printer William Wooddy issued a rebuttal to Garrison's aspersions on the Maryland judiciary. The anonymous *Proceedings against William Lloyd Garrison, for a Libel* (1847) devotes its thirty-two pages to disproving Garrison's print allegation that Baltimore "judges must be men tainted with the leprosy of oppression, with whom it would be useless to contend—men, morally incapable of giving an impartial verdict, from the very nature of their pursuit."[44] To this end, Wooddy's pamphlet presents signed "affidavits" by members of the grand jury that indicted Garrison, members of the juries for both the criminal and civil trials, and the presiding judges in both cases, expressing the "conviction that slavery is a great national and moral evil."[45] That the author of *Proceedings* chose to challenge not Garrison's "intemperate and misguided course on the subject of slavery" but his attack on Southern justice and that Garrison himself emphasized the dangers of a corrupt judicial process and a restricted press over those of human bondage highlights the importance to the slavery debate of changing attitudes toward law and print culture—and the proper relation between the two.[46]

Making Readers Judges

Garrison and the national antislavery movement commenced their print campaign just as the period's new commercial press was complicating earlier views of the bourgeois public sphere as a space for private citizens to limit the domination of political authorities through rational criticism articulated in print.[47] If those views emerged most vividly in the landmark 1735 libel trial of John Peter Zenger, they continued to inform popular assumptions about the press well into the antebellum period, as both Garrison's pamphlet and a treatise by proslavery ideologue Thomas Cooper illustrate.

Zenger was charged with seditious libel after printing criticism of New York Governor William Cosby's colonial administration in the *New-York Weekly Journal*. Legal historians often cite the Zenger trial, in which the jury disregarded instructions from the bench, as an instance of the kind of jury autonomy that would be eroded in the nineteenth century as a result of the growing professionalization of the bar and the greater influence of commercial interests on American legal practice.[48] From the alternative perspective of book history, critic Michael Warner has argued that the Zenger case, along with the print controversy surrounding it, ushered the concept of freedom of the press into eighteenth-century America. Specifically, Warner has demonstrated how the notion of freedom of the press rested on the novel idea of a supervisory regulative press that appealed to a court of public opinion, making "Readers Judges" whose impersonal adjudication would ascertain the validity of published political assertions.[49] This republican view of press freedom differed markedly from the more restrictive British common law tradition associated with Blackstone, which understood free speech largely as absence of prior restraint, with the very real possibility of punishment upon publication.[50]

According to Warner, the outcome of the Zenger trial reinforced the new understanding of the reader's adjudicative function by uniting readers and jurors in opposition to the bench. At first, the trial's verdict seemed inevitable: not only did Zenger face as judges Governor Cosby's cronies but, because of the restriction of the jury to deciding the fact of publication rather than the truth of its contents, contemporary libel law itself worked against him.[51] But, after the court rejected defense counsel Alexander Hamilton's argument that criticism of a government official should be considered not a status violation but an instance of civic virtue, Hamilton called on the jury "to decide not just the facts of the case, as precedent prescribed . . . but the law of the case as well," justifying this "appeal to the jury in the same language of deferred authority, supervision, and negativity" with which the defense had characterized the republican press.[52] The circle was complete when, ignoring the court's instructions, the jury acquitted Zenger, and the cheering spectators carried his lawyer into the streets outside.[53] The triumphant egress from the courtroom to the streets enacted the very point stressed by Hamilton (and Lundy and Garrison after him): that the press offers an extralegal forum for the reading public, instead of the government, to settle disputes of interest to the "imagined community" of the nation.[54]

The early republic remained torn between the two approaches to free speech, as indicated by the controversy over the Sedition Act of 1798. Charting the development of ideas about freedom of expression from the Sedition Act through the Civil War, legal historian Michael Kent Curtis has concluded that the repressive measures of the former ultimately yielded a vigorous and expanded popular defense of free speech in the antebellum North, as constitutional guarantees against federal censorship were increasingly understood to extend to the states as well.[55] The continued influence in the Jacksonian period of the republican assumption that, in the words of the *New York Journal*, "*public grievances* can never be redressed but by *public complaints*; and they cannot well be made *without the Press*" is evident from a work published the same year as Garrison's pamphlet, Thomas Cooper's *Treatise on the Law of Libel and the Liberty of the Press* (1830).[56] Beyond his own libel conviction and imprisonment under the Sedition Act, slavery apologist and secessionist preceptor Cooper had little in common with Garrison or Lundy.[57] Nevertheless, his *Treatise* solicits our attention because, like the abolitionist editors' commentary on the *Genius* libel cases, it rests on republican notions of the appropriate relationship between jurisprudence and print culture. In Cooper's assessment of libel law, not only does freedom of the press depend on the jury's right to try both law and fact, but print also offers an indispensable alternative to litigation.

Opposing (in Lundy's terms) "the ermine of judicial power" to "freedom of the press," Cooper linked the criminal law of libel to "an usurpation on the rights of the jury" by emphasizing judicial encroachment upon the jury's right to judge questions of libelous intent or veracity of content.[58] To drive home his point, Cooper imagined a scenario that, even as it illustrated the need for juries to decide questions of both law and fact, constructed print publication as a kind of surrogate trial. Supposing a situation in which he accused in print another man of bribing a legislator to pass a bill that would further the man's own interests and further supposing that the man in question then indicted him for libel, Cooper asked whether under such circumstances a jury could render a verdict if it were prohibited from hearing evidence as to the truth of the alleged libel. Abruptly shifting the responsibility of adjudication from "the jury" in the courtroom to "the public" outside of it, Cooper next suggested that the primary purpose of freedom of the press was to accomplish extrajudicial arbitration of questions concerning the common weal. "Why am I to be put to the trouble and expense of indicting" the unscrupulous man for bribery "when the ends of the public are fully answered by the course I have taken?" Cooper demanded.[59] "Compelling a man to become a prosecutor, at the hazard of his character, the loss of his time, his trouble, and his money, is a sure way to screen the guilty," he contended, adding that, after all, "if the fact I assert be not true, he can compel me to the proof by a civil action."[60] The court of public opinion, not the criminal court, was the correct venue to adjudicate such civic concerns; only when the public tribunal was abused should citizens turn to law for remedy. Instead of going to "the trouble and expense of indicting" those "guilty" of placing personal interest above public good, the virtuous citizen best served "the ends of the public" by bringing his charge before that public through the alternative tribunal offered by print.

Precisely this view of the press as a surrogate tribunal drove Garrison in his pamphlet of the same year to criticize what he portrayed as Francis Todd's inappropriate response to the *Genius* editorial. In keeping with the promise made in his article, Garrison had mailed a copy of the paper to Todd, but "instead of vindicating his conduct in the columns of the Genius, and endeavoring to show that [the] statement was materially false," Todd immediately "entered a civil action against" Garrison, "estimating damages at five thousand dollars."[61] If Todd were motivated by a sense of civic responsibility rather than a desire for personal gain, Garrison implied, he would have engaged the editor in an edifying print debate rather than (or at least prior to) suing him in a court of law.

Conversely, Garrison suggested that his own allegiance to republican notions of the supervisory capacity of print and the adjudicative role of the reader had motivated his initial publication of the *Genius* editorial, as well as his ensuing pamphlet on the libel trial. Contrasting his own willingness "to be persecuted, imprisoned and bound, for advocating African rights" with the trepidation of his colleagues on the "Baltimore presses," Garrison lamented that the "loss of an advertisement, or the withdrawal of a subscriber, is of far greater consequence than the exposure of corruption, or the reform of abuses."[62] Drawing on the lingering commitment to a supervisory press and heightened anxieties about a corrupt judiciary, Garrison left little doubt that it was the press's financial self-interest, epitomized by the Slave Power's influence, that had compromised both the press and jurisprudence in the Southern city of Baltimore: "In which of the city papers can an intelligent censor gain admittance, if his strictures apply to any thing that exists in the city, county or state?" he asked rhetorically.[63] On second thought, he added, "Since the result of my trial, I ought not to marvel that they carry the fear of his honor judge Brice before their eyes!"[64] Refusing to bow to coercion, Garrison instead offered a renewed call to the adjudicative reader by publishing the pamphlet on his libel case. Inviting "the attention of the public" to his efforts to put "the case in a plain, intelligible form" and thereby "exposing the defectiveness of the indictment and the arbitrary conduct of the court," Garrison presented "the facts . . . before the public" confident that "the people" would hand down "a change of the verdict."[65]

Banditti and Desperadoes, Incendiaries and Traitors

Garrison's response to the libel trial set a pattern that would be followed for the remainder of the decade. Akin to the editor's own bewilderment upon becoming the defendant in a libel case was the bemusement of early abolitionists upon discovering themselves the target of not just riots and lynch mobs but grand jury indictments and extradition proceedings. And just as Garrison deployed extralegal print tactics to transform himself from "convicted felon" into antislavery "advocate," his abolitionist colleagues sought to decriminalize their movement by pitting the press against the bench and bar in a determined struggle for American civil liberties.

The controversy began in earnest with the abolitionist postal campaign. In 1835, taking advantage of recent improvements in printing and transportation technology, the American Anti-Slavery Society (AASS) had sent print propaganda to Southern regions where even the most intrepid reformer feared to tread. In late July of that year, a mob in Charleston, South Carolina, stole mail bags from the local U.S. post office, burned antislavery materials, and hung effigies of leading abolitionists on gallows constructed for the occasion.[66] Rather than condemnation, the mob's action received support from the city council, the local postmaster, and, eventually, President Andrew Jackson, who urged the outlawing of such incendiary material.[67] The Charleston mob's mock gallows spoke to the assumption on both sides of the Mason-Dixon line that, more than mere "fanaticism," abolitionist agitation constituted criminal activity worthy of punishment.

Such attitudes led abolitionist William Jay, son of the Supreme Court's venerable first chief justice, to devote a chapter of his *Inquiry into the Character and Tendency of the American Colonization and American Anti-Slavery Societies* (1835) to refuting the common accusation that abolitionists were "incendiaries and traitors."[68] Trained as a lawyer himself, Jay cited charges by members of "the legal profession" to the effect that abolitionists were guilty of "seeking to destroy our happy Union; of contemplating a violation of property, secured by the Constitution they had sworn to support; of pursuing measures which would lead to a civil war; and of being guilty of direct and palpable nullification."[69] Assuming a defensive pose that would soon become more typical of his proslavery adversaries, Jay asserted that "to all these charges . . . the members of the Anti-Slavery Society plead NOT GUILTY, and desire to be tried by God and their country."[70] "But alas," he continued, "no trial is vouchsafed to them: judgment has already been given, and execution awarded against them, without trial and without evidence, solely on the finding of a voluntary and irresponsible inquest."[71] Under such circumstances, "all they can now do, is ask for a reversal of judgment as false and illegal, cruel and oppressive."[72]

By decade's end, the antislavery movement would win its appeal for a "reversal of judgment" in the court of public opinion—and, as with Garrison, this reversal would be accomplished through the medium of print. In 1835, however, such a reversal was by no means certain. In addition to the persistent hostility reformers encountered from local mobs and in the mainstream press, there was afoot, as Jay well knew, a concerted attempt by government authorities to criminalize abolitionism itself. Such efforts were most successful in the South, where a wave of legislation outlawed the publication or circulation of antislavery materials as well as other forms of abolitionist activism.[73] (An 1860 Virginia *Guide to Magistrates: with Practical Forms for the Discharge of Their Duties Out of Court* conveniently provided arrest warrant forms "for writing a pamphlet . . . with intent to incite rebellion," "for knowingly circulating pamphlets . . . denying the right of the master to property in slaves, with intent to aid the purposes of such pamphlet," and "against a subscriber for an incendiary pamphlet, who receives it to aid abolitionists.")[74] But official antiabolitionist repression was by no means a sectional phenomenon. Although the proposed incendiary publications bill was ultimately defeated in the Senate, such measures nevertheless received prolonged attention in Congress. Even more unsettling was the serious consideration some Northern state legislatures gave to resolutions by their slave-state counterparts requesting that, in the words of a South Carolina petition, it be made "highly penal to print, publish, and distribute newspapers, pamphlets, tracts, and pictorial representations, calculated and having an obvious tendency to excite the slaves . . . to insurrection and revolt."[75] It was only after careful deliberation that Northerners declined the invitation to extend censorship of abolitionist materials into their own states. Many would have agreed with the *New York Sunday Morning News*'s insistence that "the leaders of the Abolitionists" were "out of the pale of the legal and conventional protection which society affords to its honest and well-meaning members" and thus should "be treated as robbers and pirates."[76]

Efforts to construe abolitionist agitation as criminal activity followed several different trajectories. The occasional attempt to construct antislavery ac-

tivism as treason foundered on the Constitution's purposefully narrow definition of that offense.[77] Far more prevalent were bids, prompted by memories
of the virtually simultaneous appearance of Walker's *Appeal* and Garrison's
Liberator with Nat Turner's uprising, to cast antislavery speech as a form of
seditious libel that threatened to disturb the public peace by inciting slave insurrection and other disruptions of law and order.[78] In October 1831, a grand
jury in Raleigh, North Carolina, found a true bill authorizing the attorney
general's indictment of Garrison and Isaac Knapp as publishers of the *Liberator*; in December, Georgia followed suit when Governor Wilson Lumpkin
signed a joint resolution by the legislature offering five thousand dollars for
the arrest, trial, and conviction of Garrison—or "any other person or persons
who shall utter, publish or circulate within the limits of this State, said paper,
called the Liberator, or any other paper, circular, pamphlet, letter or address,
of a seditious character."[79] Over the winter of 1835–36, Connecticut scientist and doctor Reuben Crandall (brother of celebrated abolitionist defendant
Prudence Crandall) was imprisoned for eight months in Washington, D.C.,
and tried on charges of seditious libel following the informal, possibly inadvertent, circulation of antislavery materials in his possession.[80] Abolitionists
were also accused of group libel. Although this attempt to broaden the concept of individual libel so as to protect slaveholders as a group does not appear
to have generated prosecutions, it did prove part of the rationale for the Gag
Rule that officially suppressed discussion of slavery in Congress from 1836 to
1844—and, by extension, contributed to the larger climate of antiabolitionist repression.[81]

Surpassing these strategies to exempt antislavery expression from the
usual legal protections accorded to free speech were calls by Southern authorities for the extradition of abolitionists for trial in slaveholding states. In
the fall of 1835, the grand jury of Tuscaloosa, Alabama, indicted *Emancipator*
publisher R. G. Williams for inciting insurrection, upon which Governor John
Gayle unsuccessfully demanded that New York Governor William Marcy extra-
dite Williams to Alabama—despite the fact that Williams had never set foot
in the state.[82] As subsequent harassment of Williams illustrated, such official persecution bore an uncomfortable resemblance to more informal threats
by local vigilance committees to kidnap and lynch well-known antislavery
leaders such as Garrison, Amos Dresser, and Arthur and Lewis Tappan.[83]

In this intolerant atmosphere, abolitionists found it necessary to defend
themselves before a hostile court of public opinion. In 1836, Garrison joined
lawyers Ellis Gray Loring, William Goodell, Samuel E. Sewall, and Charles
Follen, along with other board members of the Massachusetts Anti-Slavery

Society (MASS), in publishing a pamphlet "Showing Why There Should Be No Penal Laws Enacted, and No Condemnatory Resolutions Passed by the Legislature; Respecting Abolitioni[s]ts and Anti-Slavery Societies."[84] As the pamphlet pointed out, the criminalization of abolitionist activity was a Southern ploy "to bring the public feeling against the Abolitionists to the highest possible point of excitement, and, more than all, to gain a general credit to the injurious charges now alleged against them."[85] But, as the same work illustrates, abolitionists refused to stay on the defensive any longer than it took to refute the charges against them: like Garrison after the libel trial, they found the prosecutorial stance of antislavery advocate more rhetorically powerful. Claiming "that Abolitionists and Anti-Slavery Societies are guilty of nothing more nor less, than a consistent vindication and exercise of the fundamental, inherent, and *inalienable rights of man*," the authors went on to insist that they could not, therefore, "be proscribed, either by penal enactments or legislative censure, without a proscription of the first principles of republican freedom."[86] Having established that "it is solely for this crime" of advocating an obnoxious natural-rights doctrine "that the Southern Authorities demand that we should be condemned," the pamphlet's authors contrasted the criminality of slaveholders with their own innocence by exposing the double standard under which "the advocacy of *despotism* [is] held a venial offence, unknown to the laws," while "the *advocacy of freedom* can be a fit subject for legislative censure, or for penal enactment," or even "held 'indictable at common law.'"[87]

It was by such invocations of "the first principles of republican freedom" that early abolitionists were able to reposition themselves in the legally inflected controversy over slavery. Willing to "be arraigned . . . as culprits under the most rigorous espionage of our words and writings," the MASS asked only "the opportunity of pleading and proving the facts of the case in our defence."[88] Of course, such an opportunity would be tantamount to victory, for it required that legislative repression be replaced by due process and the inevitable print coverage.[89] Elaborating on their somewhat cryptic claim that "the forms of law afford no illustration in the premises," the pamphleteers explained that "a writ, and a constable at the heels, or on the shoulder of an Abolitionist, would supply no evidence against his statements or his principles," just as "there would be no logic in the walls of a prison to confute his reasonings."[90] Reminding their American readers that "the dungeon would emit no additional illumination on the disputed question," that "gibbets are not arguments," and that "racks cannot force men's conclusions," the MASS maintained that the "truth or falsehood" of antislavery principles, therefore, "must be determined by intuitive perception, by the power of conscience, by the clearness of illustration, by the weight of evidence, by the force of argument."[91] Opposing the apparatus of a medieval legal system (dungeons, gibbets, and racks) to the tools of the adversarial criminal trial (evidence and argument), the Massachusetts pamphleteers belied their claim that "the forms of law afford no illustration." Indeed, the early abolitionists' success in reversing the popular judgment against them lay precisely in their importation of the adversarial "forms of law" into the print debate over slavery, as they grounded their "advocacy of freedom" in those indispensable civil liberties, freedom of speech and due process.[92]

The Typographical Tribunal

Inheritors of republican values though they may have been, Garrison, Lundy, Cooper, Jay, and the MASS published their polemics in a very different print culture than that of John Peter Zenger.[93] For if the Zenger case appeared to offer an American vindication of rational-critical print debate, the popular legal spectatorship that accompanied the new commercial press in the 1830s has been associated with the breakdown of the bourgeois public sphere.[94] Discussing "consumer culture's distortion of publicity in the judicial realm," Jürgen Habermas contends in The Structural Transformation of the Public Sphere that "the trials in criminal court that are interesting enough to be documented and hawked by a mass media reverse the critical principle of publicity"; that is, "instead of serving the control of the jurisdictional process by the assembled citizens of the state, publicity increasingly serves the packaging of court proceedings for the mass culture of assembled consumers."[95] However much this observation may resonate with those of us who live in the cultural climate that has produced Judge Judy, Court TV, and Celebrity Justice, scholarship on the early penny press has complicated Habermas's claim that "it paid for the maximization of its sales with the depoliticization of its content."[96]

As Habermas acknowledged, the period's well-publicized scandals often had legal origins. For just as the economic success of the penny press resulted from technological and managerial innovations, its popularity arose from the signature crime reporting that exponentially increased circulation by capitalizing on and cultivating mass fascination with tales of crime and justice. Journalism historian Frank Luther Mott attributed the ascendancy of the nation's first successful penny paper, the New York Sun (1833), largely to the police-court reports of George W. Wisner.[97] Such reports soon became a staple of the Sun and competitors like the New York Transcript (1834–39). According to Mott, the "great field-day for the penny press" arrived in 1836, when Manhattan clerk Richard P. Robinson was arrested for the murder of the prostitute Helen Jewett. Throughout the trial, James Gordon Bennett's *Herald* led other penny papers in New York, Boston, and Philadelphia in publishing "verbatim reports of the testimony . . . with questions and answers"—coverage that tripled the paper's circulation.[98] By the mid- to late 1840s, the popular appetite for crime narratives and trial reports made George Wilkes's *National Police Gazette*, with its popular "Lives of the Felons" series, one of the most widely read national newspapers of the antebellum period.[99]

Tracing the penny dailies' crime coverage back to that of the labor press of the late 1820s and early 1830s, communication historian Dan Schiller has argued that the desire for crime news arose from a residual artisanal republicanism wary of state subservience to private interests.[100] Targeting a legal culture whose rife corruption appeared to impede justice, the early penny press regularly published exposés of "the changing legal system and its evident abuses."[101] In such reporting, Schiller notes, "not only did the cheap press ritualistically oversee the operations of justice, in police and crime reports and commentary, to ensure that justice was acceptably attained, but also, more defensively, perhaps, commercial journals kept an eye on what was being *done* to justice by virtue of the transformation of the legal system."[102]

As it became more established, the penny press authorized its increasingly lurid voyeurism by appealing to this popular constitutionalist tradition of civic scrutiny and corresponding republican assumptions about the supervisory capacity of the press. For example, when Massachusetts Attorney General Perez Morton tried to restrict press coverage of one of the most infamous murder trials of the early 1830s, the "Salem Murder Case," *Herald* founder Bennett dismissed the "old, worm-eaten, Gothic dogma of the Courts, to consider the publicity given to every event by the Press, as destructive to the interests of law and justice," insisting instead that "the honesty, the purity, the integrity of legal practice and decisions throughout this country, are more indebted to the American Press, than to the whole tribe of lawyers and judges, who issue their decrees."[103] He added, "*the Press is the living Jury of the Nation.*"[104] Significantly, however, Bennett was prompted to mount his passionate defense of the supervisory function of a free press by a case that featured not an alleged libel against government authorities but the appalling murder-by-hire of one family member by another. Under such circumstances, the act of reading crime accounts implied not so much disinterested supervision as morbid scopophilia. As supervision gave way to voyeurism, and the rational criticism of the republican public sphere yielded to the grisly sensationalism of the penny press, the press usurped the adjudicative function formerly assigned to the reading public while the individual reader risked sliding into guilty complicity with the criminal.[105] Tellingly, it is "the Press"—not its readers—that Bennett characterizes as "the living Jury of the Nation."

Almost thirty years later, the ongoing fear that, in its efforts to feed the antebellum hunger for legal spectatorship, the cheap press risked endangering the very republican institutions it claimed to reinforce drove disgruntled former editor Lambert A. Wilmer to publish *Our Press Gang; or a Complete Exposition of the Corruptions and Crimes of the American Newspapers* (1859). Quoting with approval Judge Kent's claim that the cheap press "*seeks to bring into contempt the sanctuary of justice itself,*" Wilmer argued that the "Typographical Tribunal" had effectively made the "trial by jury . . . a mere nullity."[106] For Wilmer, it was the newspapers' detailed reconstruction of court cases in print that enabled them to ignite "that terrible engine called Public Opinion" and thus to obtain "an almost irresistible mastery over the misnomered 'Courts of Justice.'"[107] Three decades after Thomas Cooper's *Treatise*, Wilmer complained that, rather than offering an alternative tribunal, the press had effectively preempted the courts.

Shrill and paranoid as Wilmer's screed is, its allusion to "that terrible engine called Public Opinion" supports Habermas's observation that in the nineteenth century, public opinion "in the form of the currently dominant opinion" had turned into "a coercive force, whereas it had once been supposed to dissolve any kind of coercion into the compulsion of reason."[108] Especially in the Jacksonian context of universal white-manhood suffrage and the mass commercial press, the "reign of public opinion appeared as the reign of the many and the mediocre," as "more of a compulsion toward conformity than as a critical force."[109] By the end of the antebellum period, the public opinion that had once represented enlightened republicanism was beginning to look like a menace to law and order.[110] In such an atmosphere, the authority of published assertions was no longer deferred to the validating inspection of the reading citizen; instead, the newly passive newspaper reader had become the recipient of a "foregone conclusion," in the form of the verdict pronounced by the press, which had arrogated to itself the role of "Jury of the Nation."[111] In this way, the cheap press legitimized sensational legal spectatorship through recourse to republican notions of the supervisory role of the press, simultaneously appropriating and undermining the authority of the American legal system.

With the exception of Garrison's abortive plan to launch a penny version of the *Liberator*, abolitionist newspapers no more adopted the cheap press's innovations in printing, pricing, and distribution than they did its largely Democratic politics.[112] Differences in production and distribution notwithstanding, the two kinds of periodicals did share similar editorial policies: both were willing to transgress social mores in the interest of realism; both sought to expose the corruption of established religious, political, legal, and economic institutions; and both rejected the traditional party affiliation and mercantile orientation of the American press.[113] Moreover, Garrison and his fellow reformers borrowed Bennett and his penny-press colleagues' extralegal tactics to gain readers' attention in a print culture saturated with the bizarre and the criminal. Just as, during Garrison's libel trial, Lundy turned to the printer's "case" to open an alternative "Court of Justice," abolitionist writers, editors, and printers convened a typographical tribunal of their own.

But if, as we have seen, the abolitionist print campaign embraced the legal spectatorship popularized by the cheap press, it was nevertheless motivated by a commitment to political change over financial profit.[114] Crucially, then, abolitionist sensationalism not only had to be legitimated by the republican concept of print in which a supervisory press enlightened, educated, and informed readers who in turn passed judgment on issues central to the civic life of the nation but also had to *reanimate* that increasingly moribund concept.[115] Only by doing so could abolitionists retain the critical principle of publicity that enabled citizens to exert control over the judicial process in the public sphere. Thus, rather than presenting the antislavery press as a kind of national jury dispensing judgment to readers, abolitionist propaganda sought to provide the reading public with the knowledge and the authority to render its own verdict; in true republican fashion, censure had to come from the people.[116]

The stakes of such an undertaking were high, as the 7 November 1837 mob murder of newspaper editor Elijah P. Lovejoy in Alton, Illinois, demonstrated. More than any other event in the turbulent 1830s, the Alton Tragedy reshaped Northern views of abolitionism by starkly aligning the antislavery movement with a free press in opposition to mob violence supported by a proslavery judiciary.[117] Although not at first an ardent abolitionist, Lovejoy, a Presbyterian minister, regularly inserted antislavery articles alongside the religious material in his virulently anti-Catholic St. Louis, Missouri, newspaper, the *Observer*. The paper and its editor first came under attack when local tensions over race and slavery heightened following the alleged theft of area slaves by white abolitionists and the murder of a white constable by an African American suspect resisting arrest. Following the South's "new code" of lynch law, the white community responded to these events by administering between one hundred and two hundred lashes to each of the two white men accused of slave-stealing and by summarily convicting and burning alive the black man, Francis J. McIntosh.[118] Already subject to harassment for his editorial discussion of slavery, Lovejoy himself became prey to mob violence when he published articles deploring the lynchings. In particular, Lovejoy criticized the aptly named Judge Luke Lawless for his charge to the grand jury that, as an incident of mob murder, the McIntosh homicide "transcends your jurisdiction—it is beyond the reach of human law."[119] After the destruction of his press by a Missouri mob, Lovejoy moved the *Observer* to nearby Alton, only to see the violence against him and his press escalate with his increasingly open endorsement of antislavery principles and the corresponding growth of abolitionist organizing in Illinois. Lovejoy died, five bullets in his heart, while defending his fourth press from an armed, arsonist mob.

Accounts of the Alton Tragedy usually stress its importance, along with James Gillespie Birney's defense of his embattled *Philanthropist*, as a test of free speech in America.[120] For although harassment of antislavery activists continued throughout antebellum America, and apologists for slavery persistently portrayed abolitionists as "accomplished criminal[s]," Lovejoy's murder marked a turning point in Northern attitudes regarding the antislavery movement's print tactics; no longer perceived as a dangerous criminal act, abolitionist print agitation was for the most part tolerated—however grudgingly—as a recognized form of free speech appropriate to a healthy democracy.[121] It bears emphasizing, however, that the saga of Lovejoy and the *Observer* was framed by terrifying moments when lynch law supplanted due process: beginning with the whippings of the two white "abolitionists" and the burning alive of McIntosh by Missouri mobs, the tragedy culminated with the Illinois mob's shooting of Lovejoy. That the editor's murder, like that of McIntosh, was followed by highly suspicious judicial pandering to the Slave Power only reinforced abolitionist efforts to associate antislavery with both freedom of expression and trial by jury.[122]

Of course, even as Lovejoy's murder and other incidents of antiabolitionist repression strengthened reformers' efforts to identify their opponents as the true criminals, such events served as a potent reminder that extralegal appeals to public opinion could provoke not only reasoned critical print debate but also that other legacy of popular constitutionalism, uncompromising mob violence. But as abolitionists and other defenders of American civil liberties never tired of insisting, mobs like those at the Boston Tea Party had no place in the new republic, for unlike colonial subjects, American citizens themselves held the power to change intolerable laws. It was to this very end that the AASS had dedicated itself in its constitution.[123] Moreover, because political progress in a republic required the active participation of an informed citizenry, abolitionist propagandists could not stop with merely exciting mass outrage through their rousing portrayals of legal crises involving slavery; antislavery writers had to educate as well as inflame their readers by coupling their promotion of popular legal spectatorship with instruction in American slave law.[124]

What the Alton Tragedy revealed was the impossibility of parsing American civil liberties: if legally tolerated mobs could brutalize not just abolitionists and blacks in the South but a white newspaper editor in Illinois as well, then slavery posed a hazard to the civil liberties of all Americans, regardless of condition, race, section, or political orientation. As sobering as the Lovejoy murder had been, it was not until the fugitive slave crisis of the 1850s that the antislavery movement finally managed to persuade Northerners of the threat the South's peculiar institution posed to American civil liberties, due process in particular.

The Courthouse in Chains

Having decriminalized their movement both legally and rhetorically by identifying antislavery activism with free speech and trial by jury throughout the 1830s, abolitionists in the following decades sought to deprive what they portrayed as an antidemocratic judiciary of authority over the slavery issue. It would take the Compromise of 1850, with its legal limitations on due process and resulting restrictions on public access to the courts, to affirm the abolitionist equation of the judiciary with government repression. The succession of fugitive slave cases that rocked Boston in the early 1850s dramatized how Jacksonian anxieties about the judiciary, when combined with the apparent erosion of Massachusetts's rights as a free state, could consolidate Northern public opinion against the Slave Power.[125] If, as suggested earlier, we read the antebellum period's virulent antijudicial sentiment and avid legal spectatorship as manifestations of an increasingly jeopardized popular constitutionalism, we can see how the extended reach of Southern slave law gave new urgency to abolitionist calls to transfer authority over slavery from the judiciary to the lay public via the medium of print. For it was in the 1850s that the Northern reading public finally understood the extent to which slavery impinged on the civil liberties of, in the *New York Atlas*'s words, "the white man as well as the black."

Less than five months after James Hamlet's capture in Manhattan, Shadrach Minkins was arrested in Boston. The city had already been the scene of one of the best-known fugitive crises before 1850, the 1842 case of George Latimer. An important outcome of that earlier case was Massachusetts's 1843 "Latimer Law," which prohibited state authorities from aiding the rendition of fugitive slaves. As a result, those seized as fugitives in Boston were not held in the local jail but in the courthouse, the use of which was leased to the federal government.[126] Accordingly, when Minkins was arrested in early 1851, he was detained in the Boston courthouse. A crowd quickly gathered outside while Deputy Marshal Riley directed all but the main entrance to the building to be closed, and the Boston Vigilance Committee scrambled to arrange legal representation for Minkins.[127] Upon the adjournment of the preliminary hearing, approximately thirty African American abolitionists burst into the courtroom and successfully liberated Minkins, who eventually escaped to Canada.

The Minkins rescue seemed to prove that the Fugitive Slave Law could not be enforced in Boston, the Cradle of Liberty. But on 3 April 1851, as local newspapers continued to carry articles on the rescue's legal fallout, in which several prominent antislavery activists were indicted for aiding and abetting the escape of a fugitive from service, the arrest of Thomas Sims offered yet another test case for Northern liberty and justice.[128] Explicitly seeking to avoid a repeat of the Minkins rescue, municipal authorities fortified the Boston courthouse—which again served as a holding cell for the suspected fugitive—by encircling it with heavy chains and armed militia companies (fig. 5).[129]

When, in the spring of 1854, a third fugitive, Anthony Burns, was arrested and imprisoned in the same building, the return of the chains and militia served as a powerful visual reminder of both earlier cases.[130] The next night, three years after the Minkins rescue, another mob "assaulted" the Boston courthouse, and in the gunfire that followed, Deputy James Batchelder fell dead (fig. 6).[131] The riot was unsuccessful, however: like remanded Georgia fugitive Sims, Burns was forcibly returned to slavery, this time amidst a tremendous military display that prompted national outrage.

Throughout the fugitive slave crises, Boston's Court Square stood at the center of the legal spectacle. As the Unitarian *Christian Register* reported after Sims's capture, "the Court House in chains has been decidedly the chief topic of conversation, and constant source of excitement for the past week."[132] Throngs of people crowded to watch as Sims's counsel, celebrated lawyer and maritime author Richard Henry Dana Jr., "hopped over the chains."[133] "Not having been two years before the mast," Chief Justice Lemuel Shaw (father-in-law of that other author-sailor, Herman Melville) and his Supreme Judicial

BOSTON COURT HOUSE.

Figure 5. "Boston Court House." (Courtesy of the Bostonian Society/Old State House)

Court colleagues "bowed themselves in the dust" and "crawl[ed] under the chain."[134] Court of Common Pleas Judge Daniel Wells "refused" to engage in such antics, requiring that "a free passage [be] made for him."[135]

Scrutiny of judicial demeanor was not limited to the judges' negotiation of the chains encircling the courthouse. In addition to calls for an elected judiciary as a means to curtail dangerous judicial independence, the cases' denouement saw Burns commissioner Judge Edward G. Loring removed from the office of probate judge in a hearing before the Massachusetts House Committee on Federal Relations—in effect, put "on trial for having been a slave commissioner."[136] Loring had already been tried in the court of public opinion: upon Burns's rendition to Virginia, crowds in Worcester and North Bridgewater hanged in effigy "Loring, the unjust Judge."[137] The *National Anti-Slavery Standard* portrayed Loring as "gathered to that small company of infamous Judges whom the world never forgets, and whose names are a byeword and a hissing to the latest posterity."[138]

NIGHT ATTACK ON THE COURT HOUSE.

Figure 6. "Night Attack on the Court House," in Charles Emory Stevens, *Anthony Burns: A History* (Boston, 1856). (Courtesy American Antiquarian Society)

Beyond such antijudicial sentiment, however, popular fascination with the trial participants' various modes of entry into what one local diarist called "the Boston Bastile" betokened more serious anxieties about public exclusion from the controversial legal proceedings.[139] Not only was the building itself chained, but the Commissioner's Court that heard Sims's case was held "in session with closed doors, strongly guarded upon the outside by an extra police force" to which "the public [was] not admitted.—None but Counsel and Reporters."[140] Of course, the officials' determination to block legal spectatorship only made the proceedings more tantalizing. In the local press, transcripts and summaries of the Sims case appeared alongside reports of the legislative and judicial inquiries into the authorities' exclusionary practices. In his testimony before a state senate investigative committee City Marshal Francis Tukey, the man responsible for chaining the courthouse, explained that he "did not exclude any persons having business with the courts, from entering the building" but that "spectators or idlers have been excluded."[141] In a contempt of court hearing over the matter, Judge Wells, the justice who had refused to go under the chains, ruled that "not only witnesses and parties, but *every spectator* has a right to be present in the Court" and "that access to the Court Room should be free."[142] Wells's ruling notwithstanding, crowding and continued security measures ensured that most people would learn about both the Sims and the Burns cases from the exhaustive newspaper coverage of the hearings. Throughout Boston's fugitive slave crisis, as in the larger antebellum slavery debate, print remained an important medium of both spectatorship and supervision.

Not everyone in Boston took umbrage at the events in Court Square. Applauding the decision to chain the courthouse, "Law and Order," a pseudonymous contributor to the Hunker Whig Courier, characterized the gesture as one of "consummate propriety and good discretion" in light of the previous Minkins rescue.[143] But if such precautions ensured the successful enforcement of the Fugitive Slave Law, they also transformed the meaning of the courthouse for many Northern spectators. Noting that "'chains and slavery' generally go hand in hand," the Christian Register speculated that it was "possibly not unfortunate for the cause of liberty, that a tribunal whose procedure was without the usual forms and safeguards of law, and whose object is the remanding of the captive to captivity, should have been obliged to sit encircled by chains, and to have the chains themselves guarded by a military force."[144] By surrounding the courthouse with the very symbol of human bondage, the journal implied, the skittish authorities had played right into the abolitionists' hands.

"Lawlessly transformed into a slave prison and a fortress of the slave power," the chained Boston courthouse offered a stunning physical expression of how the denial of liberty and justice to enslaved African Americans required the simultaneous restriction of free Northern citizens' civil liberties.[145] Could Northerners help but join the Free Soil Boston Commonwealth in asking, "Are not the chains around the Court House emblematical of our present position?" — "chains which even our judges are obliged to pass under, and which serve to keep respectable citizens (who have the right to enter the courts, and perhaps have business there) out, turned away, or rudely questioned by insolent officials, who have no more right to act than their prisoner"?[146] Under such conditions, the chains around the courthouse came to represent not only the Slave Power but also the ideological fetters "which bind the hearts and the consciences of so many of our citizens, that they suffer chains, bayonets, revolvers, soldiers and police, to be used by this great free government" in order "to crush liberty, to destroy the trial by jury and the rights of all men at the dictation of a set of tyrants, who will only despise us and trample upon us in proportion as we succeed in riveting our own chains."[147] Originally intending to keep out insurgent African Americans and their abolitionist supporters, the authorities who chained the Boston courthouse in 1851 and 1854 effectively prohibited members of the general public from participating in the

American legal process, thus encouraging them to identify their "own chains" with those of the slave.

Nowhere was this identification so palpable as on the night of 26 May 1854, when an angry mob stormed the Boston courthouse. In a reversal of the Alton Tragedy and other instances of antiabolitionist mobbing, the riot in Court Square manifested not the mob's desire to preempt or circumvent due process but Northerners' frustration with their perceived exclusion from the legal system. That the Court Square riot represented as much an assertion of Northern citizens' democratic rights as an attempt to free Southern slave Anthony Burns is indicated by subsequent trial testimony, which suggested that the courthouse itself, rather than the fugitive imprisoned within, was the main object of contention. Estimating that a crowd of about five hundred people filled Court Square, Police Chief Robert Taylor described the riot: "I heard a number of pistol shots or gun shots," he testified, "I heard the glass rattling; I heard bricks striking against the glass; there was a continual rattling of glass & bricks."[148] Through the chaos, Taylor claimed, he "saw men at the door with axes, striking against the door" as well another "fifteen or twenty men . . . drawing off & striking the door" with "a stick of timber which we generally call a battering-ram."[149] As the testimony of Taylor's subordinates makes clear, the mob's physical assault on the building evinced not so much an effort to get Burns out as a bid to let the rioters in. Police officer William Lassell recalled his heated exchange with Boston Vigilance Committee member, temperance lecturer, and labor activist John C. Cluer: "I told him he could not pass into the Court House; he said that he knew the laws of the Commonwealth; that the Court House belonged to the people, that I had no right to stop him, & that he should not be stopped by a contemptible puppy like me."[150] Another policeman, Daniel M. Hill, who also heard Cluer say to the crowd "that the Court House belonged to the citizens of Boston, & he had as good a right to go in as any other person," testified that "while they were working the timber" he "heard voices say—'Stove down the door' —'Damn the building'—'Tear it down.'"[151] The expressed desire of at least some of the Court Square rioters to demolish the Boston courthouse itself indicates that the antijudicialism that had percolated throughout the antebellum period finally came to a boiling point with the fugitive slave crisis of the 1850s when Northerners increasingly came to identify the extension of slavery's legal reach as an imposition on their own civil liberties.

Less dramatic, but equally revealing, was the rumor that swirled around Boston during first the Sims and then the Burns hearings. In an item headed

"Southern Court-House," the Commonwealth reported that the "only way of getting in" to the Boston courthouse was to "give the pass-word that [one] was a Southern gentleman, and the way would be open."[152] The message seemed clear: when the Slave Power could close the courts to Northern citizens, only Southern gentlemen could be certain of gaining access to justice in post–Fugitive Slave Law America.

Court Day

The precise connotation that "Southern Court-House" may have had for a Northern readership may be discerned by turning our attention to an antislavery novel advertised in an issue of the Boston Daily Morning Commonwealth emblazoned with an engraving of "Sims Leaving the Boston Courthouse . . . under a guard of two hundred Policemen, with U.S. cutlasses."[153] The proximity of the advertisement and the engraving is suggestive: if the Commonwealth's coverage of the Sims rendition presented the Boston courthouse as the symbol of Northern complicity with the Slave Power, Emily Catharine Pierson's Jamie Parker, the Fugitive (1851) presents the courthouse and its environs as the primary site of Southern slavery.

Juxtaposing scenes of brutal plantation justice with those depicting slave auctions in "Court House Village," Pierson's novel portrays the South as a society in which law serves primarily as a pretext for repression and injustice.[154] The plot commences when the young title character is caught learning to read the Bible in the slave quarters, and "the judge, jury, executioner, all vested in the person of the overseer, proceeded to take summary vengeance for the broken laws of the State, by applying the ever-at-hand cow-hide to the naked back and shoulders of the poor child."[155] Years later, the same overseer frames the adult Jamie and his siblings for a turkey theft they did not commit. The travesty of justice is complete when the morning arrives for Jamie and his brothers to receive their punishment. Arriving at their cabin, the overseer calls, "Come, stir yourselves! go with me; it's court day, and you are wanted at the court house!"[156]

As Pierson suggests, for slaves the Southern courthouse represented not justice but its opposite, the total denial of African Americans' rights through their sale as chattel personal on "Court Day."[157] In a study of antebellum South Carolina, legal historian Thomas D. Russell has found that "the courts acted as the state's greatest auctioneering firm."[158] Emphasizing the local sheriff's centrality to economic transactions in nineteenth-century America, Russell points out that a considerable part of a sheriff's work arose from civil litigation, most notably the task of conducting the execution sales through which judicial decisions were carried out.[159] Such transactions, Russell contends, put "the courts . . . at the center of the domestic slave trade."[160] Acknowledging that "the slave auction is perhaps the most powerful and disturbing image from the history of the United States," Russell insists that "a more accurate vision of the slave auction would make clearer the full involvement of law and legal officials." Contrary to what we might imagine, "the site of these sales was not an auction block beside an urban wharf, but rather the steps of any district's courthouse. The stirring metaphor of the slave auction ought, then, to bring to mind an image of courts and law and a vision of these courthouse steps, on which each month one-half of all slave sales took place."[161]

Harriet Beecher Stowe offered just such a vision in *Uncle Tom's Cabin*, when the slave trader Haley, spotting a newspaper ad for an "EXECUTOR'S SALE" of "NEGROES" to be held "before the Court-house door," joins the "mixed throng . . . gathered around the court-house steps" before making the purchase that will separate an elderly slave mother from her last remaining child.[162] Whereas Stowe foregrounds the sacrifice of black familial rights to white property rights, Pierson presents Jamie Parker's sale as a tableau of African Americans' legal outsidership. On Court Day, the slaves to be sold are "led in by the constables," while "the auctioneer, hammer in hand, takes his stand directly in front of the village tavern, the jail being on the right and the court house in the rear."[163] Made "the gazing-stock of gentlemen of the bar" and "judges," Jamie stands "perfectly calm and self-possessed . . . [w]rapt in the consciousness of his own title to himself, which no conveyance to another can destroy."[164] Accused of a crime he did not commit, Jamie does not get his day in court but instead becomes a victim of Court Day. And, rather than gaining access to the court and its representatives to prove his "title to himself" under the principles of natural law, Jamie is subjected to the gaze of legal professionals who view him against the backdrop of the court that sanctions such transactions.

As illustrated by sentimental fiction and press coverage of Boston's fugitive slave crisis, after the Compromise of 1850 the antebellum courthouse, whether North or South, could no longer stand as the architectural symbol of impartial justice. Deeply implicated in the legal and economic workings of slavery, the once-revered "Temple of Justice" had too often done double duty as an auction block, "a barracoon," "a slave pen," or "a besieged fortress."[165] Little surprise, then, that novelists like Pierson and Stowe joined antislavery activists in urging their audiences to divest a corrupt judiciary of its authority and to reinvest that power in a popular tribunal conducted through the medium of print.

Judge of the Judge

"It is to some extent fatal to the courts, when the people are compelled to go behind them," Henry David Thoreau observed on 4 July 1854, a little more than a month after Anthony Burns had been marched under a suspended coffin inscribed "Liberty," through streets hung with black crepe, past law offices and stores closed in protest, while in nearby towns "church bells tolled a requiem for dead liberty," and Judge Loring swung in effigy on the commons.[166] Thoreau's audience was the hundreds, perhaps thousands, of people who had gathered in Framingham, Massachusetts, for a day of picnicking and lectures by such abolitionist luminaries as William Lloyd Garrison, Wendell Phillips, Charles Remond, Sojourner Truth, and Lucy Stone.[167] Organized by the MASS to counter what many saw as the city of Boston's perverse Fourth of July festivities—complete with a fireworks display featuring "'statues of Liberty and Justice' . . . emblazoned in fiery forms"—the Framingham Grove meeting quickly became famous for its own controversial pyrotechnics, when Garrison burned a copy of the Constitution to mingled applause and hisses.[168] Less frequently remembered is that Garrison had prefaced this act by setting fire, in quick succession, to a copy of the Fugitive Slave Law, "the decision of Edward G. Loring in the case of Anthony Burns, and the late charge of Judge Benjamin R. Curtis to the United States Grand Jury in reference to the 'treasonable' assault upon the Court House."[169] In mid-afternoon, well after the ashes from the incinerated legal documents had settled, Thoreau took the stage, flanked by "banners depicting a downcast Massachusetts chained to a triumphant Virginia."[170] Although his speech marked the Transcendentalist social critic's first public appearance at an abolitionist-sponsored function, Thoreau's lecture hewed to what had by 1854 become a well-established antislavery tactic.[171] Much as Garrison had done with his (literally) inflammatory speech that morning, Thoreau seized the occasion of a legal crisis over slavery to wrest authority from the American legal system in order to place justice in the hands of the people.

In words that would inspire the New York Tribune's Horace Greeley to direct the attention of the nation's "lower-law journals" to "a genuine Higher Law Speech," Thoreau asserted that the Burns rendition had illustrated the necessity of shifting the burden of just government from officials and institutions to the individual conscience.[172] "It behooves every man," he insisted, "to see that his influence is on the side of justice, and let the courts make their own characters."[173] Unlike the judges of the sitting bench, whom the Constitution and the Fugitive Slave Law had reduced to "merely the inspectors of a pick-lock and murderer's tools, to tell him whether they are in working order or not," the *real* judge, Thoreau maintained, "is not he who merely pronounces the verdict of the law" but rather he who "finds himself constituted judge of the judge."[174] Noting that recent events had revealed "what are the true resources of justice in any community," Thoreau observed sadly that "it has come to this, that the friends of liberty, the friends of the slave, have shuddered when they understood that his fate was left to the legal tribunals of the country to be decided."[175] Appealing to prevalent fears of expanded judicial power, Thoreau affirmed that he would prefer to trust such a case "to the sentiment of the people" than to "the trammelled judgment of an individual, of no significance" who "is not a competent authority in so important a case."[176]

The question was how to put such higher law reasoning into practice. The speech provided several possibilities, from finding hope in nature's regenerative ability to create the "purity" of the water lily from "the slime and muck of earth" to enjoining that "each inhabitant of the State dissolve his union with her, as long as she delays to do her duty" of "dissolv[ing] her union with the slaveholder."[177] But Thoreau himself did not retreat into Romantic contemplativeness any more than he acted on his "involuntar[y]" urge to plot "murder to the State."[178] Unlike John Brown, whom he would fervently eulogize five years later, Thoreau did not "endeavor to blow up" the slave "system" by "touch[ing]" a "match" to it.[179] Instead, he published his speech in the *Liberator* as "Slavery in Massachusetts," where it was quickly picked up and republished by the *New York Tribune* and the *Anti-Slavery Standard*.[180]

Thus, despite Thoreau's support for the Court Square rioters ("only they are guiltless, who commit the crime of contempt of such a Court") and his call for an "earnest and vigorous . . . assault on the Press," "Slavery in Massachusetts" implies that print—not the mob—remained the best venue for redressing public wrongs.[181] Unquestionably, Thoreau, who claimed he could hear "the gurgling of the sewer through every column" of local newspapers, deprecated the press's "pernicious influence" on the nation.[182] Lambasting newspaper and magazine editors as "a class of tyrants" who "live and rule only by their servility, and [by] appealing to the worst, and not the better nature of man," Thoreau accused them of putting their readers "in the condition of the dog that returns to his vomit."[183] Yet, even as he insisted that the press was as badly in need of reformation as the Church once was, Thoreau nevertheless distinguished "noble exceptions" like the *Liberator* and the *Commonwealth* on the basis of their coverage of Boston's fugitive slave crisis.[184] In order to offer a viable substitute for corrupt courts of law, the nation's newspapers (in effect, "the only book which America has printed, and which America reads") had to do more than distract their readers from injustice with sensationalism.[185] Following the example of the antislavery and Free Soil papers, the press had to educate the public about such matters by "condemn[ing] . . . the cowardice and meanness of the authorities" when circumstances required— much as Thoreau's published speech itself did.[186]

That speech culminated in an evocation of the reciprocal relationship between print and slavery. If the press was to be evaluated on the basis of its treatment of human bondage, slavery itself was to be reviled as a threat to intellectual and artistic inquiry conducted through the medium of print. No one, with the exception of Emerson, was as well positioned to make this point as Thoreau, who was known to his Framingham audience as "a representative of Concord, of science and letters."[187] This identification of Thoreau with the liberal arts would have intensified the impact of the nightmarish scene with which he concluded his discussion of slavery, law, and print. Shunning the Union-preserving quietism characteristic of most contemporary calls for American literary nationalism, Thoreau asked his audience to "suppose you have a small library, with pictures to adorn the walls, . . . and contemplate scientific and literary pursuits," only to "discover all at once that your villa, with all its contents, is located in hell, and that the justice of the peace has a cloven foot and a forked tail."[188] "Do not these things suddenly lose their value in your eyes?" he demanded abruptly.[189] Like Pierson, Stowe, and other abolitionist authors, Thoreau realized that America's newly emerging print culture would acquire "value" only by confronting—not ignoring—the injustice of slavery. In a world where their proslavery rulings made judges appear more and more demonic, print had the special task of providing a forum in which members of the reading public could try the issue of slavery according to their conscientious sense of higher law. Only after thus resolving the issue, Thoreau suggested, would the American writer ("and every man") be free— not simply to pass uninterrupted "through Court street on errands of trade" but, far more importantly—to pursue "his onward and upward path, on which he had trusted soon to leave Court street far behind."[190] Until that day, American literature would stand in the sinister shadow of American slave law.

In the thirty years before the Civil War, abolitionists repeatedly issued print appeals to American readers not only to judge those judges who collaborated with the Slave Power but also to adjudicate the legal status of slavery. Accordingly, most Americans would enter the nation's courtrooms not as the Court

Square rioters did, with a battering ram, but as the diverse readerships of the *Atlas*, the *Commonwealth*, the *Courier*, the *Christian Register*, and the *Liberator* did, through print. For, as impervious as the Boston courthouse may have been to such violent assaults—Anthony Burns was, after all, returned to slavery—the hearings conducted within proved far more porous. Their discursive contents, like that of the era's other famous slave cases, spilled onto the pages of daily and weekly newspapers, broadsides, engravings, pamphlets, and novels. From Garrison's libel trial onward, antislavery print propaganda strove to remove authority over slavery from the judiciary and bestow it on an American reading public assumed to be thoroughly versed in both the facts and the law of such crises. In this way, each of the era's highly publicized trials became a synecdoche for the larger debate over slavery, in which readers were expected carefully to review the testimony of slaves and slaveholders, to follow the arguments of both abolitionists and defenders of slavery, and, finally, to render a verdict that would not only reverse the decisions reached by the nation's atrocious judges but, more importantly, put an end to the crime of slavery. By turning to this thriving print culture, Northerners demonstrated their willingness to "go behind" the courts—and thus their distrust for American law and their corresponding commitment to seek an alternative forum for justice.

That slavery and its perpetrators—and *not* abolitionists—could convincingly be portrayed as criminal in antebellum print culture represented one of the victories of the early antislavery movement. Successfully countering legal and rhetorical efforts to criminalize abolitionist agitation, Garrison, Lundy, Jay, Lovejoy, and other early reformers radically repositioned their movement with respect to Northern public opinion. The next challenge would be to effect a corresponding decriminalization of the black subject in American print culture, transforming the representative African American from guilty malefactor to outspoken eyewitness.

2 | PRECARIOUS EVIDENCE

Sojourner Truth and the Matthias Scandal

Along with his friend Henry David Thoreau's criticism of Judge Loring and William Lloyd Garrison's incineration of legal documents, the third of the "striking incidents" that Unitarian minister and abolitionist Moncure Daniel Conway recalled of the 4 July 1854 Framingham Grove gathering was the devastating dismissal of a fellow Southerner by "a very aged negro woman named 'Sojourner Truth.'"[1] "Lank, shrivelled, but picturesque," Truth sat on the platform, listening to a proslavery Carolinian whom Garrison had invited, impromptu, to address the crowd.[2] "The young man complied, and in the course of his defence of slavery and affirming his sincerity, twice exclaimed, 'As God is my witness!'"—upon which, Conway recalled, Truth interjected: 'Young man. . . . I don't believe God Almighty ever hearn tell of you!'"[3] "Her shrill voice," he recollected, "sounded through the grove like a bugle; shouts of laughter responded, and the poor Southerner could not recover from that only interruption."[4]

Whether the story is accurate or, like so many other contemporary white accounts of Truth's speech, either heavily embroidered or fabricated out of whole cloth, Conway's anecdote captures the testimonial posture that authorized formerly enslaved African Americans' contributions to the debate over the South's peculiar institution. Implicitly contrasting the moral obscurity of the would-be defender of slavery with her own intimate knowledge of both "God Almighty" and bound servitude, Truth in this account trumped the Southerner's Pauline invocation of divine authority with her own authoritative self-fashioning as God's witness. Her testimonial intervention was so powerful that it provoked a crisis of conscience in the rising young minister from Virginia as well. "Did that old African Fate," Moncure Conway wondered, "tell the truth about me also?"[5]

The Southerners' faltering in the face of the irresistible "truth" articulated by the slave witness indicates the moral and political potency that black testimonial speech had acquired by the late antebellum period—a potency registered in the formerly enslaved Isabella Van Wagenen's choice of the name "Sojourner Truth."[6] The most recent avatar of the black print subject whose suffering and exemplary piety authorized him or her to critique the society in which he or she lived, the slave witness also drew rhetorical power from black vernacular linguistic and religious practices in which "testifying" or "witnessing" was an important form of spontaneous yet authoritative speech based in intense personal spiritual experience.[7] But if the image of the righteous testifying slave witness can be traced to both early Anglo-American print culture and African American expressive traditions, it also needs to be viewed in light of the popular legal consciousness that endowed the words "witness" and "testimony" with juridical as well as religious meaning in Jacksonian America.

This point is illustrated by an anecdote that surfaced in both Olive Gilbert's *Narrative of Sojourner Truth* (1850) and Harriet Beecher Stowe's influential *Atlantic Monthly* essay, "Sojourner Truth, the Libyan Sybil" (1863).[8] In the latter account, Truth, "aged and worn with many hardships," tells how her mystical Christian conversion and her harsh experience of slavery inspire her to "go round a-testifyin'" as an evangelical abolitionist lecturer.[9] Embedded in her testimonial conversion narrative, however, is a story that highlights how the authority of the slave witness could be complicated—even compromised—by African Americans' perceived legal outsidership. In 1826, on the eve of New York's legislative emancipation, Isabella Van Wagenen learned that her son Peter had been illegally sold by his New York master and transported to Alabama.[10] In Stowe's version of the story, Truth recalls how she came to initiate the legal proceedings that would eventually force her son's return and manumission: "I talked with people, an' they said I must git the case before a grand jury. So I went into the town when they was holdin' a court, to see ef I could find any grand jury. An' I stood round the court-house, an' when they was a-comin' out, I walked right up to the grandest-lookin' one I could see, an' says I to him,—'Sir, be you a grand jury?'"[11] In keeping with Truth's "whole air," which according to Stowe "had at times a gloomy sort of drollery," her tragicomic tale's punch line turns on that minstrel-show commonplace, the black speaker's malapropian efforts to master an authoritative, alien white discourse.[12] Here, as in other versions of the tale, the morally upright, "testifyin'" ex-slave woman is ignorant of, awed by, and emphatically *outside* law, even as her personal narrative of racial exploitation provides irrefutable evidence for the abolitionist case against slavery.[13]

The historical Isabella Van Wagenen was no legal naif, however; by the time she encountered Conway, Gilbert, and Stowe, Truth had had more direct contact with law than most women of her generation, black or white. Not only did Truth have a thoroughgoing familiarity with law but—astonishingly, given the widespread denial of procedural rights to blacks in antebellum America—she appears to have had successfully instituted two separate lawsuits against comparatively wealthy white men. In 1827–28, she initiated the legal proceedings that would force slaveholder Solomon Gedney to journey to Alabama in order to return her son to her.[14] And sometime in the winter of 1834–35, she sued renowned New York businessman Benjamin Folger for slander, reportedly receiving a $125 settlement and public recognition that she was not the murderer Folger and his wife Ann had painted her to be.[15] Furthermore, during the same period, she seems to have played an important behind-the-scenes role in arranging defense counsel for Robert Matthews, alias "the Prophet Matthias," in three highly publicized trials in which he was charged with embezzlement, fraud, murder, and assault following the collapse of the religious cult he had established at the Folgers' mansion in Westchester, New York.[16]

But this bizarre penny-press scandal, one of the nation's first, reveals much more than merely the legal resourcefulness of the woman who would become Sojourner Truth and the inaccuracy of white abolitionist portrayals of her.[17] Truth's early foray into print publicity provides a vantage point from which to examine the black print subject's transformation in the shadow of American law by revealing how the contemporary fascination with legal spectatorship informed African Americans' acquisition of testimonial authority in early antebellum print culture. For if the discursive fashioning of former slaves as the antislavery movement's most powerful witnesses drew considerable power from the moral rectitude of their personal testimony, it also acquired meaning in legal and print contexts that potentially impeded the development of an authoritative extralegal black literary persona. Excavating those contexts, this chapter examines how the production and reception of African American personal narrative was shaped by the conjunction of procedural restrictions on black courtroom speech with a gallows literature tradition disproportionately devoted to malefactors of color.[18] The prevalent critical truism notwithstanding, slaves were not "silenced" in early America; quite the opposite, in law, as in popular literature, they were often enjoined to engage in a particular kind of speech, confession.[19] Marshaling the moral authority of the afflicted Christian witness, the testifying former slave had to overcome the pervasive tendency in law and print culture to reduce black testimony to confession. To a far greater extent than the white abolitionists with whom they would collaborate in the coming decades, African Americans who entered the print debate over slavery had to shed any possible association with criminality in order to gain a hearing at the bar of public opinion.

Initially portrayed in the Matthias scandal as "the most wicked of the wicked," a wanton black servant suspected of poisoning the family for whom she worked, Isabella Van Wagenen emerged from that scandal in a role much like the one she occupied in subsequent abolitionist accounts: as a victimized ex-slave testifying to the crimes of corrupt whites. By analyzing this transfiguration in a set of texts contemporaneous with but not explicitly directed to the early antebellum debate over slavery, we can better understand the rhetorical conditions that made possible the abolitionist movement's promotion of formerly enslaved authors as "witnesses" and their narratives as "testimony" in the 1840s and 1850s.[20]

For contemporary observers and historians alike, the cult that Robert Matthews founded on Zion Hill exposed the fissures in Jacksonian views of religion, sex, class, and family—not race and slavery.[21] But the New York–based scandal burst into public consciousness in the fall of 1834, when that city was still reeling from a wave of antiabolitionist riots. In the wake of those riots—and coinciding with the abolitionist postal campaign and the Charleston mail riots—two competing books on the Matthias scandal appeared. The first, *Matthias and His Impostures* (1835), was published by antiabolitionist editor (and riot fomenter) William Leete Stone in collaboration with two former Matthias disciples, Benjamin and Ann Folger. Stone's book joins earlier pamphlet and press accounts of the scandal in assigning Isabella Van Wagenen a role familiar from early American crime literature: that of the guilty black slave who threatens the established social order with her criminal acts. The same year, however, Stone's rival journalist, the radical freethinker and antislavery activist Gilbert Vale, worked with Van Wagenen to produce a counterattack, the two-volume *Fanaticism; Its Source and Influence* (1835). Rejecting its predecessor's attempt to cast blame on Van Wagenen, the subtitle of Vale's "Reply to W. L. Stone" presents "the Simple Narrative of Isabella in the Case of Matthias" in testimonial terms, as "the Whole Truth—and Nothing but the Truth." Published the year before the first American abolitionist–sponsored slave narrative appeared in print, Isabella Van Wagenen's "Simple Narrative" offers a revealing early example of an innocent former slave systematically exposing the private crimes of a corrupt white household.[22] Turning the leaves of these now-forgotten volumes, we glimpse a telling moment in the development of a new kind of African American literary authority, as the black print subject metamorphosed from the confessing criminal of the New England gallows tradition into the testifying eyewitness of antislavery literature.

In this odd scandal, as in the national print debate over slavery, that transformation occurred in the interstices between the court of law and the court of public opinion. Our inquiry begins, then, with a brief survey of black speech in the early American courtroom and on its print periphery.

Precarious Evidence

The same year that Isabella Van Wagenen commenced legal proceedings for the return of her son Peter, abolitionist legal scholar George M. Stroud published a treatise on American slave law in which he identified the exclusion of enslaved witnesses as "the cause of the greatest evils of slavery."[23] Almost thirty years later Harriet Beecher Stowe, relying heavily on the work of Stroud and other "legal gentlemen," would affirm in her *Key to Uncle Tom's Cabin* that "the very keystone of Southern jurisprudence is the rejection of colored testimony."[24]

This had not always been the case, however. One of the earliest known references to a black person in colonial jurisprudence is the General Court of Virginia's ruling in 1624 that "John Philip A negro, . . . was qualified as a free man and Christian to give testimony, because he had been 'Christened in England 12 years since.'"[25] But the ruling is notable primarily for the precedent that it *failed* to set. As the court's language suggests, under seventeenth-century Anglo-American law, it was blacks' presumed status as non-Christians that rendered their testimony inadmissible in most courtrooms. The inadmissibility of slave testimony arose, in part, from colonial courts' reservations as to whether Africans and their descendents were capable of appreciating the unique significance of the oath in Judeo-Christian culture.[26] Of course, the emergence of African American Christianity called this logic into question. But the religious rationale against the competency of black witnesses was supplemented by a legal one that rested on their status as slaves: their complete subjugation to their masters deprived them of free will, thereby undermining the authority and integrity of their testimony.[27] Thus, even as increasing numbers of slaves became, like John Philip, Christians, unlike him, they were not qualified as free people to give testimony.

The preamble to a 1732 Virginia statute "to disable certain Persons . . . to be Witnesses" indicates that racial ideology had come to play as important a role as religion or status in rendering the testimony of nonwhites suspect. The statute was prompted by the inconsistent practices of the Virginia courts: the legislature noted that "negros, mulattos, and Indians, have lately been frequently allowed to give testimony as lawful witnesses in the general court, and other courts of this colony, when they have professed themselves to be christians"; at other times, however, "forasmuch as they are people of such base and corrupt natures, that the credit of their testimony cannot be certainly depended upon . . . some juries have altogether rejected their evidence."[28] In order to put an end to such inconsistency and to prevent "the mischiefs that may possibly happen by admitting such precarious evidence," the legislature passed a law "that no negro, mulatto, or indian, either a slave or free, shall hereafter be admitted in any court of this colony, to be sworn as a witness, or give evidence in any cause whatsoever."[29] The only exceptions were to be the capital trials of slaves, "in which case they shall be allowed to give evidence, in the manner directed" by an earlier 1723 statute.[30]

The designated manner in which such evidence was to be admitted suggests the danger testimony involved for black witnesses from the very beginnings of American jurisprudence. Like their white counterparts, nonwhites in colonial Virginia were charged, "You are brought hither as a witness; and . . . you must tell the truth, the whole truth, and nothing but the truth."[31] Unlike white witnesses who risked fines and imprisonment for perjury, however, witnesses of color were admonished, if "you tell a lie, and give false testimony in this matter, you must, for so doing, have both your ears nailed to the pillory, and cut off, and receive thirty-nine lashes on your bare back, well laid on, at the common whipping-post."[32] By restricting black courtroom speech to either confession or testimony against other nonwhites under penalty of severe bodily harm for perjury, such laws made clear that the racial exclusion of nonwhite witnesses in cases involving whites resulted not simply from their unfree status or their position as cultural outsiders.[33] It was their intrinsic racial inferiority, their "base and corrupt natures" that made their evidence so "precarious." Over a century later, acknowledging that the "disqualification" of slave testimony "has been the prolific theme for much complaint and abuse of the system," proslavery legal theorist Thomas R. R. Cobb insisted that such exclusionary rules are "founded not only upon the servile condition of the negro, but also his known disposition to disregard the truth"—adding, conveniently, "that the negro, as a general rule, is mendacious, is a fact too well established to require the production of proof, either from history, travels, or craniology."[34]

For abolitionist treatise-writer William Goodell, however, the prohibition reflected not the mendacity of blacks but the perverse logic of slave law. Ironically defending the "reasonableness of the rule," he pointed out that "it would be an absurdity for chattels to come into Court and bear testimony against their owners!"[35] As Goodell well knew, it was precisely the impossibility of consistently treating human beings as objects of property that had led to the legal fiction of slaves' "double character," which credited enslaved African Americans with criminal agency while maintaining their incapacity for civic agency.[36] As the Court succinctly put it in an 1861 Alabama case, *Creswell's Executors v. Walker*, "because they are rational *human beings*, they are capable of committing crimes; and, in reference to acts which are crimes, are regarded as *persons*. Because they are *slaves*, they are incapable of performing civil acts; and, in reference to all such, they are *things*, not persons."[37] The decision's careful parallel structure clearly conveys the double standard at the core of American slave law: slaves were understood as having criminal but not civic agency.[38] Throughout the South and in some Northern states, this contradictory principle was encapsulated by statutory rules of evidence that, like Virginia's 1732 act, refused to recognize slaves (and often free blacks, mulattos, and Indians) as witnesses in cases involving whites, while providing for them to be tried on criminal charges and to testify against other nonwhites.[39]

While imputations of "negro" criminality effectively limited black courtroom speech to confession (or testimony to other blacks' guilt) in many jurisdictions, this legally mandated confessional posture was supplemented outside the courthouse by a print culture in which nonwhites were disproportionately represented in sermons and confessions published as part of the early American execution ritual.[40] From Cotton Mather's *Pillars of Salt* (1699) to Thomas R. Gray's *Confessions of Nat Turner* (1831), published portrayals of condemned blacks buttressed long-standing cultural associations of blackness with sin and criminality.[41] The credibility of such confessions resided not only in the widespread belief in the truth-provoking nature of the gallows but also in the racialized presumption of guilt. Although blacks' reputed mendacity made their testimony against whites "precarious evidence," no such reservations attended African American confessional discourse: to accept the veracity of such narratives, after all, was merely to affirm black criminality.

Like others in the early antislavery movement, African Americans had to reject any identification with crime in order to speak authoritatively on the slavery issue; due to the common legal and cultural association of blackness with criminality, however, they faced a far more daunting rhetorical challenge. As we have seen, early antebellum abolitionists rejected the legal and rhetorical criminalization of specific political acts—writing, publishing, or circulating incendiary literature—by aligning themselves and their movement with those key civil liberties, freedom of speech and trial by jury. But unlike the white male reformers considered in the previous chapter, African American activists were precluded by a history of racial exclusion from laying claim to such core civic values and traditions; on the contrary, their contributions to the legally inflected slavery controversy were articulated under a legal regime that rendered black civic acts largely unintelligible (at best) or downright criminal (at worst) and in a print culture fascinated by the familiar figure of the confessing black criminal.[42]

Of course, the black print subject did not exclusively address early American readers from behind bars or atop the scaffold. Other black voices acquired authority from their far-flung travels or their access to the Holy Spirit. Such cosmopolitan and spiritual perspectives would continue to inform black discursive authority in the antebellum slavery controversy.[43] But, as Frances Smith Foster notes in her classic study of the development of the slave narrative, "before the nineteenth century, it was rare that a writing was primarily concerned with relating the experiences of a particular black person. . . . When the black person as statistic or [literary] subject gave way to the black person as narrator, the most common protagonist was the social degenerate," the criminal in particular.[44] Given the extralegal cast of the print debate over slavery, the daunting rhetorical legacy of the black gallows tradition should not be underestimated. In the 1830s, for African Americans even more than for their white abolitionist counterparts, the question was how to construct a form of civic agency in print—a form, ultimately, of authorship—that was not by definition criminal.

Van Wagenen's participation in the Matthias scandal provides one answer. By publicizing her version of the cult and its dissolution, Van Wagenen expanded her role in the proceedings by substituting one kind of first-person narrative evidence for another, testifying to the crimes of others instead of confessing her own guilt. Her collaboration with Vale advanced an alternative model of extralegal black literary authority that, situated in law's shadow, envisioned an African American agency grounded in civic participation, not criminality. The shift in authorial posture was, of course, neither immediate nor irreversible. But even as white Americans stubbornly clung to their long-held association of blackness with crime, they slowly began to attend to extralegal African American speech—especially when that speech took the form of the printed personal narrative—no longer as guilty confession but, increasingly, as testimony against the crimes of slaveholding whites. Of course, the fact that Vale felt compelled to corroborate Van Wagenen's story with what he called "legal white evidence" indicates that, even as testimony gradually came to replace confession as the dominant form of African American personal narrative, such eyewitness accounts would remain precarious evidence in antebellum print culture.[45]

Matthias and His Impostures

The Kingdom of Matthias had its origins in the rapidly changing religious, political, and commercial climate of early nineteenth-century New York City. Although Robert Matthews, better known as the Prophet Matthias, was himself a poor carpenter from Albany, several of his disciples—notably, Elijah Pierson and Benjamin Folger—were recently established Manhattan merchants who, along with their wives, had been active in the city's evangelical reform movements. In the coming decade, the reformist impulse associated with this evangelical merchant class would be linked to the nascent abolitionist movement through the celebrated philanthropists Arthur Tappan and Lewis Tappan, who joined William Lloyd Garrison and others in 1833 to found the American Anti-Slavery Society (AASS).[46] Not surprisingly, these perfectionist religious communities also attracted African American members, who were responsive to evangelical calls for individual spiritual transformation and collective social reformation.[47] Along with "another black woman, named Katy," Isabella Van Wagenen joined the independent church founded by Elijah Pierson.[48] Like Pierson and Arthur Tappan, Van Wagenen was active in the Magdalen Society, the nation's first organized antiprostitution endeavor, and, for many, a crucial stepping-stone to what would soon be the all-consuming reform of abolitionism.[49]

Matthews became acquainted with both Pierson and Van Wagenen in the summer of 1832. A year later, the three had moved into the Sing Sing, New York, mansion of Benjamin and Ann Folger and their three children. The house was soon to be known as Zion Hill, the Kingdom of Matthias, who was, in turn, "the Spirit of Truth—the male governing spirit, or God."[50] As historians Paul E. Johnson and Sean Wilentz have shown, Zion Hill in many ways represented an attempt to return to an earlier, rigidly patriarchal social order. For example, work was divided along gender, race, and class lines: in the house, "Isabella performed heavy household work and did most of the cooking" with the help of a white woman named Catherine Galloway, whereas Ann Folger was "appointed . . . to wash and groom the children, help with light housework, and direct the kitchen as Father's delegate."[51] Like the labor of the wealthy white woman they would come to call "Mother," that of the white servant and the African American former slave was unpaid.[52]

What exactly occurred in the year between the establishment of the Zion Hill household in August 1833 and its breakup a year later is the subject of the print affray between, on the one hand, William Leete Stone and the Folgers and, on the other, Gilbert Vale and Isabella Van Wagenen. The only facts that seem certain are that in March 1834, Benjamin Folger became bankrupt; that on 28 June 1834, Elijah Pierson, after an increasingly troubling series of "fits," died at Zion Hill without medical attention; and that in November 1834 and April 1835, Matthias was tried first for defrauding Folger, then for murdering Pierson and for assaulting his own daughter, Isabella Laisdell.[53] Ultimately, however, it was not the religious fanaticism, dubious finances, and physical violence that fueled the Matthias scandal but rather the rampant rumors of unconventional sexuality and multiple poisonings—in both of which Isabella Van Wagenen figured prominently.

If the Matthias cult erupted from the religious, political, economic, and social changes bubbling in early nineteenth-century New York, its scandal burst on to a print culture that, as historian Louis P. Masur has demonstrated, was radically reconstituting traditional understandings of the relations among crime, publicity, and the printed word. The Matthias story broke in 1834, the same year that Pennsylvania held the nation's first private execution; in the following year, when New York, along with New Jersey and Massachusetts, passed legislation mandating private executions, Matthews was tried on the capital charge of murdering Pierson. As a result of the contemporary debate over capital punishment, executions were relocated "from the town commons to behind prison walls," symbolizing "a broader trend toward social privatization and class segmentation" by turning "the execution of criminals into an elite event structured around class and gender exclusion rather than communal instruction."[54] Among the select group of professional men invited to witness these recently privatized executions were representatives of the new penny press, which appealed to the very masses who were now excluded from viewing hangings in person.[55] And, whereas the purpose of execution-day sermons and criminal confessions published from the 1670s to the mid-eighteenth century was to teach that the murderer, like other criminals, was an "example not only of deep depravity but of spiritual hope, pointing to her spiritual progress and dying confession as a model for the larger community to emulate," cultural historian Karen Halttunen has found that the more secular late eighteenth- and nineteenth-century crime narratives that circulated in the penny press and as cheap pamphlets encouraged their readers to see such figures as monstrously alien embodiments of the dangers that lurked both within and outside of the newly private domestic spaces of middle-class society.[56]

As "one of the first penny-press sensations in American history—the main protagonist in a deeply disturbing scandal that received unprecedented national attention," the Prophet Matthias stood at the center of a spectacle that was covered by newspapers from Boston to Richmond.[57] This press coverage generated, in turn, at least ten pamphlets or books on the case between 1834 and 1879.[58] Prior to the advent of the penny press in 1833, newspapers had been organs of political parties, religious organizations, or commercial interests, circulating on a weekly basis to well-heeled subscribers who spread out the unwieldy sheets in their homes or offices, squinting at the large, closely printed pages. Beginning with the New York Sun, however, the penny press appeared daily, its publishers relying on the new easily pocketable format, cheap cost, and sensational stories to capture the passing fancy of a mass readership.[59] Sales depended on the papers' ability to catch and maintain readers' interest, which meant exhaustively covering every angle of a popular news story—more often than not, one of the era's melodramatic trials.

With legal spectatorship blurring the boundaries between the court of law and the court of public opinion, print coverage of famous cases mimicked the trial's adversarial structure. Arguing that nineteenth-century nonfiction crime narratives demonstrate "the historical triumph of the legal discourse of murder over the theological," Halttunen has demonstrated that just as "the new adversarial trial made legal truth a matter of formal argument," these narratives were indeterminate and contestatory: they "effectively treated readers as jurors who had to take an active role in crafting the murder narrative" by processing "the chaos of trial testimony and physical evidence to make sense of what really happened."[60] Like the burgeoning print debate over slavery, coverage of the Matthias scandal joined this trend.

The trial's adversarial structure was most vividly reenacted by the books published on behalf of each of the opposing parties in the actual legal proceedings. Commercial Advertiser editor William Leete Stone collaborated with the Folgers to publish Matthias and His Impostures after the New York Sun published a pamphlet detailing some of the more salacious rumors circulating about the Prophet's sexual relations with his disciples.[61] In contrast to the cheap pamphlets typically generated by this and subsequent scandals, Stone's book was published by the respected Harper and Brothers firm in an attractive stereotyped edition that garnered an extensive, laudatory article in the highbrow North American Review.[62] In an effort to clear the Folgers' names, Matthias and His Impostures refuted some of the most damaging rumors put forth by the Sun pamphlet and offered, largely through the Folgers' own interpolated account, an alternative tale of misguided religious "delusion" that nevertheless remained firmly within the bounds of acceptable bourgeois domesticity.

In the same year, radical British deist and Citizen of the World editor Gilbert Vale collaborated with Isabella Van Wagenen on Fanaticism.[63] The first volume of this work conducts a rather tedious line-by-line rebuttal of Stone's book; the spicier second volume offers a counter-exposé that gives "names, dates, places, and facts, without reserve" in order to reveal "the assumption of supernatural power in more than one case, uncleanness, seduction, and adultery, committed in the name of the Lord" in an effort to disprove the Folgers' "reciprocal charges of something like murder and theft."[64] By the time the second volume of *Fanaticism* had been published, the Folgers and Van Wagenen had been on opposite sides of two different court cases; even more emphatically than usual, then, their competing print versions of the mysterious doings at Zion Hill placed the reader in the role of juror.

Although Stone and Vale provided dramatically divergent behind-the-scenes views of what both referred to as "the family" at Zion Hill, their contrasting accounts nevertheless offered their readers the characters, settings, themes, and plots that were rapidly becoming familiar to consumers of the popular nonfiction murder mysteries of the day.[65] The scandal centered on the body-horror represented by poor Elijah Pierson.[66] In life Pierson's unexplained "fits" produced ugly contusions, "occasioned by his knocking his feet together" and, worse, led him to call out Ann Folger's name, "endeavouring to approach her with one hand extended" while "feel[ing] about his person with the other within his clothes."[67] In his final illness, Pierson remained largely unattended, covered in his own vomit, urine, and feces.[68] And in death, he was exhumed and autopsied twice, his corpse the subject of detailed (and gruesome) forensic medical examination and discussion.[69] In contrast to the grotesque horror of Pierson's diseased body was the pornography of violence involving the scandal's women: notably, Pierson's anointing of his wife's dead body in oil and Matthias's cowhide whipping of his own adult daughter.[70] The combined revulsion and voyeurism encouraged by such horrific representations, Halttunen has argued, served the dual purpose of heightening the nineteenth-century reader's sense of distance from the human evil entailed in the crime of murder even as it reinforced that reader's sense of vicarious complicity in that evil.[71]

In the Matthias scandal, much of this horror occurred in the appropriately gothic setting of the Folger mansion, Zion Hill, which perverted the newly established ideal of middle-class domesticity in one of two ways, depending on whether one subscribed to the version of events put forth by Stone and the Folgers or that of Vale and Van Wagenen. The Stone narrative depicted a model bourgeois family, part of a community of "highly respectable and intelligent citizens—ladies, educated, accomplished, virtuous—and gentlemen of character—acute in business—men of wealth, of information, and of great public and private worth," who were regrettably but understandably caught up in "the great error of the times in which we live, and especially in our own country . . . a tendency to ultraism," or religious extremism, which in turn led them to subject themselves to the tyranny of an impostor whose monomania was complemented by the "shrewdness and cunning" of a confidence man.[72]

The Vale version told a very different story. Rather than depicting the Folgers as pious Christians, who, after "pure and blameless lives," "God . . . allow[ed] to wander into error," Vale depicted the Folgers *themselves* as classic examples of the confidence man and the painted woman, pretenders to a sentimental bourgeois identity whose values they exploited rather than shared.[73] Vale's Mr. Folger emerges as a "poor lad" turned speculator whose "rather showy style of living," "rather . . . handsome" looks, and "extreme politeness" allowed him to become "connected with the best society" and "effectually concea[l] a rather defective education" as well as "some vices and weaknesses in his character, which counterbalance his virtues."[74] For her part, Mrs. Folger, although "not properly a beautiful woman," "dressed with much taste, highly scented," spoke in "tones insinuating," and assumed an "innocence and harmlessness" that "appear[ed] natural"; once fallen, however, she manifested an insatiable sexual appetite that led her to neglect her responsibilities to her husband, children, and housework.[75]

When these social impostors themselves became involved in the even greater imposture of Matthias, the result was "a family" that on the outside "differed in appearance very little from other well conducted families" but concealed a "mystery within" that offered a grotesque parody of the idealized middle-class household.[76] Headed by a tyrannical, ranting "Father" (Matthias) and a scheming, adulterous "Mother" (Mrs. Folger), this perverse "family" transgressed bourgeois sentimental notions of companionate marriage and child nurture: to compensate for her own dalliances, the fashionable Ann Folger adorned two of her husband Benjamin's working-class paramours (sometimes in her own clothes) in order to render them more appealing to him, whereas Mr. Folger, deprived by Matthias of his own wife, had sex with the prophet's newly married daughter in the bedroom (and possibly the bed) she shared with her ten-year-old brother.[77]

The uncertainty posed by these two competing versions of the events at Zion Hill was heightened by the ambiguous outcome of the legal proceedings that had prompted such extensive print coverage in the first place. Although Matthias was eventually sentenced to three months' imprisonment for the assault on his daughter, the fraud suit was dismissed, and the erstwhile prophet was ultimately acquitted of both insanity and the murder charge. The lack of any resolution to the latter case—no one else was charged with Pierson's murder—only intensified the mystery that the Stone and Vale books sought to solve. Whether one accepted the Stone-Folger or the Vale–Van Wagenen account, the same troubling question remained: if the gross perversion of Christian domesticity that culminated in the gruesome death of Elijah Pierson could not be blamed on Matthias, as either a dangerous lunatic or a wily confidence man, who or what was to blame for the breakdown of this particular household that differed in appearance very little from other well-conducted families? Where did the source of evil lie?

The Black Servant Isabella

Isabella Van Wagenen was never charged in the murder of Elijah Pierson; nevertheless, many accounts of the scandal—notably Stone's authoritative *Matthias and His Impostures*—offered a narrative resolution to the mystery of Pierson's death and the troubling questions it raised by resorting to racial scapegoating and tracing the crime to "the black servant Isabella." For example, just prior to reporting the disappointing legal conclusion of the scandal, the *New York Sun*'s pamphlet related the following anecdote regarding Matthias's final day at Zion Hill, after the prophet had been dismissed by Mr. Folger: "A breakfast of coffee was placed on the table, which had been prepared by Isabella Van Wagenen, the black servant, and disciple of Matthias. He declined to partake of it, saying that his bodily person was somewhat indisposed.—Mr. and Mrs. Folger, however, and their children, drunk of it as usual, but found fault with it, as ill-f[l]avored and disagreeable. In a very short time afterwards, the whole family, except Matthias and the black servant, who alone had not partaken of the coffee, were taken violently sick; but though they all escaped death, several of them had not recovered from its effects at the termination of nearly three months. Matthias had left the city before the breakfast was concluded, and the place of his destination was unknown."[78] Anecdotes like this one, with their implicit charge that Van Wagenen poisoned the Folger household under Matthias's direction, magnified the importance of one frequently reported detail in the circumstances surrounding Pierson's death. As Stone has it, "Mr. Pierson's sickness, which terminated in his death, commenced" after he had eaten "freely of some blackberries picked by Matthias . . . and prepared with sugar for the table, as is supposed, by the coloured woman."[79] Soon Pierson was incapacitated with "severe fits," vomiting, and diarrhea.[80] Once again, the circumstantial evidence seemed to point to "the coloured woman."

Beyond solving the mystery of Pierson's death, these stories could help allay the larger concerns the scandal posed. With Isabella as the culprit, the question of Matthias's exact mental state became less pressing; after all, he had only conspired to murder Pierson and the Folgers—it was "the black servant" who actually committed the crime. If, as Halttunen suggests, the figures of the partially insane murderer and the confidence man forced middle-class Americans to face, on the one hand, their own potential capacity for evil and, on the other, the artificiality of their own performance of bourgeois identity, the oddly reassuring figure of the black criminal presented no such uncomfortable dilemmas to white readers. More significantly, the coffee-poisoning tale suggests that the danger extended beyond the clearly mad Pierson to the very core of the pious (albeit deluded) white Christian middle-class family. Like "the black servant" whose task it was to maintain "the family" through her household labor (especially her cooking), poison is an agent that, usually masquerading as a source of sustenance, destroys the health of the body from within. The rumors of poisoning, then, voice greater anxieties about the very traits that helped to distinguish the model nineteenth-century American family: nurturing, femininity, and domesticity. If the idealized bourgeois domesticity the Folger family claimed to represent was in danger, these accounts suggest, it was neither the erring parents nor even Matthias, the "mental alien" in their midst, who posed the mortal threat but Isabella, "the coloured woman."[81]

What is particularly striking about most print treatments of the Matthias scandal is that even as these stories illustrate radical transformations both in early nineteenth-century American society and in the narrative means by which the culture addressed such changes, they nevertheless demonstrate the comparative stasis of images of the African American in the popular imagination. If, as Johnson and Wilentz contend, "in the newspaper accounts, each of the Kingdom's major characters appeared to be emblematic of a more general social type; and almost every twist in the plot seemed indicative of some larger trend" with respect to "the contests over family life, sexuality, and social class that accompanied the rise of market society," then "Isabella, the black servant," stands out as a remarkably timeless, ahistorical figure—an almost mythical embodiment of entrenched associations of blackness, criminality, and sexuality.[82] Contrasting sharply with the dramatically shifting narrative of human evil articulated by the nonfiction murder accounts from the Puritan to the antebellum eras would appear to be the profoundly static story of black criminality repeatedly told over the same period.

The bulk of the print coverage of the Matthias scandal is consistent with the nineteenth-century turn of crime narratives to gothic and horror as a means to negotiate larger cultural changes; tellingly, however, at a time of such powerful reevaluation of the meanings of everything from gender, family, and the home to violence, crime, and evil, the specific literary constructions of *race* and criminality in these accounts do not radically transform the figure of the consistently alien, sexualized, black criminal.[83] Although in both verbal and visual texts, the European "association of the black with concupiscence reaches back into the Middle Ages," critic Sander Gilman has found that it is in the eighteenth century that "the sexuality of the black, both male and female, becomes an icon for deviant sexuality in general."[84] In early America, the chain of associations from blackness through deviant sexuality to criminality was reinforced by the steady stream of gallows literature devoted to the sexualized black criminal. Antebellum accounts of the Matthias scandal follow this logic of criminal black deviance: first, by mapping the sexual perversity associated with the scandal onto "the coloured woman"; then, having established her as "among the most wicked of the wicked," by identifying her as the source of the crime itself.[85]

The sensational *New York Sun* pamphlet gives the best sense of the kind of rumors that were swirling about Matthias and his disciples. Matthias, it disclosed, had "instituted a revolting domestic ceremony or religious rite," called, perversely, "the Purification from Marriage," or "the Fountain of Eden."[86] In this unseemly ritual, "all the members of his household, both male and female, including the black servant Isabella," stripped and stood in a circle, so that Matthias could wash each with a sponge that "had first been consecrated by the ablution of his own person," pronouncing them " 'virgins of the garden,' and children of his kingdom."[87] In another wanton distortion of biblical precedent, it was reported that "of the seven females, including Isabella Van Wagenen, the black servant, which composed his harem," Matthias "appointed" one "to each working day in the week," with "the black one consecrated for Sundays."[88] Withholding the identities of the white participants, "in pity to their scarcely pardonable fatuity" (and, perhaps, in fear of a libel suit), the *Sun* writer nevertheless clearly identifies "the black servant" twice by name.[89] In both anecdotes, the presence of "Isabella Van Wagenen, the black servant" accomplishes the verbal equivalent of the insertion of the black servant in visual depictions of deviant (white) sexuality from Hogarth's *A Harlot's Progress* (1731) and *A Rake's Progress* (1733–34) to Manet's *Olympia* (1863). In American popular literature as in European fine art, "one of the black servant's central functions in . . . the eighteenth and nineteenth centuries was to sexualize the society in which he or she was found."[90]

As prevalent as the figure of the sexualized black servant may have been, this image was particularly explosive at the very moment and in the very place that the Matthias scandal entered public consciousness. For, as Elijah Pierson's seizures worsened in the spring and summer of 1834, New York City was itself convulsed by riots. The worst uprising in this "year of the riots" occurred from 9 to 11 July, when "violent mobs of as many as twenty-thousand persons formed on anti-abolitionist, anti-black lines" and "held the city at bay, destroyed at least sixty dwellings, demolished six churches, and seriously damaged other homes and meeting houses."[91] Particular targets were antislavery meetings and abolitionist-owned property, most notably the home of wealthy philanthropist-reformer Lewis Tappan.[92] In the weeks leading up to the July riot, two newspapers, James Watson Webb's *Courier and Enquirer* and William Leete Stone's *Commercial Advertiser*, encouraged antiabolitionist violence by stoking the inflammatory rumors that abolitionists advocated interracial marriage.[93] In the days following the riot, even as Stone repudiated the mobs, he persisted in accusing abolitionists of "kindling the fury of the rioters by seeking to '*mulattoize* our posterity' and degrade 'a nation of white men . . . to the condition of mongrels.' "[94] By the fall and winter of 1834, then, New Yorkers were well primed for a scandal involving violence, race, and perverse sexuality. And William Leete Stone was just the man to give it to them.

In doing so, however, he faced a challenge. Committed to defending the Folgers, his longtime friends, of any moral and legal wrongdoing, Stone had to refute charges of aberrant sexuality while still maintaining the plausibility of Isabella's guilt—to shift the blame from the white hardware merchant and his wife onto the black servant. He had, somehow, to stir up the embers of racialized criminal deviance without burning the Folgers (especially Mrs. Folger) in the process. In his book, Stone accomplishes this task by associating Isabella with illicit practices prior to her arrival at Zion Hill and, once in that household, identifying her with a racialized brutality from which the Folgers are consistently excluded. Accordingly, Stone introduces "Isabella, a black woman" to his readers as one of the dozen or so original members of Elijah Pierson's church, noting that not only did she enter "into all the vagaries and delusions of Mr. Pierson" but also "was probably, before the end came, among the most wicked of the wicked."[95] In Stone's hands, Isabella has an inherent, almost occult, capacity for evil. This cryptic early reference to Isabella's wickedness shades with mystery Stone's subsequent portrayals of her. She next appears at the gothic "ceremony" in which the dead Mrs. Pierson is anointed with oil: Stone notes that "the black woman Isabella . . . was very forward and active" in the ritual and that, "according to the impressions of persons in the adjoining apartment, who were too much shocked by the procedure to be present, Isabella must have been one of the principal actors and speakers in the religious rites and ceremonies that were observed."[96] Isabella's inappropriately "forward" behavior contravenes expectations for the class and racial deference that a black servant would be expected to perform before her employer and his white guests. At the same time, her "active" involvement in the fanatical and implicitly immoral "rites and ceremonies" heightens the contrast between her and the decorous, pious, middle-class observers whose horror keeps them from participating in such proceedings. Indeed, by noting that Ann Folger "consented to attend" the ceremony but omitting any further reference to her, Stone dissociates the white woman from the sexual deviance of the "wicked" black servant by implicitly grouping her with those blameless, unnamed "persons in the adjoining apartment."

It is imperative to Stone's vindication of the Folgers that whatever Zion Hill's inhabitants' theological errors, no sexual perversity tainted the household. The account insists, therefore, that "there was no indecorous washing, as has been rumoured" and that the "impression abroad that marriages were rejected by" Matthias and his disciples "is an error."[97] In place of sexual indecorum, Stone offers violent scenes that would doubtless resonate, in at least some readers' minds, with the sensational imagery of sexualized brutality that was already beginning to characterize the abolitionist movement's portrayal of female slaves in works such as Lydia Maria Child's *Appeal in Favor of That Class of Americans Called Africans*.[98] That Stone and Child may have reached overlapping audiences with these volumes is suggested by the fact that they were reviewed in consecutive issues of the *North American Review*.[99]

In a tableau more suited to the antebellum South than upstate New York, the Folgers recall how "Matthias once whipped the coloured woman" when she "undertook to intercede" for one of Matthias's sons, "quickly lash[ing] her with his cowhide."[100] The Folgers conclude their account by speculating, "We presume we all should have submitted to stripes in time," adding as an afterthought, "Indeed, we would rather have taken stripes sometimes, than hear his long vollies [sic] of threats, and curses."[101] The possibility that the Folgers *could* have themselves "submitted to stripes" is raised only to underscore that—unlike "the coloured woman"—they have *not* been active participants in the gothic-domestic violence of Zion Hill. Analyzing print portrayals of brutality against slave women in abolitionist literature, Karen Sánchez-Eppler demonstrates how white Northern women exploited such imagery to address their own sexual oppression, noting that "it is the very indelicacy of the slave woman's position that makes her a useful proxy in such indelicate matters."[102] Here, the black woman's subjection throws into relief the gentility of both Mr. and Mrs. Folger: unlike the brutalized ex-slave, they remain "not accustomed to such scenes" of domestic violence. Indeed, their immunity from the horror induced by such brutality is evident in their abstraction of physical violence as a form of suffering equivalent to the verbal violence of Matthias's harangues.

Having associated "the coloured woman" with Matthias's tyrannical violence in the whipping scene and having established her guilty involvement in the anointing ceremony, Stone depicts Isabella as the aggressor in a final scene of gothic violence. The day before Elijah Pierson's death, Mrs. Folger, finding him "insensible, his eyes closed, but his mouth opened . . . asked if she might give him drink, or wet his lips, as they appeared dry." When Matthias refused on the basis of his deluded notion that illness represented visitation by evil spirits, Mrs. Folger made sure she "visited his room frequently to drive the flies" from the dying man.[103] Hours later, when bathing the unconscious Pierson, "the coloured woman perceiving a fit coming upon him, slapped him in the face, saying 'Come out of your hellish sleep!'"[104] Soon afterward, according to the Folgers, Isabella joined Matthias in pouring water down Pierson's throat from "some four or five feet above him," a procedure that "caused a shocking noise or gurgling in the throat, which Mrs. Folger could not remain to hear, and hastened from the sound."[105] Here, Isabella is simultaneously passive and transgressive: she obeys the fanatical Matthias but not the dictates of conscience and physically and verbally chastises Pierson, her vulnerable white employer. Both scenes play on the earlier rumors of perverse bathing rituals, once again placing Isabella at their center but carefully exonerating the Folgers from any direct involvement. As in the anointing and whipping scenes, Mr. Folger is altogether absent from the household, leaving Mrs. Folger on her own as a reluctant spectator. The brutality described in the bathing and water-pitcher scenes derives its horror from its travesty of feminine caregiving, simultaneously contrasting with Mrs. Folger's attempts at traditional nursing and anticipating Isabella's alleged poisoning of the family. Indeed, the water-pitcher incident reinforces Isabella's complicity in Pierson's death in that it presents a gothic-domestic tableau in which the black servant, under the direction of the tyrannical fanatic, proffers sustenance that quickly becomes bane. The portrayal of Isabella in Stone draws on the century-old convention in Western art and literature of depicting "the black servant" as the embodiment of both perverse sexuality and violent criminality even as such depictions participate in the distinctly antebellum tendency to represent the brutalized "coloured woman," in particular, as a foil for genteel, idealized white womanhood.

The Folgers' interpolated narrative in *Matthias and His Impostures* concludes with an account of the servant Catherine Galloway's "interview with the coloured woman" after the dissolution of Zion Hill. When asked by Catherine "why she had told so many falsehoods about Mrs. Folger," Isabella purportedly responded by saying that, given the besieged position of Matthias's disciples, "we cannot help telling lies; besides it's no harm to lie to these devils," and vowing to "crush Mrs. Folger yet."[106] If Stone's Isabella evoked the familiar image of the sexualized, criminal black servant, she also confirmed widespread expectations that the speech of the mendacious black witness, when not self-incriminatory, ultimately remained precarious evidence.

Good White Evidence

The feuding former Matthias disciples shared an appreciation for the power of antebellum print culture as a typographical tribunal, waging battles that moved from the courtroom into print and back again. Immediately upon Matthias's arrest, Benjamin Folger apparently "circulated the poison story, and declared that Isabella, in conjunction with Matthias, had attempted to poison his family."[107] Folger's eleventh-hour effort "to injure the character of Isabella," Gilbert Vale suggests in *Fanaticism*, was specifically intended "to affect the testimony she was expected to give in favour of Matthias" by damaging her credibility as a legal witness.[108] Finding herself "met, in every direction, with the charge of poisoning," Van Wagenen first "took . . . the very wise precaution of getting written characters from all her former employers" and then arranging for Henry B. Western, one of New York's most prominent lawyers, to conduct the prophet's defense.[109] Her choice was a good one: Western "undertook the defence of Matthias, and advised also the prosecution of Mr. B. Folger for slander, as the only means to establish her character, and make her an effective witness."[110] Displaying remarkable legal sagacity, Van Wagenen not only lined up impressive defense representation for Matthews but conducted a campaign to salvage her own credibility. Determined to present her version of events in court, Van Wagenen was examined by the grand jury in preparation for Matthias's murder trial, only to be denied the opportunity to testify by Western's successful motion that the case be dismissed on grounds of insufficient evidence.[111] (Belying his own emphasis on Van Wagenen's resourcefulness, Vale portrays her as a legal naif, much as Stowe would three decades later: "Isabella was grievously disappointed in not giving her unsophisticated narrative in the court.")[112] Denied a hearing in the court of law, Van Wagenen, like so many of her African American contemporaries, turned to print. According to Vale, at some point during the long months between the original trial date of 25 November 1834 and the actual commencement of the proceedings on 17 April of the following year, interloper Catherine Galloway reported to Isabella, "All this blessed winter Mrs. B. Folger has been writing against you and Matthias," adding, "She will overcome you, and Matthias will be hung."[113] "Thus informed, that a formidable book was coming out against her and Matthias, by Mrs. Folger," Isabella responded, "I have got the truth, and I know it, and I will crush them with the truth."[114]

Both books depict desperate attempts by the Folgers and Van Wagenen to influence legal outcomes through print. *Matthias and His Impostures* has "the coloured woman" vowing to "crush" the Folgers with calculated lies; *Fanaticism*, with the undeniable "truth." At the crux of these competing accounts is the probative value of black testimony. Much more was at stake in the print battle over the Matthias scandal than how Elijah Pierson died and whether the Folgers engaged in adultery. For these questions could not be resolved without addressing the larger issue of whether the testimony of a former slave (in or out of court) could persuasively refute that of bourgeois white citizens regarding crimes of brutality and licentiousness that allegedly occurred in the genteel household of the latter. In this sense, Van Wagenen and Vale faced a rhetorical challenge much like the one former slaves and their abolitionist amanuenses and editors would encounter in the coming years: to overcome the powerful cultural and legal identification of blackness with criminality in order to present credible African American testimony of white guilt. Not surprisingly, then, many of the same strategies to rehabilitate black speech appear in *Fanaticism* and the print campaign against slavery: the portrayal of the former slave as an innocent victim; the emphasis on her role as observer in the white household; and the insistence on corroborating her version of events with what Vale repeatedly calls "white evidence."

Just as Stone inserted the Folgers' narrative into his larger account of the cult, Vale framed Van Wagenen's "Simple Narrative" with his own editorial commentary—making *Fanaticism*, like the antebellum slave narrative, a "black message" in a "white envelope."[115] Vale's inspiration to publish *Fanaticism* seems to have arisen as much from his editorial rivalry with Stone as from any altruistic desire to "rescu[e] an injured person from the private malice of an abuser of the press."[116] Portraying Van Wagenen in this light, however, allowed Vale to appeal any verdict the public may have reached after reading Stone's book. Claiming to be driven by a commitment "to satisfy the public curiosity" and a desire "to do justice to the parties concerned," Vale vows in what sounds like defense counsel's opening statement to "expose the crimes and follies of some individuals" and "at the same time, remove the guilt from comparatively innocent shoulders, and place the burden where it ought to be."[117] In order to charge Stone with racial scapegoating (and the Folgers with more serious offenses), Vale must first establish Van Wagenen's status as innocent victim. Accordingly, he charges that Stone "meanly attempts to transfer the sins of those he has taken under his protection, to others, not guilty of those crimes; but unfortunately, poor, uneducated, and coloured"; after all, the renowned editor and author "could expect no defence from a woman, formerly a slave[,] incapable of reading or writing."[118]

Inverting the Stone-Folger strategy, Vale cites Van Wagenen's previous bondage (along with her illiteracy, poverty, and gender) as proof not of her sexuality, criminality, or mendacity but of her victimization. Reversing conventional thought about the relationship between race and law, which assumed that blacks' criminality and mendacity rendered their nonconfessional testimony inadmissible, Vale insists that, on the contrary, it is whites' trepidation about black testimony that leads to false accusations of guilt. Or, as Vale fulminates about Stone's book, "Why thus so *falsely* point to Isabella, with the impression in the mind of the reader that she is . . . the 'most wicked of the wicked,' but for the purpose of destroying her character, in order to invalidate her testimony! why all this, but from the FEAR of her testimony!"[119]

Rather than compromising that testimony, it is precisely her status as innocent (ex-)slave that, in Vale's account, perfectly positions Van Wagenen to witness the perversity, crimes, and lies of her white social superiors. Vale's "Sketch of Isabella's Life" begins by noting, "ISABELLA VAN WAGENEN, in early life, was a slave," and although her emancipation is acknowledged in passing, throughout the book she effectively remains in that role.[120] At Zion Hill, the reader is told, Van Wagenen "had no wages" but nevertheless was expected to do "the common work" in the kitchen; it is in this way that "the family . . . differed in appearance very little from other well conducted families" who relied on unpaid, black domestic labor.[121] Appearances, however, are deceptive: not only do the Folgers' pretensions to bourgeois domesticity mask their profligacy but Isabella's apparent conformity to the role of ignorant black servant veils her underlying knowledge. In an aside to the reader, Vale notes, "from our listening to this coloured female, questioning her frequently, and often recurring to very curious and doubtful subjects, we have discovered that she, too, like Mrs. B. Folger, is not exactly what she seems." Vale explains that although a New York native, "she has African features, and no apparent mixture of blood; she is not exactly bad looking, but there is nothing prepossessing or very observant or intelligent in her looks."[122] Despite Van Wagenen's dull mien, Vale nevertheless "finds her reflecting, [that] 'she had her own or private opinion on every thing,'" and, moreover, that "these opinions of her *own* we have frequently found very correct; yet she is not communicative, and if circumstances did not prompt her to tell all she knows, it would be difficult to get at it."[123] In a world characterized by white "impostures"—whether that of wily Robert Matthews to divinity, social-climbing Benjamin Folger to bourgeois respectability, or lascivious Ann Folger to feminine virtue—the qualities traditionally associated with "African features" could be called into question as well. In such a world, Vale suggests, the seemingly ignorant, unobservant, taciturn "coloured female" could, under the right "circumstances," become just the person to expose the corruption lying beneath the surface in the apparently exemplary white household.

Instead of disqualifying her, then, Van Wagenen's blackness makes her the perfect witness by giving her a unique point of view from which to observe the mysterious goings-on around her. In the Zion Hill household, we are told, Van Wagenen quickly became "the depository of very curious, if not valuable information," a capacity in which "even her colour assisted."[124] Exploiting Van Wagenen's former slave status, Vale supports this claim by noting that "persons who have travelled in the south know the manner in which the coloured people, and especially slaves, are treated,"—namely, "they are scarcely regarded as being present."[125] Commenting that "this trait in our American character has been frequently noticed by foreign travellers," Vale mentions in particular the remarks of an "English lady" who "discovered in course of conversation with a southern married gentleman, that a coloured girl slept in his bedroom, in which also was his wife." When the Englishwoman's interlocutor "saw that this occasioned some surprise, he remarked 'What would he do if he wanted a glass of water in the night?'"[126] Noting further that "other travellers have remarked that the presence of coloured people never seemed to interrupt conversation of any kind for one moment," Vale concludes, "thus the peculiar . . . characteristics of Isabella, gave opportunities which none other had, and circumstances have induced her, nay rendered it necessary that she should keep back nothing, but . . . tell the whole truth."[127] Conveniently ignoring Van Wagenen's Northern origins, Vale implicitly compares the suspicious behavior of Zion Hill's white inhabitants to the notoriously decadent habits of Southern slaveholders. By making this association, Vale does more than simply "rever[t] to racist stereotypes"; he converts subsequent accounts of Van Wagenen's eavesdropping (a behavior that inappropriately crosses race and class lines) into a kind of inadvertent witnessing that arises from her racial invisibility and her socially sanctioned role as servant.[128] The slave, it would appear, is the perfect witness.

The English lady's suggestive tale of white slaveholders' unorthodox nocturnal arrangements is particularly well suited to Vale's purposes. Playing on the same cultural association of blackness with sexuality that the *Sun* and others relied upon to sensationalize their accounts of the Matthias scandal, this story discovers perversity not in the powerless slave woman but in the dissipated Southern gentleman and his complacent wife. Accordingly, throughout *Fanaticism*, Vale repeatedly characterizes Van Wagenen as "a coloured woman who is neither very young or beautiful."[129] Rather than allowing his informant to be compromised by the pervasive identification of blackness with criminal sexuality, Vale insists that it is precisely Van Wagenen's physical appearance that desexualizes her and thus guarantees her integrity. At one point, he goes so far as to note, "Isabella . . . is candid enough to say, that if she has escaped the peculiar pollution which threatened to affect the whole community at Sing Sing, that she believes she owes it to circumstances, as much as anything—(she is near forty, not handsome, and coloured)."[130] Such sexual and racial outsidership, Vale implies, perfectly situates Van Wagenen for the role of witness. Thus, when Matthias conducts the bizarre ceremony to sanction Benjamin Folger's adulterous union with Matthias's married daughter, we are told that "Isabella, the coloured woman, . . . took her place by the door, rather without the party than among them, but admirably situated for observation."[131] Similarly, indirect confirmation of Ann Folger's adultery comes through an account of words said "to Isabella in Matthias' bedroom, where he and Mrs. Folger were then in bed; for as the fire was lighted in their room before they got up, she was frequently there while they were in bed."[132] No longer "the black servant Isabella" whose presence sexualizes the whites around her, Van Wagenen becomes the "middle aged, not handsome[,] coloured" woman whose involuntary witnessing exposes the domestic corruption and religious hypocrisy of the bourgeois white household.

Having cleansed the taint of criminality and sexuality from Van Wagenen and shown that, due to her ubiquitous but invisible place in the private white household, the (former) slave was well-placed to witness the secret actions of its inhabitants, *Fanaticism* still had to establish the validity of African American testimony to a culture that persistently refused black witnesses a hearing in many of its courts of law. In order to accomplish this, Vale did in 1835 what abolitionist editors of slave narratives would do throughout the 1840s and 1850s: he corroborated the ex-slave's story with white-authored endorsements. In his first chapter, Vale assures the reader, "We have taken some pains to ascertain the personal character of Isabella, and before we lay her testimony before the public, we wish to show what confidence was placed in her by those families in which she lived from her womenhood [sic] or even childhood."[133] The character references Van Wagenen had collected from her employers in response to the Folgers' slanderous rumormongering came in handy in dealing with her white advocate, too: "On our expressing a wish to know her character previous to her connexion with Mr. Pierson, Matthias, or Folger," Vale recalls, "she thrust into our hands a lot of papers containing written characters from a regular succession of her employers, even from the time of her slavery."[134] Noting that "these papers will speak for themselves," Vale presents "copies of the documents," assuring the reader that "the originals of these documents may be seen at our office."[135]

Vale's words echo those prefacing the first book published by an African American, Phillis Wheatley's *Poems on Various Subjects, Religious and Moral* (1773): in order to prove that "an uncultivated Barbarian from Africa" could have written polished neoclassical verse, the publisher reprints an "Attestation" by eighteen white Boston gentlemen, noting that the original "may be seen by applying to *Archibald Bell Bookseller, No. 8, Aldgate-Street.*"[136] The best-known use of such authenticating documents, however, appears in the slave narratives published by various antebellum abolitionist organizations. Typically, the first-person account of the former slave was framed—and made legitimate—by prefaces or appendixes in which respectable whites would endorse the truthfulness of the story and the authenticity of its author's identity. Additional documentary materials might be included, such as facsimile bills of sale and other legal documents, correspondence between master and slave, or reproduced newspaper advertisements for the runaway. Such documents, many critics have argued, not only proved that the former slave was who he or she claimed to be but also had the effect of restoring, in freedom, many of the oppressive race and status relationships of slavery.[137] Celebrated author, editor, and reformer Lydia Maria Child recommended the incriminating pseudonymous "autobiography" of escaped North Carolina slave Harriet Jacobs on the grounds that "during the last seventeen years, she has lived the greater part of the time with a distinguished family in New York, and has so deported herself as to be highly esteemed by them"; that the distinguished family was white and the former slave their servant went without saying.[138] The well-known conclusion to *Incidents in the Life of a Slave Girl* underscores the parallels between Northern and Southern servitude by portraying the former slave woman as figuratively bound to the side of the New York mistress who

purchased (and manumitted) her and her children.[139] Similarly, Vale's introduction of Van Wagenen's character references effectively returns her to "the
time of her slavery" by subordinating her words to those of her previous white
employers, including her erstwhile owners.

Vale believed he was justified in anticipating a hostile readership. In the
busy months that separated the publication of the first volume of *Fanaticism*
from the second, Vale assiduously sent copies of his book to the New York
papers.[140] Although no one challenged him in print, "in private," he averred,
"we have heard the remark, that we rested our evidence that Mrs. B. Folger
seduced . . . Matthias, on the credit of a coloured woman; and although we
had given other evidence for other important facts, for this, we had not; and
that it was so incredible, that they never could believe it."[141] Attributing these
doubts to a friend of the Folgers, Vale is nevertheless careful to accommodate
the man's concerns about such "incredible" testimony, explaining that with
this second volume, "We have now given him and others white evidence for
this fact."[142]

Any evidence would do, apparently, as long as it came from white sources.
"Not to be depended on" for "any independent information," even the slip-
pery Catherine Galloway offers valuable "confirmation of *all* the important
facts in Isabella's narrative," providing the "important *white* evidence, which
the public so much seek after."[143] Indeed, Vale goes so far as to trumpet
the recently imprisoned, possibly insane Matthias's verification of "the chief
points" in Van Wagenen's story as proof that *Fanaticism* has been endorsed "by
the leading members of the kingdom—forming a perfect white evidence."[144]

Vale's efforts to validate Van Wagenen's account, like the white-authored
endorsements of antebellum slave narratives, reveal underlying anxieties
about black veracity and reliability. These anxieties come floating to the surface in the series of rhetorical questions Vale poses regarding his print antagonists. Alluding to Van Wagenen's references, he demands, "Could Mr. Stone"
or the Folgers "get a better character? They may be whiter in skin, more ele-
gant in manners, able to read and write, [and] of literary fame . . . ; but are
they more honest, can we depend on their testimony . . . ?"[145] His concluding question, however, betrays his dilemma: "And what shall we do in cases
where the single testimony of one of them is opposed to the single testimony
of this black woman?"[146] The answer is clear: although the white-authored
attestations to Van Wagenen's character may well "speak for themselves," Van
Wagenen's own extralegal testimony cannot. Instead, despite his insistence
that "we can depend on Isabella's statements, because we have not detected
her in inconsistencies or opposite statements," Vale ultimately defers final

authority to Van Wagenen's white corroborators, however compromised they may be. "On all important subjects," he assures his reader, "we have collateral evidence of the most respectable character." [147]

Certificates of Character

The Matthias scandal would gradually fade from public memory, displaced by the titillating deaths of glamorous prostitute Helen Jewett and "beautiful Cigar Girl" Mary Rogers. But, by transforming "the black servant Isabella" from sexualized criminal into observant witness, Vale and Van Wagenen's effort in *Fanaticism* to authorize African American testimony of white "crimes" employed strategies that would persist in antislavery literature for the next quarter-century.

Fanaticism bridged the gallows literature and slave narrative traditions by presenting a popular crime account from a distinctively black perspective in which the authority of the first-person narrative was no longer grounded in the guilt of the speaker but in her witnessing of others' crimes. Implicitly rejecting blacks' legally mandated confessional posture, *Fanaticism* urged its readers to detach race from criminality and, thus, to acknowledge what critic Saidiya Hartman has called "white culpability." [148] This shift from a confessional to a testimonial stance entailed a profound shift in the authority of the black speaking subject. "The indiscriminate admission and giving credit to negro testimony" in the courtroom, as proslavery treatise writer Thomas R. R. Cobb acknowledged, "would be productive of innumerable evils in the relation between master and slave"; his abolitionist counterpart William Goodell concurred, insisting that the very act of testifying would ensure that slaves "could not *remain* chattels at all." [149] Publishing her "Simple Narrative" as "the Whole Truth and Nothing but the Truth," Isabella Van Wagenen asserted a testimonial black literary authority in the shadow of law; rejecting the doctrinal attenuation of African American agency to criminality, she presented extralegal textual production as a form of black civic participation.

But even as it represents an important attempt to dissociate black personal narrative from confession, the "Simple Narrative of Isabella" also reveals the problems such a testimonial posture would pose for a black activist like Frederick Douglass—or Sojourner Truth herself. For if the former slave's testimony exposed the crimes committed by guilty whites, it had a tendency simultaneously to victimize the black speaking subject; as Hartman notes, criminality and abjection are virtually impossible positions from which to claim legal personhood. [150] It is perhaps not surprising, then, that Harriet Beecher Stowe and Olive Gilbert joined Gilbert Vale in portraying Van Wagenen as a legal naif: the victim merely offers an eyewitness narrative of personal experience, not a forensic argument. In such a dependent role, the black witness, seemingly incapable of autonomous authorship, required white collaboration and corroboration.

No longer confessional, published African American personal narratives in the 1840s and 1850s would continue to betray cultural anxieties about the credibility of black speech. Thus, much as lawyer Henry Western and editor Gilbert Vale had done during the Matthias scandal, sympathetic abolitionist advocates for the slave would assiduously corroborate his or her potentially "incredible" testimony with "good white evidence." Indeed, Van Wagenen would affirm her testimonial identity first by renaming herself Sojourner Truth and then by collaborating with another white reformer to publish the *Narrative of Sojourner Truth, a Northern Slave*. But fifteen years after the publication of *Fanaticism*, such gestures of self-authentication remained insufficient for the black witness. On the *Narrative*'s final page, Truth and her amanuensis, Olive Gilbert, following what had by then become an established convention of the genre, printed as "Certificates of Character" the references Van Wagenen had collected from her former masters at the height of the Matthias scandal—alongside more recent ones contributed by abolitionist luminaries such as William Lloyd Garrison.[151] Even as the antislavery movement constructed a forum in which formerly enslaved African Americans could gain a hearing for their testimony against those whom Frederick Douglass would call "the perpetrators of slaveholding villainy," that testimonial speech (as Douglass himself would protest) remained subject to authentication and interpretation by their well-meaning white advocates.

PART II   AT THE BAR OF
           PUBLIC OPINION

3 EYEWITNESS TO THE CRUELTY

Frederick Douglass's 1845 Narrative

While William Lloyd Garrison was convening a court of popular opinion in which to gain a hearing for his appeals on behalf of the slave, Frederick Douglass was still Frederick Bailey, a Maryland bondsman. In the summer and fall of 1834, as the Zion Hill household disintegrated and the first newspaper reports of the Matthias scandal began to appear, Bailey was waging physical and psychological battle with notorious "nigger breaker" Edward Covey.[1] Then, in 1845, a decade after Gilbert Vale presented the "Simple Narrative of Isabella in the Case of Matthias" as "the Whole Truth—and Nothing but the Truth," the Boston Anti-Slavery Office published the *Narrative of the Life of Frederick Douglass, an American Slave, Written by Himself*.

Almost as familiar as the *Narrative*'s depiction of the enslaved Frederick Bailey's transformation into abolitionist author and orator Frederick Douglass is the scholarly account of Douglass's political and professional metamorphosis following the publication of his first book and subsequent lecture tour of the British Isles. Prior to the journey, the fugitive worked as an abolitionist lecture agent, giving speeches based on his life in slavery and documenting that experience with his popular *Narrative*. Afterward, Douglass, now an international celebrity, purchased his freedom, founded his own antislavery newspaper, reversed his position on the U.S. Constitution, rejected disunionism, broke with the Garrisonians, embraced political abolitionism, and published a second personal narrative, *My Bondage and My Freedom* (1855).[2]

Well-trodden as the path that bore Douglass from the *Narrative* to *My Bondage and My Freedom* may be, retracing it here in light of the antislavery movement's appeals to popular legal consciousness allows us to clear away one of its stumbling blocks, namely the apparent discrepancy between Douglass's retrospective account of his career as Garrisonian abolitionist and the historical record of his oratory and writing from 1841 to 1845. Meticulous reconstruction of Douglass's early career as an agent has effectively debunked "the standard view," derived largely from *My Bondage and My Freedom*, that

initially Douglass, awed by Garrison and the Massachusetts Anti-Slavery Society (MASS), "limited his remarks to a simple narrative of his slave experiences."[3] Douglass's transcribed early speeches and documented participation
in abolitionist meetings show him actively debating and analyzing the central issues facing the movement in its middle decade, from moral suasion,
Northern racism, disunionism, and church complicity in slavery, to the ad-
visability of petitioning, legal crises like the *Latimer* and *Creole* cases, and the
constitutionality of slavery. Why, then, does Douglass in *My Bondage and My
Freedom* appear, in historian John W. Blassingame's words, to have "exaggerated the restrictions placed on him during his first months as an antislavery
lecturer"?[4] Although familiarity with the Douglass-Garrison split makes it
impossible to rule out the influence of an acrimony that was at once intensely
political and deeply personal, Douglass's revisionist self-presentation in the
late 1840s and 1850s does not seem contradictory when viewed in the context of the slavery debate's pervasive juridical rhetoric. If we focus attention
not merely on the content of Douglass's contributions to the slavery controversy but on the rhetorical frames by which he authorized them, the shift in
posture is undeniable.[5]

Compare, for example, Douglass's speech "The Dred Scott Decision"
(1857) with two documents from the early 1840s addressing, respectively,
Latimer and the Constitution. All three center on pressing legal issues; none
recounts Douglass's personal experience in detail. Yet, the two earlier texts,
written during Douglass's Garrisonian phase, authorize their claims through
recourse to his slave identity, whereas the later speech replaces such testimonial authority with that of a distinctly African American civic persona. In
his first known antislavery publication, apparently written in lieu of a speech
he had intended to give on the capture in Boston of Virginia fugitive George
Latimer, Douglass urges the Northern reader to "follow me to your courts of
justice" and, specifically, to "mark him who sits upon the bench." But rather
than joining his abolitionist colleagues in stoking Jacksonian antijudicialism
or probing the case's precedent-setting legal questions, Douglass characterizes the judge (Lemuel Shaw) in sentimental terms as one with the power to
"tear Latimer from a beloved wife and tender infant."[6] After this fleeting visit
to the courtroom, Douglass takes his reader to Latimer's cell, where his highly
sensational untagged, first-person evocation of the slave's thoughts effectively collapses the distinctions between the fugitive author and his fugitive
subject: "I . . . must be torn from a wife and tender babe," Douglass imagines
Latimer musing, "to be murdered, though not in the ordinary way—not to
have my heart pierced through with a dagger—not to have my brains blown

out. . . . No: I am to be killed by inches . . . perhaps by cat-hauling until my back is torn all to pieces, my flesh is to be cut with the bleeding lash . . . warm brine must now be poured into my bleeding wounds . . . until death shall end my sufferings." [7] If, as Douglass explains, "I can sympathize with George Latimer, having myself been cast into a miserable jail, on suspicion of my intending to do what he is said to have done, viz. appropriating my own body to my use," Douglass's authority in this passage arises as much from his experiential identification with the enslaved victim's pained body as from his familiarity with the legal predicament attending the fugitive's unsuccessful (and unlawful) appropriation of that body.[8] Similarly, in an 1844 disunionist speech maintaining the proslavery character of the Constitution, Douglass follows up his opening disclaimer — "I am here more to bear testimony, than to argue the question" — by disavowing "a minute examination of every clause" of the Constitution, proclaiming that "it is sufficient for me to prove its character, that I am a slave under the Constitution." [9] Here again, personal experience, not legal exegesis, provides the basis for his antislavery argument.

In marked contrast to the testimonial posture of such earlier legally oriented lectures is the stance that Douglass adopted thirteen years later in a speech to the American Anti-Slavery Society on the U.S. Supreme Court's recent Dred Scott decision. Rhetorically distancing himself from "the person of Dred Scott, or the humblest and most whip-scarred bondman in the land," Douglass introduces his detailed analysis of the decision (presented in accordance with "well known rules of legal interpretation" and a strict construction of the Constitution) by proclaiming that "as a man, an American, a citizen, a colored man of both Anglo-Saxon and African descent, I denounce this representation as a most scandalous and devilish perversion of the Constitution, and a brazen misstatement of the facts of history." [10] No longer defined by a proslavery Constitution or his sympathetic identification with the slave, Douglass bases his critical challenge to Dred Scott on the very black civic authority that the ruling sought to eradicate.

The change in Douglass's self-fashioning cannot be attributed solely to the greater maturity and knowledge Douglass had acquired by the end of his second decade of public speaking.[11] An attentive survey of Douglass's oratory and journalism before and after his British lecture tour reveals a radical revision in Douglass's public persona — a revision that, in keeping with the movement's own juridical rhetoric, can best be described as a shift from a testimonial to a prosecutorial posture.[12] During the decade that separated the Narrative from My Bondage and My Freedom — not coincidentally, the same decade that saw the beginnings of an African American bar in the United

States—Douglass, reevaluating both the goals of abolitionism and his own place in the movement, sought not so much to abandon his designated role as slave witness but, instead, to incorporate it into the more authoritative persona of black advocate. Realizing that slavery was only the most daunting of many obstacles blocking African Americans' access to full citizenship, Douglass became increasingly aware that striking the posture of antislavery witness risked affirming the persistent imputations of racial inferiority that underwrote the African Americans' legal outsidership. Like so many other African American abolitionists in the 1840s and 1850s, Douglass came to believe that black self-representation in the court of public opinion was imperative to the larger project of black civic inclusion in the nation.[13]

But even as, in the familiar phrasing of *My Bondage and My Freedom*, Douglass sought to frame the well-rehearsed "narrations of [his] own personal experience as a slave" with more philosophical denunciations of "slaveholding villainy"—and thereby to exchange his public identity as the representative "American Slave" for that of "Representative American man"—he retained an appreciation for the power of the antislavery movement's rhetorical engagement with popular legal consciousness.[14] Thus, following his return from Great Britain in 1846, Douglass figured the two decisive acts in his break with Garrisonian abolitionism in the language of the courtroom, now revised to accommodate his new, expanded role. Launching the *North Star* in 1847 with fellow African American activist Martin R. Delany, Douglass echoed his editorial predecessors Samuel Cornish and John Russwurm when he once again asserted the need for a black-owned abolitionist newspaper: "It is evident that we must be our own representatives and advocates, not exclusively, but peculiarly—not distinct from, but in connection with our white friends."[15] Even more significantly, perhaps, after initially avowing his reluctance to enter the interpretive fray over the Constitution and "talk 'lawyer like' about law," Douglass proceeded to do just that.[16] In an 1851 *North Star* editorial, he announced his rejection of the Garrisonian view of the Constitution as a proslavery document: "We had arrived at the firm conviction that the Constitution, construed in the light of well established rules of legal interpretation," could, in fact, "be wielded in behalf of emancipation."[17] In the years that followed, Douglass provided increasingly detailed, authoritative, and insightful commentary on controversial legislation and landmark judicial decisions.[18] No longer merely the "eye-witness to the cruelty" of slavery whose primary role was to support the extralegal arguments of white abolitionist advocates with his moving testimony, Douglass became the race's own representative and advocate, talking lawyerlike about law to demand immediate emancipation and full citizenship for African Americans. Indispensable to that undertaking, Douglass insisted in *My Bondage and My Freedom*, was the ability of African Americans themselves to "apprehend"—in the dual sense of understanding and seizing—"their rights."[19] Only black advocacy grounded in the lived experience of African Americans could enable slaves—and, indeed, all American blacks—fully to apprehend their rights as citizens.

If Douglass's post-1845 oratory and journalism offer the substance of this new black advocacy, it is in the constitutive genre of the witness—the autobiographical account—that we find Douglass *narrating* his revised self-fashioning within the abolitionist movement and the larger slavery debate by telling the story of his transformation from slave witness to black advocate. When read along these lines, Douglass's narrative reassessment of abolitionist rhetoric in *My Bondage and My Freedom* can itself be reevaluated as a valuable internal, African American critique of the antislavery movement's ubiquitous trial trope. Refiguring his own discursive contributions as advocacy rather than testimony, Douglass deployed the projective capacities of metaphor and narrative to envision African Americans not as victims in need of protection but as autonomous citizens.[20]

This chapter discusses in further detail the cultural significance of the legal exclusion of black testimony. Such an approach enables us to take a fresh look at the *Narrative*, focusing in particular on how it initiates the trajectory from victim to witness to advocate in a series of scenes that persistently link witnessing, physical vulnerability, and Southern slavery in opposition to testifying, physical autonomy, and Northern freedom.

Legal Strangers

The abolitionist promotion of extralegal slave testimony was driven by the conviction that, as the *Boston Chronotype* put it in a review of the *Narrative of the Life and Adventures of Henry Bibb, an American Slave* (1849), "argument provokes argument, reason is met by sophistry. But narratives of slaves go right to the hearts of men."[21] This principle can be traced back to the Aristotelian assumption that the most powerful literary and legal performances were those eyewitness accounts that, by engaging the imagination in conjunction with the emotions, sought not merely to entertain or educate their audiences but to move them to exemplary civic action.[22] Yet, precisely because it "springs not from the precepts of the law, but from the propensity of our nature," the virtually irresistible affective impact of testimonial narrative could pose an impediment to the administration of justice, as James Wilson pointed out.[23]

Explaining rules of evidence in America's first law course, Wilson elaborated that "experience has found it necessary and useful, that, at least in legal proceedings, the indulgence of this natural and original propensity should be regulated and restrained."[24] Hence the legal attempt to differentiate between hearing and believing a witness: "The law has said, that, unless a witness appears . . . to be honest and upright, credible and disinterested; and unless he delivers his testimony under all the solemnities and obligations of religion, and all the dangers and penalties of perjury; you shall not—" here Wilson interrupted himself to emphasize his point—"it does not say, you shall not *believe* him."[25] After all, "To prevent this act or operation of the mind might be impracticable on hearing the witness."[26] But he resumed, "It says—you shall not *hear* him."[27] Thus, such "qualifications and solemnities . . . are requisite to the competency, not to the credibility, of the witness—to the admission, not to the operation, of his testimony."[28] The subtle but crucial distinction between, on the one hand, the witness's competency and his or her credibility and, on the other, testimony's admissibility and its operation or effect was important enough for Wilson to underscore in a series of neat oppositions: "The propensity to believe testimony i[s] a natural propensity. It is unnecessary to encourage it; sometimes it is impracticable to restrain it. The law will not order that which is unnecessary: it will not attempt that which is impracticable. In no case, therefore, does it order a witness to be believed; for jurors are the triers of the credibility of witnesses, as well as the truth of facts. . . . In no case, likewise, does the law order a witness not to be believed; for belief might be the unavoidable result of his testimony. To prevent that unavoidable, but sometimes improper result, the law orders, that, without the observance of certain precautions, which experience has evinced to be wise and salutary, the witness shall not be heard."[29] Although Wilson does not address here the inadmissibility of testimony by slaves or people of color, his lesson, "Of The Nature and Philosophy of Evidence," can teach us a great deal about the potential threat such testimony could pose, in the courtroom and beyond.

If, as discussed in the previous chapter, the slave's subordinate status made his or her evidence "precarious" in the archaic sense of being "dependent upon the will or favor of another" (i.e., the master), it also made that testimony "dangerously lacking in stability or security."[30] This instability and insecurity arose not from nonwhites' "base and corrupt natures," as colonial Virginia's legislature would have it, nor from the negro's "known disposition to disregard the truth," as Cobb maintained, but from the slave's double character. Resting on the fiction that slaves, as objects of property, were "incapable of performing civil acts" (except, of course, "in reference to acts which are crimes" when they "are regarded as *persons*"), American law could not include the slaves' first-person accounts of white criminality and itself remain stable and secure.[31] For rather than reinforcing the larger fiction that the formal procedures of American jurisprudence ensured its neutrality and universality, such stories threatened to expose that fiction by placing law in a broader historical context and viewing it from an alternative social reality.[32]

This view of the insurgent potential of African American personal narrative has driven the legal academy's Critical Race Theory (CRT) movement to endorse storytelling as a political and legal strategy.[33] In the words of Richard Delgado, "counterstories" told by people of color "attack and subvert the very 'institutional logic' of the [legal] system."[34] And, as legal scholar Thomas Ross has found, since the nineteenth century, an important, if unspoken, component of American law's institutional logic has been the complementary myths of "white innocence" and "black abstraction."[35] Absolving contemporary whites of any responsibility for racial oppression, this phenomenon obscures black humanity by decontextualizing racism and its impact, thus blocking any empathy that would require those in power to redress such inequality.[36] Allowing white antebellum juries to hear the all-too-credible testimony of slaves and others whose civic exclusion rendered them incompetent witnesses in cases involving whites thus risked (to borrow Wilson's phrase) the highly "improper result" of calling the legal regime itself into question through a disruptive counternarrative of white guilt and black humanity.[37]

This point is vividly illustrated in one of the period's most notorious slave cases. The case (or, rather, the series of cases) had its origin in the events of July 1855 when the enslaved Jane Johnson and her two children accompanied John H. Wheeler, their master and U.S. Minister to Nicaragua, on a visit to Philadelphia en route from Washington, D.C., to New York. Johnson communicated her desire to be free to a member of Philadelphia's black community, and just before the boat on which Wheeler, Johnson, and the children were passengers left the dock, Passmore Williamson, a white reformer, boarded the boat with African American abolitionists William Still, Isaiah Moore, William Custis, John Ballard, James Martin, and James S. Braddock. The activists informed Johnson that she and her children were free under the laws of Pennsylvania, whereupon she disembarked and effectively escaped from Wheeler. Wheeler then acquired a writ of habeas corpus from Federal District Judge John K. Kane (who would thereby become Richard Hildreth's American model of an "atrocious judge"). When the writ was served on Williamson, he insisted that Johnson, as a free woman, had never been in his custody. Williamson spent from July to November 1855 imprisoned for contempt of court for his return on the habeas corpus writ while lawyers wrangled over the cluster of issues raised by the case.[38]

As the Pennsylvania Anti-Slavery Society's (PASS) pamphlet on the case explained, the habeas corpus proceedings were premised on "a double falsehood, *viz*: that Jane Johnson did not desire her freedom and was forcibly abducted by Passmore Williamson."[39] This was because, in Judge Kane's words, "of all the parties to the act of violence, he was the only white man, the only citizen, the only individual having recognized political rights, the only person whose social training could certainly interpret either his own duties or the rights of others under the constitution of the land"—in other words, the only participant in the escape who, in the eyes of law, possessed any civic agency.[40] In such a situation, according to Kane's logic, "the so-called rescue" could be construed as an instance of "unlawful restraint": "For persons in servitude do . . . often possess those personal attachments which prove stronger than the love of liberty; and no one, certainly, has the right to force them to be free."[41]

The court's story of white agency and black passivity was threatened, however, by the counternarrative offered by a petition from Jane Johnson herself— an account that, like Johnson's dramatic testimony on behalf of Williamson's African American colleagues in the separate criminal case, emphasized her own active role in the incident.[42] Judge Kane protected the coherence of the court's version of the events, however, by resorting to a legal technicality that allowed him to ignore Johnson's petition. Because Wheeler, in keeping with plantation usage, had identified his slave "Jane" only by her first name in his habeas-corpus petition (a usage reproduced in the writ itself), the court refused to recognize Jane *Johnson* "as a party" to the case, explaining that "our records cannot be opened to every stranger who volunteers to us a suggestion, as to what may have been our errors, and how we may repair them."[43] This legal loophole allowed Kane to find that Jane Johnson "has therefore no status whatever in this Court."[44] Johnson's lawyer Joseph B. Townsend pointed to the irony of this logic when, noting that the case was "virtually her proceeding," he demanded, "Why cannot she be heard? . . . Surely, no one is so competent to satisfy the Court . . . as the woman herself; her declaration is the best evidence attainable, all others being but secondary."[45]

Like Judge Kane's contorted (but successful) efforts to portray would-be witness Jane Johnson as a "stranger" to the civil hearing that was "virtually her proceeding," the extensive legislation restricting African American testimony in courtrooms both North and South put Wilson's logic into racialized practice. Given the impracticability of restricting the operation of incriminating black testimony on the minds of its auditors, of enforcing disbelief in African American witnesses, the American legal system had to silence this testimony altogether by excluding such evidence from its proceedings. In order to do so, it had to call into question not the credibility of black testimony but the very competency of the black witness.

"Eye-Witness to the Cruelty"

While nonwhite testimony remained inadmissible in many American courtrooms throughout the antebellum period, the development of the slave narrative as a new genre of literature made African Americans' personal stories of slavery indispensable to the court of public opinion. The argument of Jane Johnson's lawyer that "no one is so competent to satisfy the Court" as the former slave and that "her declaration is the best evidence attainable, all others being but secondary" echoed the similar claims with which abolitionist editors had introduced slave narratives as the most powerful "evidence" they presented in their case against Southern slaveholders. In his preface to the first slave narrative published by the AASS, the *Narrative of James Williams* (1838), Quaker poet John Greenleaf Whittier opened his discussion of Southern inhumanity by citing "the testimony and admissions of slave-holders," which he acknowledged were "only [those] of the . . . wrong-doer himself" and must therefore be "partial and incomplete."[46] He insisted that "for a full revelation of the secrets of the prison-house, we must look to the slave himself."[47] The representation of the former slave as testifying witness quickly became a staple of abolitionist discourse. A decade later, Henry Watson, who had been enslaved in Virginia and Mississippi, authorized his *Narrative* (1848) by reflecting that "twenty-six years, the prime of my life, had passed away in slavery, I having witnessed it in all its forms."[48] By the end of the period, fugitive slave J. H. Banks would emblazon the title page of his *Narrative* (1861) with the slogan, "I am a witness against American slavery and all its horrors," and Harriet A. Jacobs would preface *Incidents in the Life of a Slave Girl* by expressing a desire "to add [her] testimony to that of abler pens to convince the people of the Free States what Slavery really is."[49]

Although the *Narrative of the Life of Frederick Douglass, an American Slave* was one of many slave narratives that appeared during the antebellum period, from the beginning of his career, Douglass stood as the apotheosis of the slave witness. An abolitionist who reported on Douglass's first speech before an interracial audience put it this way in the *National Anti-Slavery Standard*: having long "indulged the hope that . . . we might have some repentant slaveholder, or powerful slave to testify 'that which they themselves did know,'" the reformers found that the "morning of the 12th instant fulfilled our hopes. One, recently from the house of bondage, spoke with great power. Flinty hearts were pierced, and cold ones melted by his eloquence. Our best pleaders for the slave held their breath for fear of interrupting him. . . . It seemed almost miraculous how he had been prepared to tell his story with so much power."[50] When, four years later, this same "powerful slave" published his *Narrative*, he recounted the acts of silent witnessing that had "prepared [him] to tell his story with so much power" before the court of public opinion. In the process, he provided the abolitionist movement, in critic John Sekora's astute formulation, "not so much a life story as an indictment, an anti-slavery document, the testimony of an eyewitness, precisely what Garrison sought."[51] For, in addition to its well-known portrayal of the journey from slavery to freedom as a passage from South to North, from brute to man, from illiteracy to authorship, and from damnation to salvation, Douglass's *Narrative* also depicts the transition from thralldom to liberty in juridical terms, as a move from silent victimization to defiant testimony.

Scholars of the genre have frequently noted how slave narratives drew on vivid forensic images to inspire white, Northern audiences to take action against slavery.[52] Others have demonstrated that such vicarious witnessing risked substituting cathartic complacency for action while tacitly reinforcing legal restrictions on slave testimony, either by allowing imaginative white identification to obscure actual black suffering or by endowing the mute, abject body of the slave with superlative evidentiary authority.[53] As important as these analyses have been in heightening critical appreciation for the rhetorical challenges facing formerly enslaved authors, the discussion has tended to focus on the responses of white audiences to portrayals of black suffering. By contrast, the reading of Douglass's *Narrative* offered here stresses not so much the transactional qualities of the ex-slave's witnessing but, instead, examines how the author's testimonial stance modeled a new form of black discursive and civic authority in the interstices of American law and antebellum print culture.[54]

As suggested in the previous chapter, the rhetorical decriminalization of the black subject in Jacksonian print culture seemingly necessitated that subject's virtually simultaneous rhetorical victimization as the surest means of detaching crime from race in order to authorize extralegal black testimony to white crimes. But even as the role of testifying eyewitness may have appeared to offer an opening wedge for broader black civic participation, the position of victim, like that of criminal, was a precarious one from which to assert civic agency, much less autonomous legal personhood.[55] In the court of law, the authority of witnesses is grounded in their corporeal experience: they gain a hearing on the basis of what they may have seen or heard. In the antebellum court of public opinion, the authority of slave witnesses was doubly predicated on their corporeality, in that they testified to the violence they had personally suffered or had seen inflicted on other pained, black bodies.[56] As Sánchez-Eppler has demonstrated, if slaves gained a hearing at the popular tribunal at the very moment when there appeared "a crack in the hegemonic rhetoric of political disembodiment" that had situated "authority" in "the impossible position of the universal and hence bodiless subject," they did so at the behest of "a political movement and a literature" that strove "to speak the body, but that in so representing the body" also "exploit[ed] and limit[ed] it."[57] The era's most self-conscious print construction of the slave as witness, Douglass's Narrative, probes this discursive dilemma by demonstrating how the seemingly liberating authority of the fugitive's testimony can only be sustained through ongoing association with the slave's definitive physical abjection.[58] A possible resolution to this dilemma appears in the Narrative's final lines, with the introduction of the figure of the black advocate.

The Narrative charts the development of its author's testimonial authority by presenting three incidents of Southern violence in which the slave Frederick Bailey is "doomed to be a witness and a participant."[59] As Frederick grows from passive, silent, terrorized witness of legally sanctioned violence against other slaves into a brutalized victim who seeks but is denied legal redress, the Narrative charts the increasing incommensurability of the young slave's maturing civic consciousness with his legal status as human property. The story culminates with the fugitive's public antislavery testimony in the North—and, implicitly, with his published testimony in the Narrative itself— thereby figuring the court of public opinion as an alternative to the court of law as a forum for African American civic participation.

The Narrative's editorial apparatus indicates that to be a Southern slave is not only to be denied physical autonomy, forced to perform backbreaking labor, and subjected to arbitrary violence but also to be a silent witness to such suffering. Garrison, playing his part of abolitionist advocate, focuses his opening argument on the laws mandating the silence of Southern slaves. Although similar laws limiting the admissibility of African American testimony existed in the North, Garrison's comments locate both violence and silence exclusively in the South.[60] Noting that "Mr. DOUGLASS has frankly disclosed . . . the names . . . of those who committed the crimes which he has alleged against them," Garrison quickly asserts, "Let it never be forgotten, that no slaveholder or overseer can be convicted of any outrage perpetrated on the person of a slave, however diabolical it may be, on the testimony of colored witnesses, whether bond or free. By the slave code, they are adjudged to be as incompetent to testify against a white man, as though they were indeed a part of the brute creation."[61] Alluding to Douglass's narrative allegation of slaveholders' "crimes" enables Garrison to expose the inadequacy of American law, which by rendering such testimony inadmissible effectively denies the criminality of such outrages. In a society in which "there is no legal protection in fact, whatever there may be in form, for the slave population; and any amount of cruelty may be inflicted upon them with impunity," the abolitionist editor appeals to popular legal consciousness by presenting the former slave's printed "testimony" to the court of public opinion as a corrective to both the legal sanction for slavery and the exclusion of African Americans from full participation in American law.[62]

In the "Letter from Wendell Phillips, Esq." that follows Garrison's introduction, the celebrated abolitionist lawyer and orator acknowledges to Douglass the absence of legal protection for fugitive slaves in the North: "The whole armory of Northern Law has no shield for you."[63] Nevertheless, Phillips suggests that in the abolitionist community of the North, Douglass "may tell [his] story in safety," anticipating that "some time or other, the humblest may stand in our streets, and bear witness in safety against the cruelties of which he has been the victim."[64] Together, Garrison and Phillips imply that if in the South, the speech of a slave witness is deferred indefinitely, in the North, witnessing and testimony can be reunited in the extralegal court of public opinion. In the South, enslaved eyes see black bodies beaten, whipped, raped, and murdered, but enslaved tongues remain silent; in the North, not only are African American eyes freed from witnessing such horrors, but African American tongues are free to testify against what Garrison refers to as "that crime of crimes, — making man the property of his fellow-man."[65] It is by testifying to the crimes he himself has endured or has witnessed his fellow bondspeople suffering, Garrison and Phillips suggest, that the fugitive slave attains true liberation.

Douglass's *Narrative* reinforces the abolitionist association of the South with silence. Young Frederick, lacking a legal record of his birth, quells his desire to ask his master for information on this point, knowing that "he deemed all such inquiries on the part of the slave improper and impertinent."[66] Similarly, Colonel Lloyd's long-suffering stablemen mutely attend their master's unfair harangues, for, "to all these complaints, no matter how unjust, the slave must never answer a word"; the place of the slave is not to speak but to "stand, listen, and tremble."[67] The fact that those who broke this code of silence were punished with beating and sale, Douglass explains, "had the effect to establish among the slaves the maxim, that a still tongue makes a wise head."[68]

The Maryland plantation's pervasive silence is broken by the inarticulate screams of tortured slaves, screams that are met with yet more silence.[69] In the *Narrative*'s first portrayal of Southern violence, Frederick receives his initiation into slavery through an act of witnessing. One of the most frequently quoted scenes in the *Narrative* describes how as a young boy Frederick witnessed the flogging of his Aunt Hester by their master, Captain Anthony:

> I have often been awakened at the dawn of day by the most heart-rending shrieks of an own aunt of mine, whom he used to tie up to a joist, and whip upon her naked back till she was literally covered with blood. No words, no tears, no prayers, from his gory victim, seemed to move his iron heart from its bloody purpose. The louder she screamed, the harder he whipped. . . . He would whip her to make her scream, and whip her to make her hush. . . . I remember the first time I ever witnessed this horrible exhibition. I was quite a child, but I well remember it. I never shall forget it whilst I remember any thing. It was the first of a long series of such outrages, of which I was doomed to be a witness and a participant. It struck me with awful force. It was the blood-stained gate, the entrance to the hell of slavery, through which I was about to pass. It was a most terrible spectacle. I wish I could commit to paper the feelings with which I beheld it.[70]

From the beating of his Aunt Hester, Frederick learns that to be a slave is to be a silent "witness" to arbitrary yet authorized cruelty against one's friends and family. Indeed, his aunt's whipping, "awaken[ing]" him "at the dawn of day," opens Frederick's eyes to the meaning of slavery and establishes his position early in the *Narrative* as an eyewitness to its cruelty. This episode represents the "blood-stained gate, the entrance to the hell of slavery," because previously Frederick had lived with his maternal grandmother "out of the way of the bloody scenes that often occurred on the plantation" and therefore "had never seen any thing like it before."[71] Underscoring the *Narrative*'s persistent association of authorship with the visual through the homonym "scene"/"seen," Douglass suggests that this first act of witnessing introduces Frederick not only to his slave identity but also to the embodied subjectivity that is inherent in the role of the slave witness.[72] Douglass's account of Frederick's frightened response to the bloody scene of his aunt's whipping vividly emphasizes the enslaved witness's physical vulnerability: "I was so terrified and horror-stricken at the sight, that I hid myself in a closet, and dared not venture out till long after the bloody transaction was over."[73] Seeing violence inflicted on the body of another, the young slave instinctively hides his own vulnerable African American body. That the body Frederick sees whipped is a female one is not insignificant, for not only does this scene introduce the young slave to the identification of blackness with abject corporeality under slavery, but also it demonstrates how the feminization of blackness serves to ungender and thus to dehumanize the enslaved male body.[74] The terror is that as interchangeable commodities, one brutalized slave can stand in for another—that young Frederick can and will replace Aunt Hester at the joist.[75] As Douglass suggests, in the context of slavery, to observe such violence is to be "doomed to be" both "a witness and a participant."

Minimizing the distinction between witnessing and participating in Southern violence, the account of Aunt Hester's beating maximizes the gap between witnessing and testimony. This first witnessing scene, which Douglass characterizes as an "exhibition" and a "spectacle," establishes the separation of the visual from the verbal that will characterize subsequent representations of Southern violence in the *Narrative*. Unlike later scenes, this one is notable for its noisiness. We should note, however, that Aunt Hester's vocalizations are incoherent "shrieks" and "screams"; her more articulate "words" and "prayers" are negated by their ineffectuality and, in the text, by the anaphoric "no" that precedes these terms. Far from putting an end to the violence of slavery—the goal of black testimony in the North—the slave's inarticulate utterances only seem to provoke more violence in the South: "The louder she screamed, the harder he whipped."

Just as the shared experience of enslavement and physical vulnerability unites young Frederick with his aunt, the incapacity for coherent verbal expression that violence fosters links the adult Douglass with the abused slave woman. For although the author breaks Frederick's silence by describing Aunt Hester's flogging, he nevertheless implies that in this instance, the very act of witnessing precludes speech well after the event itself has passed; even the famously articulate Douglass cannot "commit to paper the feelings" with which he beheld this violent scene.[76] Here the trauma of witnessing threatens to overwhelm the ability to testify; the visual threatens to exceed, and thereby to suppress, the verbal. The remaining "bloody scenes," then, chart Frederick's quest to gain a hearing for his eyewitness testimony against slavery as well as Douglass's growing determination to "commit to paper" his increasingly detailed testimonial account of Southern violence. For it is only through such extralegal print testimony, the Narrative implies, that the black subject will be able to assert the civic identity denied to him as a slave.

The Narrative's second witnessing scene powerfully illustrates how the act of observing violence against other slaves reinforces both the silence and the embodied subjectivity of the witnessing self through the logic of the slave's fungibility as a commodity.[77] Douglass describes how an overseer, aptly named Mr. Gore, shoots and kills the slave Demby for openly resisting punishment. In the middle of a whipping by Gore, Douglass explains, Demby had broken free and "plunged himself into a creek, and stood there at the depth of his shoulders, refusing to come out."[78] Warned that if he does not leave the water after three calls, he will be shot, Demby refuses, and Gore carries out his threat. As in his account of Aunt Hester's flogging, here Douglass emphasizes the scene's spectatorial aspect. The deliberate, dramatic pace at which it unfolds ("The first call was given. Demby made no response . . ." etc.) climaxes with the repressed reaction of the slaves forced to be passive witnesses to this violence: "A thrill of horror flashed through every soul upon the plantation."[79] And just as watching his Aunt Hester's whipping introduces young Frederick to his own physical vulnerability, Gore's murder of Demby is explicitly intended as an object lesson to the enslaved onlookers.[80] When asked by Frederick's master "why he resorted to this extraordinary expedient," Gore replies that Demby "was setting a dangerous example to the other slaves, — one which, if suffered to pass . . . would finally lead to the total subversion of all rule and order upon the plantation," for "if one slave refused to be corrected, and escaped with his life, the other slaves would soon copy the example; the result of which would be, the freedom of the slaves, and the enslavement of the whites."[81] Demby's body serves as a surrogate for those of his fellow slaves: if that body is recalcitrant, the entire corporate body of the slaves will become resistant, resulting in a cataclysmic reversal of racial power relations. If, however, that body is successfully subdued through exemplary violence, the enslaved collective will become tractable, and plantation order will be preserved. As Gore understands, in the context of Southern slavery, to witness brutality is to experience it vicariously. The logic of Gore's monitory murder of Demby rests on the equation of the roles of "witness" and "participant," an equation that in turn rests on both the witness's physical vulnerability and the slave's commodity status.

In this second violent scene, Douglass emphasizes that in the South, black witnessing must always be silent. Noting that "the guilty perpetrator of one of the bloodiest and most foul murders goes unwhipped of justice, and uncensured by the community in which he lives," Douglass explains that Mr.

Gore's "horrid crime was not even submitted to judicial investigation" because "it was committed in the presence of slaves, and they of course could neither institute a suit, nor testify against him."[82] The enforced silence of the slave witnesses means that just as the material evidence of Gore's crime is rendered invisible by the physical setting in which it occurs (Demby's "mangled body sank out of sight," the creek's running water "marked" only temporarily by his "blood and brains"), any testimonial evidence of Demby's murder is similarly effaced by the legal environment of the South, in which white violence evaporates in a haze of black silence.[83]

Even as Douglass's account of Demby's murder once again calls attention to the persistent separation of the seen from the said under slavery, however, it serves to narrow the gap between witnessing and testimony in the *Narrative*. Like the other terrorized slaves on Colonel Lloyd's plantation, Frederick is as powerless to take legal action against Demby's murderer as he is to intervene in the murder itself. An important distinction, however, sets this scene apart from the one in which he witnesses his Aunt Hester's flogging. Here, although the young slave is once again silenced by the trauma of witnessing, the adult fugitive is not. Unable to "institute a suit or testify against" Gore in a court of law, Douglass redresses Frederick's silence and that of the other enslaved witnesses with his retrospective print incrimination of the "guilty perpetrator": he thus exposes the murderous overseer before the court of public opinion with his extralegal testimony that "Mr. Gore lived in St. Michael's, Talbot county, Maryland, when I left there; and if he is still alive, he very probably lives there now."[84] Following the *Narrative*'s trajectory from slavery in the South to freedom in the North, this scene places the narrator one step closer to the latter by associating him not only with the visual, as a frightened witness to Southern violence, but also with the verbal, as one prepared to give detailed factual testimony against the perpetrators of such violence. Appropriating the language of the jettisoned "judicial investigation," Douglass endows his enslaved self a legal consciousness that belies his property status as a "nigger"—"worth a half-cent to kill . . . and a half-cent to bury."[85]

Critics of the *Narrative* have traditionally stressed the structural and thematic importance of another violent scene, Frederick's fight with the slave-breaker Covey. Douglass himself highlights the encounter with his acclaimed chiasmus: "You have seen how a man was made a slave; you shall see how a slave was made a man."[86] This observation, together with Frederick's vow that "the white man who expected to succeed in whipping, must also succeed in killing me," appears to signal his achievement of masculinity, maturity, and physical autonomy and, therefore, to represent his symbolic emancipation.[87] But, as Douglass himself points out, Frederick "remained a slave for four years afterwards," encouraging us to read this scene not as the Narrative's turning point but, like Frederick's earlier attainment of literacy, one of many steps on "the pathway from slavery to freedom."[88]

Instead of prefacing Frederick's liberating flight to the North, the fight with Covey introduces the abortive escape attempt that in turn brings Frederick into his first direct contact with law. Far from censuring the plantation justice represented by Covey's violence, the court of law effectively extends it by reinforcing legal restrictions on slave speech. When the would-be runaways are caught in their escape attempt, Henry literally eats Frederick's words by consuming in a biscuit the pass he had forged. Next, Frederick urges Henry to "own nothing."[89] Repeating the phrase twice more, Douglass writes, "And we passed the word around, 'Own nothing;' and 'Own nothing!' said we all."[90] Playing on the dual meaning of the verb "to own," as "to admit" and "to possess," Douglass's repetition alerts us to how silence mediates the slave's civic exclusion. As objects of property who literally can "own nothing," and especially not the property in whiteness through which to claim the procedural rights that will allow their speech to be exculpatory rather than incriminatory, Frederick and his comrades seek refuge in silence.[91] Due to the slave's double character, all he or she can "own," it would seem, is guilt. Under Southern law, the slave's testimonial speech can only be an admission of guilt, whether one's own or that of another slave. (And indeed, Douglass reports, "We found the evidence against us to be the testimony of one person," clearly an enslaved "informant.")[92] Thus, when the runaways "reached St. Michael's, [they] underwent a sort of examination"—Douglass's language here signaling that slaves were subject to a very different "sort" of legal proceeding than whites—in which the captured fugitives deny any intention to abscond.[93] When the slaves briefly break their silence, their few words are strategic rather than expressive: Frederick and his co-conspirators speak "more to bring out the evidence against" them "than from any hope of getting clear of being sold," the standard punishment for runaways.[94] The episode ends not with Frederick "safe in a land of freedom" as he had hoped but, rather, held fast by Southern slave law, immured "within the walls of a stone prison."[95] In the very next paragraph, however, Frederick's unexpected release returns him to Baltimore, where, in keeping with the Narrative's testimonial trajectory, the book reaches its climax when an injury to the slave's eye propels his escape from Southern brutality, silence, and law.

As the final instance of violence Douglass recounts in the Narrative, this critically neglected scene depicts a crisis of witnessing that cannot be resolved in the South. Frederick, working as an apprentice in a racially mixed Fells Point shipyard, struggles to obey the journeymen carpenters' often conflicting orders. But when four armed white apprentices gang up on him, Frederick, keeping "the vow [he] made after the fight with Mr. Covey," fights back and is beaten badly.[96] He recounts his experience to his master, who immediately takes him to an attorney with the intention of suing his attackers, only to discover that blacks can neither institute a suit nor testify against whites in a court of law. Significantly, this scene, which calls attention to the physical vulnerability and silence inherent in Frederick's role as an "eye-witness to the cruelty" of Southern violence, directly precedes the chapter in which Douglass recounts how Frederick "planned, and finally succeeded in making, [his] escape from slavery."[97]

Like the fight with Covey, the shipyard beating differs from the other bloody scenes in the *Narrative* in that Frederick, no longer merely a witness to the violence inflicted on the enslaved black body, becomes its direct target. In contrast to the Covey episode, however, this experience produces in Frederick a heightened awareness of the inescapability of the slave's embodied subjectivity. As the shipyard beating and its sequel suggest, it is precisely this definitive corporeality that denies the slave witness the right to testify against that violence, making it impossible for him to fulfill his civic responsibilities in the South. Frederick's eye injury represents not only the slave's physical vulnerability, but also the necessity of the would-be slave witness's escape to the North, for it is only there, the *Narrative* suggests, that the fugitive can replace silent victimization with resistant testimony.

Douglass introduces the shipyard scene with a montage of disparate body parts, thereby linking the ruthless exploitation of the black body to the violence of Southern slavery: "At times I needed a dozen pair of hands. . . . Three or four voices would strike my ear. . . . 'I say, Fred., bear a hand['] . . . 'I say, darky, blast your eyes, why don't you heat up some pitch?' . . . [']Damn you, if you move, I'll knock your brains out!'"[98] Douglass continues to focus on body parts in his description of Frederick's beating, associating the labor of the shipyard "hands" with the violence that white hands—and "fists"—commit: "I fell, and with this they all ran upon me, and fell to beating me with their fists. I let them lay on for a while, gathering strength. In an instant, I gave a sudden surge, and rose to my hands and knees. Just as I did that, one of their number gave me, with his heavy boot, a powerful kick in the left eye. My eyeball seemed to have burst. When they saw my eye closed, and badly swollen, they left me. With this I seized the handspike, and for a time pursued them. But here the carpenters interfered, and I thought I might as well give it up. It was impossible to stand my hand against so many. All this took place in the sight of not less than fifty white ship-carpenters."[99] Frederick, first prostrate under others' "fists," begins to rise heroically, only to rest servilely on his "hands and knees," finally concluding in the odd locution that completes his rise even as it signals his defeat, the impossibility of "stand[ing]" his "hand." Syllepsis links his white antagonists to Frederick's own degraded posture: Frederick "fell," and his aggressors "fell to beating him"; he lay on the ground, letting them "lay on" their blows; when his "left eye" shut, his attackers finally "left" him.

Crucial to this scene is the injury to Frederick's eye—the same eye that was opened at the dawn of day by his Aunt Hester's shrieks, the same eye that witnessed her flogging and Demby's murder. Now, when Frederick himself is the helpless target of slavery's violence, his own sight is disabled by a kick to his eye. The spectatorial distance that characterizes Douglass's description of Aunt Hester's whipping and Demby's murder has, quite literally, vanished, replaced with a new tactile immediacy. The momentarily blinded Frederick literally cannot see his own beating as a "terrible spectacle" or a "horrible exhibition," but he *can* attempt to witness this inhumanity after the fact by testifying against his white coworkers.

Following the shipyard scene, the visual and the verbal seem, at last, to come together in what appears to be a set-piece of slaveholding paternalism: Frederick tells "the story of [his] wrongs to Master Hugh," while his mistress, Sophia Auld, "moved . . . to tears" by Frederick's "puffed-out eye and blood-covered face," "bound up [his] head, covering the wounded eye with a lean piece of fresh beef."[100] Like Sophia's ministrations to his eye, Frederick's private testimony seems to restore his identity as a witness, not only to the cruelty of slavery but also to this rare instance of benevolence. As Master Hugh "listened attentively to [his] narration of the circumstances leading to the savage outrage, and gave many proofs of his strong indignation at it," Frederick finds that "it was almost compensation for [his] suffering to witness, once more, a manifestation of kindness from this, [his] once affectionate old mistress," whose flowing tears sympathetically (albeit colorlessly) mimic her slave's bleeding eye.[101]

Douglass disrupts this scene of benign plantation justice, however, by demonstrating the inadequacy of private redress to the public wrongs suffered by the slave. As a reminder that the gap between witnessing and testimony can never be closed in the South due to restrictions on slaves' courtroom speech, Frederick's restored status as witness is quickly overturned when Hugh Auld consults with Esquire Watson, an attorney: "His answer was, he could do nothing in the case, unless some white man would come forward and testify. He could issue no warrant on my word. If I had been killed in the presence of a thousand colored people, their testimony combined would have been insufficient to have arrested one of the murderers. Master Hugh, for once, was compelled to say this state of things was too bad. Of course, it was impossible to get any white man to volunteer his testimony in my behalf, and against the young white men. . . . There was nothing done, and probably nothing would have been done if I had been killed. Such was, and such remains, the state of things in the Christian city of Baltimore." [102] As Shoshana Felman has argued of the trials involving brutalized Los Angeles motorist Rodney King and wife-abuser O. J. Simpson, Frederick's encounter with Esquire Watson is, crucially, "about an *unseen* beating, about an inexplicable, recalcitrant relation between beating and blindness, beating and invisibility, an invisibility that cannot be dispelled in spite of the most probatory visual evidence." [103] But whereas for Felman (following Althusser) it is the jury in each case whose ideological blinders keep it from seeing beatings of the black citizen or the female spouse as physical manifestations of deep cultural hatred in the form of racism or misogyny, in this scene from the *Narrative*, it is the legal inadmissibility of black testimony that illustrates how justice can "in effect be blind — in ways other than the ones in which it is normally expected to be." [104] In the topsy-turvy world of the slaveholding South, the willful blindness of justice implies not impartiality but its reverse, (racial) discrimination. And through the legislated legal incompetence of the slave, law overlooks the very racist violence that endangers the sight of the would-be black witness.

As in his account of Demby's murder, here Douglass provides literary testimony that arraigns the slaveholding South's criminality before the popular tribunal as it protests the exclusion of blacks from the American legal system by directing attention to the inadmissibility of African American testimony in the American courtroom.[105] Frederick's legal exclusion represents the penultimate phase in his transformation from silent enslaved victim to outspoken antislavery witness. Denied the opportunity to give his testimony in a Southern court of law, Frederick must turn to the Northern court of public opinion.

In the logic of the antislavery movement's juridical metaphor, the attack on Frederick and its aftermath become a metaphor for the authorship of the *Narrative* itself. Just as earlier the murdered Demby stands in for "every soul on the plantation," Frederick embodies the "thousand[s] of colored people" beaten, silenced, and rendered invisible by white supremacy, represented here by the murderous, bullying white shipyard workers. Douglass's "narration" of the "outrage" of slavery is intended to provoke "indignation" in the attentive antebellum reader, who, like Frederick's master Hugh Auld, may well be complicit in the peculiar institution of slavery yet fair-minded enough to be persuaded by what Douglass pointedly calls the "facts in the case." [106] It is no coincidence that the beating immediately precedes Frederick's flight from slavery. Refusing to remain physically vulnerable and silent any longer, Frederick directly engages the legal system, personified by Esquire Watson. The inadequacy of plantation justice, the inadmissibility of his own eyewitness testimony, the refusal of the Southern attorney to represent him, the failure of any white coworkers to come forward as witnesses, and the highly racialized blindness of Southern justice precipitate, even require, Frederick's escape to the abolitionist North, where he encounters passionate white advocates for the slave and the opportunity to take the witness stand against the guilty perpetrators before the popular tribunal.

But even as the pivotal scene of Frederick's shipyard beating seems to justify the antislavery movement's adoption of the language of criminal litigation, it also threatens to undo the power of that rhetoric. This scene, with its emphasis on the eye's physicality, poses but does not resolve some disturbing questions about the reliability of the slave victim's firsthand testimony of Southern violence. Like the "lean piece of fresh beef" with which his wounded eye is covered, Frederick's injury reminds us of the corporeality and, hence, physiological vulnerability and fallibility of that organ. Although the reader, like Hugh Auld, is meant to be outraged by the injustice of a legal system in which slave testimony is inadmissible, Douglass's account of the assault potentially reinforces the well-documented anxieties of white readers about the veracity of African American accounts of slavery and the trustworthiness of their authors. [107] After all, how reliable is an eyewitness whose "eye [is] closed, and badly swollen"? [108]

Douglass strives to resolve this dilemma in his story's brief but subtle conclusion. The final image that the *Narrative* offers of its protagonist/narrator seems to represent the culmination of the witnessing scenes that have gone before: three years after his arrival in the North, the former bondsman, attending a Nantucket antislavery convention, "felt strongly moved to speak." [109] Although he "felt [him]self a slave, and the idea of speaking to white people weighed [him] down," the fugitive "spoke but a few moments" before he "felt a degree of freedom, and said what [he] desired with considerable ease." [110] It is not his first, exhilarated view of New York nor his subsequent preaching and lecturing at "the colored people's meeting at New Bedford" that provides Douglass with "a degree of freedom" but the act, years later, of telling his story to a racially mixed audience. [111] The liberating experience of testifying in the North, the *Narrative* seems to imply, provides the discursive antidote to the oppressive trauma of witnessing in the South. Rising to address the Nantucket antislavery meeting in the *Narrative*'s closing lines, the fugitive completes his transformation from slave to freeman: no longer forced silently to witness violence in the South, he is now free publicly to testify in the North against that violence.

Intriguingly, however, Douglass vacates his testimonial role at the moment of its fulfillment. Instead of providing an account of that landmark Nantucket speech—an abbreviated version, as Garrison's preface makes clear, of the *Narrative* we hold in our hands—Douglass notes that "from that time until now, I have been engaged in pleading the cause of my brethren." [112] Shifting in the *Narrative*'s last sentence from the posture of the witness to that of advocate, Douglass locates his identity as slave victim and witness firmly in the South, implicitly resisting abolitionist pressure to retain that identity in the North. No longer the "powerful slave" whose moving testimony caused "the best pleaders for the slave" to catch their breath in Nantucket, Douglass now pleads his fellow slaves' cause himself. With this concluding image of professional black advocacy, Douglass claimed a role usually reserved for white antislavery activists, asserted a civic agency denied to African Americans in the North as well as the South, and thereby assumed a discursive authority as unprecedented in the court of public opinion as it had been in the court of law.

A decade later, Frederick Douglass would follow his best-selling *Narrative* with *My Bondage and My Freedom*, published the same year that Jane Johnson's "bold and perilous" reappearance in Philadelphia as a witness for the defense caused "amazement and confusion" in her former master John Wheeler's criminal case against William Still and his fellow activists. [113] The timing is suggestive: for if the case clearly demonstrated the precariousness of black speech (slave or free) in the nation's courtrooms (North or South), it offered a more subtle indication of the challenges of black advocacy. As we have seen, Wheeler's habeas-corpus suit effectively asserted that of the seven men who participated in Johnson's rescue, the only one capable of civic agency was Passmore Williamson, whom Judge Kane designated as "the only white man, the only citizen, the only individual having recognized political rights." [114] The federal court's denial of black civic agency meant that the parallel actions of Williamson's six African American colleagues could only be construed as criminal acts, as their role as defendants in the state criminal trial suggests. (Tellingly, despite Williamson's inclusion in the indictment, his involvement in the civil proceedings effectively exempted him from the criminal case.) Thus, although it was Williamson who was imprisoned and his African American colleagues who were acquitted or received light sentences, federal and state courts cooperated to support a narrative of white civic agency (no matter how misguided) and black criminality (no matter how dubious). Because the voluminous print coverage that ensued focused on Johnson's dramatic reappearance as a heavily veiled witness in the criminal trial and on Williamson's lengthy imprisonment for contempt of court, the cases became identified with the testifying former slave and the white citizen rather than with the free black activists.[115]

Similarly, the complicated position of free African Americans could not easily be assimilated to the rudimentary trial model upon which so much of the debate over slavery was fashioned.[116] As the antebellum career and writings of Frederick Douglass illustrate, the prevalent emphasis on slave testimony provided a platform for black print agitation, but it also tended to restrict formerly enslaved writers and activists to the comparatively confined, newly racialized discursive space of the witness stand. Those black abolitionists who could not (or would not) base their interventions on their firsthand experience of slavery did not have their white colleagues' option of authorizing their contributions to the slavery debate on their "recognized political rights" as citizens.[117]

4 TALKING LAWYERLIKE ABOUT LAW

Black Advocacy and *My Bondage*
and *My Freedom*

Upon the publication of his *Narrative*, Frederick Douglass boarded the steamship *Cambria* for an eighteen-month lecture tour of the British Isles. On 27 August 1845, the day before the *Cambria* docked in Liverpool, Douglass—who had spent the voyage segregated from first class—was invited to give his fellow voyagers a sample of his celebrated oratory. Soon after he began speaking, however, a small riot broke out, ending only when the captain threatened to put the rioters in irons.[1] In subsequent accounts of the shipboard events, Douglass indicated that the riot began when he substituted his autobiographical testimony with a dramatic reading of Southern slave laws.[2]

Eight years later, in his only work of fiction, a novella based on the *Creole* case, Douglass would have his eponymous "Heroic Slave," Madison Washington, proclaim in the midst of a slave ship uprising, "You cannot write the bloody laws of slavery on those restless billows. The ocean, if not the land, is free."[3] But the very different kind of shipboard rebellion prompted by Douglass's reading of "the bloody laws of slavery" on the *Cambria* illustrates the considerable hostility with which black advocacy had to contend in the antebellum period. For, as the discussion of the *Cambria* riot at the end of this chapter will address in greater detail, it was not Douglass's antislavery lecture itself that sparked the riot. When Douglass confined himself to reading passages from his *Narrative*, his antagonists limited themselves to verbal heckling; it was only when he began to read the slave code that they turned to violence.[4] That nationalist display of violence, I suggest, vividly dramatized white Americans' widespread refusal (or incapacity) to conceptualize African Americans as active participants in civil society.[5]

A portent of the tremendous resistance that awaited those African Americans who, like Douglass, were determined to talk lawyerlike about law, the *Cambria* incident occurred just over two months after the nation's first black attorney, Macon Bolling Allen, was admitted to practice law in Massachusetts.[6] Responding to the call to reconstruct "the everyday world of the historically situated lawyer" and seeking to provide a historical grounding for Douglass's efforts to theorize and enact a form of black advocacy in print, this chapter begins by recounting the experiences of two of Allen's African American colleagues, John Mercer Langston and Robert Morris.[7] Then, placing *My Bondage and My Freedom* (with emphasis on James McCune Smith's introduction) alongside Thomas Jefferson's *Notes on the State of Virginia* (1787) and Caleb Bingham's *Columbian Orator* (1797), I argue that Douglass presented black advocacy as an alternative to the "plain narration" required of the antislavery witness in order to combat the long-standing allegations of black intellectual inferiority that underwrote African American civic exclusion as well as the racialized hierarchy of antebellum abolitionist discourse.[8] Douglass's own reassessment of his role in the antislavery movement, I conclude, should prompt a corresponding reevaluation of the ongoing critical emphasis in African American studies and in the legal academy on black testimony's purportedly liberating quality. As Douglass's account of the *Cambria* riot suggests, African American civic participation required a black advocacy that foregrounded forensic argumentation even as it retained the personal narrative of racial oppression.

The Little Darkey Lawyer

In 1829, African American pamphleteer David Walker challenged "the American people . . . to show me a man of colour, who holds the low office of a Constable, or one who sits in a Juror Box, even on a case of one of his wretched brethren," noting that he would not go so far as to ask his countrymen "to show me a coloured President, a Governor, a Legislator, a Senator, a Mayor, or an Attorney at the Bar."[9] The nation would wait a long time before blacks would be elected to such high offices (to say nothing of the presidency). But during the 1840s and 1850s, the same decades that saw Frederick Douglass's transformation from antislavery witness into black advocate, the first African American lawyers were admitted to the bar in the United States (among them, perhaps, Walker's own son).[10] The period would also see the emergence of African American legal-reform movements, from the New York Legal Rights Association's struggle against segregation on public conveyances to the black state conventions' efforts to combat restrictions on testimony in Ohio, Indiana, and California.[11]

The tumultuous early careers of two of the period's first black lawyers, Robert Morris and John Mercer Langston, provide insight into the antagonism Douglass could expect to encounter as black advocate, for these men encountered firsthand the virulent opposition that met antebellum displays of African American civic agency. Legal historian Kenneth Walter Mack's insight regarding resistance to women's postbellum entry into the legal profession can be applied to would-be African American lawyers in Jacksonian America: "Given the close nexus between the attorney's role as a public officer and suffrage rights, granting [African Americans] the right to practice law" could be seen as tantamount to "grant[ing] them the right to vote."[12] In a culture that tenaciously clung to notions of black criminality and intellectual inferiority in order to reject the possibility of African American citizenship, the testimony of former slaves may have been precarious evidence, but free black advocacy was virtually unimaginable.

Although Allen was the first African American lawyer and first black justice of the peace, far better known is his successor, Robert Morris, who, after clerking in the Boston office of white abolitionist lawyer Ellis Gray Loring, was admitted to the Massachusetts bar in February 1847. In addition to maintaining a successful practice, serving as the nation's second black justice of the peace, running as Free Soil candidate for mayor, and playing a central role in the school-desegregation and black-militia movements, Boston Vigilance Committee member Morris attained notoriety for his involvement in that city's fugitive slave crisis of the 1850s. He was tried and acquitted for joining the mob of African American Bostonians in aiding and abetting the rescue of alleged fugitive Shadrach Minkins, for whom he had briefly served as co-counsel.[13] John Mercer Langston, Morris's Western colleague, emancipated Virginia slave, and Oberlin graduate, was admitted to the Ohio bar in 1854 and is known largely for his involvement in the black-convention movement, his postwar deanship of Howard University Law School, his position as the first African American elected to the U.S. Congress, and his status as grand-uncle to poet Langston Hughes.[14] For Morris and Langston, as for other early African American lawyers, the legal profession provided an essential point of entry for black participation in local, state, and federal governance.

The experiences of these men illustrate how the widespread denial of African American civic agency rendered the concept of black advocacy incomprehensible, if not ludicrous, for many whites in Jacksonian America. Retrospective accounts published at century's end provide some sense of the obstacles each man encountered in his efforts to join the antebellum bar. From the Virginia Plantation to the National Capitol (1894), Langston's third-person autobiography, tells the Horatio Algeresque story of how the youngest child of a Virginia slaveholder and his manumitted African American–Indian partner eventually became, as described in the book's subtitle, "The First and Only Negro Representative in Congress from the Old Dominion." Langston recounts that after being denied admission to law schools in Ohio and New York, he followed the advice of one of his Oberlin professors to become the first student of color to enroll in an American theological seminary; having thus proven his intellectual capacity, he embarked on private study of law in the office of Philemon Bliss, an Ohio abolitionist judge.[15] As Langston recalls, "There was no public sentiment in any part of the country favoring such course on the part of any young colored man however endowed, educated, qualified, and well situated for such profession. The public feeling of the country seemed to be entirely against it, and no promise of success in such behalf could be discovered in any quarter."[16] Once in practice, new difficulties arose from the insecure legal status of African Americans. As Langston explains, even when African Americans had legal business to conduct, they were hesitant to employ a lawyer of their own color, "for the courts were all composed of white men and so were all the juries, and on the part of the former and the latter alike prejudice, strong and inveterate, existed against the colored litigant"; moreover, "the very language of the law was so positively against the colored man . . . that he very justly felt that he must do his utmost, even in the employment of his lawyer, to gain so far as practicable, favor with the court and jury. He felt that he must not certainly do the least thing to engender or arouse any feeling or sentiment against himself as a suitor for justice."[17]

Whereas potential African American clients were reluctant further to diminish their scant chances for legal justice by hiring a black lawyer, the pervasive racism of the virtually all-white legal profession is clearly evident from the published account of two memorial "bar meeting[s] in Boston," on 16 December 1882 and 5 March 1883, "called to commemorate the life and death of Mr. Robert Morris."[18] Eulogizing Morris on the basis of an "acquaintance . . . reaching back nearly forty years, to the time when he was clerk," one lawyer recalled a "highly respectable member of the Suffolk Bar who told me many years ago that he did not care to practise in the courts now, since they had got to 'letting niggers in.' "[19] Likewise, a Judge Russell, remembering "how slight was the encouragement for such a youth" and recollecting "the 'unnumbered smiling' that rippled through Court Street when his purpose was announced," noted that against Morris's "success was leagued every mean prejudice and every great interest in the community."[20]

Both Morris and Langston were forced to respond to expressions of prejudice that far exceeded the reticence of black clients and the condescension of white colleagues, however. When trying his first case, Morris faced opposing counsel who not only refused to cooperate with him but verbally abused him. According to Edwin Garrison Walker, Morris's friend, legal colleague, and fellow black Bostonian, "Mr. Morris . . . said that he left the man's office with a heavy heart, and with a feeling that, if that was the way he was to be treated by the members of the bar in his practice, for the moment he doubted his ability to face the storm." [21] Walker recalled Morris telling him, "I went to my office. I sat down and I cried. I thought of the mighty odds against which I had to contend, and then it was that I made the vow that I have never broken. It was this: I would prove myself to be a man and a gentleman, and succeed in the practice of the law, or I would die." [22]

Langston's more tumultuous experience speaks less to the differences between the two men, perhaps, than to the contrast between the Boston bar's civil incivility and the Ohio legal community's frontier ruffianism. In order "to show what the public feeling was which the colored lawyer had to encounter and overcome in the early days of his professional career," Langston tells of one case when he and his client were warned not to come to "court on the day of trial, and that if the colored lawyer did appear, he might be compelled to confront even violence." [23] Ignoring such warnings, Langston met "threatening looks" and "menacing words" from the gathered spectators, one of whom "went so far as to declare as the colored lawyer passed him on the street, that 'The community has reached a pitiable condition when a nigger lawyer goes in pompous manner about this town.'" [24] Worse yet, "the attorney on the opposite side" joined in the "offensive, vulgar language, in accordance with the apparent desire of the rabble." [25] The lawyer's unprofessional behavior led the genteel Langston to conclude the anecdote: "If blows were used it was because they were necessary." [26] Langston recounts how, on another occasion, in response to a litigant's slur, he "immediately struck" the man "with his fist, felling him to the floor." [27] Just as quickly, the black lawyer approached the bench and "confessed himself as in contempt of the court and ready to accept any punishment, fine or even imprisonment," insisting, "however, that no man should ever refer to his color, even in a court room and in the presence of the judge and jury engaged in their judicial labors, to insult and degrade him, without prompt and immediate attempt on his part to resent it, with any and every means and method at his command." [28] True to his word, Langston "administered" to another racist colleague "not only a sound slapping of the face, but a round thorough kicking as he ran crying for help"; upon arriving in the courtroom, Langston found his obtuse opponent "with a bloody nose, smarting under the deserved castigation" and mulishly "making a very serious and solemn complaint of vexatious and outrageous assault and battery against him by this *nigger* lawyer!"[29]

Whether met by the determined gentlemanly sensibility of a Morris or the firm physical resistance of a Langston, the hostile "public feeling" displayed toward black lawyers starkly demonstrated the reluctance, even inability, of many white Americans to conceive of African Americans in a legal capacity other than that of property, criminals, victims, or (most recently) witnesses. As we can see if we return to the legal fallout of the Shadrach Minkins rescue for one final account of black advocacy, it was the African American attorney's role as an officially recognized representative of the American legal system, more than his "pompous" class status, that made the idea of a "*nigger* lawyer" seem a contradiction in terms. The telling moment occurred not in the trial of Morris himself but in that of his white colleague Charles G. Davis, who, like Morris, was represented by Richard Henry Dana Jr. and whose case, also like that of Morris, attracted extensive print coverage.[30] In the pamphlet *Report*, and, indeed, at the trial itself, portrayals of Morris illustrate how exemplary black advocacy was imaginable to most antebellum whites only through uplift ideology (at best) or racial caricature (at worst).

According to the *Report*, Dana commenced his defense of Davis by establishing the white lawyer's character, referring not only to his official position as "Justice of the Peace, sworn to sustain the laws, a counsellor of this court and of all courts of the United States in this State, sworn doubly to sustain the laws," but also to his class status and ethnic heritage as "a gentleman of property and education, whose professional reputation and emolument depend upon sustaining law against force; a man whose ancestors, of the ancient Pilgrim stock of Plymouth, are among those who laid the foundations of the institutions that we enjoy."[31] Dana's depiction of Davis's considerable investment in "personal pride, historical recollections, property, in family, reputation, honor and emolument in these courts" contrasts sharply with his characterization of the abolitionist lawyer's clients: those "mostly poor" African Americans who are the "plebeians, while we are the patricians of our community."[32] It is in this class-inflected racial context, not in the professional or elite milieux in which he cast Davis, that Dana referred to his colleague at the bar, Robert Morris. Seizing the opportunity to document what otherwise would have been a passing racial slur, Dana concluded his comments to the court by referring to a disruption in the previous day's proceedings:

> While we uphold the public peace and the dignity of all laws, let us
> regard with tenderness and consideration that poor class of oppressed

men, our negro population, on whom the [Fugitive Slave Law] statute falls with the terrors and blackness of night. When one of their number [Robert Morris], by his industry and abilities has raised himself to the dignity of a place in this bar, it was with mortification I heard him insulted, yesterday, on the stand, by an officer of this court, who pointed him out, in giving his evidence, as "the little darkey lawyer[.]" While I rejoiced at the rebuke administered to that officer from the bench, it was with deep regret that I saw the representative of the government [District Attorney George Lunt] lead off the laugh of the audience against him.

Mr. Lunt—This is false.

Mr. Dana—Do you deny you did so? It was seen and noticed by us all. I spoke to you at the time.

Mr. Lunt—I only smiled. I cannot always control my muscles.

Mr. Dana—I am sorry you could not control them on this occasion. It led off and encouraged others, who take their cue from persons in high positions.[33]

Characterizing Morris as "the little darkey lawyer," the court officer's testimony reduced him to a caricature of black advocacy that diminished his professional stature through its exaggerated attention to his racialized physical attributes. The judge's rebuke notwithstanding, this testimony and the gales of laughter that it provoked from "the audience" effectively transformed the legal proceeding into popular entertainment—a performance that, like the minstrel show, turned on the figure of the dandified black who implausibly mimics authoritative white discourse. Taken together, Dana's earlier remarks on Davis, Lunt's retort to Dana, and Dana's rejoinder all highlight how, in the American courtroom, the lawyer's authority was premised not only on behaviors that one could attempt to "control," in acts of exemplary bourgeois physical restraint, but also on the ungovernable history of one's body—whether one was the descendent of "ancient Pilgrim stock" or a "darkey" from that "poor class of oppressed men," the "negro population."[34] Whereas the pained African American body legitimized former slaves' testimony, the requisite (but impossible) effacement of the African American lawyer's body effectively reduced black advocacy to an oxymoron for many white Americans.[35]

To Apprehend Their Rights

The same tumultuous years that saw Robert Morris and John Mercer Langston struggling to integrate the American bar found Frederick Douglass meditating on the challenges and responsibilities of the black advocate in antebellum print culture. Retaining the popular legal consciousness that pervaded abolitionist rhetoric, Douglass increasingly adopted the prosecutorial posture hitherto reserved for his white colleagues in an effort to expand his role—and, by extension, that of other African Americans—in the movement. Nowhere is this shift in stance so evident as in the autobiography Douglass published a decade after his 1845 Narrative. For if the Narrative of the Life of Frederick Douglass is the consummate portrayal of the bondsman as victim of and witness to the crime of slavery, My Bondage and My Freedom offers the period's most thorough articulation of the dilemma of the free black abolitionist facing the bar of public opinion. In the Narrative, prefaces by well-known white advocates for the slave mimic the prosecutor's opening argument by introducing and framing the testimonial evidence that follows; appropriately, then, the prefatory materials with which Douglass begins his second narrative foreground the conundrum of black advocacy itself.

In a letter reproduced in the unsigned "Editor's Preface" to My Bondage and My Freedom, Douglass, responding to his editor's "urgent solicitation for such a work," reminds his reader, "I have often refused to narrate my personal experience in public anti-slavery meetings, and in sympathizing circles, when urged to do so by friends, with whose views and wishes, ordinarily, it were a pleasure to comply." [36] Instead, Douglass maintains, in "letters and speeches, I have generally aimed to discuss the question of Slavery in the light of fundamental principles, and upon facts, notorious and open to all; making, I trust, no more of the fact of my own enslavement, than circumstances seemed absolutely to require." [37] Picking up where the Narrative left off, Douglass's autobiography portrays its author as pleading the cause of his brethren in preference to narrating his "personal experience." Still, Douglass's claims seem more than a little disingenuous. After all, he had become an international celebrity through recitations of his "own enslavement" in print and on the lecture platform; he would retell the story of his "Bondage" in the current volume; and he would go on to recount that story yet again in a third autobiographical narrative, the Life and Times of Frederick Douglass (1881), publishing two further revised and expanded editions of that work before his death in 1895.

But in an era when, in Habermas's words, the "publicizing of private biographies" was beginning to supplant the ideal of reasoned debate in the public sphere, circumstances frequently seemed "absolutely to require" that Douglass root his philosophical antislavery argument in what critic Eric J. Sundquist has called the "wrenchingly personal" facts of his own enslavement.[38] Indeed, later in the same introductory letter, Douglass would draw on the very juridical language that Garrison had used to authorize the *Narrative* in order to elaborate his reasons for publishing this sequel. Emphasizing that *My Bondage and My Freedom* was intended "not to illustrate any heroic achievements of a man" but, rather, to shine "the light of truth upon a system, esteemed by some as a blessing, and by others as a curse and a crime," Douglass moved from a religious to a legal register to explain that "this system [slavery] is now at the bar of public opinion—not only of this country, but of the whole civilized world—for judgment."[39] Because "its friends have made for it the usual plea—'not guilty;' the case must, therefore, proceed. Any facts, either from slaves, slave-holders, or by-standers, calculated to enlighten the public mind, by revealing the true nature, character, and tendency of the slave system, are in order, and can scarcely be innocently withheld."[40] However eager he may have been to step down from the witness stand, Douglass implied, his autobiographical testimony had been effectively subpoenaed by the popular tribunal.

At the moment that he offered one of the era's most vivid evocations of the slavery debate as a trial before "the bar of public opinion," however, Douglass (always an astute observer of the racial politics of antebellum print culture) called attention to the unique rhetorical challenges such legal language posed for African Americans. Citing "special reasons why I should write my own biography, in preference to employing another to do it," Douglass explained, "Not only is slavery on trial, but unfortunately, the enslaved people are also on trial. It is alleged, that they are, naturally, inferior; that they are *so low* in the scale of humanity, and so utterly stupid, that they are unconscious of their wrongs, and do not apprehend their rights."[41] Linking the imputed criminality of slaves to their presumptive inferiority, Douglass acknowledged the importance of black literary production to demonstrating African Americans' ability to "apprehend their rights"—perceiving the fundamental principles of natural law that guaranteed those rights, as well as laying claim to the rights themselves.

As if to lend support to Douglass's observation, three years later proslavery legal theorist Thomas R. R. Cobb would employ precisely such courtroom imagery to affirm black cultural and intellectual deficiency: adverting to claims that ancient Ethiopia offers "an example of negro civilization," Cobb placidly conceded that, "when discovered, and its monuments, and people, and works of art, and records of history, are brought before the world, we will be called on to examine the witness, and determine his competency and credibility."[42] As Douglass understood, persistent allegations of intellectual inferiority called into question both blacks' "competency" and their "credibility" before the bar of public opinion. The challenge for Douglass and his

African American colleagues, then, was to prove black intellectual, physiological, and civic equality through the authorship and publication of a distinctively black literature and, thus, to vindicate the enslaved people at the popular tribunal.

But, as Douglass's shrewd use of the word "apprehend" implies, due to the nature of the inferiority ascribed to blacks, such vindication could not be accomplished merely by casting the former slave in the role of testifying eyewitness.[43] It was not enough, in other words, that "the narrated, descriptive 'eye' was put into service as a literary form to posit both the individual 'I' of the black author as well as the collective 'I' of the race."[44] For, as radical as the abolitionist call for black testimony may have seemed, that appeal was nevertheless rooted in Enlightenment racial thought, which conceded blacks to be skillful in description and other mimetic techniques associated with the production of narrative but deficient in a higher capacity for analysis and interpretation. Thomas Jefferson's classic formulation of this thesis in "Laws," Query XIV of his *Notes on the State of Virginia*, builds on the philosophy of David Hume and Immanuel Kant to justify Virginian legislators' refusal to "incorporate the blacks into the state" (and by extension the nation) largely on the basis of this deficiency.[45] Framing his well-known elaboration of the "physical and moral" qualities of blacks that require their postemancipation deportation and colonization, Jefferson's discussion of Virginia law first presents slaves as criminals receiving limited due process and as chattel in a section on conveyances.[46] Later, Jefferson acknowledges that it is their status as property that explains slaves' criminality. Rather than innate, slaves' "disposition to theft" is the product of the repressive legal environment in which they find themselves.[47] Jefferson notes, "When arguing for ourselves, we lay it down as a fundamental, that laws, to be just, must give a reciprocation of right: that, without this, they are merely arbitrary rules of conduct, founded in force, and not in conscience."[48] Little wonder, then, that the "man, in whose favor no laws of property exist, probably feels himself less bound to respect those made in favor of others."[49] But as Jefferson takes pains to demonstrate, ultimately this legal double standard arises not from the hypocrisy or tyranny of white slaveholding legislators but from blacks' intrinsic racial inferiority.

"Comparing [blacks] by their faculties of memory, reason, and imagination," Jefferson finds "that in memory they are equal to the whites; in reason much inferior," and "in imagination they are dull, tasteless, and anomalous"; thus, like animals, "their existence appears to participate more of sensation than reflection."[50] Restricting his "judgment" to blacks of the diaspora, amongst whom "some have been liberally educated, and all have lived in countries where the arts and sciences are cultivated to a considerable degree, and have had before their eyes samples of the best works from abroad," Jefferson concludes, "Never yet, could I find that a black had uttered a thought above the level of plain narration." [51] Assigning Ignatius Sancho, Douglass's eighteenth-century Afro-British counterpart, "to the first place among those of his own colour who have presented themselves to the public judgment" but at the "bottom" of "the writers of the race among whom he lived," Jefferson explains that Sancho's writing suffers from his "wild and extravagant" imagination that "escapes incessantly from every restraint of reason and taste, and, in the course of its vagaries, leaves a tract of thought as incoherent and eccentric, as is the course of a meteor through the sky." [52] Sancho's posthumously published Letters (1782), which often addresses racial themes, does "more honour to the heart than the head," Jefferson suggests.[53] "His subjects should often have led him to a process of sober reasoning; yet we always find him substituting sentiment for demonstration." [54] Although Jefferson's language anticipates both the scientific racism and the romantic racialism that would increasingly characterize nineteenth-century racial thought, his conclusions were particularly devastating in the bourgeois Enlightenment world that both he and Sancho inhabited, for in that milieu, civic inclusion was premised, at least theoretically, on the display of reason rather than social status.[55] To lack reason was to lack humanity; to be denied admission to the republic of letters authorized one's exclusion from the republic of laws.[56]

Identifying Notes on the State of Virginia as the leading example of "the emerging paradoxical association of racial thinking and egalitarian philosophy," historian Alexander O. Boulton has pointed out that "by the middle of the nineteenth century, many Northern abolitionists held the same combination of antislavery ideas and scientific racism that were earlier proposed by Jefferson." [57] It is precisely his white colleagues' inheritance of Jeffersonian racial thought, and most notably the opposition of blacks' "plain narration" to whites' "sober reasoning," that Douglass critiques in My Bondage and My Freedom's best-known passage, from the chapter "Introduced to the Abolitionists":

During the first three or four months, my speeches were almost exclusively made up of narrations of my own personal experience as a slave. "Let us have the facts," said the people. So also said Friend George Foster, who always wished to pin me down to my simple narrative. "Give us the facts," said Collins, "we will take care of the philosophy." . . . "Tell your story, Frederick," would whisper my then revered friend, William

Lloyd Garrison, as I stepped upon the platform. I could not always obey, for I was now reading and thinking. New views of the subject were presented to my mind. It did not entirely satisfy me to *narrate* wrongs; I felt like *denouncing* them. I could not always curb my moral indignation for the perpetrators of slaveholding villainy, long enough for a circumstantial statement of the facts which I felt almost everybody must know. Besides, I was growing, and needed room.[58]

Rejecting the Garrisonian demand that he limit his public speaking to a "circumstantial statement of the facts," Douglass identifies a dynamic that Holocaust scholar James E. Young sees as a defining characteristic of testimonial literature.[59] Young describes testimony as " 'factually insistent' narrative" that "accomplishes not so much the unmediated rendition of facts as it does a 'rhetoric of fact.' "[60] As a result, Young explains, both testimonial texts and their authors are assigned the impossible task of becoming "traces" or "material fragments of experiences."[61] Hence, the need for formerly enslaved lecturers and writers to authorize their political interventions on the basis of the physical victimization against which they testified.

Douglass's earliest surviving transcribed speech shows this dynamic at work. "My friends," Douglass addressed his Lynn, Massachusetts, audience in October 1841, "I have come to tell you something about slavery—what I *know* of it, as I have *felt* it."[62] Recalling that "when I came North, I was astonished to find that the abolitionists knew so much about it, that they were acquainted with its deadly effects as well as if they had lived in its midst," Douglass then proceeded to emphasize his unique qualifications as a former slave.[63] Northern abolitionists, he acknowledged, "can give you its history—. . . they can depict its horrors," but, Douglass maintained, "they cannot speak as I can from *experience*; they cannot refer you to a back covered with scars, as I can; for I have felt these wounds; I have suffered under the lash without the power of resisting. Yes, my blood has sprung out as the lash embedded itself in my flesh."[64] As noted, Douglass offered little in the way of autobiographical detail in his early speeches; at the same time, his rhetoric spoke to African American reformers' sense that there were, in effect, "two abolitionisms": the theoretical concept of individual liberty embraced by most white activists and the more pragmatic understanding held by black abolitionists of everyday racial oppression.[65] Nonetheless, as *My Bondage and My Freedom* suggests, in such early lectures, Douglass explicitly grounded his oratorical authority in his firsthand experience of slavery as victim and witness, which he contrasted to the abolitionists' more abstract knowledge of the peculiar institution. Just prior to the publication of his *Narrative*, for instance, he assured a New York audience, "I can tell you what I have seen with my own eyes" and "felt on my own person."[66]

The problem with this "rhetoric of fact" was not so much its claim to unmediated representation as its tendency to separate, in the words of Douglass's white colleague, John Collins, "fact" from "philosophy."[67] Mimicking the adversarial trial's apparent distinction between facts and analysis, narration and interpretation, the antislavery movement endowed its black witnesses with "testimonial authority"—recognition of the authenticity and facticity of their texts—at the expense of what we might call exegetical authority, recognition of their ability and right to construct meaning from these texts.[68] It is this exegetical authority (or "hermaneutic [sic] function," in Foucauldian terms), reinforced by Jeffersonian racial thought, that created a demand for black testimony to be framed by white advocacy even as it made autonomous black advocacy virtually unthinkable in the antebellum period.[69] Perhaps it is not surprising to find Boston lawyer George W. Searle—in phrasing much like that Douglass attributes to Collins—recalling of his late colleague Robert Morris, "He tried cases on facts, and left the refinements and technicalities of law to others who had mastered them."[70]

The Polemical Slave

In early nineteenth-century print culture, personal storytelling—whether confessional or testimonial, spiritual or extralegal—was not the only discursive mode available to the politically engaged African American writer and orator. As Douglass well knew, an alternative model of black political speech, one that powerfully illustrated the slave's capacity for sober reasoning, was readily available in households and schoolrooms across the nation. Identified by Douglass as the first book he ever purchased as a slave, Caleb Bingham's *Columbian Orator*, a primer and elocution manual, was one of the few books to be found in many early American homes, reaching over twenty editions by 1860, with total sales approaching 200,000 copies.[71] Influenced by Bingham's oratorical exemplars, Douglass devoted special attention in his personal narratives to the selection from John Aikin's "Dialogue between a Master and a Slave," in which a slave is recaptured in his second escape attempt by his master, who demands an explanation for the bondsman's lack of "gratitude."[72] "In this dialogue," Douglass recalled, "the whole argument in behalf of slavery was brought forward by the master, all of which was disposed of by the slave."[73] Indeed, "the slave was made to say some very smart as well as impressive things in reply to his master—things which had the desired though unexpected effect; for the conversation resulted in the voluntary emancipation of the slave on the part of the master."[74]

Critics have long recognized the importance of the *Columbian Orator*, and this moral suasionist "Dialogue" in particular, to Douglass's preparation for—and publicizing of—his subsequent abolitionist career.[75] But what is seldom, if ever, acknowledged is the significant discrepancy between the rhetorical strategies adopted by the *Columbian Orator*'s idealized republican slave and those employed by Douglass as Garrisonian "eye-witness to the cruelty."[76] From this exchange, historian David Blight points out, young Frederick Bailey learned "that slavery was something subject to 'argument,' even between master and slave"—a discovery that offered a valuable example of "reason winning over power" to an adolescent "surrounded and imprisoned by the opposite message."[77] But, like Garrison, Douglass grew up in a print culture shaped by the lingering ideals of republicanism only to find himself contributing to a very different one, in which sensationalism and biographical storytelling increasingly trumped reason and argument. Strictly speaking, Aikin's eloquent slave devotes only two sentences to autobiographical narrative, sentences that are subordinated to a larger philosophical discussion about "power" versus "right."[78]

It is this kind of reasoned adversarial dialogue that Douglass in *My Bondage and My Freedom* claims Garrisonians reserved for themselves while restricting the former slave to a "circumstantial statement of the facts." But as the archival work of Newman, Rael, and Lapsansky shows us, Aikin's eighteenth-century fictive slave had his counterpart in the first generation of black pamphleteers whose turn to print culture as a court of public opinion would influence Garrisonian tactics. From the 1790s onward, these scholars note, autobiography provided the ballast for black political writing; for African American pamphleteers "the first-person perspective was an important method of clarifying, critiquing, and illuminating the issues at hand: racist laws, white stereotypes, black nationhood. Autobiographical frames of reference broadened outward into a world of analysis, formal social debate, and intellectual activity."[79] In contrast to the antebellum slave narrative, however, "the trick was to go beyond the personal to the transcendent."[80] Thus, it is only in the fourth and last article of David Walker's *Appeal* that the author assures his reader, "I do not speak from hear say—what I have written, is what I have seen and heard myself"; by contrast, Walker devotes Article I to demonstrating the need for black forensics: "Unless we try to refute Mr. Jefferson's arguments respecting us, we will only establish them."[81]

We can see these antecedents resurfacing in Douglass's revised self-fashioning in *My Bondage and My Freedom*. As James McCune Smith's introduction suggests, Douglass's second personal narrative represents his determined attempt, through a consolidation of the roles of antislavery witness and black advocate, to reconcile the proven extralegal tactics of Garrisonian abolitionism with the still-influential republican association of reason with citizenship, especially where blacks were concerned.[82] Thus, even as McCune Smith's prefatory comments seem to affirm the volume's generic status as slave narrative by replicating traditional authenticating documents, his introduction radically revises that model, effectively following Aikin's "Dialogue" and black pamphleteers in subsuming the former slave's narrated "personal experience" to his impassioned but well-reasoned advocacy on behalf of his fellow African Americans.[83]

Signaling Douglass's independence from Garrisonian abolitionism in his opening paragraphs, the free African American doctor, activist, and author begins his introduction by reminding his readers that the "real object" of "the American anti-slavery movement" was "not only to disenthrall" but "also, to bestow upon the negro the exercise of all those rights, from the possession of which he has been so long debarred."[84] Presenting Douglass not merely "as a representative" to "the downtrodden" of "what they may themselves become," McCune Smith maintained that he was "a Representative American man—a type of his countrymen" and that *My Bondage and My Freedom* was, therefore, "an American book, for Americans, in the fullest sense of the idea."[85]

Because Douglass's eligibility as representative American was jeopardized by racism in the form of perennial murmurs that the famous orator's "descriptive and declamatory powers, admitted to be of the very highest order, take precedence of his logical force," McCune Smith carefully refuted such Jeffersonian slurs by insistently coupling the author's "uncommon memory" with his "keen and accurate insight into men and things," his "passion" with his "intellect," and (again) his "unfailing memory" with his "keen and telling wit."[86] In McCune Smith's account, Douglass's "plantation education," far from suppressing these "original gifts," actually "prepare[d] him for the high calling on which he has since entered—the advocacy of emancipation by the people who are not slaves" by providing the necessary "facts and experiences, welded to acutely wrought up sympathies" that could not be acquired elsewhere.[87] (The awkwardness of his reference to "the advocacy of emancipation by the people who are not slaves" betrays the strain of articulating a black advocacy premised not on previous condition of servitude but on current assertions of civic agency.)

The Garrisonians' mistake, McCune Smith made clear, was to limit Douglass to such "facts and experiences" rather than encouraging that free play of "memory, logic, wit, sarcasm, invective, pathos, and bold imagery of rare structural beauty" that gave Douglass's post-*Narrative* oratory and writing its tremendous power.[88] Of "Wendell Phillips, Edmund Quincy, William Lloyd Garrison," and other white "men of earnest faith and refined culture," McCune Smith wrote, "these gentlemen, although proud of Frederick Douglass, failed to fathom, and bring out to the light of day, the highest qualities of his mind; the force of their own education stood in their own way: they did not delve into the mind of a colored man for capacities which the pride of race led them to believe to be restricted to their own Saxon blood."[89] In short, the movement's racism produced a crowd-pleasing but narrow representation of African American identity: "Bitter and vindictive sarcasm, irresistible mimicry, and a pathetic narrative of his own experiences of slavery, were the intellectual manifestations which they encouraged him to exhibit on the platform or in the lecture desk."[90]

More than simply exposing and condemning the prejudices of white abolitionists, however, McCune Smith's account turns such racial thought on its head. "Whilst the schools might have trained" Douglass "to the exhibition of the formulas of deductive logic," as they did his Yankee colleagues, "nature and circumstances," McCune Smith cannily asserts, "forced him into the exercise of the higher faculties required by induction":

> The first ninety pages of this "Life in Bondage," afford specimens of observing, comparing, and careful classifying, of such superior character, that it is difficult to believe them the results of a child's thinking; he questions the earth, and the children and the slaves around him again and again, and finally looks to "*God in the sky*" for the why and the wherefore of the unnatural thing, slavery. . . .
>
> To such a mind, the ordinary processes of logical deduction are like proving that two and two make four. Mastering the intermediate steps by an intuitive glance . . . it goes down to the deeper relation of things, and brings out what may seem, to some, mere statements, but which are new and brilliant generalizations, each resting on a broad and stable basis. Thus, Chief Justice Marshall gave his decisions, and then told Brother Story to look up the authorities—and they never differed from him.[91]

McCune Smith's identification of Douglass with American Colonization Society officer and slaveholder John Marshall is a comparison as apt as it is unexpected. After all, Jefferson's nemesis, Federalist lawyer and Supreme Court

Chief Justice Marshall, not only stood as the personification of American constitutional law but was also known for his comparative lack of formal legal training, his corresponding disinclination to "blackletter scholarship," and his uncommon mixture of "those qualities essential to legal greatness: a capacious, retentive, and quick mind; sharp analytical skills; and a logical prose style that bordered on eloquence"—the exact qualities that McCune Smith has been careful to attribute to Douglass.[92] Like Marshall, characterized by the "exercise of the higher faculties required by induction," Douglass is, along with McCune Smith's masculinist roll call of black abolitionists (Samuel Ringgold Ward, Henry Highland Garnet, William Wells Brown, James W. C. Pennington, and Jermaine Wesley Loguen), uniquely qualified for the "high calling" of advocating for the "full recognition of the colored man to the right, and the entire admission of the same to the full privileges, political, religious and social, of manhood."[93]

The comparison of Douglass to Marshall further implies that such African Americans' firsthand experience of slavery or racism, far from constraining them to the subordinate position of antislavery witness, fits them to lead the movement. The image of Marshall telling "Brother Story to look up the authorities" thus offers an alternative model of abolitionist collaboration. In place of the unequal relationship between the testifying slave witness and the white advocate who represents him, McCune Smith provides the example of Marshall and Story as legal colleagues; characterized by mutual respect, this fraternal model nevertheless grants authority and leadership to the "Brother" with the greater experience and skill.

McCune Smith's inversion of Jeffersonian claims to blacks' intellectual inferiority through his emphasis on Douglass's superior capacity for induction retraces a similar movement in the Columbian Orator's "Dialogue between a Master and a Slave."[94] Opening with the master's accusatory address to his runaway slave—"NOW, villain!"—the "Discourse" begins with the premise of black criminality that, in the master's deductive logic, is proven by the slave's illegal theft of himself.[95] But the slave wins both the argument and his freedom by demonstrating inductively from his own experience that it is the perpetrators of slavery, not slaves, who are the guilty criminals. Briefly recounting his own "treacherous kidnapp[ing]" in Africa as a preface to his philosophical query, "What step in all this progress of violence and injustice can give a right?" the slave clinches his argument with his pointed appropriation of the slaveholder's inaugural epithet: "Was it in the villain who stole me, in the slave-merchant who tempted him to do so, or in you who encouraged the slave merchant to bring his cargo of human cattle to cultivate your lands?"[96] Lest the connection between the villainy of the African slave trade and the crime of slaveholding remain unclear, the slave's next contribution to the dialogue dispatches the master's earlier appeal to providential design by responding, "You cannot but be sensible, that the robber who puts a pistol to your breast may make just the same plea. Providence gives him a power over your life and property; it gave my enemies a power over my liberty."[97]

Bingham's lesson was lost on neither the young Frederick Bailey nor the adult Frederick Douglass. Immediately following his discussion of the *Columbian Orator*, Douglass recalls in the *Narrative* that "the more I read, the more I was led to abhor and detest my enslavers," culminating in the realization that slaveholders are merely "a band of successful robbers, who had left their homes, and gone to Africa, and stolen us from our homes."[98] Through a combination of reading and the "reflection" Jefferson found wanting in blacks, the rhetoric of the abolitionist advocate becomes second nature to the slave child.

Douglass drives this point home in the expanded treatment of the *Columbian Orator* in *My Bondage and My Freedom*, where the author explicitly identifies himself with Bingham's exemplary slave: "It is scarcely necessary to say, that a dialogue, with such an origin, and such an ending . . . powerfully affected me; and I could not help feeling that the day might come, when the well-directed answers made by the slave to the master, in this instance, would find their counterpart in myself."[99] For Douglass, what was "finely illustrated in the dialogue" was "the mighty power and heart-searching directness of truth, penetrating even the heart of a slaveholder, compelling him to yield up his earthly interests to the claims of eternal justice."[100] Complicating the abolitionist adage that "argument provokes argument, reason is met by sophistry; but the narratives of slaves go right to the hearts of men," Douglass here insists upon the "mighty power" of a black-authored antislavery argument that irresistibly employs forceful inductive reasoning grounded in personal experience.[101]

As *My Bondage and My Freedom* illustrates, by 1855 Frederick Douglass had become convinced of the need for black abolitionists to leave the confines of the witness stand in order to advocate for both immediate emancipation and the full citizenship of all African Americans.[102] Far from rejecting the adversarial trial model that had provided the print debate over slavery with both its structure and its rhetorical power, Douglass's determined efforts to combine personal narrative and advocacy indicated his growing awareness of the extent to which, in the words of legal scholar Paul Gewirtz, "storytelling in law is narrative within a culture of argument," that "the trial process" is "a struggle over narratives."[103] For however much law may appear to assign discrete functions to the different personages in the criminal trial—that is, the witness's task is storytelling; the lawyer's, argumentation; the judge's, adjudication of law; and the jury's, adjudication of facts—the tendency of the adversarial process is inevitably to fragment, multiply, and disperse these activities.[104] Putting this insight into discursive practice, Douglass demonstrated how thoroughly he had learned to talk lawyerlike about law.

Evidentiary Imperatives

Before returning to the *Cambria* riot and its aftermath as a final example of Douglass's fusion of the role of antislavery witness into that of black advocate, it bears noting that, despite Douglass's efforts to distance himself from the antislavery movement's testimonial rhetoric, scholarship on the slave narrative continues to carry strains of that rhetoric. For example, the *Oxford Companion to African American Literature* asserts that the genre has "provided some of the most graphic and damning documentary evidence of the horrors of slavery," noting that the "most widely read slave narratives . . . became virtual testaments in the hands of abolitionists," at the same time giving "incontestable evidence of the humanity of the African American."[105] Likewise, in his introduction to *The Classic Slave Narratives*, Henry Louis Gates Jr. observes that formerly enslaved authors "created a *genre* of literature that at once testified against their captors and bore witness to the urge of every black to be free and literate."[106] Explaining that the "black slave narrators sought to indict both those who enslaved them and the metaphysical system drawn upon to justify their enslavement," Gates maintains that "no group of slaves anywhere . . . has left such a large repository of testimony about the horror of becoming the legal property of another human being."[107]

The tone of the examples suggests how the institutional and political climate in which African American studies programs and scholarship have developed since their disciplinary establishment in the 1960s and 1970s has produced a new set of evidentiary imperatives that have obscured the implications of abolitionists' juridical rhetoric from scholars who themselves relied upon the "testimony" of former slaves as "evidence" of the validity of their field.[108] The contemporaneous deconstructive turn notwithstanding, such "disciplines in formation" tended to be "evidence-heavy," due to the fact that critics in these emergent fields were required to prove the legitimacy of their objects of study.[109] This evidentiary pressure was even greater in fields that, like African American studies and women's studies, focus on the cultural production of historically marginalized groups, the same "people who have traditionally been seen as unreliable witnesses."[110] Since the field's inception, scholars in African American studies have had to prove the legitimacy of black-authored texts and the importance of African American history and culture as well as to establish the value and relevance of their own research and their own authority as scholars. (That, more often than not, these early scholars were themselves African Americans in a newly integrated academy only intensified these pressures.) The debate over the authenticity of *Incidents in the Life of a Slave Girl* and the identity of its author serves as a reminder of the particularly embattled status of the slave narrative genre, which, until its rediscovery by African Americanists, was widely considered to be an unreliable historical source and a dubious literary one.[111] This academic environment, in which African Americanists were constantly required to make a case for the cultural worth of their intellectual enterprise, may help to explain why so many felt compelled to adopt rather than critique the rhetorical strategies originally designed to give black authors and activists a hearing in antebellum print culture.[112]

Even among those scholars best positioned to think critically about intersections of race, law, and narrative, there has been a tendency to recapitulate rather than to interrogate antebellum calls for black testimony. In the debate over "perspectivism" that flared up in the legal academy during the 1990s, the promotion of storytelling by Critical Race Theory (CRT) scholars resuscitated the emphasis on African American testimonial writing through specific reference to nineteenth-century slave narratives. As noted in the previous chapter, Richard Delgado's influential article offers storytelling, or, more precisely, "counterstorytelling," as the "cure" for the oppressive narratives generated by dominant cultural ideology and thus as an indispensable weapon in "the struggle for racial reform."[113] Although the counternarratives envisioned by Delgado are not necessarily autobiographical in nature, many of the most frequently cited examples are. Along with African American folktales and slave songs, Delgado himself cites slave narratives by Henry Bibb, William Wells Brown, and Solomon Northup as an example of how "ironic or satiric" counternarratives "can shatter complacency and challenge the status quo."[114] Similarly, for storytelling-advocate Jerome McCristal Culp Jr., the "work that begins this forward-looking approach to autobiography by black intellectuals is the autobiography of Frederick Douglass."[115]

But when Delgado maintains that "counterstories" should "invite the reader to suspend judgment, listen to their point or message, and then decide what measure of truth they contain," he comes uncomfortably close to returning the relationship between the African American narrator and the "majority-race reader" to an all-too-familiar footing.[116] By endowing the majority-race reader with Young's exegetical authority or Foucault's hermeneutic function,

CRT's insistence on storytelling recalls the abolitionist practice of rhetorically framing (black) testimony with (white) forensic argumentation, rendering the authenticity and veracity of that testimony subject to the (no longer suspended) judgment of the dominant-culture reader.[117]

Fraught as it may be, the "turn to narrative" by Delgado, Culp, and other CRT scholars has been driven by the urgent need for a viable solution to the persistent rhetorical dehumanization and abstraction of black people, both within and beyond the American justice system.[118] The call for African American legal storytelling arises from the valid insight that "by ignoring the experiences of black people, we are limiting our vision of law to one that reflects a white male perspective" and that "by leaving out the personal . . . we simply replace our personal stories with mythic assumptions about race."[119] But if, in fact, "it does not seem possible to find a neutral place to observe how race interacts with legal decisionmaking," this is not to say that narrative must *replace* argumentation, that testimony must *supplant* advocacy.[120]

Consider that set piece of oppositional legal storytelling and its transformative potential for "empathetic understanding": Thurgood Marshall's decision in *Brown v. Board of Education I* (1954) to move from "conventional modes of legal argumentation" to a firsthand "narrative of the experience, the harm, the evil, and the irrationality of racism"—when, in other words, he "departed from the usual forms of oral argument to 'testify' as a black and to include his own observations of segregation in the South."[121] Crucially, however, Marshall did not abandon the role of lawyer for that of witness; his antisegregationist testimony did not supersede his advocacy on behalf of African Americans' claims to civil rights. Instead, Marshall grounded that advocacy in a testimonial account of a personal experience shaped, if not defined, by race in America.[122] When, a century earlier, Douglass stepped into the role of advocate with *My Bondage and My Freedom*, his understanding of that role was closer to that of Thurgood Marshall or of lawyer-turned-autobiographer John Mercer Langston than it was to that of Wendell Phillips or Phillips's Southern colleague, the *Narrative*'s Esquire Watson. For, even while striking the posture of advocate, Douglass continued to draw on his firsthand knowledge of slavery in the task of pleading the cause of his brethren.

If we return now to the *Cambria* riot, we can see how Douglass's efforts to cultivate a distinctly black advocacy—based in, but no longer authorized by, his well-known testimonial narrative—were inspired by his appreciation for the ways in which, as Culp puts it, "stories can alter public debate by attacking and questioning the underlying stories that we tell about public policy and the law" and that such stories may even influence "public policy by adding aspects to the stories currently being told, or by introducing questions that are not being discussed."[123]

Abolition Riot on the Atlantic

In October 1845, two months after the *Cambria* had docked in Liverpool, Douglass provided his Irish audience with his version of the events leading up to the notorious shipboard fisticuffs — the exhaustive press coverage of which Douglass would later describe as "a sort of national announcement of my arrival in England."[124] That speech, "American Prejudice against Color" — an address that, fittingly, situated Southern slavery in the larger context of American racism — recounted Douglass's public transition from fugitive witness to black advocate:

> The Captain . . . invited me to address the passengers on slavery. I consented — commenced — but soon observed a determination on the part of some half a dozen to prevent my speaking, who I found were slave owners. I had not uttered more than a sentence before up started a man from Connecticut, and said, "that's a lie." I proceeded without taking notice of him, then shaking his fist he said, again — that's a lie. Some said I should not speak, others that I should — I wanted to inform the English, Scotch and Irish on board on Slavery. . . . Well, said I, ladies and gentleman, since what I have said has been pronounced lies, I will read not what I have written but what the southern legislators themselves have written — I mean the law. I proceeded to read — this raised a general clamour, for they did not wish the laws exposed. They hated facts, they knew that the people of these countries who were on the deck would draw their own references from them.[125]

We cannot be certain of the exact content of Douglass's original *Cambria* speech, but we can safely assume from Douglass's allusion to reading "what [he] had written" that he was offering the assembled passengers excerpts from his *Narrative* when he was first interrupted by hecklers challenging his veracity — a common occurrence on the abolitionist lecture circuit.[126] Indeed, it was to silence such challenges that Douglass had published his *Narrative*, which established his testimonial authority by offering "such a revelation of facts as could not be made by any other than a genuine fugitive."[127] This time, however — afloat on "the restless billows" of the Atlantic — Douglass did *not* revert to his autobiographical *Narrative* but instead switched to another set of "facts," those of the American slave code, most likely taken from Stroud's

Sketch of the Laws Relating to Slavery.[128] But Douglass did not simply replace one neutral set of facts with another; by substituting Southern laws for his own testimonial narrative, Douglass subtly but effectively reshuffled the power relations that had structured his lectures up to this point. In this account, the audience still exercises its hermeneutic function or its exegetical authority—as Douglass points out, the rioters "knew that the people . . . who were on deck would draw their own references from" the laws he read—but rather than being directed toward the former slave's testimony, this critical judgment now centers on the culpable Southern legislators and their incriminating slave laws. And, more importantly, Douglass himself has crossed the bar separating narration from interpretation and thus changed his status *within* the bar of public opinion. Temporarily abandoning his autobiographical testimony and, with it, the confines of the witness stand, Douglass strikes a prosecutorial posture by presenting Southern laws themselves as evidence in order to indict slavery's perpetrators before the popular tribunal.

The *Cambria* speech appears to have been the first time Douglass read slave laws to an audience, a tactic that would become a staple of his subsequent public speaking in both Britain and the United States. Revealingly, in the Irish speech from which this account is drawn, Douglass's version of the *Cambria* incident is directly preceded by his discussion of the laws prohibiting slave literacy, an implicit but pointed response to Jefferson's *Notes on the State of Virginia*. Right after asserting "I plead here for man," Douglass makes the disarming concession "that the Negroes in America are inferior to the Whites"; exposing the racist logic of Jefferson's Query XIV on "Laws," Douglass attributes this so-called inferiority to African Americans' condition and particularly to their legally mandated ignorance.[129] "The people of America deprive us of every privilege," then "they turn round and taunt us with our inferiority!" he thundered.[130] "That is the position of America in the present time, the laws forbid education, the mother must not teach her child the letters of the Lord's prayer; and while this unfortunate state of things exist[s] they turn round and ask, why we are not moral and intelligent; and tell us, because we are not, that they have the right to enslave" African Americans.[131] At this point, Douglass must have opened his well-worn copy of Stroud's *Sketch of the Laws* as he entreated his audience, "Now let me read a few the laws of that democratic country":

> In South Carolina in 1770, this law was passed. "Whereas the teaching
> of slaves to write is sometimes connected with an inconvenience, be it
> enacted that every person who shall teach a slave to write, for every such

offence shall forfeit the penalty of £100." Mark, we are an inferior race, morally and intellectually. Hence 'tis right to enslave us. The same hypocrites make laws to prevent our improvement. In Georgia in 1770 similar laws were passed; and in Virginia. South Carolina, in 1800, passed the following—that the assemblage of slaves and Mulattos for the purpose of instruction may be dissolved. In Louisiana the penalty of . . . teaching a black in a Sunday school is, for the first offence 500 dollars fine, for the second death. This is in America, a Christian country, a democratic, a republican country, the land of the free, the home of the brave—the nation that . . . pledged itself to the declaration that all men are born free and equal, making it at the same time a penalty punishable by death for the second offense to teach a slave his letters.[132]

As Jefferson did in Query XIV, Douglass here links race to law and republican education. But rather than justifying the civic exclusion of African Americans through imputations of their intellectual inferiority, Douglass demonstrates how the laws of "a democratic, a republican country" *create* civic inequality by prohibiting black education.

Having exposed the illogic of that peculiarly American—indeed, Jeffersonian—paradox of racial thought and egalitarian philosophy, Douglass immediately moves in the speech's next sentence to what only seems to be a new topic, his account of the *Cambria* riot: "Now I will briefly tell you what past during my voyage to this country. In taking up one of your papers this morning I saw an extract from the *New York Herald* by Gordon Bennett, one of the greatest slave haters in the world. It relates that a remarkable occurrence took place in the *Cambria* on its passage to England: — 'A coloured slave named Douglas[s] is said to have spoken on anti-Slavery, and that a row took place in consequence.'"[133] In this speech, Douglass situates his public persona in the charged interplay of literacy and its legal proscription. Here, as on the *Cambria*, he selectively reads the laws of slavery in order to critique the hypocrisy of not only slaveholders but so-called American democracy as well. His selection, moreover, is not arbitrary: in a wonderfully ironic act of verbal resistance, the fugitive Douglass, "a coloured slave" (in the *Herald*'s phrasing), *reads* the laws that should preclude such an action, laws proscribing slave literacy. The irony intensifies as Douglass segues into his account of the shipboard incident, which is accomplished by reference to yet another act of reading, this time of the proslavery *New York Herald*'s dismissive account of the "row" on the *Cambria*—a gesture that not only gives Douglass the final word on the events in question but also reaffirms the discursive authority the *Herald* seeks to deny him. For, by reenacting his shipboard reading of slave law and then interrupting himself with the Herald's account of the incident, Douglass places the Herald in the same position as the "man from Connecticut"—the disempowered, dependent position of heckler, one whose speech is not in itself authorized but who boorishly seeks to usurp the authority and audience of another.

Furthermore, Douglass's account of the Cambria incident employs a series of narrative frames that work to break down the prevailing distinctions between advocacy and testimony. Douglass prefaces his account by reading the laws that establish the legal and historical contexts for his insurgent act of reading on board the Cambria; he then turns to his personal experience ("in taking up one of your papers this morning I saw . . .") to frame the Herald's interpretation of the events, an interpretation which he counters with his own firsthand testimony as evidence of (in the speech's title) "American Prejudice against Color." This testimony in turn recounts how he replaced firsthand personal testimony with exegesis of the laws of slavery. In the process, the racialized hierarchy of extralegal abolitionist discourse—in which white advocacy introduces and gives meaning to the raw materials of black testimony—yields to a model of autonomous African American political speech that encompasses but is not confined to the speaker's firsthand experience of racial oppression.

Douglass's growing commitment to talking lawyerlike about law represented not only a significant transformation in his post-Narrative self-fashioning, from witness to advocate, but also a determined effort to join his fellow black abolitionists in their efforts to expand and redefine African American participation in both the antislavery movement and the civic life of the nation.[134] Like his interpretation of the founding legal documents of the United States, his reading of Southern slave laws suggests that for Douglass, black advocacy meant not just breaking free of the discursive constraints associating blackness with plain narration and claiming the right to denounce as well as to narrate wrong—not just liberating himself from the racial hierarchy of the antebellum antislavery movement and asserting the necessary autonomy of black political speech. Far more powerfully, black advocacy meant rejecting the legal marginalization of African Americans and demanding full legal and political enfranchisement, beginning, but by no means ending, with emancipation and the right to due process.

5   REPRESENTING THE SLAVE

White Advocacy and Black Testimony in Harriet Beecher Stowe's Dred

Combing through the trial transcripts and newspaper clippings in *A Key to Uncle Tom's Cabin*, a dedicated reader of Harriet Beecher Stowe's first antislavery novel might have been pleased to come across a fictional vignette featuring two of the book's best-known characters, Simon Legree and Tom. Unlike the novel, however, in which the cruel master's brutality leads to the humble slave's death, this scene imagines the conflict between slaveholder and bondsman not in sentimental terms, as demonic violence and Christian martyrdom, but in juridical terms, as a legal dispute mediated by a benevolent white man.

Stowe offers the scene to demonstrate the futility of a South Carolina protective act that ostensibly guaranteed basic necessities to slaves by allowing concerned whites "to make complaint to the next neighboring justice in the parish" on their behalf.[1] "Now suppose," Stowe introduces the scene, that Simon Legree's slaves, "getting tired of being hungry and cold, form themselves into a committee of the whole, to see what is to be done."[2] The leader who quickly emerges in this scene of nascent organized resistance is a "broad-shouldered, courageous fellow" named Tom, who, "having by some means become acquainted with this benevolent protective act, resolves to make an appeal to the horns of this legislative altar . . . determined that, if there is such a thing as justice to be got, he will have it."[3] "After considerable research," Tom finds a "white man . . . verdant enough to enter the complaint for him," a Master Shallow.[4] In due time, Legree is brought before the justice of the peace to answer the charges against him. After some whiskey and conversation, the judge finally turns to "this nigger business," demanding, "How plagued did you ever hear of that act, Shallow? I'm sure I'm forgot all about it."[5] Cursing and rifling through his law books, Justice Dogberry reminds Shallow, "The act says you must make proof, you observe":

> Mr. Shallow. [Stuttering and hesitating] Good land! why, don't everybody see that them ar niggers are most starved! Only see how ragged they are!
>
> Justice. I can't say as I've observed it particular. Seem to be very well contented.
>
> Shallow. [Eagerly] But just ask Pomp, or Sambo, or Dinah, or Tom!
>
> Justice Dogberry. [With dignity.] I'm astonished at you, Mr. Shallow! You think of producing negro testimony? I hope I know the law better than that! We must have direct proof, you know.[6]

The scene ends with Legree acquitting himself by swearing his own innocence, in accord with a provision in the act that permits a negligent slaveholder to "exculpate or clear himself from the charge, by his or her own oath."[7] The vignette thus illustrates the Key's claim that "the very keystone of Southern jurisprudence is the rejection of colored testimony" as it depicts the predicament facing the slave's white advocate—two themes that would become central to Stowe's second antislavery novel, Dred: A Tale of the Great Dismal Swamp.[8]

A Key to Uncle Tom's Cabin, published a year after its namesake and three years before Dred, is often read as a kind of nonfiction "bridge between Stowe's two anti-slavery novels."[9] That Stowe should revise her depiction of the slave Tom and the master Legree in this transitional text and that she should do so by shifting from a sentimental to a juridical register reveals her increasing tendency, in the wake of Uncle Tom's Cabin, to conceptualize slavery in legal terms. That she should interpose a well-meaning but ineffectual white mediator between master and slave, as she would again in Dred, also indicates that at the height of her own fame as spokesperson for the slave, Stowe shared with Frederick Douglass a growing ambivalence about the trial trope that structured so much of the print debate over slavery.

But whereas Douglass protested the restriction of African Americans to the witness stand, Stowe concerns herself, fittingly, with the other main figure in the abolitionist case against slavery, the slave's white advocate. Like Shallow, Stowe and other sympathetic whites acknowledged the indispensability of slave testimony to the case they presented to the popular tribunal. Also like Shallow, however, they knew that their very presence and authority in the proceedings arose from the same anxieties about black speech that mandated the inadmissibility of slave testimony. If Shallow's position resembles that of abolitionist advocates for the slave, the "stuttering and hesitating" speech of "the infatuated white man who has undertaken this fool's errand" reveals another difficulty with white advocacy: its tendency to misrepresent the slave.[10] From an activist "committee of the whole" aware of their own exploitation and possible means of redress, Tom and his fellow slaves are reduced by Shallow's words to "niggers . . . most starved" and "ragged." As suggested in chapters 2 and 3, the rhetorical decriminalization of extralegal African American speech involved a corresponding rhetorical victimization of the black print subject through the figure of the testifying eyewitness. And, whereas Douglass's call for black advocacy can be read as an attempt to assert a form of African American discursive authority that is grounded in neither criminality nor victimization, here Stowe makes it clear that black victimization, even debility, is white advocacy's raison d'être. The problem with white advocacy, Stowe's vignette implies, is not simply its potential to reinforce restrictions on black political speech and the racial logic that underlies them but also that white speech cannot represent the enslaved without simultaneously misrepresenting them.[11] Much as Dred would three years later, the Key raises this conundrum without resolving it. The Key's final chapter demonstrates the ineluctability of the problem it poses by rehearsing once more the "Shallow" claims of the white advocate. After more than two hundred and fifty pages of "corroborative statements verifying the truth" of her first novel, much of which were derived from oral and written "testimony," Stowe asserts that because the slave is "poor, uneducated and ignorant, and cannot speak for himself," benevolent Northerners must not only "guard his rights" but also "speak for him."[12] The following year, Stowe would dramatize this tendency of white advocacy to misrepresent, even silence, the slave on whose behalf it claims to speak in Dred's Edward Clayton, slaveholding lawyer turned antislavery legal reformer—although, like the Key, Stowe's second antislavery novel would merely rehearse, not resolve, the dilemma of white advocacy.

Just as Uncle Tom's Cabin, with its emphasis on domesticity, moral suasion, and the political power of sympathy, has been the touchstone for critical reevaluations of the antebellum culture of sentiment, Dred, with its focus on the legal profession, court cases, and law reform, has been central to the more recent scholarly reorientation toward "the jurisprudential dimensions of Stowe's sentiment."[13] This chapter also addresses the novel's treatment of what Stowe called "the legal relations of slavery," but it differs from these studies in that it does not consider (except in passing) the novel's fictional treatment of law vis-à-vis actual court cases or Stowe's mingling of legal and sentimental discourses.[14] Instead, situating Dred in the context of the discursive politics of the antislavery movement, this chapter demonstrates that the novel can be productively read as an allegory of the fraught relations between the slavery debate's black witnesses and their white advocates. Such a reading requires an awareness of the implications of legal rhetoric in antebellum representations of slavery. In order to see more clearly how the series of legal crises in Dred's second volume manifests the tensions of interracial abolitionist collaboration, we need briefly to review Stowe's career, focusing on the simultaneous emergence of her own fame as advocate for the slave and her sharpened interest in slavery's legal aspect. Stowe's misgivings about her new role, I suggest, are evident not just in Dred's legally oriented plot and characters but in the novel's first appendix, which reproduces much of Virginia slaveholder and lawyer Thomas R. Gray's ventriloquized Confessions of Nat Turner (1831).[15] Written at the height of her celebrity as antislavery author, Dred evinces Stowe's increasing ambivalence about both black testimony and white advocacy, suggesting her growing sense that any attempt by whites to represent the slave, whether in the courtroom or on the literary page, would only further entrench white paternalism and black oppression by silencing, not liberating, enslaved African Americans.

Stowe's Jurisprudence of Love and Sentiment

The sentimental and the legal were intertwined from the beginning of Harriet Beecher Stowe's career as a literary abolitionist. Stowe maintained that she was inspired to write Uncle Tom's Cabin by both the death of her infant son Charley and the passage of the Fugitive Slave Act of 1850.[16] Accordingly, her first novel depicts slavery as occurring "beneath the shadow of American law, and the shadow of the cross of Christ."[17] As George Sand observed, Uncle Tom's Cabin "shows us human law on one side, and God on the other."[18] Indeed, legal scholar Alfred L. Brophy credits Stowe's first novel with developing and popularizing an evangelical "jurisprudence of love and sentiment" that invoked higher law to reject both the property claims of slaveholders and the conservative legal thinking that placed law and order above moral considerations of humanity.[19] Further, Brophy reminds us that "Stowe's contemporaries realized that she attacked law as well as slavery" and that, in particular, "Southern readers were acutely aware of her condemnation of slave law," publishing reviews, book-length rebuttals, and fiction that stressed the importance of law and order over sentiment.[20]

Responding to such criticism, Stowe indicated the extent to which contemporary legal discourse about slavery had informed the composition of Uncle Tom's Cabin. She claimed to have had "on hand for reference, while writing, the Code Noir of Louisiana, and a sketch of the laws relating to slavery in the different states, by Judge Stroud," adding archly that "this work, professing to have been compiled with the greatest care from the latest editions of the statute books of the several states, the author supposed to be a sufficient guide for the writing of a work of fiction."[21] She purportedly claimed to have kept *American Slavery as It Is: Testimony of a Thousand Witnesses*, which features numerous slave cases and statutes, "in her work basket by day, and slept with it under her pillow by night, till its facts crystallized into Uncle Tom."[22]

Despite its legal influences and its critique of slave law, *Uncle Tom's Cabin* nevertheless portrays slavery primarily in sentimental terms, as a national sin that could be rectified through sympathy and prayer. It was when she was writing the *Key*, drawing on technical assistance from "legal gentlemen" to refute charges of inaccuracy in *Uncle Tom's Cabin*, that Stowe came to see slavery as a peculiarly legal institution.[23] Originally planned as an appendix to her celebrated novel, the *Key* quickly swelled to over 250 pages, largely due to Stowe's detailed citation and analysis of statutes and court cases involving slavery. Much of this legal material, including an almost verbatim citation of Judge Ruffin's decision in the 1829 North Carolina case, *State v. Mann*, reappears in Stowe's second antislavery novel; indeed, as Judie S. Newman notes, Stowe's transitional nonfiction factbook "might more properly be described as the key to *Dred*."[24]

Dred does not represent a radical departure from Stowe's earlier sentimentalism. In addition to its overwrought prose, richly described domestic settings, and highly stereotyped slave characters, the novel also features an ill-fated romance between an idealistic planter who sacrifices his career for his principles and a flighty young belle who succumbs to cholera upon her religious conversion.[25] *Dred*, however, borrows as liberally from slave codes and trial transcripts as it does from the Bible and the sentimental tradition, demonstrating Stowe's conviction that "slavery in itself, as legally defined in lawbooks and expressed in the records of courts, is the SUM AND ESSENCE OF ALL ABUSE."[26]

Stowe began *Dred* in early 1856, just as the national controversy over the legal status of slavery was reaching its height. As her brother Henry Ward Beecher was encouraging his Brooklyn congregation to send rifles ("Beecher's Bibles") to the antislavery faction in Kansas, her friend Charles Sumner was brutally beaten on the floor of the Senate by his colleague Preston S. Brooks in response to Sumner's speech "The Crime against Kansas."[27] Stowe herself had opposed the Kansas-Nebraska Bill through both her writing and political activism. In February 1854, she published in the *New York Independent* an "Appeal to the Women of the Free States" and soon afterward organized a drive to present the U.S. Senate with a two-hundred-foot-long petition signed by over three thousand members of the New England clergy.[28] The passage of the controversial Kansas-Nebraska Act of 1854 coincided with another legal crisis involving slavery, the highly publicized trial of fugitive slave Anthony Burns. Although Stowe did not comment publicly on these events, she was in Boston during the Burns crisis, when the city was placed under a state of emergency and buildings were draped with black crepe to protest Judge Edward G. Loring's ruling. If the passage of the Fugitive Slave Act of 1850 had inspired Stowe to write *Uncle Tom's Cabin*, the controversial law's aftermath certainly informed her second antislavery novel. As critic Lisa Whitney has observed, "Legal matters are so central to *Dred* that it seems to have been written primarily to give them a context."[29]

Dred's title, of course, recalls the era's best-known court case involving slavery, *Dred Scott v. Sandford*, which was decided in 1857, a year *after* the novel's publication. Although the exact relationship of the novel's title to the famous slave litigant remains cloudy, Gregg D. Crane suggests that Stowe was at least aware of the case, pointing out that Stowe drafted much of the novel over the summer of 1856 and that "*Dred Scott* began to receive considerable attention from the press after it arrived at the Supreme Court in February of the same year."[30]

Whatever the origin of his name, *Dred*'s title character is clearly a composite of the defendants in the two most famous cases involving slave conspiracies, Nat Turner and Denmark Vesey.[31] *Dred*'s thoroughgoing concern with the legal aspect of slavery is further evidenced by the fact that many of the novel's white male characters are members of the legal profession, and much of the plot is driven by legal proceedings resembling those documented in the *Key* and in legal treatises like George M. Stroud's.[32] Moreover, for readers of *Dred* unfamiliar with such reference sources, Stowe reproduces in the novel's appendix many of the same legal materials she had incorporated into the *Key*: summaries of slave cases *Souther v. Commonwealth* and *State v. Castleman* and slave outlawry statutes from North Carolina and Virginia. In this sense, *Dred* marks the culmination of Stowe's literary abolitionist jurisprudence: whereas *Uncle Tom's Cabin* presented its critique of American law and calls for legal reform indirectly through vivid sentimental scenes, and the *Key* exhaustively documented the harsh legal and historical facts behind the fiction, *Dred* powerfully illustrates the mutually constitutive nature of law and everyday life under slavery.

White Advocacy

In the years following *Uncle Tom's Cabin*, Stowe became, along with William Lloyd Garrison, the era's best-known white advocate for the slave, making her central to debates over the politics of representative identity within the antislavery movement.[33] In everything from gift-book fiction to newspaper articles and political tracts, black activists such as Frederick Douglass, Martin Delany, William C. Nell, Henry Bibb, and Mary Ann Shadd Cary consistently questioned the role of benevolent whites in representing African Americans.[34] It is in the context of these exchanges, critics have argued, that we must read the literary productions of Douglass and Stowe in the 1850s, particularly Douglass's short story "The Heroic Slave" (1853).[35] Central to Douglass's fictional account of the *Creole* slave-ship uprising is the Northerner Mr. Listwell, who becomes converted to abolitionism after overhearing the fugitive Madison Washington's anguished antislavery soliloquy. As Shelley Fisher Fishkin and Carla L. Peterson note, the "primary function" of this white reformer is, in keeping with the name Douglass bestows on him, "to *listen well* . . . clearly the role that Douglass, the journalist and public speaker, wants white abolitionists to play: to listen well to what the black slave has to say."[36] In his only work of fiction, published the year after *Uncle Tom's Cabin* appeared in book form, Douglass thus creates "a narrative situation that he must have desired": in short, "an interdependent relationship between the black slave as speaking and experiencing subject, on the one hand, and the white abolitionist, who both listens well and takes an active role in his cause, on the other, guided by an authoritative black leader whose role it is to write the black back on the page of human existence."[37] Reading *Dred* as "the result of Stowe's creative exchanges with Douglass," we find that although she may no longer resemble "Garrison and other New Englanders Douglass grew to distrust, the very sort of 'blind' abolitionist he sought to enlighten in 'The Heroic Slave,'" Stowe could not — or would not — allow her insights about the politics of representative identity to yield an alternative vision of interracial collaboration in *Dred*'s conclusion.[38] Instead, the narrative, along with its first appendix, a lengthy excerpt from the *Confessions of Nat Turner*, alerts Stowe's readers to the dangers of white advocacy.

Like Douglass's *Narrative* and Stowe's *Key*, Gray's *Confessions of Nat Turner* presents itself as the product of interracial collaboration.[39] The *Confessions's* structure and format anticipate abolitionist-sponsored slave narratives of the 1840s and 1850s. Framed by authenticating documents, the narrative presents Nat Turner's life in slavery as told to his white amanuensis, who claims to

"commit his statements to writing, and publish them, with little or no variation, from his own words."[40] Published before the rhetorical decriminalization of extralegal black speech, however, the text presents Turner, not his
master, as the guilty perpetrator, and his narrative, rather than providing "testimony . . . [to] what slavery really is" as did those of later slave witnesses,
instead offers the confessions of "the great Bandit" (as Gray, perhaps ironically, calls him).[41]

At first glance, the appendix titled "Nat Turner's Confessions" serves primarily to underscore the similarities between Stowe's fictional prophet-rebel,
Dred, and the notorious insurrectionist.[42] The *Confessions* characterize Nat
Turner as a "gloomy fanatic . . . revolving in the recesses of his own dark,
bewildered, and overwrought mind, schemes of indiscriminate massacre to
the whites."[43] Placed in the appendix, this description simultaneously anticipates and echoes *Dred*'s portrayal of its title character as one who, "cut off
from all human companionship, often going weeks without seeing a human
face," with "no recurrence of every-day and prosaic ideas to check the current
of enthusiasm," creates a "wild and hopeless . . . scheme" of insurrection.[44]
It is possible, however, to read Stowe's extended extracts from the *Confessions*
less as authentication of the novel's portrayal of Dred than as a continuation
of her novel's exploration of the politics of interracial collaboration between
the slave and his or her white advocate. Gray, it bears recalling, was not just
a down-at-the-heels Virginia slaveholder who hoped to reap profits from his
hastily compiled sensationalist pamphlet. He was also the court-appointed
defense attorney for Turner's alleged co-conspirators.[45] Like his Northern
counterpart John Jolliffe, an abolitionist lawyer-turned-author, Gray moved
fluidly between representing slaves in court and on the printed page. And like
Stowe's slaveholding lawyer Edward Clayton, Gray seems incapable of attending to the resistant message of slave speech, transforming his representation
of that speech into a justification for slavery. In Stowe's excerpt of the *Confessions*, Gray asserts that Nat Turner's "own account of the conspiracy is submitted to the public, without comment. It reads an awful, and it is hoped, useful
lesson, as to the operations of a mind like his, endeavoring to grapple with
things beyond its reach."[46] Simultaneously claiming to present the *Confessions*
"without comment" *and* as "an awful, and . . . useful lesson," Gray demonstrates the apparent impossibility of unmediated, neutral transcription, especially when the transcriber is white, the narrator black, and the subject slavery.
Stowe's reprinting of the *Confessions*—at the conclusion of a novel whose plot
often turns on a white slaveholding lawyer's relationships with local slave
insurgents—urges us to consider the structural similarities in the relation-

ship between, on the one hand, Nat Turner and Thomas R. Gray and, on the other, Stowe's revolutionary slave Dred and Southern lawyer Edward Clayton (or, for that matter, between Frederick Douglass and Wendell Phillips). The appendix, featuring a self-interested slaveholding Southern attorney in place of a benevolent Northern abolitionist advocate, begs the question: could the very structure of the relationship between black witness and white advocate trump the specific political intentions motivating such extralegal interracial collaborations?

Inspired by actual abolitionist attorneys like Phillips and Salmon P. Chase, Northern advocates for the slave saw themselves playing a distinctly emancipatory role.[47] But in the South, where Nat Turner and his co-conspirators were tried and where Dred's legal proceedings occur, the slave's advocate occupied a very different ideological position. There, the legal profession was widely seen as a "springboard" to the coveted position of planter, and lawyers were known to accept slaves "in lieu of legal fees."[48] Moreover, with the rise of the legal profession in the late eighteenth century, several Southern states had introduced statutes making the slaveholder responsible for providing counsel for slaves in criminal cases.[49] As legal historian Thomas D. Morris explains, "The imposition of liability rested on the idea that the master owed a duty to the slave in exchange for his or her labor and the power he exercised over the slave."[50] A Georgia court clarified the logic of this assumption by inserting it into a larger ethos of slaveholding paternalism: "This duty of procuring counsel for his slave . . . is in return for the profits of the bondsman's labor and toil, [and] is as binding on the master, as the obligation to procure for that slave, medical attendance in his sickness, or food and clothing at all times."[51] In contrast to the imaginary trial conjured by abolitionist print propaganda, Southern statutes treated legal representation of the slave as an extension of mastery, one that reinforced the slave's legal and cultural status as property capable only of criminal agency.[52]

By having slaveholding lawyer Edward Clayton occupy a dual role as Dred's antislavery legal reformer, Stowe implicitly draws attention to the paternalist logic that unites the slave's white advocates on both sides of the Mason-Dixon line, in and outside of the courtroom. In this sense, the placement of "Nat Turner's Confessions" directly after the narrative's oddly quietist conclusion underscores not just Dred's affinity to the historical Nat Turner but also that of the benevolent Edward Clayton to the far less attractive Thomas R. Gray—and perhaps, by extension, that of the author herself to such equivocal white advocates for the slave. Like the narrative proper, Stowe's first appendix to Dred nudges the reader to question the reliability and authenticity of white-authored representations of African American resistance, insurgent black testimony in particular.

Their Accuser at the Bar of the World

Although several critics have noted similarities between Edward Clayton and his creator with respect to legal concerns, others may find the parallel forced, given the legal status of women and antebellum separate-spheres ideology.[53] How could Harriet Beecher Stowe, that paragon of literary domesticity, claim the requisite civic agency—however rhetorical—to imagine herself an advocate for the slave on par with Edward Clayton, Wendell Phillips, or Gerrit Smith?

That other abolitionists, male and female, could imagine women in precisely such a role is indicated by an early letter from Theodore Dwight Weld to exiled South Carolinians Angelina Grimké and Sarah Grimké. Emphasizing the Grimkés' unique position, Weld urged them into the abolitionist field, reminding them, "Slavery is *on trial*. The people of the north are the court. You are summoned as *witnesses* to sustain the prosecution."[54] But even as he giddily emphasized their distinctiveness—"You are *southern* women, *once in law* slaveholders, your friends all slave holders, etc., hence your testimony; *testimony* TESTIMONY is the great desideratum"—Weld also acknowledged the more conventional role the sisters would be expected to play as abolitionists in the North: "True, it is incumbent on you to appear also as *advocates* arguing upon the evidence and as *examiners* cross questioning and sifting counter testimony," like fellow reformers "Mrs. Child, Mrs. Chapman, Lucretia Mott, etc."[55] What is striking about Weld's letter is his offhand application of the antislavery movement's pervasive juridical rhetoric to female abolitionists. Of course, these particular women would become as renowned for their feminism as for their abolitionism; Weld's own support for women's rights is, perhaps, what led him so comfortably to imagine his female colleagues undertaking the forensic tasks of what was still an exclusively male profession. The ease with which he figured these women as "advocates" is consistent with the conviction he shared with the Grimkés that separate-spheres ideology should not constrain women's antislavery activism.[56]

An even more vivid instance of white female abolitionist advocacy filled the pages of the *National Anti-Slavery Standard* as Stowe was composing *Dred*. In Stowe's former home of Cincinnati, one of the era's most tragic slave cases was unfolding, the trial of Kentucky fugitive Margaret Garner, who like *Dred*'s Cora Gordon, had elected to kill her children rather than see them returned to slavery. Once the attorneys on both sides had completed their arguments, a fascinating scene occurred that dramatized the abolitionist determination to put slavery on trial even as it revealed a tacit acceptance of extralegal female advocacy. Local reformer Lucy Stone, accused by the claimant's attorney of offering the bereaved slave mother a knife to kill herself if remanded to slavery, was given the opportunity to reply to the charge in court. Stone, the *Standard* reported, "preferred not to speak at the bar, but . . . requested the audience to remain a few moments after the adjournment."[57] As "a practiced antislavery activist," notes Steven Weisenburger in his study of the case, "Stone resisted answering a court whose legitimacy the movement questioned," opting instead to "take her case before the tribunal of American public opinion."[58] She did just that when she spoke of the slave woman's "silent agony" to the packed courtroom—the attorneys for the claimants and the defense still seated at their respective tables.[59] Affirmation of her extralegal authority came when the lawyer for Garner's master rose in response to Stone's speech in order "to speak to a point of law to prevent a claim."[60] At a time when women were not admitted to the American bar, a committed abolitionist like Stone could nevertheless play the slave's advocate quite convincingly before the popular tribunal.

That one need not have been a feminist like Weld or Stone to imagine women promoting legal change through extralegal advocacy is evident throughout antebellum print culture. Consider the example of one of Stowe's harshest critics, conservative essayist, proslavery political theorist, and plantation mistress Louisa McCord. Like Stowe, McCord "was not a lawyer, but she thought"—and wrote—"about legal issues."[61] In a similar vein, Confederate novelist Augusta Jane Evans depicts her stunningly beautiful heroine Irene Huntington "gravely discussing the tariff question" with a suitor, "pronounced the most promising lawyer of her acquaintance." That superior legal acumen and feminine social graces could go hand in hand is clear from Irene's "politely listening to" the young attorney's "stereotyped reasoning."[62] Stowe shared with McCord and the fictional Irene a distaste for the kind of radical feminism that inspired Angelina Grimké to brave widespread criticism for addressing mixed-gender audiences (criticism supplied, most notably, by Harriet's sister Catharine E. Beecher). Finding herself in the public eye after her first novel's success, Stowe assiduously performed the practices of true womanhood, sitting silently as her husband, Calvin, either read her written speeches or, more frequently, delivered lectures of his own.[63] Further, under the law of couverture, in which a married woman's legal identity was "covered" by that of her husband, Harriet's legal transactions, from signing book contracts to suing an unauthorized German translator of *Uncle Tom's*

Cabin, were necessarily conducted in the name of Calvin Stowe.[64] As we have seen, however, Harriet Beecher Stowe's more traditional understanding of women's role did not inhibit her from developing and promoting in her antislavery writing an alternative "jurisprudence of sentiment" that offered a profound critique of American law.[65] Nor did it keep her from acknowledging in an 1853 letter to North Carolinian abolitionist Daniel R. Goodloe that Southerners resented her "as their accuser at the bar of the world."[66] Nor, finally, did it prevent her, in the final work of her "trilogy on slave law" at the peak of her own fame as literary abolitionist, from allegorizing the dilemma of white advocacy in the only way she plausibly could, through the figure of a reform-minded male lawyer.[67]

Dred

Dred is set primarily on Canema, a plantation in rural North Carolina run by young Nina Gordon with the assistance of Harry, her devoted mulatto slave and (unbeknownst to her) half-brother. The capricious Nina is gradually transformed into an introspective and religious young woman largely through her engagement to Edward Clayton, an upstanding lawyer who has made his plantation, Magnolia Grove, a model of slaveholding paternalism. Before Nina and Edward can marry, however, a cholera epidemic sweeps the region, and Nina, after heroically nursing the slaves on her plantation, succumbs and dies. Her death places Canema in the unscrupulous hands of her cruel, alcoholic brother, Tom Gordon, who resents his slave and suspected half-brother Harry and torments him by openly coveting Harry's wife, Lisette. This change of affairs, combined with Harry's heightened sense of his legal disenfranchisement, leads Harry to venture into the Great Dismal Swamp to join the maroon community led by the mysterious Dred. The son of martyred slave rebel Denmark Vesey, Dred speaks like an Old Testament prophet and, recalling Nat Turner, reads the natural world for signs of divine sanction for the slave rebellion he plans to lead. In the meantime, Nina's fiancé, Clayton, disillusioned with Southern law, resigns from the bar and embarks on a crusade for legal reform, pressing in particular for the admission of slave testimony as a means to gradual emancipation. Repeatedly threatened by Tom Gordon's lynch mobs, eventually Clayton, too, moves into the swamp for safety. The novel ends when Dred is killed as an outlaw by Tom Gordon and his mob, and Clayton finances the remaining slaves' escape from the South to an émigré settlement he founds in Canada.

Dred's second volume is driven by a series of legal crises, many of which have their precedent in actual cases cited by Stowe in *A Key to Uncle Tom's Cabin*.

The central crisis revolves around Milly, an elderly slave who is shot by the man to whom she is hired by the Gordons. A second legal event involves Cora Gordon, who, in the tangled skeins of plantation kinship, is at once the sister of Harry Gordon, the illegitimate half-sister of Nina and Tom, and the emancipated quadroon wife of the Gordons' Mississippi plantation-owner cousin. Upon her husband's death, Cora Gordon is remanded with her two children into slavery by Tom Gordon and his morally bankrupt lawyer, Mr. Jekyl. This legal crisis begets another when, after being captured by Jekyl during her abortive escape to Cincinnati with her children, Cora is tried and executed for murdering her children in preference to seeing them sold into slavery in Virginia. This series of legal events reaches its climax when Mr. Jekyl declares the contract guaranteeing Harry Gordon's emancipation invalid, leading Harry to join the maroons in the swamp, which in turn provokes Tom Gordon to swear out an act of outlawry upon him. Figuring prominently in each of these crises is lawyer, gradual emancipationist, and benevolent slaveholder Edward Clayton. Although over the course of the narrative Stowe places Clayton in increasing proximity to both individual slaves and the larger enslaved community, and thus to African American speech, Clayton nevertheless consistently fails to respond appropriately to this testimony. Indeed, notwithstanding his own legal crusade on behalf of the slave, his determined advocacy has the ironic effect of inhibiting African American resistance by silencing black speech and blocking revolutionary action.

The profound lack of interracial communication that characterizes the uneasy dialogue in the novel between resistant slave testimony and uninformed, often self-serving white advocacy registers Stowe's growing awareness that the antislavery movement's legal rhetoric tended to reinforce the racial hierarchy in abolitionist discourse. Despite her seeming dissatisfaction with the juridical model, Stowe nevertheless fails to envision an alternative to the custodial role it assigned white advocates for the slave, as evidenced in the novel's conclusion, which unconvincingly offers white paternalism as a solution to legal and moral injustice.

In the context of Dred's sentimental plot, Edward Clayton's prosecution of Milly's case is notable as the "maiden plea" of a young, principled lawyer, who, although enamored with the theory of law, has been reluctant to engage in its practice.[68] (As Clayton himself puts it, "If I practised law according to my conscience, I should be chased out of court in a week.")[69] Literary critics and legal historians have extensively explored the relationship of law to morality in both Dred and State v. Mann, the 1829 North Carolina case on which Stowe based her fictional portrayal of Milly's case.[70] More relevant to our purposes, however, is the interplay between black testimony and white advocacy that *Dred*'s legal crises enact, especially as it mimics the discursive relations between African American and white abolitionists in the slavery controversy. In her depiction of Milly's case, Stowe offers the first of four models of black speech and white response, one that demonstrates the danger inherent in the white advocate's effort to represent or speak for the slave.

Consistent with Southern laws regarding the inadmissibility of slave testimony, Stowe situates Milly's first-person account of the events that precipitate her case outside the courtroom, in the domestic space of Canema, where she tells her story to Nina Gordon, much as Frederick Bailey recounted his shipyard beating to the sympathetic Aulds. Milly tells Nina in a lengthy dialect monologue that her employer, Mr. Barker, threatened to kill a slave child who "blacked one of his clean shirts" with a burnt stick.[71] When Milly intervened on behalf of the child, she reports, "he turned on me, and he got a cowhide, and he beat me over de head," upon which she "broke away from him, and run," which in turn led Barker to shoot her in the arm.[72] Outraged, Nina vows to Milly, "I tell you what, I'm going to have that man prosecuted!"[73] Her paternalistic (maternalistic?) intervention at once echoes Milly's own protection of the slave child and anticipates Edward Clayton's prosecutorial emphasis on the custodial aspect of slavery; Nina then "despatche[s] a long letter to Clayton, full of all the particulars."[74] The benevolent slaveholding lawyer agrees to take this, his first case, in order "to prove the efficiency of the law in behalf of that class of our population whose helplessness places them more particularly under our protection," noting that "they are to us in the condition of children under age; and any violation of their rights should be more particularly attended to."[75]

The mediated fashion of Clayton's encounter with Milly's testimony (through Nina's letter) resembles the indirect means by which many white Northerners accessed the testimonial accounts of former slaves, through texts transcribed and edited by white amanuenses. Like Nina's letter, slave narratives called for readers to respond to black testimony by taking immediate action on the slave's behalf. The alacrity with which Clayton answers this call would thus seem to offer a model of appropriate response to such witnessing: if in the legal context of the South, acting on behalf of the slave meant representing her in the courtroom, in the discursive climate of the North, it entailed "speak[ing] for him" in print. Both forms of advocacy meshed well with a white paternalism predicated upon the restricted speech of the racial other: the superior ability of an educated, articulate white advocate, whether Clayton or Stowe herself, to represent the slave seemed to mitigate the circumscription of black speech, whether in the court of law or in the court of public opinion.

But here, as in the *Key*, rather than accurately representing the slave, white advocacy almost inevitably ends up defending its own interests, as Clayton's closing argument in Milly's trial demonstrates. "No consideration can justify us holding this people in slavery an hour, unless we make this slavery a guardian relation, in which our superior strength and intelligence is made the protector and educator of their simplicity and weakness," Clayton maintains.[76] "The eyes of the world are fastened upon us," he acknowledges.[77] "Our continuing in this position at all is, in many quarters, matter of severe animadversion," Clayton reminds the court, urging, "Let us therefore show, by the spirit in which we administer our laws, by the impartiality with which we protect their rights, that the master of the helpless African is his best and truest friend."[78]

Clayton's paternalism is, of course, consistent with his position as a Southern slaveholder. But such paternalism, Stowe implies through her portrayal of Clayton's involvement in Milly's case and *Dred*'s subsequent legal crises, also seems to be inherent in white advocacy. Advocacy for the slave has quietly become advocacy for *slavery*. Instead of representing Milly, Clayton misrepresents her by replacing the agency foregrounded in her own extralegal testimony with a narrative of dependency. Milly's resistant intervention on behalf of the slave child disappears in Clayton's portrayal of slaves themselves as "helpless," infantile, and in need of protection, just as in Stowe's *Key*, the political organizing of Tom and the slave "committee" vanish in Shallow's sentimental depiction of them as "most starved" and "ragged." Clayton's misrepresentation of Milly demonstrates how black testimony, when mediated by layers of white advocacy, could be transformed from a discursive tool for protesting the injustice of slavery and asserting the humanity of enslaved people into a means by which to defend the peculiar institution in the "eyes of the world" and to cast African Americans as childlike dependents. Depicting Clayton's well-meaning but ultimately self-serving perversion of slave speech, Stowe seems to acknowledge how easily discursive representation of the racial other could slip into highly motivated misrepresentation.

Pointedly, Edward Clayton occupies what, in the abolitionists' imaginary trial, would have been perceived as two conflicting roles. Striking the defensive posture of a Southern slaveholder seeking to "justify" slavery as a "guardian" institution, he also claims to speak on behalf of the slave as a sympathetic white advocate. The glue that holds together these apparently opposite positions is Clayton's paternalism, suggesting that this quality characterized the relations of both the benevolent slaveholder *and* the white abolitionist with enslaved African Americans. Indeed, *Dred*'s second model of white advocacy highlights the affinities between the two roles. When Milly's case is overturned on appeal, Clayton acknowledges the incommensurability of paternalism with the harsh injustice of the slave law (represented, significantly, by the judicial decision of his own father, Judge Clayton) by resigning from the bar in order to embark on a crusade to reform Southern slave codes. What prompts Clayton to act is his observation of Harry's silent response to the appeal decision. The sight produces an epiphany in the white lawyer: "Never had Clayton so forcibly realized the horrors of slavery as when he heard them thus so calmly defined in the presence of one into whose soul the iron had entered."[79]

Just as Milly recounts her story to Nina in the extralegal space of the plantation, Harry, in keeping with the exclusion of slave testimony from the courtroom, does not speak. Instead, his nonverbal response forcefully articulates his firsthand knowledge of "the horrors of slavery." And much as Wedgwood's icon of the chained, kneeling, close-mouthed slave silently imploring, "Am I not a man, and a brother?" inspired Garrisonians to reject their rights and responsibilities as citizens of a corrupt government and take action against slavery through nonresistant moral suasionist tactics, Harry's mute testimony leads Clayton to reject advocacy of the slave within the corrupt Southern legal system. Like the abstentionist Wendell Phillips, whose moral commitment to abolitionism conflicted with his formalist understanding of law, Clayton relinquishes the legal profession in order to devote himself to antislavery activism in the social and political sphere.[80] As Clayton later explains to his father, he seeks to "excite the public mind on the injustice of the present slave-law, with a view to altering it" and thus "give to the slave the right to bring suit for injury, and to be a legal witness in court."[81] To this end, Clayton vows to engage in reform activities that closely resemble those of real-life lawyers turned antislavery activists: "He would give his time to journeyings though the state; he would deliver addresses, write in the newspapers, and do what otherwise lies in the power of a free man who wishes to reach an utterly unjust law."[82] Clayton's career change not only casts him in a role similar to that played by Northern abolitionists but also appears to offer a revised model for the relationship between black testimony and white advocacy, in which the latter, no longer supplanting the former in the courtroom, seeks to enable and legitimize it in the court of public opinion.

Like Stowe's first model of white advocacy, however, this one is weakened by the paternalism at its core. Clayton resigns from the legal profession not because he rejects Southern legal paternalism but because law is *insuf-*

ficiently paternalistic. In his farewell speech, delivered in court immediately upon the epiphany provoked by Harry's unspoken testimony, he laments that slave law cannot be "administered so as to protect the defenceless" and therefore cannot support his view of slavery as "a guardian institution, by which a stronger race might assume the care and instruction of the weaker one."[83] Even after realizing "the horrors of slavery" by seeing the effect of the slave code on "one into whose soul the iron had entered," Clayton preserves both his paternalist commitment to slavery and the underlying belief in a preordained racial hierarchy. Rather than serving as a corrective to his earlier misguided efforts to represent the slave in the legal sphere, Clayton's new reformist approach to advocacy seems merely to perpetuate the custodial relationship of slavery itself. The contradictions inherent in Clayton's advocacy for the slave are most evident in his response to a question posed by his father, Judge Clayton, who is modeled after the emphatically nonpaternalist Judge Thomas Ruffin. Asked whether his "conscience" will "allow [him] to retain the position of a slave-holder," Clayton answers somewhat sophistically, "I have already relinquished it, so far as my own intentions are concerned. I retain the legal relation as owner simply as a means of protecting my servants from the cruelties of the law, and of securing the opportunity to educate and elevate them."[84] Of course, for the enslaved "servants," the master's "intentions," however benevolent, would be insufficient as long as he retains "the legal relation as owner"; Clayton's determination to remain a slaveholder as a means of shielding his slaves from law's cruelty illustrates yet again how sympathetic white advocacy, far from being incompatible with the prerogatives of white supremacy, can actually serve to rationalize and enforce them. By having her exemplary advocate for the slave reject the legal profession but not "the legal relation" of slave ownership, Stowe implies that the paternalism of extralegal white advocacy is not far removed from that of slaveholding.

In *Dred*'s next legal crisis, or cluster of legal crises, Edward Clayton for the first time comes into contact with unmediated slave testimony, both in and out of the courtroom. In each case, however, rather than allowing these direct encounters with African American speech to inform his advocacy on behalf of the slave, Clayton once again turns them into occasions to supplant black resistance with white trusteeship. *Dred*'s third model of white advocacy emerges when at Harry's request, Clayton makes inquiries into the case of Cora Gordon, who, although emancipated by her late husband, has been remanded into slavery and stands trial in Alexandria, Virginia, for murdering her two children. Clayton, bound by a deathbed promise to "take care of" Nina Gordon's "poor people," recognizes his duty to serve as Cora's advocate.[85] Yet, notwithstanding the combined claims of chivalry and paternalism that require Clayton to intervene on Cora's behalf, Cora's testimony has the effect of releasing Clayton from responsibility for directly confronting the corrupt Southern legal system and the peculiar institution it supports.

Following her confession in a preliminary examination before the magistrate's court, Cora Gordon explains, "I was the lawful wife of a man of honor, who did what he could to evade your cruel laws, and set me free. My children were born to liberty . . . till my father's son entered a suit for us, and made us *slaves*. Judge and jury helped him—all your laws and your officers helped him—to take away the rights of the widow and the fatherless!"[86] Much like Linda Brent in Harriet A. Jacobs's *Incidents in the Life of a Slave Girl*, Cora Gordon strikes a confessional stance in order to gain a hearing for her resistant autobiographical testimony, which sentimentally depicts how the "cruel laws" of slavery disrupt home and family.[87] Clayton's reaction to Cora's testimony, however, is precisely the kind of response Jacobs tries to preempt in her preface to *Incidents*, when she insists that she has not written about her experiences "to excite sympathy for [her] own sufferings" but rather "to arouse" white Northerners, especially women, "to a realizing sense of the condition of two millions of women at the South . . . suffering what I suffered."[88] Like Jacobs's "testimony . . . [of] what Slavery really is" and like the slave testimonies that will form a "heap of witness" near *Dred*'s conclusion, Cora's courtroom speech offers one slave's experience as evidence of the larger collective's intolerable condition in a bid to provoke political and social change.[89] After hearing Cora's testimony, however, the slaveholding lawyer focuses exclusively on the plight of the individual: "Clayton determined, in his own mind, to do what he could for her. Her own declaration seemed to make the form of a trial unnecessary. He resolved, however, to do what he could to enlist for her the sympathy of some friends of his in the city."[90] Instead of heeding the slave woman's testimonial speech and rising up in behalf of her persecuted people, as Jacobs and other antislavery witnesses urged their audiences to do, Clayton responds to Cora's testimony by seeking to enlist white "sympathy," which, although temporarily ameliorating the condition of a single bondwoman, ultimately does nothing to liberate or enfranchise African Americans as a group.[91]

More importantly, Clayton's unilateral decision that Cora's courtroom speech "seemed to make the form of a trial unnecessary" forecloses the possibility of any further insurgent testimony by the slave and therefore of any antislavery action in response to that testimony. Cora's defiant confession, like her dramatic sacrifice of her own children, is a resistant act that publicly exposes and challenges the injustice and hypocrisy of the South's "cruel laws." But here, as in Milly's case, apparently well-intentioned white mediation deprives resistant black speech of its power by interpreting it as a plea for a paternalist protection and private sympathy predicated upon the silence and passivity of the enslaved racial other. In this third model of white advocacy and black testimony, the lawyer, when confronted with dissident slave witnessing, employs a paternalist logic to suppress rather than to encourage further African American speech, thus ensuring his own discursive prerogatives and neutralizing any challenge to the status quo.[92]

Framing Cora Gordon's trial in *Dred* is the ongoing debate between Cora's brother Harry and Clayton regarding the most appropriate response to slavery. Harry, like Douglass's Madison Washington, draws on his reading of the Declaration of Independence to call for armed resistance, whereas Clayton, despite his "belief in the inalienable right of every man to liberty," nonetheless fears the consequences of "bloody insurrection."[93] The exchange, which offers the novel's final, and perhaps most telling, model of black testimony and white advocacy, occurs after Harry escapes into the swamp, where the fugitive prophet Dred proclaims him "a witness and commander to the people."[94] Tom Gordon retaliates by having an act of outlawry prepared that certifies that "any person or persons may kill and destroy the said slave by such means as he or they may think fit, without accusation or impeachment of any crime or offense for so doing, and without incurring any penalty or forfeiture."[95] This legal crisis, combined with Clayton's own departure into the swamp after a beating by Tom Gordon's lynch mob, exposes the sympathetic white advocate to extralegal black testimony and reorients the novel away from the white-dominated plantation culture of Canema and Magnolia Grove and toward the rebellious slave culture of Dred's maroon community.

Stowe signals this move with an editorial aside that emphasizes the indispensability of slave testimony to a complete understanding of the South's peculiar institution. "We have been accustomed, even those of us who feel most, to look on the arguments for and against the system of slavery with the eyes of those who are at ease," Stowe acknowledges, pointing out, however, that "we shall never have all the materials for absolute truth on this subject, till we take into account, with our own views and reasonings, the views and reasonings of those who have bowed down to the yoke, and felt the iron enter their souls."[96] In the "Concluding Remarks" to *Uncle Tom's Cabin*, Stowe had famously asserted her faith in the power of "sympathetic influence" and thus Christian moral suasion, encouraging her readers to address the national problem of slavery by endeavoring to "*feel right*" and to "*pray*."[97] Here, however, in an implicit reference to her earlier novel, Stowe suggests that even those white abolitionists "who feel most" have a limited perspective on slavery if they do not take into account African American "views and reasonings." Suggesting the inadequacy of sympathetic white advocacy uninformed by black testimony, Dred thus represents a profound revision of Stowe's approach to slavery and abolitionism. Of course, as critic Robert B. Stepto notes, even when writing Uncle Tom's Cabin, Stowe was "rather assiduous . . . in seeking the forms of black testimony that could both counter and corroborate the white testimony she already had in hand.[98] But as Robert Levine demonstrates, in the years after Uncle Tom's Cabin, Stowe became even more attuned to the need to incorporate African American perspectives into her portrayals of slavery.[99] Thus, in her Key, Stowe extensively cites and often reproduces long passages from the oral and written narratives of such former slaves as Frederick Douglass, Josiah Henson, Lunsford Lane, Lewis Clarke, Solomon Northup, and Milly Edmondson.[100]

Dred reenacts this accumulation of black testimony in a chapter titled "Jegar Sahadutha," or "heap of witness," in which Harry, in an act of Douglass-like black advocacy, reads to his fellow slaves from the Declaration of Independence, contrasting "the long train of abuses and usurpations" suffered by the colonists with the slaves' own suffering under their descendants.[101] Harry concludes by calling upon the Lord to "judge between us and them, if the laws that they put upon us be not worse than any that lay upon them."[102] Noting that the Founders "complained that they could not get justice done to them in the courts," Harry demands, "But how stands it with us, who cannot even come into a court to plead?" thereby echoing Clayton's (and Stowe's) emphasis on the denial of slaves' procedural rights, as well as perhaps Douglass's call for black advocacy.[103] This allusion to African American legal outsidership becomes an invitation to testify, as one by one, the "dark witness[es]" rise to speak of their experiences under slavery.[104] These experiences have their historical counterparts in cases cited by Stowe in both Key and Dred's appendix 2, cases in which slave testimony is notably absent.[105] Like the stones gathered by Jacob and Laban in Genesis, these individual stories are amassed into a heap of witness. And, like the hundreds of slave narratives that were recorded and published in the antebellum period, the accumulated "narrations" of these dark witnesses stand as extralegal testimony against the crime of slavery.[106] But although this collective testimony helps to consolidate slave unity and resistance in the swamp, like Clayton's ineffectual campaign for legal reform, it accomplishes no real social or political change in the novel.

It is to such a heap of witness, Stowe implies, that the literary abolitionist and her audience must turn for those "crucial materials for absolute truth" about slavery; such materials were indispensable to white abolitionists in their role as (in Weld's formulation) "*advocates* arguing upon the evidence and . . . *examiners* cross questioning and sifting counter testimony."[107] But to assert that such advocates "must" attend to "the feelings and reasonings of the slave" is not to say that they *will* do so.[108] Indeed, Stowe's characterization of enslaved African Americans as "those who have . . . felt the iron enter their souls"—the same words she uses earlier in the novel to describe Harry from Edward Clayton's perspective—underscores not only the representative role of Harry as a black antislavery "witness" but also the corresponding parallel between white advocates for the slave in the abolitionist movement and the inattentive Edward Clayton. Tellingly, therefore, although Clayton follows Harry and *Dred*'s other black characters "to the fastness in the Dismal Swamp," where he encounters the heap of witness, he does not, like Douglass's exemplary Listwell or like real-life advocate Fanny Kemble, either listen well or take an active role in the slaves' cause as they have defined it.[109] In the swamp, Dred finds Clayton "a sympathetic listener," whereas the white man takes "a quaint and poetic interest" in the slave rebel "as a psychological study."[110] Refusing to allow Dred's "views and reasonings" to revise or even inform his own, Clayton instead casts the slave's testimony in a discursive frame that reduces it to an unintelligibly "wild jargon of hebraistic phrases, names, and allusions."[111]

It is after Dred's death, however, that Clayton's tendency to engage in advocacy that supplants, rather than attends to, black testimony becomes most apparent. Dred's funeral ends with the slave Hannibal, his hopes for prophetic deliverance "extinguished," resignedly looking forward to Judgment Day, when "our testimony will be took . . . if it never was afore; and the Lord will judge atween us and our oppressors."[112] And indeed, for the remainder of the novel, black testimony is all but silenced.[113] Emphasizing Stowe's inability or reluctance to take the plot of her potentially radical second antislavery novel to its logically revolutionary conclusion, critics have located the slaves' failure to achieve their rebellion in Dred's determination to await a divine portent that never appears, or, alternatively, in Milly's success in countering Dred's Old Testament vengefulness and wrath with her New Testament patience and faith.[114] But it is crucial to note that in the wake of their charismatic leader's murder, some slaves remain prepared for a bloody insurrection and that it is only Clayton's intervention that wards off the violent climax to which the novel has been building.[115] The abortiveness of the rebellion, then, symbolizes not so much Stowe's doubts about the capacity of blacks for leadership nor her faith in the triumph of feminine Christian forbearance over masculine Hebraic militarism as it does her awareness of the tendency of white advocacy to act as a check on black resistance. Although Clayton, by bankrolling the maroons' escape to the North, saves the outnumbered insurgents from certain death, his intervention also rescues the plantation community from bloody insurrection and preserves the slave system intact. In the swamp, as he has throughout the novel, Clayton responds to slave testimony with a paternalist advocacy that may help individual slaves but, overall, tends to buttress rather than dismantle the institution of slavery and the racial hierarchy upon which it is built. Stowe depicts Clayton's intervention as a discursive accomplishment. Following Dred's funeral, feeling that "there was a perilous degree of excitement in some of the actors before him, which, unless some escape-valve were opened, might lead to most fatal results," Clayton "talked with Harry, wisely and kindly, assuming nothing to himself on the ground either of birth or position; showing him the undesirableness and hopelessness, under present circumstances, of any attempt to right by force the wrongs under which his class were suffering, and opening to him and his associates a prospect of a safer way by flight to the Free States."[116] Seemingly incapable of listening to "the feelings and reasonings of the slave" as they are articulated by Dred, Harry, or the other slave witnesses in the swamp, Clayton (his principled condescension notwithstanding) claims the prerogative to speak. Moreover, upon escaping to the North, the previously voluble Harry does not testify to his experience of slavery, nor does he consolidate his emerging role as black advocate. Quite the contrary: from Clayton's speech onward, Harry, although still a central character, no longer has a speaking part in the novel.[117]

"It's Rather the Fashion to Move about That a Little"

A final scene from Dred highlights the parallels between Edward Clayton and Northern white antislavery activists even as it calls attention to Stowe's own revised approach to literary abolitionism. This scene, which seems to reject religious and sentimental solutions to the problem of slavery in favor of legal ones, ultimately points to what, after Uncle Tom's Cabin, had become a discursive dilemma for Stowe: the apparent inadequacy and inefficacy of any attempts by sympathetic whites to represent the slave—legally, politically, or artistically.[118]

Soon after Clayton begins his career as a reformer, he makes an artless (and unsuccessful) antislavery appeal to an ecumenical conference of clergymen, but, disgusted with clerical infighting and hypocrisy, he quickly abandons a moral suasionist approach grounded in religious activism for a political one centered on legal reform. Having "determined to petition the legislature to grant to the slave the right of seeking legal redress in cases of injury; and, as a necessary step to this, the right of bearing testimony in legal action," Clayton seeks support from his old friend Frank Russell, now a candidate for Congress.[119] The cynical Russell, who throughout the novel has served as a foil to the idealistic Clayton, responds to his friend's plan for legal reform by asking, "Say, Clayton, what do you want to get up a petition on that point for? Why don't you get up one to prevent the separation of families?"[120] After all, Russell points out, "there's been such a muss made about that in Europe, and all around the world, that it's rather the fashion to move about that a little," adding, "Politicians like to appear to intend to begin to do something about it. It has a pleasing effect, and gives the Northern editors and ministers something to say, as an apology for our sins. Besides, there are a good many simple-hearted folks, who don't see very deep into things, that really think it possible to do something effective on this subject."[121]

The dispute between Frank Russell and Edward Clayton offers a suggestive meditation on abolitionist strategy. Both men agree that antislavery activism should employ political measures (in the form of petitions to Congress) in order to achieve legislative reform (a statute preventing the separation of slave families or guaranteeing slaves due process). But Russell, like many abolitionists and especially the thousands of abolitionists who flooded Congress with petitions, sees political activism in instrumental terms, as a means to bring the problem of slavery to public attention.[122] He therefore sanctions a sentimental approach whose popularity is guaranteed despite—or perhaps because of—its paternalism and ineffectuality. Clayton, on the other hand, seeks here to undermine the legal basis of slavery by proposing a law that would grant civic agency to the slave in the courtroom.

Keeping in mind critic Sarah Meer's insight that *Dred* should itself be understood as part of the *Uncle Tom* phenomenon, we can read the Russell-Clayton debate as an allegory for Stowe's own literary abolitionist agon.[123] Referring to the "muss made . . . in Europe, and all around the world" about "the separation of families," Stowe alludes to the international outcry provoked by her first novel, with its sentimental emphasis on slavery's destruction of both black and white domesticity. Frank Russell's trivialization of the kind of public outrage the novel inspired—"It's rather the fashion to move about that a little"—registers Stowe's growing doubts, after *Uncle Tom's Cabin*, about the political impact of sentimental appeals on behalf of the slave. Indeed, Russell's comments insinuate that, due to the opportunism of cultural leaders ("Northern editors and ministers") and the naiveté of the larger public ("simple-hearted folks, who don't see very deep into things"), such a sentimental approach to the national problem of slavery creates the "effect" of change while avoiding any real social, political, or economic transformation —a conclusion similar to that reached by some modern critics of Stowe's first novel and of sentimentalism in general.[124] ("Moral sentiment," Russell admits, "is a humbug!")[125] Here Stowe seems to imply that Dred, with its juridical take on slavery, may be a more "effective" piece of literary abolitionism than her previous novel, with its sentimental approach.

We must read this scene, however, in light of the novel as a whole, and especially its conclusion. I have suggested that Dred not only participates in the widespread antebellum tendency to understand slavery in legal terms but also offers a revealing critique of the trial trope that structured abolitionist discourse. The roles played by Stowe's imaginary Southern characters correlate, along racial lines, to those adopted by their real-life Northern counterparts. Just as Theodore Dwight Weld cast the Grimkés and their white colleagues as "advocates" for the slave, and Frederick Douglass portrayed himself as "eye-witness to the cruelty" of slavery, Stowe's novel features a crusading white lawyer and testifying slave witnesses. In this rhetorical context, Russell's comments, along with Clayton's rejoinder—that "it's no use to pass laws" protecting slave families "without giving slaves the power to sue or give evidence, in case of violation"—would seem to imply that sympathetic white advocacy on behalf of the slave is meaningless without black testimony.[126] Yet, as we have seen, in Dred, Stowe's slaveholding white advocate, rather than representing the slaves on whose behalf he claims to speak, consistently misrepresents them by disregarding slave testimony, denying African American political agency, and impeding black resistance. Furthermore, the novel's conclusion, frequently criticized for its substitution of black revolution with white trusteeship, is perhaps even more unsettling for its silencing of African American voices.

The debate between Russell and Clayton, like the novel itself, ultimately seems not to valorize one discursive approach to the problem of slavery over another but, instead, to question the very attempt by sympathetic white advocates to represent the slave. Thus, if Stowe's first antislavery novel dramatically illustrated the power of literature to influence public opinion over the issue of slavery, her second not only demonstrates the inadequacy of religious, legal, and revolutionary solutions to the problem of slavery, but also calls into question the efficacy of *any* literary approach to that problem.[127] Similarly, whereas Uncle Tom's Cabin has dominated the ongoing critical debate over sentimental reform, the primary significance of *Dred*, with its notorious failure to offer a viable resolution, may be precisely that it indicates a crisis of representation not just in Stowe's post-*Tom* writing about slavery but in late antebellum print culture more generally, as a number of authors began to question the appropriateness of white efforts to "speak for" the slave.[128]

Nowhere, perhaps, is white authorial ambivalence about representing the slave more legible than in "Benito Cereno," published the same year as *Dred*. The novella, Herman Melville's only sustained portrayal of slavery, appeared serially in *Putnam's Monthly Magazine*, with one installment accompanying a favorable review of Douglass's *My Bondage and My Freedom*.[129] Like Stowe's novel, Melville's novella features a slave insurrection that is aborted due to a benevolent white man's well-meaning intervention—and, like *Dred*, "Benito Cereno" features interpolated legal documents based on an actual slave case.[130] As critics have noted, the contrast of these two works with that other legally inflected account of a slave uprising, Douglass's "Heroic Slave," is instructive.[131] The only one of the three to portray a triumphant black insurrection, Douglass's story is also the only one in which white speakers document and celebrate the authentic speech of the slave rebel rather than distorting it or suppressing it altogether.[132] As brilliant as Madison Washington, as powerful as Dred, and as authoritative as Harry, Melville's Babo differs from the decade's other heroic slaves in his abstention from impassioned antislavery eloquence. Scripting the words of his erstwhile captor, Benito Cereno, Babo either dissembles a loyal slave's speech or, upon his own capture, remains steadfastly silent; like Peter Poyas in the Denmark Vesey conspiracy or Frederick Bailey in the runaway plot, Babo owns nothing.[133] In the face of the judicially administered injustice of New World slavery, Babo's undissembling, revolutionary voice is insistently, defiantly absent from the literary and legal retellings of the events aboard the *San Dominick*—the basis for the "criminal cause" that will redefine as criminality the civic agency Babo's plot entails, thereby returning the fugitive rebel to the role of silent witness.[134] Refusing to settle for the constrained agency of the confessing black criminal or the abject slave victim, yet denied the autonomous speech of the self-possessed individual, Babo at the conclusion of "Benito Cereno" is not only meted death, like Dred, but, like Harry, meets "his voiceless end."[135] Following Babo's decapitation by order of Lima's viceregal court, his head is "fixed on a pole in the Plaza" where it "met, unabashed, the gaze of the whites."[136]

Babo's fate, when read alongside Harry's in the context of the antebellum slavery debate's juridical rhetoric, suggests that Melville, like Stowe, understood himself to be writing in (yet could not imagine an alternative to) a world in which the legal and literary discourses set in motion by slavery authorized white representations of the enslaved—from the historical Benito Cereno's deposition to the real-life Captain Delano's *Narrative of Voyages and Travels* (1817) to Melville's "Benito Cereno" and Stowe's *Dred*—at the expense of an insurgent black speech that is inevitably criminalized, silenced, or both. How fitting, then, is Melville's haunting last image of his heroic slave as the ultimate posthumous witness: decaying eye sockets eternally gaping, rotting tongue eternally silent, "the black" is reduced, finally, to a grotesque spectacle for white consumption.[137] It was precisely such a spectacle, Southerner William MacCreary Burwell insisted in a proslavery novel published the same year as *Dred* and "Benito Cereno," that abolitionists produced in their extralegal print promotion of the fugitive slave as "eye-witness to the cruelty."

6   THE SOUTH'S COUNTERSUIT

William MacCreary Burwell's *White Acre vs. Black Acre*

In its notice of *Dred*, the influential Southern periodical *DeBow's Review* presented Stowe's novel as "another exhibition of abolition spite and spleen, which, as it is productive of the cent and dollar, makes very good charity, religion, and philanthropy in that quarter."[1] This view of abolitionist print propaganda as a cynical moneymaking enterprise is humorously exhibited in a work featured in the same "Book Notices," *White Acre vs. Black Acre, a Case at Law*. Lauded by *DeBow's* as an "admirable burlesque," this odd proslavery novel does not appear to have reached Stowe's audiences in the North and abroad.[2] It was, however, puffed by the *Southern Literary Messenger* as an "allegory" that "relates with great humour the history of the quarrel between the North and the South with reference to slavery."[3] And the following year, the novel appeared alongside such proslavery classics as J. H. Van Evrie's *Negroes and Negro "Slavery"* (1853), Albert Taylor Bledsoe's *Essay on Liberty and Slavery* (1856), and George Fitzhugh's *Cannibals All!* (1857) in the "list of *Works relating to Slavery and the South*" that *DeBow's* followed the *New Orleans Delta* in recommending "to Southern men . . . for their libraries."[4]

Appearing the same year that *Dred* was displayed in bookshops on both sides of the Atlantic, *White Acre vs. Black Acre* was written by William MacCreary Burwell.[5] Having spent his childhood at Monticello (his father was Thomas Jefferson's personal secretary) and his college years at the University of Virginia (he was Edgar Allan Poe's classmate), Burwell pursued a career that comprised both political and literary pursuits, serving for two decades in the Virginia legislature, founding a Whig daily, the *Virginia Patriot*, and eventually replacing James D. B. DeBow in the editor's chair at *DeBow's Review*.[6]

Part of the surge of proslavery and Southern responses to *Uncle Tom's Cabin* that deluged transatlantic print culture throughout the 1850s, Burwell's allegory cannot, strictly speaking, be counted among the thirty-plus anti-*Tom* novels that have attracted critical attention in recent years.[7] Published in Richmond, Virginia, *White Acre vs. Black Acre* did not garner the same kind of attention as Northern-published works like Mary Eastman's *Aunt Phillis's Cabin* (1852) or William Gilmore Simms's *Woodcraft* (1854).[8] Nevertheless, this novelistic attempt to respond to devastating abolitionist print portrayals of the peculiar institution features stock characters ubiquitous in the better-known "Cabin Literature," including the disappointed fugitive, the charlatan slave lecturer, and the mercenary ultra-abolitionist, as well as those imports from the plantation novel tradition, the benevolent planter patriarch and the contented slave.[9] Like other responses to Stowe, *White Acre vs. Black Acre* offers an alternative point of access to antebellum print culture, allowing us to step for a moment off the abolitionists' well-worn paper trail. Moreover, Burwell's allegory of the sectional dispute as "a case at law" is especially noteworthy for the changes it wrought on the slavery debate's trial trope, which by 1856 had become well established if not downright hackneyed. An outspoken counterpoint to the ambivalent insider critiques of Douglass and Stowe, Burwell's allegory provides valuable contemporary criticism of abolitionist print tactics by an author determined to turn those tactics to his own proslavery ends.

In particular, *White Acre vs. Black Acre* presents a creative response to the rhetorical dilemma faced by Southern propagandists: how to gain a hearing for slaveholders when the terms of the debate placed them in a disadvantageous defensive posture. Despite a sectional appreciation for the interrelatedness of law and literature, many Southern writers tended to find other discourses more congenial to the discussion of slavery than the juridical one so fervently embraced by the North; in addition to the scriptural and moral approach prevalent on both sides of the Mason-Dixon line, Southerners developed distinct rhetorical models consistent with their agrarian, honor-based society.[10] What sets Burwell's novel apart from other literary interventions in the slavery debate is that it retains the culturally compelling structure and procedures of the trial even as it boldly recalibrates the roles of the participants and thus the meaning of the proceedings.[11] By reframing the case against slaveholders as a freedom suit instigated by intrusive, acquisitive abolitionists on behalf of ignorant, reluctant slaves, Burwell reoriented the imaginary proceedings away from Northern reformers' persistent concerns about higher law and natural rights to the perennial Southern themes of property and paternalism.[12] And by reversing the roles of the plaintiffs and the defendants in the novel's final pages, Burwell rejected abolitionists' self-representation as altruistic advocates for the slave, exposing them instead as amoral exploiters of hapless free blacks. In the process, Burwell offered a trenchant parody of the strategies through which the antislavery movement brought the crime of slavery before the popular tribunal. With its South-side view of antebellum legal spectatorship and popular legal consciousness, Burwell's quirky contribution to the slavery debate bears consideration as an instructive counterpoint to literary abolitionist engagements with juridical rhetoric. As one of the most fully developed attempts to articulate proslavery ideology in the legal idiom of the larger print controversy, Burwell's elaborate allegory of the slavery debate as trial represents one Southerner's determination to engage and refute — rather than merely protest and dismiss — the powerful abolitionist indictment of slavery and its perpetrators.[13]

The Duty of Southern Authors

The *Southern Literary Messenger* in which the review of *White Acre vs. Black Acre* appears opens with an article outlining "The Duty of Southern Authors." If we come to Burwell's novel as a *Messenger* subscriber might have, by first reading this manifesto for Southern literature — one of many that issued from the South's numerous, often short-lived, antebellum literary periodicals — we can better situate this proslavery burlesque in the sectional politics of print publication.[14]

The call for the South to produce its own distinctive literature was not a new one. With its founding more than two decades earlier, in 1834, the *Messenger* had sought "to stimulate the pride and genius of the south, and awaken from its long slumber the literary exertion of this portion of our country."[15] The phrasing, of course, anticipated Ralph Waldo Emerson's famous appeal, three years later, for "the sluggard intellect of this continent [to] look from under its iron lids, and fulfill the postponed expectation of the world with something better than the exertions of mechanical skill."[16] But whereas Emerson's image of literary nationalism pictured the American scholar rousing the nation from its industrial torpor with his energetic engagement in "fit actions," the *Messenger*'s vision of literary sectionalism depicted a Southern author both liberated and enervated by the limitless leisure that an enslaved agricultural labor force promised.[17] This "mud-sill" logic surfaces in the puffs by well-known Northern cultural figures featured in the *Messenger*'s introductory "Publisher's Notice."[18] Novelist James Fenimore Cooper observed that "the south is full of talent, and the leisure of its gentlemen ought to enable them to bring it freely into action."[19] His fellow author and New Yorker James Kirke Paulding was even more explicit when he pointed out that "the situation of so many well educated men, placed above the necessity of laboring either manually or professionally, affords ample leisure for the cultivation of literature."[20] Contrasting sharply with Emerson's Transcendentalist account of activist literary inspiration, Southern cultural creativity was predicated upon the physical inaction that slavery entailed on elite whites.

Rather than fostering literary "progress, civilization, and refinement," however, the leisure of the slaveholding elite seemed only to reinforce what Edgar Allan Poe referred to as "the long indulged literary supineness of the South."[21] Accordingly, two decades after its founding, the *Southern Literary Messenger*, in response to the phenomenal worldwide success of *Uncle Tom's Cabin* and at the moment when Stowe herself seemed to be questioning the efficacy of abolitionist literary tactics, issued a renewed—and newly urgent—call for Southern literature. Like others published in the 1850s, this updated manifesto, "The Duty of Southern Authors," identified slavery no longer primarily as a precondition for literary activity but instead presented defense of the peculiar institution as the guiding subject and purpose of the section's belles-lettres.[22] In addition to the usual "inducements and incentives to literary labors" that spurred "the authors of *all* nations," the *Messenger* noted that the "*Southern* writer" should be further driven by the fact that "he lives in a community in which African slavery subsists": although Southerners "recognize it as a great social, moral and political blessing—beneficial alike to us and to the slave," it had to be acknowledged that "the rest of Christendom stands united against us, and are almost unanimous in pronouncing a verdict of condemnation."[23] Citing "the success of 'Uncle Tom's Cabin,'" as "evidence of the manner in which our enemies are employing literature for our overthrow," the *Messenger* urged Southerners to fight fire with fire: "As literature has been the most powerful weapon which the enemies of African slavery have used in their attacks, so, also, to literature we must look for the maintenance of our position, and our justification before the world."[24] Given that "the literary workshops of the North are even now resounding with the noisy and fanatical labors of those who, with Mrs. Stowe as their model, are forging calumnies, and hammering falsehood into the semblance of truth," Southerners had to join University of Virginia law professor James Holcombe in the realization that "we can no longer cover the salient points of our institutions through the halls of Congress," for "the voice of the statesman and orator cannot reach the masses, with whom lie the issues of life and death."[25] That sort of mass democratic appeal was the province of "literature alone."[26]

Acknowledging the important contributions made by Thomas Roderick Dew, Bledsoe, and Fitzhugh, the *Messenger* went on to suggest that the coordinated industrialized print propaganda of Northern abolitionists had rendered such piecemeal individual efforts, often addressed to Southern audiences, ineffectual. In a climate of mass print production, the duty of Southern authors was to publish "A GREAT AND COMPREHENSIVE HISTORY OF AFRICAN SLAVERY AT THE SOUTH—a work that would take up the subject from the first introduction of slaves in 1620 . . . and bring it down to the present day"; such a "*History of Slavery* would be its strongest defence, and its clearest vindication before the world."[27] Needless to say, that history would be a revisionist one; it should document "how earnestly we resisted [slavery's] original imposition, how consistently we have labored for its subsequent amelioration, how uniformly we have sustained every measure of policy which promised for it a peaceful euthanasia," and, finally, "how fiercely those who still roll in the unblessed wealth of that bloody commerce from which it sprung"—well-off Yankee abolitionists like Wendell Phillips—"have sought to close every avenue for its gradual extinction, and hem it in, to perish amid social and national convulsion."[28]

Just as Emerson's "iron lids" connote the industrialization that simultaneously sustained Northern print culture with "exertions of mechanical skill" and threatened to stultify its "intellect," the rhetoric in which the *Southern Literary Messenger* issued its calls for literary sectionalism speaks to the economic and political conditions shaping cultural production in antebellum America. The periodical's inaugural issue figured its task in language that revealed Southern literature's dependence upon not only slave labor but the agricultural expansionism that assured its continued viability. Thus, "the first number of the 'Messenger'" was "sent forth by its Publisher, as a kind of pioneer, to spy out the land of literary promise, and to report whether the same be fruitful or barren."[29] Twenty years later, "The Duty of Southern Authors" employed the same agricultural and chivalric imagery that animated the magazine's prospectus; tellingly, however, it ultimately conceded the need for Southern writers to exchange such rhetorical tactics for the adversarial model of their antislavery opponents. "When we would *convince* men," the article explained, "we must store their minds with *facts*, upon which to base and support the arguments we intend employing for their conviction. Until we do *that*, the strength of our logic will neither be felt nor acknowledged."[30] Beyond this remedial tutorial in rhetorical practice, the essay modeled the forensic discourse it sought by incorporating legal terminology into its appeal for a newly effective Southern defense of slavery. In contrast to earlier "*ex parte*" accounts of slavery, the *Messenger* maintained, slavery's next generation of "advocates" had to "prove by evidence" the superiority of their institution to skeptical "advocates of abolition" and their followers.[31] Hence the pressing need to "raise up a native literature," for even "if it could perform no other function than be our witness before posterity," it would serve to "divide the public opinion of the world" and "break the force of its sympathy."[32] Almost as an afterthought, the *Messenger* added, "The efforts of Southern authors" should not "be altogether defensive"—rather, "Let southern authors protect slavery by attacking free society."[33]

The summons to produce such an all-encompassing narrative of the South and its relation to slavery was as serious as it was daunting. It was ironic, then, that the "admirable burlesque" blurbed eighty pages later in the same issue of the *Messenger* would fulfill virtually every duty the opening manifesto had assigned to Southern literature and its authors: it offered a comprehensive revisionist history of slavery in the South, from the arrival of the first slave ship to the current sectional dispute; it illustrated, through its parody of antislavery print agitation, the superior political power of literature; and it decisively rejected Southerners' prescribed defensive posture. By depicting a Southern countersuit against the North—and by "attacking free society" with an exposé of exploitative wage labor and corporate capital—Burwell's *White Acre vs. Black Acre* responded to the *Messenger*'s call to engage abolitionists on their own adversarial terms, using extralegal print strategies quite literally to "prove by evidence" that the case against Southern slaveholders in the court of public opinion should be dismissed as a criminal imposition on the American public.

White Acre vs. Black Acre

The novel presents itself as a lost manuscript, "Reported by J. G., Esq., a Retired Barrister," now "published because it shows light upon the origin of an old and still pending action at law, in which, few who read are not more or less interested."[34] *White Acre vs. Black Acre* recounts the founding of both the American nation and the South's peculiar institution, culminating in the allegorical trial of the title. The story begins with the settlement of "a new country" by the firm of Bull, McSnatch & Co., which is composed of the hard-drinking "capitalist" Mr. Bull (England) and his lesser partners, Sandy McSnatch (Scotland) and Pat Ragan (Ireland), whose land and labor Bull has appropriated.[35] Colonization of the new country is accomplished by Robert Careless, an unsuccessful tobacco farmer. Careless's cares increase when a slave ship anchors near his plantation, upon which Ragan and McSnatch try to convince Careless to accept the Africans as laborers. Furious, Careless resists. When the ship captain refuses to take the "black creatures" elsewhere, however, Careless's own "humane" character leads him to protect them in a good-natured effort to ensure that his landlord Mr. Bull won't take a financial loss—with the proviso that the temporary arrangement can be terminated at Careless's request.[36] Finding the "thievish and sleepy headed" blacks far more trouble and expense than they are worth, Careless annually appeals to Mr. Bull to "send them back to their own country or some other farm," only to be rudely rebuffed.[37] The presence of the blacks, who are naturally lazy, immoral, and impervious to physical injury, soon runs the Careless plantation into the ground.

The situation changes, however, with the conclusion of Careless's seven-year lawsuit against Bull, McSnatch & Co., upon which some Careless heirs receive northern lands known as White Acre, while others settle "around the old homestead and called like that, the plantation of Black Acre."[38] The blacks are distributed "amongst other property and effects" in keeping with the court's finding that they are indebted to the Careless heirs for their maintenance.[39] The White Acre inhabitants quickly dispose of most of their slaves, while Black Acre's slaves become more valuable with training.

Relations between the neighboring sections remain good until White Acre, finding slavery unprofitable, proclaims a general emancipation—although many of its inhabitants opportunely sell off their remaining slaves. Instantly envious of the comparatively happy Black Acre, some in White Acre begin scheming to "break up this happy family," hoping that "the blacks[,] being enticed away from their masters, could be persuaded to labor at very low wages for those who 'took them out of the house of bondage.' "[40] To this end, a pair of ne'er-do-wells initiates a lawsuit against the inhabitants of Black Acre through a shady Mr. Sneakright, who presents himself as the unsuspecting slaves' "gardeen and best friend."[41] After a prolonged trial, the case—and with it, the novel—ends with the slaveholding defendants filing a countersuit to prove that the plaintiffs' case arises from a conspiracy to defraud the court by appropriating any awarded damages for their own profit.

Like Dred's Edward Clayton, Burwell idealizes slavery as an inegalitarian yet humane arrangement in which benevolent whites provide for vulnerable blacks in exchange for the labor that underwrites such care. And, like many in his proslavery cohort, Burwell offers this custodial vision of slavery as far preferable to the cruel system of wage labor under corporate capitalism, a system that inevitably exploits and ultimately destroys society's weakest members: blacks, women, children, the sick, and the elderly.[42] This point is illustrated in White Acre's subplot, in which the banjo-playing slave Henry is decoyed away from his happy plantation home only to succumb to poverty and disease. When his incessant labor for the pious abolitionists of White Acre yields only religious tracts and cold indifference, the ailing Henry vows to return to Black Acre or die trying. Incapable of acquiring funds himself, Henry is saved by Bowery Boy Joe Grant, who, thriving in the very dog-eat-dog capitalist world that destroys Henry, kindly buys his ticket home.[43] In a stock scene from the plantation tradition, the "prodigal nigger," emaciated and prematurely aged, returns to the arms of his loving mother and his forgiving master and mistress.[44] Just as the depiction of Henry dramatizes black dependency, the sympathetic portrayal of the crass, striving Joe Grant illustrates the progress and citizenship attainable by working-class whites. Unlike George Fitzhugh, who took Southern elitists' logic to its extreme and advocated the extension of slaveholding paternalism to poor whites as well as blacks, Burwell depicts slavery as the cornerstone to a Herrenvolk democracy promoting white racial unity and egalitarianism.[45]

The greatest threat to that ideal society, Burwell implies, is the antislavery movement. Far from disinterested, benevolent reformers, Burwell's abolitionists are greedy, hypocritical Northerners who, envious of their Southern neighbors, have found in wage labor an efficient means of exploiting vulnerable blacks while shedding the responsibilities of paternalism. Burwell joins other Southern writers in locating the movement's power in an unholy alliance between incautious Northerners and interfering Britons.[46] In his allegory, the slave trade, having been initiated by Mr. Bull's spinster Aunt Lizzy, is continued by Bull as a compromise in his "long lawsuit with one Don Armado" (Spain).[47] Belatedly discovering the trade's unprofitability, Mr. Bull becomes "very thick all of a sudden with the White Acre people," assuring them (in a White Acre denizen's folksy paraphrase) that "the Black Acre people has no right to them black creatures, an' whoever tries it at law will find it so, only let them subpoeny me as a witness . . . and I'll prove it clear as a whistle."[48] Alluding to the Mansfield decision and Clarkson's parliamentary testimony, Burwell's novel joins the chorus of Southern voices protesting British abolitionism as a thinly disguised attempt to sabotage the prosperity and unity of the fledgling American nation.

That the military contests between Spain and England, or between England and the American colonies, should appear in the novel as lawsuits seems surprising, given the apparent Southern preference for alternative discursive models, particularly that of chivalric military contest. But *White Acre* parodies the Northern fondness for juridical rhetoric by turning *every* conflict into a lawsuit. Thus, the English Civil War becomes the "suit of 'the King against Oliver and others'"; the War of 1812 makes a brief appearance as Mr. Bull's failed "great appeal case"; and even the Louisiana Purchase is transacted as a desperate out-of-court settlement quickly followed by a case involving one Miss Houri—and which, like the Missouri Compromise, establishes precedent for subsequent sectional disputes between White Acre and Black Acre.[49] But if Burwell plays on the Northern fascination with litigation, he gives it a distinctly Southern accent: each of the cases mentioned pertains, in one way or another, to questions of property. And it is this property orientation that makes the trial between abolitionist White Acre and slaveholding Black Acre very different than the one imagined by Burwell's print antagonists.

A Joint-Stock Nigger

Seeking to redirect Southern energies toward literature, away from the honor code, political economy, and oratory, the Southern Literary Messenger insisted that the success of Uncle Tom's Cabin had demonstrated that American writers were living "in an age when the power of the pen exceeds that of the sword, purse and tongue."[50] Registering this state of affairs with its acute sendup of antislavery print tactics, Burwell's novel joins other fictional rejoinders to Stowe in calling attention to abolitionism's pervasive impact on American print culture. But whereas a sentimentalist like Caroline Lee Hentz put antislavery print agitation in the service of her romantic narrative—in The Planter's Northern Bride (1854), the titular bride's father is an abolitionist pamphleteer and editor of the Emancipator—Burwell's subplot of Henry's stint in White Acre as a fugitive slave lecturer reveals the potency of abolitionists' trademark brew of political agitation, print propaganda, and legal spectatorship while exposing ruthless exploitation of the slave as the reformers' secret ingredient.[51]

Print is indispensable to the power wielded by White Acre's most prominent activists. Initially, Henry's loyalty and complacent legal outsidership lead him to resist Sneakright's urgings that he burn down his master's house or, at the very least, steal his money ("dis chile aint gwine to de court house on dat account")—until Sneakright, a former colporteur, uses trite religious homilies to convince Henry to steal himself.[52] Once arrived in White Acre, Sneakright and Henry give a lecture to "the Wanderer's Welcome"—a pitch-perfect parody of an antislavery gathering.[53] If the meeting's organizer, dissenting minister Ananias Thistle, recalls the evangelicals who preached (and published) antislavery sermons, its most wealthy participant, factory owner Deacon Grubb, evokes the era's best-known capitalist philanthropists, Arthur Tappan and Lewis Tappan, who funded much of the early print campaign against slavery. The two women present, Mistress Keziah Clam and Miss Maria Mule, are caricatures of female writer-activists who, like Angelina Grimké and Lydia Maria Child, gained both influence and notoriety through their involvement in antebellum print culture. As a schoolteacher in Black Acre, Mistress

Clam "filled her portfolio with narratives, of everything she had ever heard of a painful or scandalous character," which "she exaggerated, for her own purposes."[54] Her younger counterpart, Mistress Mule, "editress of the Emancipator, the object of which was to liberate women and black people from servitude," addresses an audience of New England mill girls.[55] Whether through religious tracts, an antislavery factbook, or a reform journal, White Acre abolitionists deceitfully manipulate print culture for their own ends.

Not surprisingly, then, the reformers accomplish their exploitation of Henry by an elaborate textualization of his body. Initially sexual in nature, this exploitation moves into the realm of the economic. When an audience member urges "the colored brother" to "exhibit the certificate of his wrongs" by removing his clothing to reveal lacerated flesh, both the slave and his advocate are taken aback.[56] But whereas Henry is reluctant to disrobe "before all dese ladies," Sneakright, "looking upon Henry much in the light of a kangaroo, with whose physical care and moral culture he had been once entrusted as part of the personel of a managerie, caught readily at a suggestion so well calculated to excite popular interest," knowing "that this might be advantageously embodied in a descriptive pamphlet, and with an essay upon the tortures to which the blacks were subjected, would add much to the value of his enterprise."[57] Displaying a disappointing lack of marks on his chest and back, Henry obligingly bares shins full of cuts and scars ("a faithful record of all the injuries he had ever inflicted upon himself, by sleeping in imprudent proximity to the fire, or by falling over logs in hunting or other nocturnal excursions"), which the audience members gaze upon, fondle, and eulogize.[58] Disclosing Burwell's own anxieties about interracial sexuality and doubts about black humanity, the scene's shrewd satire of the reformers' fetishization of black corporal suffering suggests that the sensational provocation of such attitudes could resonate with white audiences regardless of sectional affiliation or political orientation.[59]

Henry's experiences in White Acre recall Frederick Douglass's account of his own early encounters with the antislavery movement, when a white abolitionist like William Lloyd Garrison or John A. Collins would take the former slave "as his text" or introduce the black man as a "graduate from the peculiar institution . . . *with* [his] *diploma written on* [his] *back!*"[60] Sneakright's "enterprising" calculations end up literalizing the phenomenon described by Douglass. Here such abolitionist intervention represents not altruistic advocacy on behalf of the slave but a cynical capitalist exploitation of the spectacularized black body through the medium of a sensationalist mass print culture. Upon the success of the Wanderer's Welcome meeting, Sneakright plans a traveling exhibition in which "Henry was, without his knowledge or consent, parcelled out amongst various stockholders who advanced the money necessary for his clothing and other expenses, with the agreement on the part of Sneakright to divide the profits of his exhibition."[61] Incapable of autonomous agency, Henry must be owned by *someone*: thus, his escape from Black Acre to White Acre, from a slave section to a free one, merely means that "from having been the property of one man, Henry had unconsciously become 'a joint stock nigger.'"[62] Such, Burwell implies, will be the fate of *any* African American no longer sheltered by the benevolent paternalism of Southern slavery from ruthless commodification under Northern corporate capitalism.[63]

Presenting the antislavery movement as a joint-stock company in which those with ties to evangelical Christianity, industrial capitalism, and reform publishing invest in the fugitive slave as a potentially profitable spectacle, Burwell emphasizes the role of print in attracting popular interest to the cause. After a few rehearsals, Sneakright travels from town to town, exhibiting Henry as the "Mutilated Fugitive," much as the scheming Brainard does with the similarly disfigured ex-slave Vulcan in The Planter's Northern Bride.[64] Anticipating the wily print tactics of the Duke and the King in The Adventures of Huckleberry Finn (1884), Sneakright's "method was to post handbills in every village, headed in large capitals, 'The Bloody Deeds of Black Acre!'"[65] Also like Twain's antebellum hucksters, Sneakright understands that, along with its capacity for labor and its status as ready capital, the value of the slave's body resides in its figurative representation. Emblazoned with "a wood cut" portraying "two white men beating a black one with clubs, whilst a third was marking his ears like those of a pig," the handbill features "a succinct narrative of Henry's birth, raising and rescue" and provides additional "engravings illustrative of every principal event"; the whole is "bordered with handcuffs with cowskin whips crossed at intervals."[66] Recalling the decorative chain borders of abolitionist pamphlets and the lurid woodcuts gracing publications like the Anti-Slavery Record, Sneakright's handbills address nonliterate as well as literate readers by combining an inflammatory written text with eye-catching illustrations and symbolically freighted iconography—which cohere through the abject black body at their center.[67]

Highlighting the indispensability of print to the construction and promotion of the brutalized slave as spectacle, White Acre vs. Black Acre also registers the extent to which the interpretation of that spectacle was shaped by rhetorical appeals to popular legal consciousness. In his role as advocate, Sneakright introduces and frames the former slave's testimony, assuring his audience, "You will now hear from an eye and ear witness, A narrative of

Enormities without a parallel in the annals of human iniquity."[68] Comparing tyrannous Black Acre with "the time-worn types of treachery and crime"—the Borgias, Nero, and Indian "Savages"—Sneakright insists that "all these have been ministers of mercy in comparison with the bloody—the inhuman—the *barbarious* treatment of their fellow creatures, by those who now disgrace the neighboring farm of Black Acre, by their abominable enormities."[69] (At this point in the lecture, "Henry was trained to tuck down his head and blubber audibly.")[70] But even as it retains the familiar juridical forms and rhetoric of abolitionist lectures, Burwell's satire dramatically revises their meanings. Rather than a well-meaning reformer, Sneakright is exposed as a Barnumesque humbug whose sensational print publication and sentimental performance are motivated by greed masquerading as disinterested benevolence. Further, with Sneakright's own criminality established through his incriminating account of his underground activities in Black Acre ("He had, upon his own testimony, been guilty of ingratitude, lying, theft, burglary, counterfeiting the current coin, and subornation of murder and arson"), his hyperbolic identification of that section with "the time-worn types of treachery and crime" is exposed as a transparent attempt to project his own guilt onto innocent slaveholders.[71] Likewise, Henry's narrative, rather than testifying to Southern brutality and African American humanity, merely affirms black dependency: throughout the scene Henry is either silent, ventriloquized by Sneakright, or made to behave like a "trained" animal.

Yet, rhetorically powerful as the white advocate's argument may be, the slave's evidence steals the show. The lecture reaches its climax when, in order to provide "proofs" of Black Acre's fabled "barbarity," "the fugitive stripped off his upper garment, to display what was generally called 'The Black Scene.'"[72] Sneakright, "profiting by the suggestions of his first exhibition, had manufactured out of harness leather, an exact representation of a roughly scarified surface, with various letters and figures branded thereon," which he "neatly secured to the natural skin by an adhesive substance, and lightly anointed with what the tanners call 'dubbin,' to resemble the adjoining surface."[73] Literally taking Henry for his text, Sneakright compensates for the missing physical evidence of slaveholding violence by turning the fugitive's back into a blank slate upon which to inscribe his own gothic antislavery fiction.[74] In the process, the abolitionist charlatan accomplishes the racial oppression he ascribes to Henry's slaveholding master: affirming the persistent identification of blacks with animals by conjoining brown skin and tanned leather, Sneakright exerts control over Henry's body with the same harness leather that keeps horses and other draft animals in trace.

Even as it lampoons abolitionists' exploitative use of print tactics and legal rhetoric to sensationalize black suffering, however, Burwell's bizarre "Black Scene" puts Henry's body in the service of its own proslavery agenda. Historian Eugene D. Genovese has suggested that in the antebellum period constituents of the two sections conceptualized slavery and freedom in profoundly different terms: whereas white Southerners sought to distinguish labor as a social relation from the economic relations of the free market, Northerners, regardless of political affiliation or racial identity, "understood freedom as absolute property in oneself—as the logical opposite of personal servitude."[75] In Burwell's novel, Henry literally embodies each of these views in turn. As a Black Acre slave, Henry has a "stout," "dark and slick" physique that is marred only by its clumsily self-inflicted cuts and scrapes; his body thus articulates the salutary reciprocity of innate black vulnerability and conscientious white paternalism.[76] Although the exposure of Henry's unmarked chest upon his arrival in White Acre suggests Locke's tabula rasa, Henry does not attain the possessive individualism that will enable him to enter as an equal into bourgeois civil society and its capitalist market economy.[77] Instead, the fugitive's body is artificially inscribed with a fiction of slaveholding brutality when Sneakright covers Henry's chest with a false history that misrepresents him as—and thereby converts him into—an object of property.[78] Elaborating on "The Black Scene," Sneakright informs his White Acre audience that "every man has his different figures and letters branded" on his slaves "jest as you have different letters and pictures on your snuff boxes, to know them from anybody else's."[79] Pointing to the series of initials branded into Henry's false skin, Sneakright explains that "every time [slaves] pass from hand to hand, they always marks them just as you endorse a note of hand."[80] It is in Sneakright's hands, though, not those of his master, that Henry is reduced to commodity status; for, like his conversion from the private (and protected) "property of one man" into "a joint stock nigger," Henry's transformation from contented slave into the "Mutilated Fugitive" indicates the beginning, rather than the end, of his economic exploitation by whites.

Crucially, that exploitation is mediated by textuality. In contrast to Henry's Black Acre master, who appropriates the fruits of his slaves' bodily labor in order to fund a system of mutually beneficial social relations, Henry's White Acre sponsors not only appropriate but exhaust the slave's body, turning it into a text whose circulation generates profit. As the comparison of Henry to both snuff boxes and multiply endorsed bills of hand suggests, in the mass print culture that epitomizes the White Acre's industrialized economy, the textualized slave body, with its inscribed history, becomes at once commodity and currency in a dizzying round of capitalist exchange. For just as the "diploma" on Frederick Douglass's back would draw audiences to abolitionist meetings where his *Narrative* would be sold, thus yielding greater income for antislavery organizations and attracting larger audiences to future meetings, the mass-produced handbills reproducing Henry's body and its fictionalized "narrative" draw paying audiences to "The Black Scene." The joint-stock company that invests in Henry speculates on the profitability of the textualized black body as spectacle, indifferent to the fate of the actual fugitive—who eventually sickens and dies. Dramatizing a familiar political economic argument in favor of proslavery paternalism, *White Acre*'s contribution is to demonstrate how the antislavery movement itself participated in—and profited from —an exploitative capitalist market economy in which the industrialization of print enabled the commodification of formerly enslaved African Americans as spectacles for mass consumption.[81]

A Case at Law

Burwell's novel derives its title from terms used in legal hypotheticals to differentiate between parcels of land in property disputes.[82] Of course, the terms "white acre" and "black acre," which may have originally referred to crops on the various pieces of land, take on distinctly racial associations in the novel: "as it was known that those who had parted with their blacks were for the suit, and those who had not were against it," the case "was always spoken of" as *White Acre vs. Black Acre*.[83] Nevertheless, the terms' origin in property litigation highlights the discrepancy between the allegorical case at law imagined by Burwell and that conjured by Northern abolitionists.

As we have seen, through their persistent use of juridical rhetoric, antislavery writers imagined the slavery debate as an adversarial trial to be adjudicated by the American reading public. Appealing to and cultivating popular legal consciousness, they sought to censure the perpetrators and abettors of slaveholding villainy in the court of public opinion and to make a case for criminalizing bondage under American law even as they presented forward-looking alternative models of race and justice in American culture. Imagining the trial as a specifically *criminal* proceeding enabled abolitionists not only to adopt adversarial procedure, admit the testimony of victimized blacks, and authorize white advocacy on behalf of the slave but, crucially, to define slavery as a "violation of the *public rights* and duties due to the whole community."[84] In his satire of the abolitionists' case, however, Burwell rejects the premise of the abolitionists' proceedings by depicting the suit as a civil rather than a criminal injury.

Brought "to set aside the title of the holders of Black Acre to the black creatures which had been bought from Mr. Bull and the White Acre family" and thus to achieve "an unconditional decree of emancipation," White Acre's suit on behalf of the blacks also seeks damages "for a sum equal to the value of [the blacks'] services and that of [their] several ancestors . . . from the earliest day of their bondage until the present."[85] As a writ *in detinue* brought by "Sneakright, who sues as the guardian and next friend of Mandingo and others against Careless and others," White Acre's case resembles the civil suit for freedom.[86] In the freedom suit, a ward claiming to be wrongfully enslaved procured a guardian to challenge the defendant's claim to a property right in him or her, with the object of obtaining emancipation as well as any damages.[87] Not unlike the case imagined by abolitionists, in such suits sympathetic whites intervened against iniquitous slaveholders on behalf of victimized blacks to prove the injustice of their enslavement and to accomplish their emancipation. From the abolitionist perspective, however, the freedom suit offered an inadequate model for the slavery debate in that it treated involuntary servitude as a civil rather than criminal injury—as "merely an infringement or privation of the civil rights which belong to individuals considered merely in their individual capacity."[88] Articulating his defense of slavery in the juridical idiom of the North but recasting the dispute as a civil rather than a criminal proceeding, Burwell affirmed the Southern view that slavery was ultimately a private rather than public concern. This deft shift from a criminal to a civil framework entailed corresponding adjustments at every level in the imaginary case presented to the public, from the motives ascribed to the participants to their assigned roles in the proceedings. For just as abolitionists marshaled the projective powers of narrative and metaphor to envision an alternative American legal regime, Burwell presents a radically different vision of race, law, and nation in his proslavery allegory.

White Acre vs. Black Acre's titular lawsuit originates in a conspiracy between out-of-favor overseer Eleazar Doubletrack and the perpetually unemployed Christopher Rant to expropriate Black Acre land from its rightful owners: the two reason that, deprived of their slaves, the citizens of Black Acre "would then be obliged to sell their farm or let it out to be farmed by others."[89] As Rant points out, the beauty of the plan lies in the opportunity it creates simultaneously to defraud Black Acre inhabitants of their property and to exploit the labor of their slaves. To Doubletrack's objection that the blacks are too poor "to hire lawyers, pay witnesses, or even get time to attend court," his co-conspirator cunningly replies, "*We'll do it for them, and they will work it out at our own wages afterwards!*"[90] So conceived, the lawsuit represents the disruptive incursion of capitalism (with its disgruntled white wage laborers and its insatiable need for land) into the mutually beneficial master-slave relations of patriarchal Black Acre—with the inevitable results of elite white dispossession and black oppression.

The ensuing trial, much like Sneakright's traveling exhibition, is more lucrative performance than sincere reform effort. Having established white advocacy as merely a pretext for black exploitation, Doubletrack and Rant quietly fade into the background, prompting "many advocates" to appear on the scene and assert "the rights of the black creatures."[91] Ultimately, the Black Acre slaves are represented by "the Clam-Thistle party," the same joint-stock company of evangelical, print, and industrial interests that finds in Henry such a profitable investment as the "Mutilated Fugitive."[92] And just as Henry's inscribed body articulates a powerful antislavery fiction in the court of public opinion, the ensemble worn by antislavery authoress Keziah Clam on the first day of the eponymous trial becomes an abolitionist text to be decoded by the spectators who pack the courtroom: "Her bonnet was modelled after the Helvœtsluys, the Dutch galliot which . . . brought the ancestors of her clients to these shores. Her cape was scollopped to resemble the outline of the coast of Africa from which they came. Her gown was figured with manacles in sprigs, a chain border in festoons, supported by handcuffs at intervals. Everything she wore was black to denote a spirit mourning for the wrongs of suffering humanity, and . . . her handkerchief was marked with a vignette, representing a colored person flying from his tormentors, who pursued him as the Furies did Orestes."[93] Reading between the seams, onlookers may discern not genuine concern for "the wrongs of suffering humanity" but, rather, a fashionable if grotesque fetishization of black suffering itself. (Indeed, Mistress Clam could have purchased her accessories at the retail establishment of Arthur Tappan and Lewis Tappan, which sold "silk prints depicting 'The Poor Slave,' in four poses, suitable" for use as "a purse covering or lamp mat.")[94] With Widow Clam's outfit, as with Sneakright's handbill, Burwell vividly parodies the excesses of an abolitionist material culture in which mass-produced representations of African American misery—on handkerchiefs, sugar bowls, and stationery and other household items—became decorative accessories in the bourgeois culture of sentiment.

The odd comparison of the fugitive slave on Widow Clam's handkerchief to Orestes seemingly acknowledges abolitionist calls to replace the personal, retributive patriarchalism of plantation justice with the public, formal due process of the jury trial.[95] But whereas abolitionists like Garrison drew on popular concerns about both the integrity of the trial by jury and the justice of

American slave law in order to place the question of slavery before a jury of the people, Burwell implies that indifference, incompetence, and bias keep the proceedings from being a genuine trial *per patriam*. Thanks to Widow Clam's intrusive involvement, the voir dire yields "twelve forlorn individuals whose business and opinions were of so little importance that they could be taken as impartial umpires of the business of others."[96] Rather than disappointed or outraged by their exclusion from the jury, the more respectable and influential members of the community "gladly withdrew, having thereby escaped confinement upon a long and exciting trial."[97] In this way, the novel distinguishes legitimate civic responsibility from the clamorous legal spectatorship that, during the trial itself, will require "sheriffs, tipstaffs, and other officers" to preserve "order with incessant activity."[98] In contrast to impassioned abolitionist efforts to place the crime of slavery before an adjudicative reading public, Burwell's novel presents the proceedings as a burden on a public either unsympathetic to the case at hand or unqualified to try that case.

Like the excluded jurors—and consistent with Southern denial of black civic agency—the slaves of Black Acre perceive the lawsuit as an undue imposition. When informed of the lawsuit, Old Mandingo, the African slave whose name appears first on the docket, becomes "very angry," whereas "the other blacks manifested much alarm at the unusual proceedings."[99] A few, like Henry, have unrealistic notions of both freedom and oppression, but most are outraged that someone is trying to separate them from their master. After this brief scene and in keeping with the routine exclusion of blacks as witnesses in freedom suits (frequently deplored by abolitionist commentators), the Black Acre slaves remain peripheral to the proceedings conducted in their name—and to the novel itself.[100]

Like its contented slaves, Black Acre's Careless family, with its careworn plantation-mistress mother, benevolent patriarch father, capricious belles, and young cavaliers, seem to have stepped out of the pages of a plantation novel. When the case comes to trial, Squire Careless meets the affront with aristocratic Southern dignity: "Dressed with great plainness, in the product of his own estate," the old squire wears his "gray hair . . . combed back from his honest face," chewing "his own tobacco with as much composure as if he were anything but the malefactor represented by the Clam-Thistle party."[101] Having served as a justice of the peace in his own community, Squire Careless sustains an honorable commitment to law and order, offering an instructive contrast to the Clam-Thistle party's sensationalism: "He had instructed his lawyers to tell the court that he wanted no advantage of law over the blacks. If they were not his property he did not want them, if they were his, he intended to hold them against the world, cost what it would."[102] Pointedly rejecting abolitionist attempts to incriminate the slaveholder, Burwell implies that the old Squire alone sees the case for what it is, a question of property rights to be adjudicated by a neutral legal system.

The abolitionists, slaves, and slaveholders in White Acre vs. Black Acre display pointedly different motives than those usually assigned to each of these groups in the case conjured by abolitionist print propaganda. Moreover, unlike that imagined trial, in which defiant testifying slaves and their sympathetic white advocates faced brutal, avaricious slaveholders at the bar of public opinion, White Acre vs. Black Acre places the reluctant slave plaintiffs, their meddlesome abolitionist guardians, and their much-maligned masters on the margins of the proceedings. Instead, the trial is dominated by opposing teams of lawyers who present competing narratives of American society and its origins.

In his opening statement, White Acre's corrupt Counsellor Whale presents a patently false tale of slavery's arrival in Black Acre. By Whale's account, in 1620 the plaintiffs' ancestors, "being bad sailors, and in great stress of weather, put into a certain port within his majesty's colonial dominions, asking help and subsistence; nothing more"; in this fictional narrative of black victimhood and white villainy, the "helpless" blacks are "reduced to bondage," a "condition they have long striven to escape," while "the proceeds of their labor has been taken to the use of the defendants, their persons held in chains and durance."[103] Indeed, if not for "the philanthropic intervention of a friend of humanity . . . the plaintiffs might have labored without reward or relief 'until Shiloh comes.'"[104] Counsellor Whale follows this questionable statement of facts with a closing argument, based on "the canons of natural law," that the slaves are free, as men and as the equals of all other men.[105] As evidence, White Acre's attorney produces with great flourish "a yellow parchment roll" that is "written in very glossy ink" and features Black Acre's signatures, to great sensation in the courtroom.[106]

Advised by the ailing but venerable Counsellor Cobweb (John C. Calhoun) and Counsellor Compromise (Henry Clay), Black Acre's defense team receives unexpected assistance from White Acre's own esteemed Counsellor Broadview (Daniel Webster). Outrage at Counsellor Whale's closing gambit leads Broadview to abandon his neutral posture and intervene on Black Acre's behalf—recalling, of course, Webster's dramatic contributions to the Great Triumvirate's Union-saving efforts in the Compromise of 1850. Appealing to inductive rather than deductive logic, Broadview argues against the precept of equality on the basis of human diversity, emphasizing the subordinate role of women and children in society. Broadview goes on to argue for the civic equality of those who enter into a social contract together. "But," Broadview asks, anticipating *Dred Scott*, "does this, gentlemen, admit others who were not partners in the contributions to this organization, to an equal participation in its administration, because, forsooth, they were born equal?"[107] Of course not, for if this were the case, "then the Mussulman, or the Hottentot, or the Hindoo may intervene, and upon the exhibition of the certificate of birth, which existence bestows upon all, may claim an equal voice in any form of human association."[108] Having established the civic exclusion of blacks (among others) as the grounds of their inequality, Broadview concludes with an appeal to White Acre to ignore the slavery question and to accept the lawsuit's dismissal in the interest of a harmonious, profitable union.

Following the example of his abolitionist adversaries, Burwell finds in the trope of the trial not only a convenient framework for presenting his case but also the ideal stage on which to model the very civic relations advocated therein. Just as the abolitionists' imaginary trial offered a pattern for African American civic inclusion based on a morally inflected, rights-based understanding of natural law, Burwell's proceedings also exemplify the society they invoke. Pushing nonwhites, women, and radicals to the margins, Burwell's trial is argued by white male legal professionals whose involvement in the case is simultaneously motivated and authorized by the property interests that guarantee their civic equality.[109] And because Burwell figures the trial in question as a civil rather than a criminal suit, even a verdict for the plaintiffs (however unjust) would not ultimately disrupt the status quo, for any awarded damages, the reader is repeatedly assured, would serve to enrich the citizens of White Acre—not to enfranchise the slaves of Black Acre.

Barratry, Champerty, and Maintenance

And, in fact, the novel *does* conclude with a verdict for the plaintiffs—thanks to a sleight of authorial hand that transforms the long-suffering slaveholders of Black Acre from falsely accused defendants into self-righteous plaintiffs in a last-minute criminal proceeding against the scheming abolitionists of White Acre.

The novel's climax occurs when Black Acre's Counsellor Flash exposes "a conspiracy to defraud these defendants."[110] Specifically, he charges "that there has been not only Barratry" on the part of White Acre's Counsellor Whale "but that the plaintiff, Sneakright, with his confederates, Keziah Clam, and Ananias Thistle have been guilty of champerty and maintenance."[111] In other words, despite claims to "have got up this suit in the name of charity," the White Acre abolitionists initiated the suit "in reality [so] that they may receive a part of the recovery to which the nominal plaintiffs may be entitled under the verdict"; furthermore, Flash alleges "that it is their design to deport and carry away into a *quasi* bondage, in another land, the deluded creatures whom they pretend to deliver from slavery in this."[112]

Whereas abolitionist print propaganda sought further to enhance the legal literacy it assumed its readers possessed, Burwell's recourse to obfuscating legal jargon suggests that his target audience was limited to those Southern gentlemen whose libraries *DeBow's* thought would benefit from inclusion of his novel among other elite "Works relating to Slavery and the South."[113] Although the novel does not define or elaborate the crimes with which the abolitionists are charged, a clear understanding of these terms is imperative to an appreciation of *White Acre vs. Black Acre*'s satire of both the antislavery movement and the juridical model it imposed on the print controversy. The crime of barratry is "vexatious incitement to litigation," especially through the solicitation of legal clients, whereas champerty, an "agreement between a stranger to a lawsuit and a litigant by which the stranger pursues the litigant's claim as consideration for receiving part of any judgment proceeds," is similar to maintenance—"meddling in someone else's litigation."[114] Significantly, a champertor has an economic investment in the case in question, having purchased "an interest in the thing in dispute, with the object of maintaining and taking part in the litigation."[115] By accusing the White Acre abolitionists of barratry, champerty, and maintenance, then, Counsellor Flash accuses them of much more than fraud, or knowingly misrepresenting the facts in the case; he accuses them, in effect, of intruding in a matter that does not concern them (and from which they seek to profit) by inciting the Black Acre slaves to engage in pointless and burdensome litigation. The novel thus rejects not only the authenticity of African American testimony against slavery and the authority of white abolitionist advocacy on behalf of the slave but also the very legitimacy of the case currently before the court of public opinion, suggesting that it amounts to nothing more than criminal harassment of the innocent South by the litigious North.

The twists and turns by which this reversal is accomplished in the novel are too labyrinthine to trace here. It bears noting, however, that the substitution of a criminal suit against abolitionists for the civil suit against slaveholders occurs when the reconciled fugitive Henry silently appears in court bearing incriminating documents compiled by Bowery Boy Joe Grant, who, in "exposing a nefarious conspiracy," seeks to "restor[e] again the peace of the community, by showing how much hypocrisy and lucre had to do with the sanctimonious profession" of the White Acre abolitionists.[116] Threatened by greedy, interfering reformers, the precious union of White Acre and Black Acre is thus preserved through a combination of Squire Careless's honorable defense of his property rights, doughface Joe Grant's timely action against his section's dangerous radicals, and Henry's obedient labor. As a result of their concerted efforts, not only is Black Acre cleared of all wrongdoing, but the court calls for the indictment of the White Acre abolitionists on the above charges. Not content with reducing the abolitionists' case against slaveholders to a civil proceeding concerned with private-property rights rather than the natural rights of citizens or even with rejecting that case as an undue imposition on the public, Burwell concludes his allegory with a countersuit casting abolitionists as the real culprits in the case before the popular tribunal.

Like the voluminous print ephemera on law and slavery, and the better-known antislavery classics by Frederick Douglass and Harriet Beecher Stowe, White Acre vs. Black Acre illustrates how thoroughly popular legal consciousness permeated print representations of the peculiar institution in the antebellum period. Indeed, by retaining abolitionists' appeal to legal spectatorship even as he parodied their tendency to portray the slavery debate as a criminal trial, Burwell demonstrated how worn the antislavery movement's legal language and imagery had become over twenty-five years of constant use.

Also like his literary abolitionist counterparts, Burwell registered profound unease with the tropological terms by which he entered the print controversy over slavery by offering yet another revision of the established trial trope. Adapting the abolitionists' legal idiom to his own proslavery purposes, Burwell portrayed slavery as a benevolent custodial institution beneficial to master and slave alike, an institution that, when threatened by a dangerous conspiracy of British interventionists, greedy corporate capitalists, disgruntled wage laborers, scribbling women, deluded fugitive slaves, and hypocritical radicals, should be defended by a coalition of Southern slaveholders and Northern whites in the interest of preserving the Union. By depicting the case before the court of public opinion as a civil rather than a criminal suit, Burwell rejected Northern efforts to cast slavery as a crime against God and man, even as, by leveling the counteraccusation of barratry, champerty, and maintenance, he suggested that the case against slaveholders should be dismissed altogether as the product of a criminal abolitionist conspiracy—recalling the strategies of his antiabolitionist predecessors in the 1830s.

But, in a final twist, by making his "great lawsuit" between a free Northern and a slaveholding Southern section only the latest in a series of lawsuits allegorizing historic military conflicts in Anglo-American history—from the

Spanish Armada and the English Civil War to the American Revolution and the War of 1812 — Burwell effectively supplanted the long-standing metaphorical identification between the slavery debate and the adversarial criminal trial with a metonymic association that linked the print debate, through the figure of the lawsuit, with war. In 1856, when *White Acre vs. Black Acre* was published, the great lawsuit of the novel's subtitle, unlike most of the other cases portrayed in Burwell's proslavery allegory, had no military referent. That would change very soon.

CONCLUSION

ALL DONE BROWN AT LAST
Illustrating Harpers Ferry

The puff in *DeBow's Review* praising William Mac-Creary Burwell's *White Acre vs. Black Acre* as an "admirable burlesque" indicates that in the mid-1850s renewed allegations of a criminal abolitionist conspiracy were as likely to prompt mirth as fear, even in the South. A mere three years later, however, such charges would be terrifyingly vindicated for many Southerners by John Brown's attack on the federal arsenal at Harpers Ferry, Virginia.[1] The prospect of a white-led, armed slave rebellion was devastating enough, but sectional paranoia heightened when Virginia Governor Henry A. Wise's investigation turned up a cache of incriminating letters between Brown and prominent abolitionists, including Frederick Douglass and the "Secret Six," a group of Northern reformers who financed Brown's deadly expedition.[2]

Some Americans, though, could still poke fun at the situation: early in its extensive coverage of the raid, *Frank Leslie's Illustrated Newspaper* ran an editorial cartoon titled, "The Way in Which Fred. Douglass Fights Wise of Virginia" (fig. 7).[3] The sketch features Douglass en route to Canada, with a trunk on his shoulder, his feet flying. The title's pun is clarified by the caption, which quotes a letter from Douglass to the *Rochester Democrat and American*, in which he explained his decision to leave the United States (where he risked indictment on treason charges) for a lecture tour of Great Britain via Canada.[4] Alluding to his celebrity as a fugitive slave, he quipped, "I have always been more distinguished for running than fighting."[5]

Clearly patterned on the iconic runaway (half-naked, frozen in space with a cloth bundle over one shoulder), the cartoon featured a stout, well-dressed Douglass burdened with an equally solid trunk—more anxious luminary than shivering fugitive.[6] This Douglass is a fugitive from justice, not from service. Strapped to the trunk is an umbrella, recalling Douglass's familiarity with England, where in 1845–46, he had consolidated his fame and received the funds to purchase his freedom. (More subtly, the umbrella offers a benign contrast

Figure 7. "The Way in Which Fred. Douglass Fights Wise of Virginia," *Frank Leslie's Illustrated Newspaper*, 12 November 1859, 382. (Courtesy American Antiquarian Society)

to the thousand pikes John Brown famously planned to distribute to Virginia slaves.) As one shoe flies off in his haste, a stray letter floats in the breeze behind Douglass, recalling at once his missive to the Rochester newspaper and his incriminating correspondence with Brown. The detail ironically suggests that if for the young bondsman literacy had been "the pathway from slavery to freedom," the adult Douglass's political writing had effectively reversed that journey, turning the freeman back into a fugitive.[7]

The cartoon appeared in *Frank Leslie's* at the height of tensions over the Brown case. John Brown, backed by an interracial force of twenty-one armed supporters, had begun his raid on slaveholding Virginia on 16 October 1859; two days later he had been captured by U.S. Marines; exactly a week afterward the severely wounded Brown was carried to court on a cot for his preliminary hearing; and eight days after that, he was sentenced to death, convicted of treason, murder, and conspiracy with slaves to rebel. (His surviving captured co-conspirators were subsequently tried and received death sentences as well.) Published in early November, a month before Brown's scheduled 2 December hanging, the cartoon deftly appeals to the political sensibilities of the illustrated weekly's increasingly divided national readership.[8] On the one hand, Douglass's guilty yet comical flight appears to substantiate slaveholders' allegations of an abolitionist conspiracy even as it ratifies the *Dred Scott* decision's exclusion of blacks from honorable citizenship.[9] On the other hand, the need for the former fugitive to flee U.S. borders a second time seemingly affirms the persistent abolitionist complaint that American ideals of freedom were more easily attainable in monarchical England than in the slaveholding republic. Susceptible of being read in different ways by different sectional and political constituencies, the cartoon in this sense resembles John Brown's raid itself. For however ineffectual the actual invasion may have been in liberating slaves or fomenting insurrection, the raid quickly became a powerful weapon in the political battles leading up to the Civil War. Far from united in their responses to Harpers Ferry, some Northerners sought to distance themselves from Brown by criticizing his actions and holding Union meetings, whereas others seized the chance to transform "Ossawattamie Brown," Kansas frontier renegade, into "Old Brown," abolitionist martyr. Despite this intrasectional dissension, Southerners tended to emphasize sympathetic Northern responses to Brown in order to authorize increasingly widespread calls for secession.[10] As scholars have noted, Harpers Ferry also marked a turning point *within* antebellum abolitionist discourse, as the moral suasionist, nonresistant "age of sentimentality" metamorphosed into a militaristic "age of heroism," or, alternatively, as abolitionist sympathy for the slave transformed itself into calls for national sacrifice on behalf of the union.[11]

Crucially, for our purposes, it was not so much the bloody battles around the arsenal but the tense trials of Brown and his co-conspirators that attracted national attention, as *Frank Leslie's* lavish coverage so vividly documents. Analysis of that coverage thus provides a fitting end to this study of popular legal consciousness in the print debate over slavery. Reporting more extensively on the crisis than other periodicals, *Frank* Leslie's published ninety-three separate illustrations of the raid and its aftermath over the fall and winter of 1859, reprinting thirty of these in a special supplement.[12] Along with majestic tableaux depicting violent encounters between the insurgents and the authorities are numerous vignettes that portray the legal proceedings in meticulous detail. Images featuring key moments in the proceedings—a feeble Brown making his way from court to prison (fig. 8); wounded raider Aaron Stevens's court appearance; and co-conspirators John E. Cook, Edwin Coppoc, Shields Green, and John Copeland hearing their death sentences pronounced—are accompanied by renderings of less dramatic subjects, from a view of the Charlestown courthouse and the cannon outside that building (fig. 8), right down to the "Sleeping Room of the Jury" (fig. 9).[13] The legal proceedings receive their most abundant treatment, however, in the outsized, four-page sup-

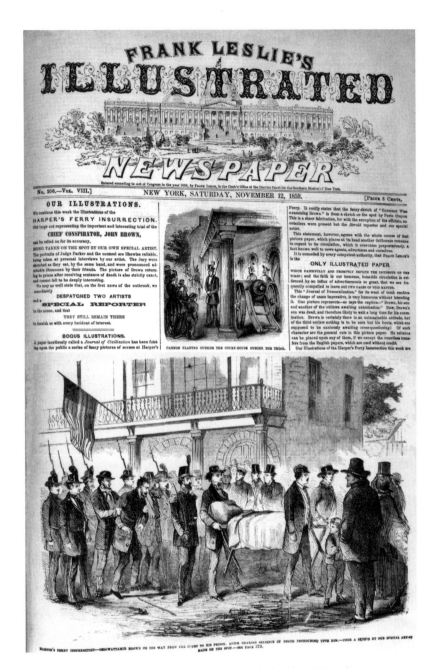

Figure 8. "Cannon Planted outside the Court-House during the Trial" and "Ossawattamie Brown on His Way from the Court to His Prison, after Hearing Sentence of Death Pronounced upon Him," *Frank Leslie's Illustrated Newspaper*, 12 November 1859, 367. (Courtesy American Antiquarian Society)

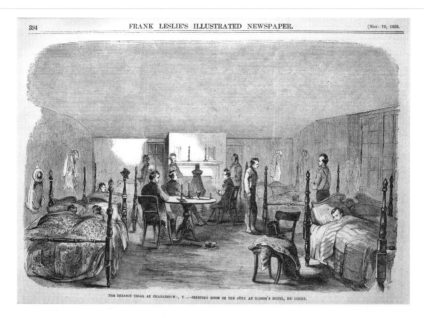

Figure 9. "Sleeping Room of the Jury at Gibson's Hotel, Belmount," *Frank Leslie's Illustrated Newspaper*, 19 November 1859, 394. (Courtesy American Antiquarian Society)

plement offering a "Pictorial History of the Harper's Ferry Insurrection" that appeared soon after Brown's hanging. Dominating the supplement's inside pages is a fourteen-by-twenty-inch engraving of the "Trial of Ossawattamie Brown," featuring a "View of the Courtroom during the Trial, with Accurate Portraits of the Presiding Judge, the Twelve Jurymen, the Counsel for the Prisoner and the Prosecution, and Brown, as He Reclined on His Couch" (fig. 10). The engraving had already been printed as a two-page foldout in the 12 November issue, where it was followed by individual "Portraits of the Judge, Counsel and Jurors," comprising seventeen cuts labeled with each participant's name (fig. 11).[14] In a magazine that had previously devoted eleven illustrations to humorously depicting "The Way a Criminal Trial is Conducted," fascination with the adversarial process ensured that the portraits of the trial participants would also resurface in the "Pictorial History."[15]

As this extravagant coverage literally illustrates, Harpers Ferry stood as the culmination of three decades of antebellum legal spectatorship over slavery. In his influential reading of the case, critic Robert Ferguson suggests that "suddenly, in Brown's trial, the context of the exchange" over slavery "was neither occasional and consensual nor loosely political, but officially adversarial," with "the rigor of legal rules" directing "formal scrutiny" toward

Conclusion   203

Figure 10. "View of the Courtroom during the Trial, with Accurate Portraits of the
Presiding Judge, the Twelve Jurymen, the Counsel for the Prisoner and Prosecution,

and Brown, as He Reclined on His Couch," *Frank Leslie's Illustrated Newspaper,*
12 November 1859, 374–75. (Courtesy American Antiquarian Society)

The Trial of Old Brown—Portraits of the Judge, Counsel and Jurors.—From Sketches made by our Special Artist.

JOHN C. WILTSHIRE.

THOMAS WATSON, JR.

JACOB J. MILLER.

HARPER'S FERRY INSURRECTION.

In our second edition of last week we gave the close of the trial of John Brown for treason and murder. We now recapitulate some of the particulars to make our narrative complete. On the last

random was not proving a murder. It will be seen, therefore, that the defence was based upon legal quibbles, and did not grapple with the crime itself, the act of commencing a civil war and inciting the slaves to insurrection.

Mr. Hunter, for the prosecution, replied, and argued that he had

after listening to the rendition of the verdict, laid down very composedly without saying a word.

There was no demonstration of any kind whatever.

Mr. Harding then announced that he was ready to proceed with the trial of Coppic, who was then brought in. The ceremony of passing him in between files of armed men was dispensed with

GEORGE W. BOYER.

WILLIAM A. MARTIN.

RICHARD TIMBERLAKE.

day of his trial the prisoner was brought in and laid on his couch as usual. He looked much better than the day previous, and seemed to be at the most perfect ease of mind.

The jurors having all answered to their names, Mr. Griswold made

proved to the satisfaction of every rational mind every count in the indictment. During the delivery of both these speeches, the prisoner remained with his eyes closed, and laid as though fast asleep on his cot.

At the conclusion of Mr. Hunter's speech the jury retired to con-

Coppic took his seat between Messrs. Griswold and Hoyt, who appeared as his counsel. He appeared calm and composed. The remainder of the day was occupied in endeavouring to obtain a jury, but the panel was not complete at five o'clock, when the Court adjourned.

GEORGE W. TAPP.

ISAAC HUST.

JOHN C. M'CLURE.

the opening speech for the defence. He argued that never having sworn allegiance to the State of Virginia, he could not commit treason. That with regard to the charge of murder, it had not been proved that he had shot any one, for proving the act of shooting at

sider their verdict. During their recess the utmost silence prevailed. At the end of half an hour the jury returned, and amid the most intense excitement rendered their verdict of Guilty on all the three indictments of inciting the slaves to revolt, of treason and of murder. The prisoner sat up in bed when the jury entered, and

The seventh day commenced by Mr. Griswold stating the points on which an arrest of judgment was asked in Brown's case. In addition to the reasons mentioned yesterday, he said it had not been proved beyond a doubt that he (Brown) was even a citizen of the United States, and argued that treason could not be committed against a State, but only against the General Government, citing the

THOMAS COCHRAN.

JOSEPH MYERS.

WILLIAM HIGHTODALE.

Figure 11. "Portraits of the Judge, Counsel and Jurors" and "Carrying the Prisoners from the Armory to the Railroad Station, En Route to Charlestown, Va.,

for Trial," *Frank Leslie's Illustrated Newspaper*, 12 November 1859, 378–79.
(Courtesy American Antiquarian Society)

"issues of universal rights and protection of property," thereby making "duty to conscience" versus "obedience to law" a matter of "prolonged debate."[16] But rather than inaugurating the phenomenon Ferguson so astutely describes, John Brown's trial represented its climax. As we have seen, dating back to William Lloyd Garrison's first antislavery speech, persistent concerns about trial by jury and freedom of the press ensured that abolitionist attempts to pattern the slavery debate on the adversarial criminal trial would resonate powerfully in antebellum print culture. Over and over again, from Garrison's libel trial in 1830 to the fugitive slave cases of the 1850s, when atrocious judges and a compromised due process failed to offer justice in the court of law, abolitionists had turned to the printer's case to gain a hearing before the court of public opinion. Coming two years after Dred Scott's affirmation of African American civic exclusion and the supremacy of a proslavery judiciary, John Brown's trial capped the series of urgent confrontations between slavery and law that only intensified after the Compromise of 1850.

Read in this context, print coverage of Harpers Ferry's legal aftermath reveals the increasingly apparent limitations of the adversarial trial as a model for the slavery debate. As Ferguson and others have observed, both Brown and the Virginia authorities used the closely watched trial for their own political purposes. By persistently disrupting trial procedures, Brown called attention to the larger injustice of slavery, whereas by assiduously observing the forms of due process, the Virginia authorities effectively sidestepped the question of justice altogether.[17] Not surprisingly, then, even as Northern reformers exploited the trial's tremendous propaganda value, some displayed a mounting willingness to question what Wendell Phillips would come to term "servility" to legal form.[18] The apparent incommensurability of justice with American law, combined with the exhaustion of the movement's own juridical trope (as evidenced by its susceptibility to Southern parody), marked an endpoint to the rhetorical power of abolitionists' appeals to popular legal consciousness —and acknowledged the seeming inevitability of Brown's military approach. As the last and the most stirring of the era's sensational courtroom dramas, Harpers Ferry demonstrated the ultimate futility of law or print in providing a peaceful resolution to the national crisis; with Brown's trial and execution in late 1859, it became evident that the civil liberties of white citizens simply could not coexist with, much less be plied to challenge, the bondage of African Americans.

That such disillusionment extended beyond the antislavery movement is indicated by the fact that Frank Leslie's Illustrated Newspaper, with its broad national audience and its antiabolitionist, pro-Union editorial posture, manifested strikingly similar doubts about the integrity of legal forms in a slave-holding nation. These doubts surface most clearly in the politically charged cartoons and engravings that subtly provide a countertext to the paper's moderate editorial commentary. In this alternative visual account of Harpers Ferry, summary Southern "justice" threatens to destroy the civil liberties of not merely enslaved blacks but free white citizens as well. Like Douglass, the pictorial countertext suggests, Northerners had to decide whether to run from or fight with a South in which justice may have had form but no substance.

A Servility to Forms

Scholars of Harpers Ferry have emphasized how John Brown, manipulating legal procedure in the courtroom and public perception outside of it, collaborated with his Northern colleagues to turn his trial into one of the most effective propaganda tools ever wielded by the antislavery movement.[19] Astutely gauging the anxieties that lay behind the national passion for legal spectatorship, Brown from the beginning raised doubts about the ability of the slaveholding South (and Virginia in particular) to provide a fair trial to the man who had instantly become the North's most infamous abolitionist.

Events before Brown's capture justified such doubts. Only the timely intervention of a local physician saved African American raider John Copeland from being lynched. Brown's son-in-law Will Thompson wasn't so fortunate. Captured and taken to the Wager House Hotel, Thompson received a reprieve when a local tavern keeper's daughter "threw herself before him" and, in the testimony of one of Thompson's lynchers, "begged us to leave him to the laws."[20] His life ended soon afterward, however, when his assailants dragged him to a bridge and dropped him into the water below with a "dozen or more balls . . . buried in him."[21] The challenge facing the Virginia authorities was to guard Brown and the state's other prisoners from Southern mobs and Northern rescuers alike while proving to the nation that the rushed trial was more than just a dressed-up lynching.

The enfeebled condition of the state's first two defendants made keeping up the appearance of due process particularly difficult. Severely wounded, Brown and fellow raider Aaron Stevens were frequently pictured with the cots on which they reclined throughout the proceedings.[22] From his first courtroom speech, during the preliminary hearing in which he and Stevens were too ill to stand without assistance, Brown seized the opportunity to call the court's legitimacy into question. "I did not ask for any quarter at the time I was taken. I did not ask to have my life spared," the veteran Kansas warrior reminded his audience; he implied, however, that the rules of engagement gave way to the rule of law when, upon his capture, "the Governor of the State of Virginia tendered me his assurance that I should have a fair trial."[23] Governor Wise's promise notwithstanding, Brown concluded that "under no circumstances whatever, will I be able to have a fair trial," citing his ill health and initial lack of access to counsel.[24] Foregrounding his own heroic vulnerability, Brown called into question Virginia's commitment to due process. "If you seek my blood, you can have it any moment, without this mockery of a trial," he admonished the court.[25] "But," he urged, "if we are to be forced with a mere form—a trial for execution—you might spare yourselves that trouble. I am ready for my fate. I do not ask a trial. I beg for no mockery of a trial—no insult—nothing but that which conscience gives, or cowardice would drive you to practise."[26] Embedded in those final words was the core issue: would the South's civic "conscience," already compromised by the section's tolerance for human bondage, ensure Brown a fair trial? Or would its "cowardice," abundantly evident from its storied brutality, lead it merely to "practise" judicial forms without endowing them with substance? Brown affirmed the latter conclusion through apophasis. Artlessly claiming, "I do not even know what the special design of this examination is. I do not know what is to be the benefit of it to the Commonwealth," Brown asked simply "that I may not be foolishly insulted, only as cowardly barbarians insult those who fall into their power."[27] In a brilliant preemptive move, Brown's earliest printed courtroom speech used Virginia's ostentatious legal decorum against the state (and, by extension, the Slave Power) to expose the proceedings as a show trial gotten up by "cowardly barbarians" intent on screening their undemocratic "power" with the forms of due process.[28]

At trial one of Brown's lawyers, Ohioan Hiram Griswold, repeated this theme in a more tempered Northern voice.[29] Claiming "no sympathy whatever with any man who could be guilty of such an offence as is charged here," Griswold further maintained on behalf of his section "that there is no sentiment in the North in accordance with that of the defendant."[30] When Griswold echoed Brown's concerns about Virginia's ability to give Brown a fair trial, then, he spoke as one committed to pragmatically preserving, not idealistically destroying, the union between the free and the slave states. In his opening statement, Griswold addressed the jury directly, posing the loaded question, "Gentlemen, what is meant by a fair trial?"[31] Answering the query himself, he implied that the jury would collude with the state to provide Brown with only the *appearance* of due process. "It is not that the mere forms of law should be invoked," he chided the Charlestown jury, reminding them that in order to ensure Brown a fair trial, "every principle of law and justice shall be made available, and every particle of evidence introduced by himself or the State shall get its fair weight and consideration in his behalf."[32] Without such substantive justice, he warned, legal forms "may be used merely to conceal, for the time being, the gallows that looms behind."[33] When, six weeks later, a hooded Brown stood with the noose around his neck, he seemed to validate his lawyer's suspicion that Virginia's legal decorum was "but the pathway to the scaffold."[34]

Although quite aware of the trial's "out-door effect and influence," special prosecutor Andrew Hunter did little to strengthen Northern faith in the legitimacy of the proceedings.[35] Insisting that "not only have the forms of a fair trial been extended to the prisoner, but the substance also," Hunter clumsily took up Griswold's gauntlet, awkwardly adding that Brown had received due process "in the midst of all temptations to the contrary" and in particular the very strong temptation of "declaring martial law and administering drum-head justice."[36] Far from assuaging Northern doubts, Hunter's assertions seemed only to verify the defense's persistent claims that the strained forms of due process only masked the Virginia authorities' preference for summary justice.

That Hunter's comments, along with those of Brown and Griswold, would reach an "out-door" audience was unquestionable; by late 1859, courthouse walls had become more permeable than ever. As Ferguson has noted, due to the introduction of the cylindrical steam press, the telegraph, the railroad, and mass-circulation daily newspapers, "Brown's trial became the first event in American history to receive intense and daily multimedia coverage."[37] Augmenting ongoing press coverage of the cases were the inevitable trial transcripts: curious readers could choose among the anonymous Life, Trial, and Execution of Capt. John Brown (1859), Thomas Drew's John Brown Invasion: An Authentic History of the Harper's Ferry Tragedy with Full Details of the Capture, Trial, and Execution of the Invaders (1860), and James Redpath's authoritative Public Life of Captain John Brown (1860), which featured chapters on "The Preliminary Examination," "Judicial Alacrity," "State Evidence," "The Defence," and "Lawyers' Pleas."[38] Such journalistic accounts were complemented by popular plays, songs, and poetry, as well as contributions from the nation's literati.[39] Lydia Maria Child garnered the highest sales of her long, prolific career when the AASS published a pamphlet reproducing her epistolary wrangles over Brown with Governor Wise and Margaretta J. Chew Mason (wife of Virginia senator James M. Mason).[40] As if on cue, Henry David Thoreau and Ralph Waldo

Emerson penned essays meditating on the case, while Child and John Green-leaf Whittier wrote elegies for Brown; far less predictably, Herman Melville and Walt Whitman also wrote poems inspired by Harpers Ferry.[41]

The almost macabre zeal with which his fellow activists exploited John Brown's martyrdom has been well documented.[42] But a telling passage from *The John Brown Invasion* reveals that abolitionists, after thirty years of cultivating legal spectatorship for antislavery purposes, had come to prioritize the propaganda value of such controversial trials over their legal significance. Commenting on Brown's trial, Drew interrupts a fairly conventional philippic against the corrupt Southern judiciary with a surprisingly transparent editorial aside: "It is certainly to be regretted, (though not in view of the progress of liberty, and of its ultimate early triumph,) that the executive and judicial authorities of Virginia proved themselves to be inadequate to the lofty, though difficult duty, of holding with even hands the reins of authority, surmounting the passions of the hour."[43] Regrettable as Brown's execution may have been, Drew implies, such rank injustice—when correctly publicized—actually accelerated "the progress of liberty" far more efficiently than a fair trial ever could have done. Drew's parentheses barely contain his delight in the public relations victory that the Virginia authorities had handed the antislavery movement with Brown's speedy conviction and execution.

But even as they converted Virginia's travesty of justice into an abolitionist triumph, some reformers found that John Brown's trial unexpectedly led them to question such perennial appeals to popular legal consciousness. John Brown "has taught us a great lesson," Wendell Phillips intoned in early November, for "he has released us from a servility to forms; he has taught us to pierce down to the essence of things."[44] Quoting the warrior himself, Emerson used remarkably similar language in his own "Remarks" on Harpers Ferry. Brown "did not believe in moral suasion, he believed in putting the thing through," the Sage of Concord told his Massachusetts audience, cutting off a burst of applause to continue, "He saw how deceptive the forms are."[45] As it had for so many other Northerners, John Brown's attack led both men to reassess abolitionist tactics, particularly moral suasion and nonresistance.[46] More subtly, however, the raid's instructive legal outcome also led thinkers as different as Phillips and Emerson to reconsider the prevalent rhetorical recourse to legal forms as a means of conceptualizing the slavery debate itself. Emerson expressed the disenchantment of his fellow Northerners when he mused in his speech, "We fancy, in Massachusetts, that we are free; yet it seems the government is quite unreliable. Great wealth, great population, men of talent in the executive, on the bench, — all the forms right, — and yet, life and freedom are not safe."[47] To appreciate the truth of this statement, he continued, one needed only to recall Boston's fugitive slave crisis, when "the honor of Massachusetts trailed in the dust, stained to all ages, once and again, by the ill-timed formalism of a venerable bench."[48] The problem lay in placing judicial procedure over justice: Northern citizens' lives and freedom were at risk precisely "because the judges rely on the forms, and do not, like John Brown, use their eyes to see the fact behind the forms."[49]

If legal form, and the adversarial structure of the criminal trial in particular, had once seemed ideally suited to expose the inhuman facts of slavery to an adjudicative American public, decades of manifestly unjust judicial decorum, culminating in Brown's trial, demonstrated the opposite. What John Brown had taught the North with his raid, but more especially with his trial, was that justice could not be found — and, thus, should not be sought — in judicial procedure. Neither in metaphor nor in reality could trial by jury protect civil liberties in a slaveholding nation; its forms could too easily be arrogated to proslavery forces, whether in a novel like Burwell's or a court like Virginia's.[50]

All Done Brown at Last

That John Brown's lesson reached a wider audience than the narrow constituencies of Phillips or Emerson is suggested by the coverage of Harpers Ferry in *Frank Leslie's Illustrated Newspaper*. In his study of the paper, social historian Joshua Brown finds that unlike *Harper's Weekly*, its highbrow competitor, *Frank Leslie's* cultivated a broad "'middle' readership, a vast and elastic range of readers that . . . stretched across the nation and into the territories, and extended from mechanics to merchants."[51] Thriving on the classic antebellum mixture of sensationalism, reform, and moral uplift, *Frank Leslie's*, which commenced publishing in late 1855 in New York, strove to maintain a neutral editorial stance throughout the escalating sectional conflict in order to sustain its hard-won national circulation.[52] Eventually, the paper would gain an even larger sectional readership through its exhaustive pictorial coverage of the Civil War, but its treatment of Harpers Ferry, unsurpassed by any other publication, represented a final sustained effort to appeal to a national public. Not surprisingly, then, reporting on Harpers Ferry in *Frank Leslie's* is riddled with the same contradictions and ambivalence that would persistently characterize its attempt to cover controversial news stories in Gilded Age America, a nation split along race, class, gender, and sectional lines. As Brown notes, these tensions often surfaced in the interstices between the paper's editorial and visual texts, where "sometimes tortured efforts to appease a divided readership" turned "illustrated journalism into a pictorial balancing act."[53]

If Frank Leslie's coverage of Harpers Ferry demonstrates the precariousness of that balancing act, the paper's treatment of the Dred Scott decision typified its cautious approach to the slavery crisis. In March 1857, Frank Leslie's published a portrait of "our venerable Chief-Justice," Roger B. Taney, acknowledging in the accompanying biography that he would be praised by "those who sympathise with the consequences of his decision" and "an object of dislike" to "those who censure it."[54] In a subsequent article, engravings of a dignified Dred Scott and his family illustrate editorial text that matter-of-factly summarizes the "principle points" in the Supreme Court decision even as it depicts the nation's most famous African American plaintiff as a minstrel-like legal naif, "laugh[ing] heartily when talking of 'de fuss dey make dar in Washington 'bout de old nigger.'"[55] The illustrated weekly's editorial policy seems clear: venerate the nation's institutions and their representatives (the Supreme Court, Taney), and trivialize those (slaves, abolitionists) who call their legitimacy into question.[56] That a similar policy governed coverage of Harpers Ferry was discernible from the first: reporting on "Wise's Interview with Brown," Frank Leslie's characterized "the miserable man," Brown, as a deluded "monomaniac" to whom the governor displayed "true Virginian courtesy" by tolerating Brown's criticism of slavery "with a sort of half-concealed regret that so much earnestness had been wasted in so bad a cause."[57]

Nowhere was the ambivalence of Frank Leslie's toward slavery more vividly dramatized than when, in the aftermath of Harpers Ferry, the paper itself became caught up in the events it was reporting. Exhaustively following the cases of John Brown and his co-conspirators in late 1859, Frank Leslie's briefly interrupted its coverage to report that the paper's artist, William S. L. Jewett, had been forced to leave Charlestown by a "special proclamation warning off strangers."[58] The print account of the artist's forced "absquatulation," when read alongside the paper's visual representations of Harpers Ferry and its legal sequel, suggests the extent to which even moderate Northerners had become concerned about the Slave Power's encroachment upon the civil liberties of white citizens, threatening not only due process but freedom of the press as well.

Contributing to the widespread editorial derision heaped on Southerners for their panicky response to Harpers Ferry, Frank Leslie's acknowledged local rumors that Jewett was "sketching the plan of the city, to enable the North to attack its weak points," only to conclude that "our artist found the 'weakest point' of the city in its over-sensitiveness."[59] "Mr. Jewett," the article avowed, "had no belligerent intentions; he did not design to surround the city, lay it under tribute, or carry Brown off on his triumphant and conquering shoulders"; quite the contrary, he had visited the Southern town "as a peaceable and well-ordered citizen in pursuit of his business" and as such "should not have been interfered with while in pursuit of his lawful occupation."[60] Committed to defending freedom of the press in the face of a distinctly Southern form of censorship, *Frank Leslie's* nevertheless sought to avoid exacerbating sectional tension. Thus, while the editorial "most strongly protest[ed] against the action of the Charlestown authorities," it expressed confidence "that the good sense of the entire South will sustain" that protest.[61] Making "every allowance for the existence of a fierce and feverish excitement," it nevertheless maintained that "the authorities should certainly have had sufficient self-reliance and cool judgment to distinguish between an artist, quietly following a line of duty inimical to no party, and a blustering demogogue whose mission is mischief."[62] *Frank Leslie's*, in other words, insisted that the Union could only be sustained if the members of both sections rose above local tensions: Northerners would distinguish the repressive "over-sensitiveness" of one Virginia town from "the good sense of the entire South" if, in turn, Southerners would prove that they could tell "a well-ordered" Northern "citizen" apart from a "blustering" abolitionist "demogogue."

In that very issue, however, appeared a cartoon that assigned a different moral to the same story. A three-panel sketch titled "The Retreat of Our Artist from Charlestown, Virginia" (fig. 12) commences with the lanky artist, knees obligingly bent, facing a porcine sheriff who stands tiptoe on a box, shouting and waving the proclamation in one hand and a pistol in the other.[63] Surrounded by an agitated, armed mob, the meek artist wields only an umbrella and a sketchbook. The caption reads, "The Virginia authorities, having come to the conclusion that our Artist is a dangerous character, invite him to absquatulate!"[64] The second sketch, bearing the caption "He takes the hint, and departs" depicts the artist running in the same direction as a Northbound train and a flock of Canadian geese.[65] The triptych ends with the artist's "arrival in New York," where he sits exhausted from his journey, slumped before a newsroom desk bearing an inkpot, blotter, and several books, his sketchpad and pen having fallen from his limp hand.[66]

Making light of Southern (or at least Virginian) "over-sensitiveness," the cartoon nevertheless highlights serious Northern anxieties about the threat posed by the Slave Power to American civil liberties. Like Brown, the artist finds himself confronted with Southern authorities whose hasty legal for-

Figure 12. "The Retreat of Our Artist from Charlestown, Virginia," *Frank Leslie's Illustrated Newspaper*, 26 November 1859, 414. (Courtesy American Antiquarian Society)

malities merely serve to legitimize a mob-driven summary justice that closely resembles lynching. The distinctly sectional nature of this repression is indicated not only by the artist's northward journey but also by the humorous vernacular demand that he "absquatulate." Contrary to the accompanying editorial, the sketch implies that when Southern "good sense" gives way to a dangerously repressive "over-sensitiveness," even the "well-ordered" Northern "citizen" may find himself in the same unenviable position as that of the "blustering demogogue."

Much of the visual humor of the cartoon lies in its freehand caricatures, which offer a marked contrast to the gravitas of the trademark engravings through which *Frank Leslie's* documented the Harpers Ferry crisis. With their panoramic views and their painstaking detail, the engravings visually asserted the authoritative neutrality mandated by the newspaper's Unionist editorial policy.[67] Unlike other visual texts in the late antebellum period, Joshua Brown notes, "wood engravings presented readers with pictorial narratives of events"—each one serving as "an elaborate normative diagram for their readers that helped make sense of the changing society surrounding them."[68] Thus, whereas in the cartoon of Jewett's "absquatulation," the narrative unfolds in three panels, it is only through careful scrutiny that a similar story about sectional concerns over civil liberties emerges from an engraving published the previous week.

Appearing a week after Brown's conviction, in the same issue as the Douglass cartoon discussed earlier, the engraving is titled "Carrying the Prisoners from the Armory to the Railroad Station, En Route to Charlestown, Va., for Trial" (fig. 11).[69] At the tableau's center is a wagon bearing the prone bodies of Brown and Stevens. Followed by two bound co-conspirators, the wagon is encircled by a uniformed guard wielding bayonets and swords who are in turn surrounded by a crowd of armed onlookers. Printed on the page facing the original portraits of the twelve jurors and below those of judge and counsel, the graphic at first seems anachronistic, depicting the prisoners "en route" to the trial that has already ended with their death sentences. A second look, however, reveals the engraving to be quite timely, for the image confirms that given the "fierce and feverish excitement" in Charlestown and the apparent Southern incapacity for "cool judgment," the prisoners' journey to their trial was all along a journey to the gallows.

Upholding the paper's Unionist sentiments, the cut sets stern but individualized U.S. troops against the blurred, anonymous faces of the mob, who hold aloft sticks, rifles, whips, and what appears to be one of Brown's confiscated spears. Yet, despite the officials' determination to maintain law and order, the prisoners' fate seems sealed. Resembling corpses in a funeral cortege, the insurgents' bodies pass under a tree, whose bare, outstretched limb evokes the gallows (and resonates with Emerson's notorious claim that Brown's death would "make the gallows glorious like the cross").[70] Tellingly, the wagon driver, who shares the mob's blunt physiognomy and shabby dress, looks backward while his whip, that icon of slaveholding brutality, points to a sign reading "Wager House." Referring by name to the combination hotel–railroad station from which Will Thompson had been dragged and killed, the sign, offering the only words in the image, stokes Northern fears about the South's perceived preference for the feudal code of honor over the republican rule of law.[71] It's a safe bet, the image seems to say, that the rushed trials of Brown and his followers under Judge Parker would end much as they would under Judge Lynch—in hanging.

If the engraving's restrained treatment of the Southern propensity for summary justice is thrown into relief by the subsequent cartoon of Jewett's confrontation with the bullying Charlestown sheriff, the sketch of the artist's "absquatulation" itself becomes more legible when read alongside the Douglass cartoon that opens this chapter. The triptych's second panel, featuring the artist's hasty sprint to New York, offers a whiteface version of Douglass's own journey north. When forced by Southern repression to choose between running and fighting, this visual echo hints, the white Northern citizen may find himself in a position disturbingly close to that of the black Southern slave. Like Douglass and other fugitives who followed the North Star (or, for that matter, Northbound trains), the artist escapes from tyrannical Southern "justice" to the safety of a free state.

More subtly, repeated visual cues unite the artist and Douglass as representatives of a Northern print culture in which, unlike the "fierce and feverish" South, divisive issues such as slavery are addressed through reasoned discussion rather than repressive mob violence. Whether the result of sheer coincidence or a printer's joke, the advertisements surrounding the Douglass cartoon are formatted so that the pistol featured in the ad for "Smith and Wesson's Seven-Shooter" points toward the black man's head, which is shielded only by the trunk with the umbrella on top. In the subsequent cartoon, the artist similarly faces the sheriff's leveled pistol armed only with an umbrella and a satchel—and a sketchbook. Like the desk, inkpot, blotter, and books that signal the artist's safe return to the North and like the envelope that floats in the air behind the fleeing Douglass, the artist's sketchbook represents print publication as an alternative to the Southern ultimatum of running or fighting. But also like Douglass's letter, the artist's sketchbook and pencil elude their owner's grasp. Has proslavery repression defeated freedom of the press as well as due process? Are Southern violence and censorship to be met only with Northern silence and passivity? The artist's dozing form, like the vacant editor's stool, says it all.

That we are not mistaken to read the humorous sketch as identifying the free white Northern citizen with the black Southern slave is confirmed by a third cartoon, published in the week intervening between the cartoons depicting Douglass's flight and that of the artist. In "The Irrepressible Conflict" (fig. 13), Virginia's Governor Wise stands at the left, pulling on lines attached to the necks of Republican politicians Joshua Giddings and William H. Seward (coiner of the titular phrase), antislavery *New York Tribune* editor Horace Greeley, and radical abolitionists Douglass and Gerrit Smith.[72] To the side stands erstwhile Brown collaborator and British soldier-of-fortune Colonel Hugh Forbes, with fencing foils and masks under one arm.[73] In the caption, Forbes, like the meddlesome Brits in Burwell's novel and other Southern propaganda, carelessly sows seeds of sectional discord, exhorting, "Pull Guv'ner

Figure 13. "The Irrepressible Conflict," *Frank Leslie's Illustrated Newspaper*, 19 November 1859, 398. (Courtesy American Antiquarian Society)

—pull niggers; I don't care which wins."[74] For his part, Governor Wise so-liloquizes, "I've got these fellows now on a string, and if I can only get 'em into Old Virginny, I'll fix 'em."[75] Among the Northerners, Giddings urges, "Hold fast, Brother Smith—if we hang, we'll all hang together"; Greeley de-spairs what will become of his "poor *Tribune*" when he's "a goner"; Douglass exclaims, "Oh, golly! I must slip out of this affair and run!"; and Smith cries, "We are all done Brown at last!"[76] Caricaturing the Northern abolitionists' fear of being charged and found guilty of criminal conspiracy with Brown, the caption maintains the newspaper's strategy of dismissing black agency as comic minstrelsy and white radicalism as embarrassing ultraism.

Here again, though, the tug-of-war between pro- and antislavery forces poses an implicit threat to the average white Northern citizen. Wise claims to hold the squirming Northerners "on a string," but in the cartoon, the twists in the rope resemble links in a chain. And although Douglass is the only African American in the picture, the onlooking Forbes addresses all the Northerners, black *and* white, as "niggers"—corroborating Smith's observation, "We're all done Brown at last." In the grips of the Slave Power, the image suggests, it is not just abolitionists like Brown but *all* white Northerners who have become,

Conclusion   **219**

effectively, as "brown" as Douglass and other African Americans whom race slavery and the recent *Dred Scott* decision have excluded from citizenship.

The cartoon's racial double entendre reveals the growing perception in the moderate North that the legal existence of slavery in the United States made it impossible to preserve for even white Northerners key civil liberties such as due process and freedom of the press. In a slaveholding republic, the trial and execution of John Brown had dramatized, all Americans would be "done Brown at last"—denied the civil liberties that had marked the tenuous boundary between white citizenship and black bondage. Instead of demarcating free American citizenship, race slavery threatened to trench upon it, rendering meaningless not only the concept of race itself (through the universal applicability of terms like "niggers" and "brown") but also of the republic's founding ideals, freedom and liberty. All done brown at last and faced with the irrepressible conflict between the North and the South, Northern citizens realized that neither print nor law could provide a solution to the slavery crisis. The foils in Colonel Forbes's hand, the armed mobs in Charlestown's streets, and the "Cannon Planted Outside the Court-House" all said as much.

If by late 1859, John Brown's trial had convinced Wendell Phillips and Ralph Waldo Emerson "how deceptive the forms" of law could be, the antislavery movement's decades of appropriating law's forms—and the language, imagery, roles, and procedures of the criminal courtroom in particular—had revealed the rhetorical power of such appeals to popular legal consciousness in an era of mass print legal spectatorship. Rejecting the criminalization of abolitionism and blacks alike in order to figure the slavery debate as a criminal trial, antislavery writers enlisted the projective capacities of metaphor and narrative to help their audiences imagine a United States in which African Americans—not human bondage—would have legal standing.

Framing the print controversy in these terms authorized testifying former slaves and their white advocates to gain a hearing at the bar of public opinion. Yet, the movement's most celebrated slave witness did not require Harpers Ferry to understand the dangers of what lawyer Phillips called "the servility to forms." Frederick Douglass's revised self-fashioning in the decade following the publication of his 1845 *Narrative* registered his growing awareness of the inadequacy of personal testimony to refute long-standing imputations of racial inferiority; only independent black advocacy, grounded in the firsthand experience of oppression, would demonstrate African Americans' ability to apprehend their rights. By the mid-1850s, Harriet Beecher Stowe, too, seemed to understand the constraints white advocacy placed on African American autonomy. But, unlike Douglass, Stowe faltered in her attempt to remold the antislavery movement's central metaphor to accommodate independent black speech and political action. For his part, Virginian William MacCreary Burwell proved only too adept at turning the trope's transformative potential to his own, proslavery, purposes. Recasting the abolitionists' imaginary trial as first a civil suit for freedom and then a criminal case in which Northern reformers are revealed as the true culprits, Burwell simultaneously rejected the South's assigned defensive posture, reasserted the Southern view of slavery as a sectional property issue, and projected a conservative social fantasy of unified white paternalism and silent black complacency. If Burwell's allegory demonstrated how pliant the figure of the trial had become as a model for the print controversy by 1856, John Brown's attack on the federal arsenal at Harpers Ferry three years later seemingly confirmed to Americans on both sides of the Mason-Dixon line the futility of print or legal solutions to the slavery crisis.

As these revisions to the trope indicate, however, the trial metaphor provided a conceptual vocabulary and corresponding set of images by which Americans holding different views of slavery could debate not merely the status of human bondage in the republic but also the related questions of social culpability, legal capacity, and civic belonging. At a time when Jacksonian politics and the industrialization of print made political debate seem chaotic and cacophonous, the abolitionists' juridical metaphor—much like the judge's gavel and the court clerk's summons—effectively called participants in the slavery debate to order by providing a set of roles and procedures that rendered the controversy intelligible while symbolically indicating its larger legal and cultural significance. Thus, when participants like Douglass, Stowe, and Burwell revised the defining roles and forms of the adversarial criminal trial, their very reevaluations of the trope served further to refine and clarify the case as it stood before the court of public opinion.

Further, at a time when judicial supremacy threatened popular constitutionalism and an apparently proslavery judiciary encroached on American civil liberties, those in the antislavery movement reasserted print as a viable, influential form of extralegal agitation. That print could remain such a powerful lever even after the decline of the rational-critical public sphere of the eighteenth century is suggested by the adaptability of nineteenth-century literary forms—the slave narrative, sentimental fiction, and the plantation novel—to the debate's guiding trial trope. Even if they could not put a stop to the individual decisions of atrocious judges, readers could nevertheless play an important role in adjudicating the ongoing case before the popular tribunal.

Along with ordering and assigning meaning to the slavery debate and contributing to the development of a diverse, activist American literature, the abolitionists' trial trope facilitated a radical reconceptualization of civic participation in America. By patterning their behavior on the personae of the criminal trial, those who approached the bar of public opinion challenged prevailing hierarchies of race, gender, class, and condition by modeling new forms of civic presence. Propertied white elites could now appear guilty of crimes ranging from the biblical manstealing to statutory offenses like battery, rape, and murder. Respectable women could be seen publicly advocating social justice. And African Americans could finally challenge their legal outsidership by exposing the danger that the crime of slavery posed to American society, thereby asserting their own human rights and demanding civic equality.

Troubled though it may have been, the practice of imagining the debate over slavery as a vast, ongoing trial had made antebellum print culture a forum for interracial collaboration while providing an alternative vision of race and justice under American law—at its most forward-looking, that still-elusive vision of full black civic inclusion.

NOTES

Abbreviations

AAS   American Antiquarian Society, Worcester, Mass.

MHS   Massachusetts Historical Society, Boston, Mass.

Introduction

1   References to "the American reading public," "Northern readers," and the like throughout this study are intended to be inclusive, given that in antebellum America "reading" could imply communal as well as individual encounters with texts, often involving the illiterate and the "semi-literate." See McHenry, *Forgotten*, 4–8, 10–14. The iconographic representations of slavery and the law that frame the current study serve as a reminder of the many points of entry by which such "readers" could access the print debate over slavery. On the target audiences of those on both sides of the slavery debate, see Wyatt-Brown, "Proslavery."

2   Douglass, *Narrative*, 30; Jacobs, *Incidents*, 2; Weld, *American Slavery*, 9.

3   Douglass, *My Bondage*, 367.

4   Thomas Auld qtd. in A. C. C. Thompson, "Narrative," 29.

5   A. C. C. Thompson, "To the Public."

6   Tocqueville, *Democracy*, 157.

7   Sewall qtd. in Abner C. Goodell Jr., "John Saffin," 85 (n. 3).

8   Saffin, *Brief and Candid Answer*. On the exchange, see Sidney Kaplan, "Samuel Sewall"; Towner, "Sewall-Saffin Dialogue"; Peterson, "Selling."

9   It remains unclear as to whether "the Negro" mentioned by Sewall in connection with his essay is the Adam Negro of Saffin's pamphlet. See Sidney Kaplan, "Samuel Sewall," 35–39. *Adam Negro's Tryall* is identified as the "first slave narrative" in Starling, *Slave Narrative*, 50. The citation, however, refers to the "Narrative" appended to Saffin's pamphlet as reproduced in Abner C. Goodell, "John Saffin," 103–12. See also Foster, *Witnessing*, 29–32; Andrews, *To Tell*, 19.

10   Saffin, *Brief and Candid Answer*, 105, 111 (emphasis omitted).

11   Ibid., 106.

12   Qtd. in Wise, *Heavens*, 182. On textual variants, see ibid., 185–91. For further discussion of the Mansfield decision and its impact, see Cover, *Justice*, 16–17, 87–88, 91; Hoare, *Memoirs*, 69–94.

13 See Hoare, *Memoirs*; Wise, *Heavens*.

14 On Sharp's informal legal training, see Hoare, *Memoirs*, 37. On the extent of Sharp's legal influence, see Wise, *Heavens*, 33, 57; Hoare, *Memoirs*, 76.

15 Benezet, *Some Historical*.

16 Wiecek, *Sources*, 28–45.

17 See Oldfield, *Popular*, 90.

18 [Clarkson], *Substance and Abstract*. Oldfield estimates that 10,000 copies of the *Abstract* were printed, roughly a third of which appeared in a widely circulated "cheap edition." (See Oldfield, *Popular*, 77).

19 See Hochschild, *Bury*, 133–34. For instances of indirect inclusion of African and slave perspectives, see [Clarkson], *Abstract*, 19–21, 26, 29, 31.

20 Cugoano's narrative prefaces his philosophical and economic treatise. See Cugoano, *Thoughts*, 12–18.

21 The works referred to are Newton's *Thoughts upon the African Slave Trade* (1788) and Falconbridge's *Account of the Slave Trade on the Coast of Africa* (1788). On Newton, see Marcus Wood, *Slavery*, 23–53.

22 Mather, *Tremenda*. See Slotkin, "Narratives," 17. Unlike other Puritan "discourses," usually published in print runs of one hundred to five hundred copies, execution sermons sold by the thousands; Daniel A. Cohen, *Pillars*, 6. On the European genealogy of early American crime literature, see ibid., 41–58. On Jacobean chapbooks, see Langbein, *Prosecuting*, 45–54. On early American gallows literature, see also Bosco, "Lectures"; Towner, "True Confessions"; McDade, *Annals*; Daniel E. Williams, *Pillars*; Daniel A. Cohen, "Social Injustice."

23 See Halttunen, *Murder*; Daniel A. Cohen, *Pillars*; Daniel E. Williams, *Pillars*.

24 See Masur, *Rites*, 93–116.

25 Richard S. Newman, *Transformation*. See also Cover, *Justice*, 160, 161.

26 Ferguson, *Law and Letters*. See also Daniel A. Cohen, *Pillars*, 192, 245. For a broader account of nineteenth-century law and literature, see Thomas, *Cross-Examinations*.

27 Richard S. Newman, *Transformation*, 23; Cover, *Justice*, 159–60.

28 Richard S. Newman, *Transformation*, 29, 30.

29 Ibid., 27. See also Cover, *Justice*, 160.
   Because the ideological use of litigation and the corresponding turn to legal rhetoric that arose in the 1830s were not unique to any one abolitionist organization or approach during the antebellum period, I do not emphasize the schisms within immediatist abolitionism or the differences within antislavery tactics (including different understandings and uses of law) except when necessary. Indeed, as Pease and Pease note, if the most enduring division in goals and strategies may have been that between African American and white abolitionists, "like many white abolitionists, most blacks readily changed affiliation and techniques of action as occasion demanded"; accordingly, "to attempt to type individuals or groups, except at a particular moment, is to impose a stasis and structure which, with rare exceptions, existed in neither white nor black abolitionism"; Pease and Pease, *They*, 281. The focus on the speeches and writing of Garrison and Douglass orients the current study more toward Garrisonian abolitionism, perhaps, but, as the examples in this

and subsequent chapters illustrate, equally significant were the publishing efforts of evangelicals Theodore Dwight Weld and the Tappans; the legal arguments of radical constitutionalists William Goodell, Lysander Spooner, and the later Douglass; the legislative strategies of political abolitionists like William H. Seward and Joshua Giddings; and the individual contributions of largely unaffiliated figures like Thoreau, Stowe, and John Brown. In addition to Pease and Pease, classic accounts of the antebellum antislavery movement are Barnes, *Antislavery Impulse*; Dumond, *Antislavery Origins*; Quarles, *Black Abolitionists*; Kraditor, *Means*; Wyatt-Brown, *Lewis Tappan*; Stewart, *Holy Warriors*; Abzug, *Passionate Liberator*. On the various legal tactics of abolitionist factions, see Cover, *Justice*, 149–93.

30 Richard S. Newman, *Transformation*, 26.

31 Ibid., 87. On the construction of African American identity through rhetorical engagements with American print culture, see Rael, *Black Identity*.

32 "To Our Patrons."

33 See Pease and Pease, *They*, 113–19.

34 Daniel A. Cohen, *Pillars*, 192. On the Cornell murder case, see Halttunen, *Murder*, 72, 89, 229; DeWaard, "Indelicate." On the Jewett case, see Patricia Cline Cohen, *Helen Jewett*; Anthony, "Helen Jewett"; Tucher, *Froth*. On the rise of the penny press, see [Pray], *Memoirs*; Mott, *American Journalism*; Schiller, *Objectivity*; Papke, *Framing*; Baldasty, *Commercialization*.

35 Patricia Cline Cohen, *Helen Jewett*, 302, 303.

36 Barber, *History*; Von Frank, *Trials*, 173. The Moyamensing register is in the Chester County Historical Society. My thanks to Phillip Lapsansky of the Library Company of Philadelphia for calling this document to my attention and to Diane Rofini and Pam Powell of the Chester County Historical Society for their assistance.

37 On Rogers, see Srebnick, *Mysterious*.

38 Grossberg, *Judgment*, 169.

39 On Partridge and other instances that "reveal how publicity opened the once-closed decision-making processes of conservative institutions to public scrutiny," see Appleby, *Inheriting*, 36–40. On the D'Hauteville case, see Grossberg, *Judgment*.

40 On the constitutional debate over slavery, see Wiecek, *Sources*. See also Wiecek, "Latimer"; Cover, *Justice*, 131–58; Cover, "Nomos," 133–38. On antislavery constitutionalism in nineteenth-century American literature, see Crane, *Race*. On the legislative struggles over slavery, see Fehrenbacher, *Dred Scott*, 74–208; Freehling, *Road*. On the Gag Rule, see William Lee Miller, *Arguing*; Zaeske, *Signatures*.

41 On the rise of legal literature, see Surrency, "Law Reports" and "Beginnings."

42 Grossberg, *Judgment*, 228. "Unlike precedents of legal rules," Grossberg explains, "such cases enter the collective memory as common references for both laypeople and lawyers to construct legal claims, conceive legal relationships, and constitute legal identities"; 227–28. Further, "as social dramas playing out the fundamental conflicts of an era, [such] cases . . . are prime illustrations of the power of legal authority in American society," revealing that law's meaning "is determined by a complex interaction between the relatively autonomous internal rules and practices of the legal system and the press of external beliefs, concerns, and commitments

on that system" (ibid., 234). On trial pamphlets as an important form of decisional literature for a professional legal readership, see Surrency, "Law Reports," 52–53.

43 Cover, *Justice*, 161.

44 See also Samuel Warner, *Authentic*. The Southampton revolt led to the slavery debate in the Virginia legislature, which in turn saw the publication of Thomas R. Dew's classic proslavery polemic, *Review of the Debate in the Virginia Legislature of 1831–32* (1832). For comprehensive overviews incorporating documentary material, see Greenberg, *Confessions*; Tragle, *Southampton*. For a literary critical approach, see Mary Kemp Davis, *Nat Turner*.

45 See Finkelman, *Slavery in the Courtroom*, 138–43; Mayer, *All on Fire*, 145–49, 171–73, 185. On the *Unionist*, see May, *Recollections*, 64–65.

46 Cover, *Justice*, 108. For a discussion of the cases' legal implications, see ibid., 108–16. On *Amistad* pamphlet literature, see Finkelman, *Slavery in the Courtroom*, 222–39. On print treatments of both cases, see Sale, *Slumbering*, 58–145. See also Thomas, *Cross-Examinations*, 102–5, and Sundquist, *To Wake*, 115–21, 175–82.

47 Finkelman, *Slavery in the Courtroom*, 29.

48 Ibid., 60–64.

49 Ibid., 64–68. See also Wiecek, "Latimer."

50 Unattributed quotation, "The Latimer Journal," Scrapbooks, Papers Related to the George Latimer Case, 1842–88, Bowditch Papers, MHS. See also Bowditch, *Proceedings*.

51 [Chandler], "Latimer" (the attribution to Chandler appears in Wiecek, "Latimer," 229 [n. 24]); Pierpont, *Discourse*; [Mann], *Virginia Philosopher*.

52 On the rescue of Jerry McHenry, see Finkelman, *Slavery in the Courtroom*, 103–7; on African American initiative in such courtroom rescues as a counterpart to white-dominated legal activism, see Pease and Pease, *They*, 206–32.

53 Finkelman, *Slavery in the Courtroom*, 123–27. See also Cheek and Cheek, *Langston*, 316–48; Langston, *Virginia Plantation*, 182–90.

54 Slaughter, *Bloody*, x, ix.

55 See Von Frank, *Trials*.

56 Prior to Toni Morrison's *Beloved* (1987), at least two abolitionist novels arose from the case: M'Keehan, *Liberty*, and [Jolliffe], *Chattanooga*. It is unclear whether Jolliffe had completed his first antislavery novel, *Belle Scott* (1856), also centered on a slave case, before his involvement in the Garner case. See Weisenburger, *Modern Medea*.

57 On Dred Scott, see Ehrlich, *No Rights*; Fehrenbacher, *Dred Scott*. On John Brown, see Oates, *Purge*; Finkelman, *His Soul*; Ferguson, "Story"; Nudelman, "Blood"; Reynolds, *John Brown*.

58 Robert J. Brent to E. Louis Lowe, 4 Dec. 1851, qtd. in Slaughter, *Bloody*, 133.

59 *North American*, 1 Dec. 1851, qtd. in ibid., 132.

60 Ibid., 120.

61 Cover divides this literature into eight categories: legal compendia on slavery; legal arguments on specific topics; treatments of the Constitution vis-à-vis slavery; "literature on legal obligation and civil disobedience"; sermons on legal issues involving slavery; academic, philosophical, and religious treatises on the same; "diatribes

against legal institutions or judges for their evil, class-ridden oppression of the downtrodden"; and trial reports. Not included in this list but also acknowledged by Cover are literary abolitionist works that address legal issues; Cover, *Justice*, 149–50.

62 Mellen, *Habeas Corpus*.

63 Ibid.

64 Ibid.

65 Stroud, *Sketch*, 1827; William Goodell, *American Slave Code*; Cobb, *Inquiry*; Hurd, *Law*; Wheeler, *Treatise*. See also Bunsen, *Law*, an excerpt from his *Hippolytus and His Age* (1854). For analysis of the former treatises, see Accomando, *Regulations*, 116–22, 164–69. On antebellum legal publishing, see Surrency, "Law Reports" and "Beginnings"; Hoeflich, "John Livingston."

66 Stroud, *Sketch*, 1856; Stroud, *Ein Abriss*; Stroud, *Southern*. See also Edward M. Davis, *Extracts*; Whipple, *Family Relation*.

67 John P. Jewett, Advertisement.

68 Wheeler, *Treatise*, n.p.

69 Hurd, *Law*, 1:v.

70 Hurd, *Topics*, iii, iv.

71 Child, *Appeal*, 36–71; Douglass, *Papers*, 2:12, 265; William Wells Brown, *Narrative*, 96; Stowe, *Key*, 67–123; Stowe, *Dred*, 571.

72 Douglass, *My Bondage*, 367; Douglass, "Letter."

73 Cain, *Selections*, 91.

74 McManus, *Law and Liberty*, 21–37.

75 Dayton, *Women*, 11.

76 It is important, however, not to overstate these somewhat artificial distinctions. See Friedman, *History*, 74–75.

77 McManus continues that "most of the developments that transformed Puritan law into the criminal law of today occurred after 1760, when the law's basic function shifted from the defense of morality to the protection of property" (McManus, *Law and Liberty*, 180).

78 Howe, *Garden*, 11.

79 For a brilliant extension of Howe's discussion of the First Amendment, see Gordon, "Blasphemy."

80 On evangelicalism and reform, see Perry Miller, *Life*, 84; Barnes, *Antislavery Impulse*; Douglas, *Feminization*; Abzug, *Cosmos*, 161.

81 Finney qtd. in Perry Miller, *Life*, 32. See also Finney, *Memoirs*, 86; Hambrick-Stowe, *Charles G. Finney*, 4, 8, 19, 35–36.

82 Antebellum higher-law thought could range from "absolutist and more conventionally religious conceptions of higher law as God's will revealed, which were offered both in defense and condemnation of slavery" to far more subtle "conceptions of American law as interplay of conscience (moral inspiration) and consent (political dialogue), which produces a plausibly universal moral consensus about the terms of justice and citizenship" (Crane, *Race*, 6). For higher-law thought in the context of Jacksonian views of law, see Kohl, *Politics*, 145–85.

83 Crosby, "Anthony." Despite Crosby's mistaken exclusion of Woolman, his discus-

sion of the importance of factual accounts provided by travel literature vis-à-vis the empiricist values of moral-sense philosophy and the corresponding development of antislavery rhetoric remains valuable. See Woolman, *Considerations*, 57, 65–70, 73, 75–76; Benezet, *Observations*, 3, 8; Benezet, *Caution*, 22; Benezet, *Some Historical*, 122–23.

84 Clark, "Sacred," 467. See also Oldfield, *Popular*, 126. On this shift in the British context, see Baucom, *Specters*, 173–305. On higher law, morally inspired narrative, and legal change, see Crane, *Race*, 12–86. On the influence of Romantic versus Enlightenment views in shaping nineteenth-century American attitudes about race and law, see Suggs, *Whispered*. The slave narrative's affinity (and perhaps indebtedness) to the Washingtonian temperance narrative bears noting here. For contemporary comparisons, see Lampe, *Frederick Douglass*, 61, 66.

85 Clark, "Sacred," 467. See also Fisher, *Hard Facts*, 104–14. On the inseparability of witnessing and spectatorship, empathy and exploitation, see Hartman, *Scenes*, 17–23.

86 According to Lakoff and Johnson, different metaphors often work together to convey or reveal diverse aspects of one concept and thus "jointly provide a coherent understanding of the concept as a whole." Such overlap characterizes figurative constructions of slavery. Antebellum Americans did not always or exclusively figure slavery in juridical terms, as a crime. They often marshaled militaristic or revolutionary rhetoric to depict it as an act of war or tyranny; even more frequently, they summoned religious or moral language to portray it as a sin. Rather than a kind of rhetorical sloppiness or incoherence, this shifting of registers should be read to indicate how each of these alternative tropes overlapped with the juridical metaphor. To depict slaveholding as tyranny, for example, was to place master and slave in antagonistic roles parallel to the adversarial positions of the defendant and the plaintiff in a criminal trial. And to imagine slavery as a sin was to draw on the early American legal understanding of crime as a moral transgression entailing both civic censure and divine judgment. The many instances when Douglass, Garrison, Stowe, and others mingle religious, juridical, and revolutionary rhetorics in their treatments of slavery offer examples of what Lakoff and Johnson call "permissible mixed metaphors"—a combining of metaphors that, although inconsistent, is nonetheless coherent (Lakoff and Johnson, *Metaphors*, 89, 96).

87 Weld, *American Slavery*, 7–8. Published anonymously by the AASS Executive Committee, the volume "sold one hundred thousand copies in its first year" of publication (ibid., 1–2). In Marcus Wood's cogent phrasing, the factbook "combines nineteenth-century legal language and evidential procedure with the rhetorical conventions of Protestant martyrology" (*Blind Memory*, 84).

88 Weld, *American Slavery*, 8.

89 William Wells Brown, *Narrative*, 25–26.

90 Sewall, *Selling of Joseph*, 9; Woolman, *Considerations*, 76–77; Benezet, *Observations*, 10. "And he that stealeth a man, and selleth him, or if he be found in his hand, he shall surely be put to death" (Exod. 21:16).

91 On antislavery "Bible politics," see Mailloux, *Reception*, 75–102.

92 Holthouse, *New Law Dictionary*, 139–40.

93 Wilson, *Works*, 1:528.

94 Ibid., 529.

95 On the criminal trial's public nature, see Gewirtz, "Victims," 149–58; Felman, *Juridical*, 81; Ferguson, "Story," 55.

96 Of the slave cases in which Sharp participated, only that of Thomas Lewis appears to have involved a slave bringing a criminal suit against his erstwhile master. See Hoare, *Memoirs*, 52–61; Wise, *Heavens*, 59–67, 81–110. Sharp's frustration with the flawed proceedings led him to circulate privately a written protest, later published as Sharp, *Appendix*. For discussion of the criminality of slaveholding in the context of scriptural and property-based arguments, see, respectively, Woolman, *Considerations*, 50; Sharp, *Representation*, 72–73.

97 See Langbein, *Origins*.

98 Ibid., 1.

99 James D. Rice, "Criminal Trial," 459, 466.

100 Weld, *American Slavery*, 4. Earlier American antislavery writers included "testimony" in their polemics, but they tended to offer a fairly limited (and repetitive) set of quotations from a rather small corpus of travel accounts, emphasizing authority over breadth in their selection of sources. See Woolman, *Considerations*, 65–70; Benezet, *Observations*, 4.

101 Weld, *American Slavery*, 4.

102 Northup, *Twelve Years*, xxvii.

103 William E. Nelson, *Americanization*, 87.

104 Bentham, *Rationale*, 18.

105 On contemporary awareness of the "truth-defeating tendencies" of the Anglo-American criminal trial, see Langbein, *Origins*, 334. For antebellum commentary, see "Abuses" and Stowe, *Dred*, 44, 390. For a psychoanalytic consideration of this dilemma, see Felman, *Juridical*, 54–105. On the influence of the adversarial trial's structure (and the discovery process in particular) on American popular culture, see Clover, "Law."

106 See Auerbach, *Justice*, 11, 47–68.

107 Felman, *Juridical*, 59. See also Grossberg, *Judgment*, 168–200, 227–39.

108 Garrison, "Dangers"; "Garrison's Second Trial."

109 Daniel A. Cohen, *Pillars*, 101. See also Bercovitch, *American Jeremiad*.

110 Walker, *Appeal*, 22.

111 Langbein attributes the "muting of the jury" and other limitations on jurors' role in the proceedings to the "lawyerization" of the criminal trial (Langbein, *Origins*, 318–31). See also Lemmings, "Criminal," 67–70; Langbein, "Response," 85–86.

112 The full title of Benezet's 1766 antislavery pamphlet is *A Caution and Warning to Great Britain and Her Colonies, in a Short Representation of the Calamitous State of the Enslaved Negroes in the British Dominions. Collected from Various Authors, and Submitted to the Serious Consideration of All, More Especially of Those in Power.*

113 Weld, *American Slavery*, 7.

114 Kramer, *People*, 29, 30. On popular constitutionalism with respect to the emerging public sphere outlined by Jürgen Habermas, see ibid., 108–9. I address the relevance of Habermas's ideas to abolitionist print propaganda in chapter 1.

115 Ibid., 63.

116 Ibid., 170–213.

117 On petitioning in this context, see Zaeske, *Signatures*.

118 Kramer, *People*, 45. On the secularization and popularization of abolitionist appeals in the 1840s and 1850s, see Wyatt-Brown, "Proslavery," 334–35.

119 Wilson, *Works*, 1:541–42, 546. Wilson played a central role in maintaining the compatibility of the common-law power of judges with the principle of popular sovereignty. See Horwitz, *Transformation*, 20.

120 Kermit Hall, *Magic*, 173. See also Horwitz, *Transformation*, 166, 176, 211. On equity in nineteenth-century American culture, see Thomas, *American Literary Realism*, 25–52.

121 Kermit Hall, *Magic*, 173.

122 Wilson, *Works*, 1:540.

123 Howe, "Juries," 589.

124 See William E. Nelson, *Americanization*, 13–35; James D. Rice, "Criminal Trial," 473 (n. 48); Kramer, *People*, 156–64.

125 "Trial by Jury," 281.

126 Perry Miller, *Life*, 180. A related issue was that of jury selection. For contemporary lampoons, see *New York Evening Post*, 20 Apr. 1834; "The Way a Criminal Trial."

127 See Grossberg, *Judgment*, 193–95.

128 "Elective Judiciary," 200.

129 *New York Evening Post*, 20 Apr. 1834.

130 "Elective Judiciary," 200. See also "Supreme Court," 143–44. For contrasting Whig and Democratic views of law in the antebellum period, see Kohl, *Politics*, 145–85.

131 On the classical legal and literary origins of this logic, see Eden, *Poetic*. On the need to distinguish the coercive power of law and its representatives from the cultural influence exerted by literature and its authors and readers, see Cover, "Violence."

132 On narrative and rhetoric in the criminal trial, see Brooks and Gewirtz, *Law's Stories*; Clover, "Law."

133 Cover, "Nomos," 95–96.

134 Ibid., 112.

135 Ibid., 133. The article theorizes issues raised by Cover's legal historical analysis of the antislavery movement and due process. See Cover, *Justice*.

136 Cover, "Nomos," 102, 137. On the transformative role of narrative in antebellum custody litigation, see Grossberg, *Judgment*, 94–167.

137 Winter, *Clearing*, 19, 20.

138 Ibid., 19, 20.

139 Lakoff and Johnson, *Metaphors*, 3. For a composite overview of the issues involved in the mid-century critical shift toward thinking of metaphor as a cognitive process, see Sacks, *On Metaphor*.

140 Tocqueville, *Democracy*, 157. Tocqueville's observation has prompted a corpus of legal scholarship focusing on how the very existence of such legal formalities in-

fluence private negotiations, notably divorce and custody settlements. See, for example, Mnookin and Kornhauser, "Bargaining," and Jacob, "Elusive." My use of the concept throughout this study is closer to that of Grossberg, who emphasizes Tocqueville's appreciation for "how the formal legal order combined with popular legal ideology and customary practices to influence individual consciousness" and thus "the existence of a conscious sense of legal entitlement that encourages individuals and groups to use legal beliefs in disputes about their status, rights, duties, and problems" (Grossberg, *Judgment*, 2).

141 Ewick and Silbey, *Common Place*, 23.

142 Ibid., 20.

143 Tocqueville, *Democracy*, 323–24.

144 The classic work is Hartog, "Constitution." See also Clark, "Sacred"; Kramer, *People*; Curtis, *Free Speech*.

145 Douglass, *My Bondage*, 367; Douglass, *Narrative*, 30.

146 The forward-looking nature of the abolitionists' juridical rhetoric helps to clarify the distinction between Garrison's nonresistant tactics, which called for withdrawal from the legal system, and his persistent vision of legal transformation. Compare, for example, "Declaration of Sentiments Adopted" and "Abolition at the Ballot-Box," in Cain, *Selections*, 101–5, 106.

147 Sewall, *Selling of Joseph*, 10; Jefferson, *Notes*, 180–81.

148 "A typical budget for the MASS [Massachusetts Anti-Slavery Society] allotted far more money to printing and distribution than any other expenditure" (Fanuzzi, "Organ," 107). See also ibid., 125 (n. 2). On interracial competition within the antislavery movement, see Sekora, "Mr. Editor"; Baxter, *Frederick Douglass's*, 31–58. On intraracial competition, see Pease and Pease, *They*, 293–97.

149 Tocqueville, *Democracy*, 316. For a contemporary portrayal of lawyerly intimidation and manipulation of witnesses, see "Abuses," 306.

150 Bruce, *Origins*, 215.

151 Garrison, for example, characterizes Douglass as "one of the most efficient advocates of the slave population" (Douglass, *Narrative*, 5). Providing a reminder that we should not be too schematic in reconstructing the schema of the criminal trial as a model for the slavery debate, such occasional discrepancies, as Garrison's preface itself illustrates, lose their significance in the far more prevalent and consistent references to black witnesses and their white advocates.

The juridical metaphor's propensity to obfuscate the part played by free black abolitionists through the emphasis on the former slave's position as victim-witness and the white abolitionist's stance as advocate for the slave is consistent with the propensity of structural metaphors simultaneously to highlight and to obscure different aspects of a given concept. See Lakoff and Johnson, *Metaphors*, 67.

152 This study's focus on the abolitionist movement's appeal to popular legal consciousness in the larger slavery debate prohibits an inquiry into the range of rhetorical postures free African American abolitionists adopted in their engagements with antebellum print culture, a topic ably addressed by other scholars. See, for example, Howard-Pitney, *African-American Jeremiad*; Glaude, *Exodus!*; Rael, *Black Identity*.

153 "Book Notices."

154 See Cornelius, *Title*; McHenry, *Forgotten*; Newman, Rael, and Lapsansky, "Theme"; Rael, *Black Identity*.

155 For the development of this view in cultural legal studies theory, see the Amherst Series in Law, Jurisprudence, and Social Thought edited by Sarat and Kearns, particularly *Law in the Domains of Culture* and *Law in Everyday Life*. Although much legal cultural studies scholarship has tended to focus on the ways in which law and culture shape each other in the present, scholars in the field frequently gesture to the nineteenth century. See Ewick and Silbey, *Common Place*, xiii, xi; Clover, "Law," 101–2; Sherwin, *Pop*, 73–105. On the integration of law and culture around the slavery debate in antebellum America, see Brophy, "Revolution."

156 Hartog calls for a legal history that attends not only to authoritative texts but to alternative forms of evidence of popular legal consciousness; Hartog, "Constitution," 1029–34. See also Hoeflich, "Legal History" and "John Livingston"; Brophy, "Revolution."

157 On the centrality of legal thought to American culture before 1900, see Ferguson, *Law and Letters*; Thomas, *Cross-Examinations* and *American Literary Realism*. For theoretical investigations of law and literature in the period, see Dimock, *Residues*; Felman, *Juridical*. Cultural historians have broadened the corpus of relevant literary and legal texts to include gallows literature, popular crime narratives, sentimental fiction, divorce proceedings, and adultery trials. See Daniel A. Cohen, *Pillars*; Halttunen, *Murder*; Goodman, *Shifting*; Grossberg, *Judgment*; Korobkin, *Criminal Conversations*; Fox, *Trials*. On slavery and abolition with respect to nineteenth-century American law and literature and the black subject's legal and discursive transformation from chattel to rights-bearing citizen, see Hartman, *Scenes*; Best, *Fugitive's Properties*; Harris, "Finding" and "Whiteness"; Suggs, *Whispered*; Crane, *Race*. Shorter works include chapters in Wald, *Constituting*, and Sundquist, *To Wake*, as well as the indispensable series of articles by Brophy. See also Daniel A. Cohen, "Social Injustice"; Ferguson, "Story"; Carla Kaplan, "Narrative." On the continuing marginalization of multiethnic literature in the law and literature movement, see Desai, Smith, and Nair, "Law."

Legal historians have long appreciated the cultural significance of slavery in its legal aspect. See the *Cardozo Law Review*'s two-volume special issue *Bondage, Freedom, and the Constitution*. The classic works are Catterall, *Judicial Cases*; Cover, *Justice*; Higginbotham, *Matter*; Wiecek, *Sources*. See also Morris, *Southern Slavery*; Gross, *Double Character*. This scholarship has been complemented by the untiring editorial labors of Kermit L. Hall and Paul Finkelman. See Hall, *Law of American Slavery*; Finkelman, *Race, Law*; Finkelman, *Slavery and the Law*; Finkelman, *Law, the Constitution, and Slavery*; Finkelman, *Slavery in the Courtroom*. See also Finkelman's pamphlet reprint series, *Slavery, Race, and the American Legal System, 1700–1872*.

As even a cursory review of titles suggests (and as chapter 4 discusses in greater depth), African Americanist scholarship has long registered the evidentiary imperatives that have shaped black history and culture, from Rebecca Chalmers Barton's *Witnesses for Freedom* (1948) to William Loren Katz's *Eyewitness: The Negro in American*

History (1967), John Blassingame's *Slave Testimony* (1977), and Frances Smith Foster's *Witnessing Slavery* (1979) to C. Peter Ripley's *Witness for Freedom* (1993) and Dwight A. McBride's *Impossible Witnesses* (2001). But even those scholars who have sought to engage the critical implications of "slave testimony" in light of official "silencing" of African Americans have not taken into account the centrality of such juridical rhetoric to the slavery debate as a whole and thus have tended to celebrate such "testimony" as an unproblematic form of discursive resistance. See Accomando, *Regulations*; McBride, *Impossible*. A notable exception is Foreman, "Sentimental Abolition."

158 My phrasing here indicates this study's indebtedness to Stephen Mailloux's rhetorical hermeneutics. Understanding "*rhetoric* as the political effectivity of trope and argument in culture"—and thus as comprising both "figurative language and persuasive action"—Mailloux proposes that "interpretive theory must become rhetorical history." Centering on "historical sets of topics, arguments, tropes, [and] ideologies . . . which determine how texts are established as meaningful through rhetorical exchanges," Mailloux's rhetorical hermeneutics seeks to excavate and analyze "the argumentative forces at work within the particular historical contexts in which interpretive knowledge emerges" (Mailloux, *Rhetorical Power*, xii, 15, 147). See also Mailloux, *Reception* and "Re-Marking."

159 Rogers M. Smith, *Civic Ideals*, 508 (n. 5). In keeping with his multiple traditions thesis, Smith acknowledges that the civic ideologies typically developed in American politics combine strains of ascriptive Americanism with more familiar liberal and democratic republican elements. See also Fitzpatrick, *Mythology*.

160 Mark S. Weiner, *Black Trials*, 11.

161 Castronovo, *Necro*, 212, 214. See also Patricia J. Williams, *Alchemy*, 146–65.

162 See, on the one hand, Michael Warner, *Letters*, and Ziff, *Writing*, and, on the other, Fliegelman, *Declaring*, and Looby, *Voicing*.

163 See David D. Hall, *Worlds of Wonder*; Kimnach, "General Introduction"; Lambert, *Inventing*, 22–179. In the legal context, see Surrency, "Law Reports" and "Beginnings."

Chapter One

1 Hamlet was returned to Baltimore and eventually redeemed from slavery for eight hundred dollars (Finkelman, *Slavery in the Courtroom*, 85–86).

2 "Fugitive Slave Law—Hamlet in Chains."

3 "Fugitive Slave Law—Hamlet in Court." The building depicted in "Hamlet in Chains" is New York City Hall, not the Halls of Justice, also known as the Tombs. The confusion seems to lie in the fact that in the antebellum period "the Halls of Justice . . . contained the entire corpus of criminal law" (Gilfoyle, "America's Greatest," 525). The engraving confirms the contemporary report that Hamlet's summary hearing was "held in a retired room on the second story of the old City Hall" (American and Foreign Anti-Slavery Society, *Fugitive*, 4). Thanks to Jean Yellin for catching this discrepancy during a presentation at the 2003 American Studies Association annual meeting.

4 A shipment of cameos bearing the image was sent to Benjamin Franklin on 28 February 1788 (Oldfield, *Popular*, 156).

5   Ibid., 155–60; Marcus Wood, Blind Memory, 22.

6   Located near Tammany Hall in Printing-House Square, the heart of Democratic journalism, and edited by Anson Herrick and John F. Ropes, who also coedited a popular two-penny daily, the New York Aurora, the Atlas was a Sunday family magazine that ran from 1838 until 1868, publishing pieces by P. T. Barnum, Louisa May Alcott, and George Washington Harris. On Printing-House Square, see Reynolds, Walt Whitman's America, 98. Ropes worked in the customhouse, and Herrick served on New York's board of aldermen (1854–56) and was elected to the House of Representatives as a Democrat (4 March 1863–3 March 1865) (Hudson, Journalism, 338–39; U.S. Congress, Biographical Dictionary, 1047).

7   "Fugitive Slave Law—Hamlet in Court." After the initial article condemning the Hamlet rendition, the Atlas prefaced this, its second Hamlet article, with an "ECLAIRCISSEMENT" asserting its commitment to law and order, its independence from "any sect or party" (including the organized antislavery movement), and its defense of state control over slavery. On New York merchants' attitudes toward slavery, the Fugitive Slave Law, and the Hamlet rendition, see Foner, Business, 1–87.

8   On Democrats' antijudicialism, see Kohl, Politics, 163–65.

9   "Fugitive Slave Law—Hamlet in Chains."

10 Stanley W. Campbell, Slave Catchers, 3–25.

11 "Fugitive Slave Law—Hamlet in Chains."

12 Ibid. On the controversial extension of judicial powers to commissioners, see Stanley W. Campbell, Slave Catchers, 37–42.

13 "Fugitive Slave Law—Hamlet in Chains."

14 Stowe, Uncle Tom's Cabin, n.p. Marcus Wood, Blind Memory, 151–82, contextualizes Cruikshank's illustrations in Anglo-American print culture.

15 On the free-speech controversy, see Savage, Controversy; Nye, Fettered, 257–81; Leonard L. Richards, Gentlemen, 162; Curtis, Free Speech, 117–299. On the Fugitive Slave Law, see Stanley W. Campbell, Slave Catchers; Nye, Fettered, 257–81; Cover, Justice, 175–91; Slaughter, Bloody; Collison, Shadrach; Von Frank, Trials. Focusing on enforcement of the Fugitive Slave Law, Campbell argues that the Kansas-Nebraska Act and the Burns rendition of 1854, not the Compromise of 1850, marked the turning point in Northerners' relationship toward the South. Campbell himself repeatedly distinguishes, however, between enforcement of the Fugitive Slave Law and popular perceptions, fostered by print, regarding the Compromise; significantly, he does not address the impact of 1852's Uncle Tom's Cabin.

16 Although the catchall phrase "Slave Power" has fallen out of favor among historians as imprecise and smacking of conspiracy theories, I follow Richards in retaining it here because of its frequent appearance in antebellum rhetoric to convey the widespread—if vague—sense among Northerners that "slaveholders had far too much power in national affairs," as a result of a combination of factors (typically, "regional unity, parity in the Senate, and the three-fifths clause of the Constitution"). With the usual imprecision of such political rhetoric, invocations of the Slave Power, Richards notes, leave it uncertain as to who exactly was included under this rubric: slaveholders, proslavery Southerners, doughfaces, and/or government

officials (Leonard L. Richards, *Slave Power*, 4, 21, 26). For a helpful overview of historiography on the Slave Power thesis, see ibid., 1–27. See also Nye, *Fettered*, 282–315; David Brion Davis, *Slave Power*.

17 Wilmer, *Our Press Gang*, 237.

18 "A jury, in criminal cases, may, indeed, be called the country of the person accused, and the trial by jury may, indeed, be denominated the trial *per patriam*" (Wilson, *Works*, 1:529).

19 On republican views of print as an impersonal, authoritative, civic, emancipatory, and supervisory medium, see Michael Warner, *Letters*. See also Anderson, *Imagined*. On the relative importance of republicanism and liberalism in American political thought, see Hartz, *Liberal*; Bailyn, *Ideological*; Gordon S. Wood, *Creation*; Pocock, *Machiavellian*; Appleby, *Liberalism and Republicanism*, 1–33. For analyses of Garrison's negotiation of these traditions, see Mayer, *All on Fire*; Fanuzzi, *Abolition's Public Sphere*; Arkin, "Federalist Trope"; Rohrbach, *Truth*, 1–27.

20 *Genius of Universal Emancipation*, 20 Nov. 1829.

21 Hinks, *Awaken*, 119.

22 *Southern Patriot* (Charleston), 4 Aug. 1835, qtd. in Wyatt-Brown, *Lewis Tappan*, 150; *Washington Globe*, 26 Feb. 1836, qtd. in Curtis, "Curious History," 828.

23 On the speech's contexts, see Mayer, *All on Fire*, 61–68.

24 Garrison, "Dangers."

25 Ibid.

26 Ibid. On the case, see Kennedy, *Memoirs*, 2:231–34.

27 Garrison, "Dangers."

28 Ibid.

29 Ibid.

30 Ibid.

31 See Garrison and Garrison, *William Lloyd Garrison*, 1:167.

32 Garrison spent forty-nine days in jail after his conviction on the criminal charge and was later ordered to pay one-fifth of the five thousand dollars Todd had sought in his civil suit. Sentenced to either six months in jail or a fifty-dollar fine plus court costs for the criminal conviction, Garrison was incarcerated from 17 April to 5 June 1830 until New York philanthropist and abolitionist Arthur Tappan, upon reading Garrison's pamphlet on the trial, sent Lundy one hundred dollars to secure his release. Payment of the one-thousand-dollar fine was not enforced. Mayer, *All on Fire*, 71–94.

33 "The Farce Ended!"

34 Ibid.

35 "The Libel Suit—Again," 35.

36 Garrison, *Brief Sketch*, 1830, 8.

37 Garrison, *Brief Sketch*, 1834, iii.

38 Ibid.

39 Ibid., iv. Based on the erroneous assertion that Garrison "was convicted under civil not criminal law for the libel of Francis Todd," Fanuzzi argues that "even though he had been convicted under civil law, [Garrison] challenged his contemporaries to judge him by criminal standards," embarking on a "campaign of self-

incrimination" in order to "make abolitionists not just outcasts from the domain of citizenship but the criminals of the state" — in effect, relying on "a legal infraction to underwrite their public identity." Awareness of Garrison's criminal conviction and imprisonment for libel, however, demonstrates that, far from suffering from what Fanuzzi calls a "prosecution complex," Garrison, through his print appeals to popular legal consciousness, sought to turn the rhetorical tables on his proslavery antagonists in order to strike the prosecutorial posture that he and other white abolitionists would maintain for the subsequent three decades (Fanuzzi, *Abolition's Public Sphere*, 13, 16, 21, 28, 40, 13).

40 See Mayer, *All on Fire*, 71–94.

41 Garrison, *Brief Sketch*, 1830, 1.

42 Ibid.

43 Ibid., 1–2.

44 Garrison, *Brief Sketch*, 1834, 17.

45 *Proceedings*, 15.

46 Ibid., 3.

47 Habermas, *Structural Transformation*. For critiques, see Craig Calhoun, *Habermas*, and particularly Schudson, "Public Sphere," and Mary P. Ryan, "Gender."

48 Kermit Hall, *Magic*, 107. See also James D. Rice, "Criminal Trial," 466 (n. 27); Horwitz, *Transformation*, 166, 176, 211; Curtis, *Free Speech*, 41–42.

49 *New-York Weekly Journal*, 18 Feb. 1734, qtd. in Michael Warner, *Letters*, 53.

50 See Curtis, *Free Speech*, 23–116.

51 Michael Warner, *Letters*, 53.

52 Ibid., 54.

53 Ibid.

54 See Anderson, *Imagined*. On the alternative imagined community evoked by abolitionist print production, see Fanuzzi, *Abolition's Public Sphere*.

55 Curtis, *Free Speech*, 117–288.

56 *New York Journal*, 15 Mar. 1770, qtd. in Michael Warner, *Letters*, 56 (emphasis in original).

57 Cooper actively supported congressional gags on discussion of antislavery petitions. See Curtis, *Free Speech*, 89–92.

58 Cooper, *Treatise*, 98. Like Garrison, Cooper was working within a larger tradition that directly linked the powers of the jury with freedom of the press. See Curtis, *Free Speech*, 23, 30–31.

59 Cooper, *Treatise*, 106.

60 Ibid.

61 Garrison, *Brief Sketch*, 1830, 3.

62 Ibid., 8, 3.

63 Ibid., 3.

64 Ibid.

65 Ibid., 8.

66 Wyatt-Brown, *Lewis Tappan*, 149. The Charleston riot was only the most extreme of

the numerous Southern crises over the distribution of antislavery literature. See also Savage, *Controversy*, 9–42.

67 Savage, *Controversy*; Wyatt-Brown, *Lewis Tappan*, 149–66; Nye, *Fettered*, 67–85; Curtis, *Free Speech*, 155–75.

68 Jay, *Inquiry*, 148.

69 Ibid., 151.

70 Ibid., 152.

71 Ibid.

72 Ibid.

73 Savage, *Controversy*, 27–60; Nye, *Fettered*, 155–71; Curtis, *Free Speech*, 131–54.

74 Mayo, *Guide*, 453, 461.

75 Qtd. in Nye, *Fettered*, 139. See also Savage, *Controversy*, 43–60; Curtis, *Free Speech*, 182–93.

76 Qtd. in May, *Recollections*, 167.

77 Curtis, *Free Speech*, 194–95. See also MASS, *Full Statement*, 11.

78 Savage, *Controversy*, 1–8; Curtis, *Free Speech*, 195–98.

79 A facsimile appears in MASS, *Full Statement*, 41. See also Garrison and Garrison, *William Lloyd Garrison*, 1:240, 247–48; Savage, *Controversy*, 37.

80 Finkelman, *Slavery in the Courtroom*, 164–70. See also Curtis, *Free Speech*, 198.

81 Curtis, *Free Speech*, 198–99. See also William Lee Miller, *Arguing*, 127–36.

82 Savage, *Controversy*, 37–38. See also Curtis, *Free Speech*, 202–5; Leonard L. Richards, *Gentlemen*, 47–49.

83 See Savage, *Controversy*, 36–37, and Leonard L. Richards, *Gentlemen*, 16–17. On Garrison, see Mayer, *All on Fire*, 122–23. For the attack on Dresser, see MASS, *Full Statement*, 44–45. Again, such activities were not restricted to the South, as the Utica riot of 21 October 1835 demonstrates; commencing with the Oneida County grand jury's declaration that those involved in organizing antislavery societies and publishing abolitionist materials were "guilty of sedition," the riot centered on the courthouse and was led by the city's leading legal professionals. See Leonard L. Richards, *Gentlemen*, 85–92; May, *Recollections*, 162–70.

84 Joseph Southwick, Samuel J. May, Amos Farnsworth, and Francis Jackson are also listed; MASS, *Full Statement*, 35. The pamphlet was published in response to hearings by the Massachusetts legislature prompted by Governor Edward Everett's speech intimating that abolitionists "were guilty of offences punishable at common law" (May, *Recollections*, 187). On the hearings, see ibid., 185–202. For attribution of the pamphlet's composition to William Goodell, see ibid., 191. See also "The Progress of Antislavery" in Cain, *Selections*, 94–96.

85 MASS, *Full Statement*, 22.

86 Ibid., 17, 18.

87 Ibid., 18, 19.

88 Ibid., 20.

89 The MASS argued to the legislature that "a penal enactment against us is less to be dreaded than condemnatory resolutions; for these are left to be enforced by Judge

Lynch and his minions" rather than through adversarial procedure (May, *Recollections*, 196).

90 MASS, *Full Statement*, 25.

91 Ibid.

92 For anecdotal evidence of the free-speech debate of 1835–36 as a turning point in public opinion, see May, *Recollections*, 167–68, 202, 400–403.

93 On generational and sectional differences in attitudes toward changes in American print culture, see Appleby, *Inheriting*, 19–23, 34–45, 50, 54–55.

94 Habermas, *Structural Transformation*, 184. See also ibid., 168–69, 184–85.

95 Ibid., 207.

96 Ibid., 169. On the politics of embodiment, antebellum abolitionism, and republican ideals, see Fanuzzi, *Abolition's Public Sphere*; on the legal and cultural implications of packaging court proceedings as mass commercial entertainment, see Sherwin, *Pop*.

97 On Wisner's abolitionist leanings, see Mott, *American Journalism*, 223.

98 Ibid., 233.

99 Schiller, *Objectivity*, 99–103.

100 Ibid., 30.

101 Ibid., 55.

102 Ibid.

103 Bennett qtd. in [Pray,] *Memoirs*, 119. In April 1830, wealthy Salem merchant captain Joseph White was murdered by a man hired by his nephew-in-law, who sought to inherit White's fortune; on the case's relevance to contemporary literature, especially with respect to antebellum antijudicial sentiment as exacerbated by the Sims crisis in Boston, see Thomas, *Cross-Examinations*, 56–70, 88–89.

104 Bennett qtd. in [Pray,] *Memoirs*, 119.

105 See Halttunen, *Murder*, 90.

106 Wilmer, *Our Press Gang*, 217, 237, 245–46.

107 Ibid., 240.

108 Habermas, *Structural Transformation*, 133.

109 Ibid.

110 See Nerone, "Newspapers."

111 Wilmer, *Our Press Gang*, 221.

112 Garrison announced his plans for the paper, to be titled the *Cradle of Liberty*, in the *Liberator*, 5 Apr. 1839 (Fanuzzi, *Abolition's Public Sphere*, xiv–xvi, 65). To contrast the pricing, printing, and circulation of the penny press with that of the *Liberator*, compare Mott, *American Journalism*, 215–52, and Mayer, *All on Fire*, 110, 113, 114, 133, 530. On the print contexts for abolitionist propaganda, see Leonard L. Richards, *Gentlemen*, 71–74.

113 For a summary of the creeds set forth by various penny papers, see Mott, *American Journalism*, 242–43. For a reevaluation of the *Liberator* that emphasizes its influence on the development on literary realism in conjunction with a nineteenth-century liberal capitalist marketplace, see Rohrbach, *Truth*, 1–27.

114 On the *Liberator's* advancement of a reform agenda within Jacksonian market capitalism, see Rohrbach, *Truth*; Fanuzzi, *Abolition's Public Sphere*.

115 On early abolitionism's anachronistic appropriation of republican values, see Fanuzzi, *Abolition's Public Sphere*, xi–82.

116 The contrast of the antislavery and the penny press is necessarily a general one; for an account of a penny paper's appeal to the adjudicative reader that emphasizes editors' "role as public legal educators" actively seeking "to promote legal change" as late as January 1841, see Grossberg, *Judgment*, 168–86.

117 Contemporary accounts include Beecher, *Narrative*; Lovejoy and Lovejoy, *Memoir*; May, *Recollections*, 221–30. See also Nye, *Fettered*, 145–53; Leonard L. Richards, *Gentlemen*, 101–11.

118 Lovejoy and Lovejoy, *Memoir*, 168.

119 Qtd. in ibid., 168–78.

120 See Nye, *Fettered*, 128–34, 145–52; Curtis, *Free Speech*, 144–51, 216–70.

121 Hentz, *Planter's*, 568.

122 "Twelve of Lovejoy's men were tried in January 1838, on the curious legal charge of resisting attack and unlawful defense of property, and were acquitted. On 19 January several members of the mob were tried for riot, and judged not guilty" (Nye, *Fettered*, 149 [n. 101]). See also Winthrop S. Gilman, *Alton Trials*.

123 Garrison and Garrison, *William Lloyd Garrison*, 1:414.

124 On rioters as self-styled Revolutionary patriots, see Leonard L. Richards, *Gentlemen*, 69, 97–98. On the new party system's co-optation of traditional forms of political expression and the resurgence of mobbing in the 1830s and 1840s, see Kramer, *People*, 168. For contemporary critiques of mobbing as unrepublican, see Curtis, *Free Speech*, 206–7, 235–36.

125 As Stanley W. Campbell notes, it is important to distinguish public perception of such well-publicized legal crises in New England with the widespread compliance and enforcement of the Fugitive Slave Law in states such as New York, Pennsylvania, and New Jersey (Stanley W. Campbell, *Slave Catchers*, 54).

126 See ibid., 173–75; Finkelman, *Slavery in the Courtroom*, 64–68; Cover, *Justice*, 169–72, 266–67; Wiecek, "Latimer" and *Sources*.

127 Collison, *Shadrach*, 115.

128 See Finkelman, *Slavery in the Courtroom*, 86–88.

129 Ibid., 88–94.

130 Burns was arrested on 25 May 1854. See Pease and Pease, *Fugitive Slave Law*; Von Frank, *Trials*; Finkelman, "Legal Ethics." For a comprehensive contemporary source, see Stevens, *Anthony Burns*. For contemporary African American perspectives, see Forten, *Journals*, 60, 65, 66, 135, 353, 405; Salvatore, *We All*, 107.

131 *Daily Commonwealth* (Boston), evening ed., 27 May 1854. See Von Frank, *Trials*, 67–68, 92–96.

132 *Christian Register*, 12 Apr. 1851, 59.

133 According to the *Courier*, Dana claimed at a speech given in Worcester to have hopped over the chains ("Chains and Slavery").

134 Ibid.; *Daily Evening Commonwealth*, 8 Apr. 1851. Shaw had already been subject to public criticism for his position in the debate over the criminal jury. "In 1845, in *Commonwealth v. Porter*, Shaw held that the judge had the sole right in a criminal

case to decide the law involved in the issue, and the jury were obligated to receive the law from him"; public protest led to legislation recognizing the jury's right to judge both fact and law—legislation that Shaw would subsequently nullify in his 1855 ruling in *Commonwealth v. Anthes*. Just prior to the fugitive slave crisis, Shaw's controversial charge to the jury in the famous Webster-Parkman murder case of 1850 prompted criticism of the chief justice in both newspapers and the legal press (Levy, *Law*, 218–28, 290–95 [quotation at 290]). On Melville and Shaw in conjunction with law and slavery, see Huntress, "Guinea"; Thomas, *Cross-Examinations*, 93–250; Susan Weiner, *Law*, 19, 39–41, 57, 59, 80.

135 "Investigation."

136 Cover, *Justice*, 179. See also Stanley W. Campbell, *Slave Catchers*, 93–94, 172–73.

137 *National Anti-Slavery Standard*, 17 June 1854, qtd. in Finkelman, "Legal Ethics," 1826. See also *Daily Commonwealth* (Boston), 6 June 1854, evening ed.

138 *National Anti-Slavery Standard*, 10 June 1854, qtd. in Finkelman, "Legal Ethics," 1827.

139 Daniel Foster, Diary and Sermon Books, 1850–84, Foster Papers, MHS, 40.

140 "The Court in Session."

141 *Daily Morning Commonwealth* (Boston), 12 April 1851.

142 "Judge Wells."

143 "Chains and Slavery."

144 *Christian Register*, 12 Apr. 1851, 59.

145 "Decision."

146 "In Chains."

147 Ibid.

148 "Testimony at the Preliminary Examination of Martin Stowell," Andrews Papers, MHS.

149 Ibid.

150 Ibid. The transcript has, variously, "Lassell," "Lascelle," and "Lascelles." On Cluer, see Von Frank, *Trials*, 93, 127, 279, 286, 293.

151 "Testimony at the Preliminary Examination of Martin Stowell," Andrews Papers, MHS.

152 "Southern Court-House"; for a similar account during the Burns crisis, see "The Chivalry on Hand."

153 *Daily Morning Commonwealth*, 25 Apr. 1851; A[d]ventures.

154 Pierson, *Jamie Parker*, 166.

155 Ibid., 22.

156 Ibid., 69.

157 On Court Day, see ibid., iii, 68. See also Roeber, *Faithful Magistrates*, 79. For a first-hand description, see Pennington, *Narrative*, 39.

158 Russell, "Slave Auctions," 329.

159 Ibid., 330. Along with execution sales, other transactions involving slaves included probate sales, tax sales, and legally sanctioned sales to convert free blacks into property.

160 Ibid., 329. See also Stroud, *Sketch*, 1827, 86–87.

161 Russell, "Slave Auctions," 355. Such court sales of slaves were not restricted to the

South. On Judge Loring's role in the abortive sale of Burns, see Finkelman, "Legal Ethics," 1819.

162 Stowe, *Uncle Tom's Cabin: Authoritative*, 101, 102.

163 Pierson, *Jamie Parker*, 71.

164 Ibid.

165 "Are Court Houses Jails?"; "Kidnapping of Sims." See also *Daily Commonwealth* (Boston), 30 May 1854, evening ed.

166 Thoreau, "Slavery," 97. Accounts of regional responses to the Burns rendition appear in the *Daily Commonwealth* (Boston), 6 June 1854, evening ed. For Thoreau's use of journal materials regarding both Burns and Sims, see Von Frank, *Trials*, 281, 277; on Thoreau's speech, the printed article, and their contexts, see ibid., 276–85.

167 Dean and Hoag, "Thoreau's Lectures," 215.

168 *Liberator*, 16 June 1854, qtd. in Von Frank, *Trials*, 278.

169 *Liberator*, 7 July 1854, qtd. in Dean and Hoag, "Thoreau's Lectures," 216.

170 Mayer, *All on Fire*, 443.

171 The MASS's *Proceedings* commemorated the Independence Day meeting as the moment when it had "the pleasure . . . to welcome Henry D. Thoreau to the public advocacy of our cause" (qtd. in Dean and Hoag, "Thoreau's Lectures," 221). On Thoreau's private connections to abolitionism, see Petrulionis, "Editorial," 207–8.

172 Horace Greeley, "A Higher Law Speech," *New-York Daily Tribune*, 2 Aug. 1854, qtd. in Dean and Hoag, "Thoreau's Lectures," 220.

173 Thoreau, "Slavery," 105.

174 Ibid., 98.

175 Ibid., 97.

176 Ibid.

177 Ibid., 108, 104. On the water-lily image, see Buell, *Environmental*, 36–38, 50; Von Frank, *Trials*, 285; Petrulionis, "Editorial," 218–20.

178 Thoreau, "Slavery," 108. For alternative readings, see Reynolds, *John Brown*, 227–28; Von Frank, *Trials*, 284.

179 Thoreau, "Slavery," 102.

180 Greeley's preface reminded his readers that the same imperiled civil liberties that had inspired Thoreau's speech authorized its republication. See Dean and Hoag, "Thoreau's Lectures," 219–20.

181 Thoreau, "Slavery," 105, 99.

182 Ibid., 101, 99.

183 Ibid., 100.

184 Ibid.

185 Ibid.

186 Ibid.

187 Conway, *Autobiography*, 184–85.

188 Thoreau, "Slavery," 107.

189 Ibid.

190 Ibid.

Chapter Two

1 Conway, *Autobiography*, 184.

2 Ibid.

3 Ibid.

4 Ibid.

5 Ibid., 186.

6 Van Wagenen changed her name to Sojourner Truth in 1843. On Truth's various names, see Washington, introduction, xiv–xv.

7 Rickford and Rickford, *Spoken Soul*, 49. See also Zeigler, "Something," 170–71. In this sense, testifying resembles those authorial eruptions of popular voice characterized as "democratic personality" in Ruttenburg, *Democratic*. On the experiential, testimonial authority of the "pious Negro" as critical observer of early America, see Bruce, *Origins*, 74, 111–15.

8 Stowe wrote an introduction for the 1855 edition of *Narrative*. It was to obtain this "puff" that Truth traveled to Stowe's Andover home in 1853 for the visit described in "Libyan Sybil." See Painter, *Sojourner Truth*, 130. Filled with inaccuracies—the New York–born, Low Dutch–speaking Truth recounts in Southern dialect her capture from Africa—Stowe's essay was crucial to the wartime transformation of Truth from "a little-noted evangelist and reformer" to "a celebrity." As Painter notes, Truth capitalized on the publicity generated by Stowe's essay. In addition to using her response to Stowe to promote her own more accurate *Narrative of Sojourner Truth*, Truth also reproduced the essay after the war in a revised edition of the *Narrative*, on which she collaborated with Frances Titus. See Painter, *Sojourner Truth*, 151–63 (quotations at 130, 163). For Truth's response to the article and its inaccuracies, see Truth, "Letter." See also Truth, *Narrative*, 1878, 151–72. For a reading emphasizing the need to "resist the parternalistic tendency of regarding blacks as always the 'victims' of racialist representations," see Levine, *Martin Delany*, 153–55.

9 Stowe, "Sojourner Truth, The Libyan Sybil," 473.

10 Peter had been sold out of state to circumvent the legislative enactment that would emancipate New York slaves in the coming year (Painter, *Sojourner Truth*, 32–33).

11 Stowe, "Sojourner Truth, The Libyan Sybil," 477–78.

12 Ibid., 473. On Stowe and minstrelsy, see Meer, *Uncle Tom*, 19–72.

13 Stowe's second antislavery novel, *Dred*, anticipates her "Libyan Sybil" with the character Milly, a thinly veiled fictionalization of Truth. A wronged slave mother, Milly finds justice in the tribunals not of man but of God. See also Judie Newman, introduction, 21–22; Levine, *Martin Delany*, 157–59.

14 Painter, *Sojourner Truth*, 32–35. The absence of any record of the case suggests a habeas corpus proceeding, which would have required neither a formal trial nor the corresponding documentation (Mabee and Mabee Newhouse, *Sojourner Truth*, 251 [n. 7]).

15 Truth's antebellum collaborators refer to the case. See Vale, *Fanaticism*, 2:110; Truth, *Narrative*, 1850, 78. Despite the recorded case pleading, *Isabella Van Wagenen v. Benjamin H. Folger*, "the records for the Supreme Court sittings in New York City and Albany show no evidence of the case actually coming to judgment." Johnson and

Wilentz nevertheless conclude the existence of a suit (*Kingdom*, 177, 220 [n. 21]). See also McDade, "Matthias," 333–34.

During Reconstruction, Truth had a Washington, D.C., conductor tried for assault and battery after he tried to block her entry to a streetcar. As in the previous two cases, the outcome of this lawsuit is uncertain. At the very least, Truth succeeded in having the conductor fired and then arrested, arranging for legal representation through the Freedman's Bureau. Mabee and Mabee Newhouse conclude that she "apparently won all three cases" she had brought against white men (*Sojourner Truth*, 134). See also Truth, *Narrative*, 1878, 186–87.

16 For histories of the cult, see Johnson and Wilentz, *Kingdom*; McDade, "Matthias." For analysis, see Jenkins, *Mystics*, 25–33. The most thorough account of Truth's New York years appears in Stetson and David, *Glorying*, 57–85.

17 For such analysis, see Accomando, *Regulations*, 51–109.

18 Starling, *Slave Narrative*; Foster, *Witnessing*; and Andrews, *To Tell*, acknowledge the slave narrative's genealogical links to gallows literature but do not explore in detail the transformation from a confessional to a testimonial stance.

19 "Legally, a black man's speech did not exist: his testimony inadmissible in court, . . . quite literally he stood mute"; Yellin, "Black Masks," 688. A similarly imprecise formulation emphasizes the slave's "nonexistent subjectivity" under law (Accomando, *Regulations*, 115, 116, 127).

20 This chapter follows Dickson D. Bruce in seeking out the "forms and conventions that seemed to provide, within a discursive world, a basis for a distinctively black intervention into the public sphere," deemphasizing authorship in order to search instead for traces of "black authority—for an authoritative literary persona and a distinctive black perspective" that may or may not have been inscribed by an African American "hand" (*Origins*, 65, xi, 32). Bruce does not discuss Truth's career, but his focus on the emergence of a distinctive African American literary presence is particularly well suited to the study of a figure who, despite her own illiteracy, contributed to print culture through a range of discursive activities. See Painter, *Sojourner Truth*, 151–99. On Truth's collaboration with her white amanuenses as well as her oral reading and writing practices, see Stetson and David, *Glorying*, 3. See also Humez, "Reading."

21 McDade, "Matthias"; Johnson and Wilentz, *Kingdom*; Jenkins, *Mystics*.

22 Although outside the scope of the current study, *The History of Mary Prince, a West Indian Slave, Related by Herself* (1831) offers a striking parallel to Truth's involvement in *Fanaticism*. Published in London in collaboration with Thomas Pringle, a radical editor-turned-abolitionist, Prince's *History* was framed by lawsuits involving Prince, her erstwhile master, and Pringle. See Salih, introduction.

23 Stroud, *Sketch*, 1827, 65.

24 Stowe, *Key*, 3, 88.

25 H. R. McIlwaine, ed., *Minutes of the Council and General Court of Colonial Virginia*, qtd. in Higginbotham, *Matter*, 21. For accounts of successful black litigants in colonial Virginia, see Breen and Innis, *Myne Owne*, 88–97, 111, 113.

26 Thus, in 1705, a Virginia "*act for establishing the general court*" establishes "that Popish

recusants, convict negroes, mulattos, and Indian servants, and others, not being Christians, shall be deemed and taken to be persons incapable in law to be witnesses in any cases whatsoever" (Hurd, *Law*, 1:239). On oath-taking, see Morris, *Southern Slavery*, 230; William E. Nelson, *Americanization*, 26–27.

27 Morris, *Southern Slavery*, 236–37. On blacks' presumptive status as slaves, see ibid., 25–29.

28 Hening, *Statutes*, 326–27.

29 Ibid., 327.

30 Ibid.

31 Ibid.

32 Ibid., 128. "Despite the vagaries of enforcement, the 1723 law remained the basis for the admission of evidence in capital trials of slaves in Virginia until the end of slavery in 1865" (Morris, *Southern Slavery*, 233).

33 See Morris, *Southern Slavery*, 231. For statutes on testimony that distinguish race from religious identity or capacity for oath-taking, see those of Maryland and Minnesota in Hurd, *Law*, 2:23, 177.

34 Cobb, *Inquiry*, 226, 233. In addition to Stroud, *Sketch*, 1856, 55–71, 105–19 (whom Cobb cites), see also Appleton, *Rules*, 271–80. For analyses of blacks' imputed mendacity from historical, literary, and legal perspectives, see, respectively, Greenberg, *Honor*, 40–41; Fabian, *Unvarnished*, 84–102; Morris, *Southern Slavery*, 232.

35 William Goodell, *American Slave Code*, 303.

36 Cobb, *Inquiry*, 83. On the "dual and contradictory character of slaves as property and persons" with specific reference to the Constitution's three-fifths clause and the exploitation of African American women, see Harris, "Whiteness," 1718–20. For elaboration of slaves' "double character" in Southern legal practice, see Gross, *Double Character*.

37 The case involved the 1856 will of John T. Creswell, which stipulated that his four slaves be given a choice between continued slavery or emancipation and emigration to a free state or Liberia (1861; Catterall, *Judicial Cases*, 3:247). On Georgia Supreme Court Chief Justice Joseph Henry Lumpkin's apparently contradictory position that although the "slave is a rational creature," the "Negro is incapable of self-government and has no common law or natural law rights," see Stephenson and Stephenson, "Protect," 527.

38 See Madison, Hamilton, and Jay, *Federalist*, 331–35. See also Hartman, *Scenes*, 62, 68; Dayan, "Legal," 65, 67.

39 The variation of such procedural rules over time and in different jurisdictions makes concise summary impossible. A composite portrait emerges, however, from Hurd's state-by-state collection of the relevant statutes. See Hurd, *Law*, 1:239, 241–44, 252–53, 281, 284, 305; 2:19–20, 23, 73–75, 77, 81–82, 89–90, 97, 117–18, 128, 131, 159, 172–73, 177, 210, 217. For a summary statement, see ibid., 2:340 (n. 2). See also O'Neall, *Negro Law*, 23. For an overview of slave testimony, see Morris, *Southern Slavery*, 229–37.

40 See Slotkin, "Narratives," 17.

41 On Western associations of evil with blackness, see Jordan, *White over Black*, 4–11;

Slotkin, "Narratives," 9–12. On African American efforts to refute notions of black criminality, see Pease and Pease, *They*, 99–101. As Turner's "not guilty" plea suggests, the *Confessions of Nat Turner* is anything but an unambiguous account of black criminality, but for the purposes of this chapter, its account of Turner's role in the uprising ("after repeated blows with a sword, I killed her by a blow to the head") places it firmly in the gallows literature and spiritual narrative traditions (Greenberg, *Confessions*, 50). See also Andrews, *To Tell*, 72–77. If we do not collapse the distinction between confession and testimony (see, for example, Sundquist, *To Wake*, 37–38), *Confessions* does not represent the kind of rhetorical break with traditional portrayals of the black print subject accomplished by Vale and Van Wagenen.

42 On the "continuum between being declared dead in law, being made a slave, and being judged a criminal," see Dayan, "Legal," 58–59. On the attribution of criminality to black agency under the logic of the slave's double character in the context of rape, see Hartman, *Scenes*, 82–86.

43 For an overview, see Bruce, *Origins*. On black cosmopolitanism, see Gilroy, *Black Atlantic*; Bolster, *Black Jacks*; Linebaugh and Rediker, *Many-Headed Hydra*; Crane, *Race*; Nwankwo, *Black Cosmopolitanism*. The scholarship on early African American politics, literature, and spirituality is substantial. See Foster, *Witnessing*; Ernest, *Resistance*; Glaude, *Exodus!* For individual examples, see Andrews, *Sisters*; Brooks and Saillant, *Face*; Sensbach, *Rebecca's*.

44 Foster, *Witnessing*, 36.

45 Vale, *Fanaticism*, 2:22.

46 Painter, *Sojourner Truth*, 62–65. On connections between evangelicalism, reform, and antislavery, see Perry Miller, *Life*, 72–84; Barnes, *Antislavery Impulse*; Wyatt-Brown, *Lewis Tappan*; Abzug, *Passionate Liberator*; Abzug, *Cosmos*, 129–62.

47 I use "perfectionist" in its broad, social sense. For a helpful clarification of the different meanings associated with the term, see Johnson and Wilentz, *Kingdom*, 190 (n. 16).

48 William L. Stone, *Matthias*, 65. On the evangelical and reform activities of Pierson and his circle, see Johnson and Wilentz, *Kingdom*, 20–37.

49 Stetson and David, *Glorying*, 67. On connections between the Magdalen Society and antislavery reform, see Barnes, *Antislavery Impulse*, 23–24; Wyatt-Brown, *Lewis Tappan*, 68–70.

50 Johnson and Wilentz, *Kingdom*, 94. Johnson and Wilentz have reconstructed Matthias's "system," locating its roots in the impoverished Scots Calvinist Robert Matthews's alienation from "the comfortable, pious, entrepreneurs who commanded the market revolution" and formed the basis of evangelical reform in the early antebellum period (*Kingdom*, 6–7). See also Jenkins, *Mystics*, 3–33.

51 Johnson and Wilentz, *Kingdom*, 105.

52 Vale, *Fanaticism*, 2:51 (emphasis omitted). Like the others in the kingdom, Van Wagenen contributed both her labor and her property to the collective enterprise. After a year of doing the bulk of the housework for a household of as many as fifteen people, Van Wagenen received a token $25 upon her departure from the Folgers. See ibid., 95.

53 Ibid., 49.

54 Masur, Rites, 5, 6.

55 Ibid., 114.

56 Halttunen, Murder, 25.

57 Johnson and Wilentz, Kingdom, 10–11. For press coverage, see 145–59, 165–72.

58 In addition to those cited below, see W. E. Drake, The Prophet! (1834); Trial of Matthias (1835); [Margaret Matthews], Matthias. By His Wife (1835); A Chapter in the History of Robert Matthews, Otherwise Called Matthias the Prophet (1835); W. E. Drake, The False Prophet! (1835); An Authentic History of Remarkable Persons, Who Have Attracted Public Attention in Various Parts of the World (1849); and Poor Little Edith Freeman (1879), which reproduces the 1834 Drake pamphlet with minor editorial changes. For a reference to "black BELLA" in a contemporary lampoon on Stone, see [Osborn], Vision, line 435.

59 Mott, American Journalism, 215–52.

60 Halttunen, Murder, 36, 97, 116. See also Daniel A. Cohen, Pillars, 191–95.

61 The pamphlet is titled Memoirs of Matthias the Prophet (1835). Stone's Commercial Advertiser was the most prestigious of the era's three prosperous mercantile dailies. See Mott, American Journalism, 181.

62 "Matthias."

63 On Vale and his freethinking labor milieu, see Wilentz, Chants, 154, 329, 337. On his abolitionism, see Johnson and Wilentz, Kingdom, 168, 169.

64 Vale, Fanaticism, 1:4.

65 William L. Stone, Matthias, 166; Vale, Fanaticism, 1:60.

66 The expressions body-horror and pornography of violence appear in Halttunen, Murder, 60, 62.

67 William L. Stone, Matthias, 209; Vale, Fanaticism, 2:75.

68 William L. Stone, Matthias, 200–203; Vale, Fanaticism, 2:76–80.

69 William L. Stone, Matthias, 335–43. See also New York Evening Post, 18 Apr. 1835. On printed medical postmortems, see Halttunen, Murder, 75–76.

70 William L. Stone, Matthias, 72, 178; Vale, Fanaticism, 1:79.

71 Halttunen, Murder, 89–90.

72 William L. Stone, Matthias, 323–24, 321, 300.

73 Ibid., 222. See Halttunen, Confidence Men.

74 Vale, Fanaticism, 2:20.

75 Ibid., 1:61.

76 Ibid., 60; 2:28.

77 Ibid., 1:76–79.

78 Memoirs, 15. William L. Stone, Matthias, 216–17, 215 varies slightly. An earlier account baldly asserts "that the woman was bribed by Mathies [sic] to poison the family" (Drake, Prophet, 5–6).

79 William L. Stone, Matthias, 193.

80 Ibid., 195.

81 Halttuen, Murder, 208. On similar racial scapegoating in an 1831 murder case, see ibid., 153.

82 Johnson and Wilentz, Kingdom, 11.

83 Cohen's analysis of print representations of black rapists complicates this claim somewhat by charting how early American crime literature followed broader literary and cultural trends. Cohen concurs, however, with other scholars in noting that the disproportionate representation of African Americans popularized more general associations of blackness with criminality in early American print culture ("Social Injustice," 484, 512, 485, 514). See also Slotkin, "Narratives"; Daniel E. Williams, Pillars, 51–58; Masur, Rites, 6.

84 Sander Gilman, "Black Bodies," 209.

85 William L. Stone, Matthias, 65.

86 Memoirs, 10.

87 Ibid.

88 Ibid., 13.

89 Ibid., 10.

90 Sander Gilman, "Black Bodies," 209.

91 Leonard L. Richards, Gentlemen, 113; Stetson and David, Glorying, 74.

92 Leonard L. Richards, Gentlemen, 117–18. See also Wyatt-Brown, Lewis Tappan, 115–22.

93 Leonard L. Richards, Gentlemen, 114–18. For abolitionist criticisms of Stone, see Wyatt-Brown, Lewis Tappan, 106.

94 Commercial Advertiser (New York), 10–14 July 1834, qtd. in Leonard L. Richards, Gentlemen, 122.

95 William L. Stone, Matthias, 65.

96 Ibid., 68.

97 Ibid., 166, 171.

98 Child, Appeal, 22–28.

99 "Slavery"; "Matthias."

100 William L. Stone, Matthias, 179. For an apparent rewriting of this scene, see Stowe, Dred, 377–81.

101 William L. Stone, Matthias, 179–80.

102 Sánchez-Eppler, Touching, 23.

103 William L. Stone, Matthias, 203.

104 Ibid., 204.

105 Ibid., 205.

106 Ibid., 220–21.

107 Vale, Fanaticism, 2:109.

108 Ibid., 110.

109 Ibid. On Western, see Johnson and Wilentz, Kingdom, 146.

110 Vale, Fanaticism, 2:112.

111 Ibid., 114.

112 Ibid., 120.

113 Ibid., 116.

114 Ibid.

115 Sekora, "Black Message."

116 Vale, Fanaticism, 1:6.

117 Ibid., 3.

118 Ibid., 7.

119 Ibid., 9.

120 Ibid., 17.

121 Ibid., 60.

122 Ibid., 62, 63.

123 Ibid., 63.

124 Ibid., 41.

125 Ibid.

126 Ibid.

127 Ibid.

128 Stetson and David, *Glorying*, 71.

129 Vale, *Fanaticism*, 1:54.

130 Ibid., 80.

131 Ibid., 2:15.

132 Ibid., 24.

133 Ibid., 1:10.

134 Ibid.

135 Ibid., 10, 13.

136 Wheatley, *Works*, 7. For an imaginative reconstruction and analysis of this "primal scene of African-American letters," see Gates, *Trials*; Gates, "Editor's Introduction: Writing 'Race,'" 7–9; Gates, "In Her Own Write." See also Shields, "Phillis Wheatley's Struggle."

137 On authenticating documents, see Sekora, "Black Message"; Stepto, "I Rose"; Accomando, *Regulations*, 36–38.

138 Jacobs, *Incidents*, 3.

139 Ibid., 201.

140 Vale, *Fanaticism*, 2:3.

141 Ibid., 13.

142 Ibid., 14.

143 Ibid., 117.

144 Ibid., 122.

145 Ibid., 1:13.

146 Ibid.

147 Ibid., 14.

148 See Hartman, *Scenes*, 82–83.

149 Cobb, *Inquiry*, 232–33; William Goodell, *American Slave Code*, 303.

150 In suggesting that the testimonial posture of the formerly enslaved victim/witness offered an alternative to the confessing stance of the black condemned in gallows literature, my account furthers Hartman's analysis by decoupling and historicizing "the pained and punitive calculation[s] of subjectivity" in antebellum culture. As violent as hanging was, this corporeal violence is not foregrounded in gallows literature. In Hartman's terms, the antislavery movement's new emphasis on the slave's "wounded body" and "mortified flesh" sought to distance the black speaking subject from the "criminal": put differently, if law defined the slave's "person"

as "little more than a pained body or a recalcitrant in need of punishment," abolitionist print propaganda sought to supplant the latter with the former (Hartman, *Scenes*, 94). See also Dayan, "Legal."

151 The statements of Isaac S. Van Wagenen and John J. Dumont, dated 13 Oct. 1834, appear alongside statements, dated March 1850, by George W. Benson, S. L. Hill, A. W. Thayer, and William Lloyd Garrison (Truth, *Narrative*, 1850, 144).

Chapter Three

1 Douglass, *Narrative*, 42.

2 See Quarles, *Frederick Douglass*, 57–79; Martin, *Mind*, 18–54; Garvey, "Change of Opinion"; McFeely, *Frederick Douglass*, 146–49, 172–78.

3 Lampe, *Frederick Douglass*, x.

4 Blassingame, introduction, xlviii.

5 See Bruce, *Origins*, 255.

6 Lung problems kept Douglass from delivering the Latimer speech. His letter to Garrison on the subject was published in the *Liberator*, 18 Nov. 1842; it is reprinted in Lampe, *Frederick Douglass*, 309–13 (quotation at 312). On the Latimer case, see Wiecek, "Latimer." For contemporary responses, see Bowditch, *Proceedings*, and Scrapbooks, Papers Related to the George Latimer Case, 1842–88, Bowditch Papers, MHS.

7 Lampe, *Frederick Douglass*, 312.

8 Ibid.

9 Originally published in the *National Anti-Slavery Standard*, 25 July 1844, the speech is reprinted in ibid., 315–19 (quotation at 315).

10 Douglass, *Life and Writings*, 2:411, 418, 421.

11 On Douglass's early oratory, see Lampe, *Frederick Douglass*, 33–56.

12 This conclusion is consistent with both Blassingame's and Lampe's accounts of Douglass's early career. As Blassingame acknowledges, "While white abolitionists theorized, Douglass drew from his own experiences to produce graphic illustrations of the peculiar institution" (introduction, xlvi–xlvii). Similarly, Lampe has Douglass "bringing forth his adversary's argument and then refuting it with personal experience, personal testimony, Garrisonian doctrine, and carefully reasoned discourse" (*Frederick Douglass*, 103). See also ibid., 106–7.

13 On black abolitionism's shift from Garrisonian moral suasion in the 1830s to greater rhetorical and political independence in the 1840s and 1850s, see Ripley, *Black Abolitionist Papers*, 3:20–57.

14 Douglass, *My Bondage*, 367, 132. On Douglass and the politics of representative identity, see Levine, *Martin Delany*; Gates, "From Wheatley"; Zafar, "Franklinian."

15 Douglass, *Life and Writings*, 1:281.

16 Ibid., 363.

17 Ibid., 2:155. See Cover, "Nomos," 135–37; Crane, *Race*, 87–130; McKivigan, "Frederick Douglass-Gerrit Smith"; Schrader, "Natural Law"; Mills, "Whose Fourth"; Garvey, "Change of Opinion"; McFeely, *Frederick Douglass*, 168–73, 204–7; Martin, *Mind*, 31–38; Quarles, *Frederick Douglass*, 71–73.

18 See Schrader, "Natural Law."

19 Douglass, *My Bondage*, 106.

20 For an alternative reading that links Douglass's change of opinion on the Constitution to his appropriation of both pro- and antislavery metaphors in *My Bondage*, see Dorsey, "Becoming."

21 Bibb, *Narrative*, 207.

22 Eden, *Poetic*, 62–111. See also Kronman, "Leontius' Tale"; Gewirtz, "Victims," 144–47.

23 Wilson, *Works*, 1:383.

24 Ibid.

25 Ibid.

26 Ibid.

27 Ibid.

28 Ibid.

29 Ibid., 383–84.

30 "Precarious," *American Heritage Dictionary*.

31 Catterall, *Judicial Cases*, 3:247.

32 On the evolution of early American attitudes toward law as neutral and universal, see Perry Miller, *Life*, 99–116. For a twentieth-century articulation that addresses race, see Wechsler, "Toward Neutral Principles."

33 For a critique, see Farber and Sherry, "Telling." For a rebuttal and overview, see Alex M. Johnson Jr., "Defending." See also *Legal Storytelling*.

34 Delgado, "Storytelling," 2415, 2429.

35 Ross, "Rhetorical."

36 Ibid., 2, 6.

37 See Hartman, *Scenes*, 82–86. For a similar conclusion regarding the legal proscription of slave literacy, see Suggs, *Whispered*, 67–68.

38 See Finkelman, *Slavery in the Courtroom*, 39–43.

39 Pennsylvania Anti-Slavery Society, *Narrative*, 10.

40 Cannon, *Case*, 12.

41 Ibid., 12; [Sheppard,] *Passmore Williamson*, 45.

42 In testimony that "utterly destroyed that of Mr. Wheeler and his witnesses," Johnson asserted, "I had made preparations before leaving Washington to get my freedom in New York; I made a suit to disguise myself in—they had never seen me wear it—to escape in when I got to New York; . . . I wasn't willing to come without my children; for I wanted to free them"; PASS, *Narrative*, 14. Higginbotham concludes that in Pennsylvania free blacks were not allowed to "be witnesses against whites in regular courts" until 1780; slave testimony under the same circumstances was inadmissible until 1847 (*Matter*, 282).

43 Cannon, *Case*, 189.

44 Ibid.

45 Ibid., 169.

46 Whittier, *Narrative*, vii, xvi, xvii.

47 Ibid., xvii.

48 Henry Watson, Narrative, 38.

49 Pennington, Narrative; Jacobs, Incidents, 1–2.

50 National Anti-Slavery Standard, 26 Aug. 1841, qtd. in Lampe, Frederick Douglass, 61.

51 Sekora, "Mr. Editor," 620.

52 On the forensic image and its effects, see Eden, Poetic, 78–83, 90. On readers as vicarious witnesses in the slave narrative, see Andrews, To Tell, 134–38; Rowe, "Between," 203–4; Foreman, "Sentimental Abolition."

53 See Fisher, Hard Facts, 103–22; Hartman, Scenes, 17–23.

54 On the criminal trial as "a forum for narrative transactions," see Gewirtz, "Victims," 135–49.

55 Hartman, Scenes, 101. See also Gewirtz, "Victims."

56 On rhetorics of corporeality in the slavery debate, see Mailloux, "Re-Marking."

57 Sánchez-Eppler, Touching, 1, 3, 8. For a complication of this point, see Castronovo, Necro, 64.

58 For a similar conclusion regarding Douglass's engagement with Scottish Common Sense philosophy, see Lee, Slavery, 93–132.

59 Douglass, Narrative, 15.

60 For Northern restrictions on African American testimony, see Pease and Pease, They, 156–58.

61 Douglass, Narrative, 8, 9.

62 Ibid., 9.

63 Ibid., 11.

64 Ibid.

65 Ibid., 8.

66 Ibid., 12.

67 Ibid., 21.

68 Ibid., 22. On Jacobs's treatment of these themes, see Garfield, "Earwitness." For a persuasive reading of Jacobs's silence as "a rejection of both the attestatory position of slave narrators and the seductive one typical of white women's romances" with reference to contract law, see Carla Kaplan, "Narrative," 97.

69 Significantly, Douglass portrays the slaves who sing tragically expressive songs as in transit, "on their way" from one of the many "out-farms" to "the home plantation," Great House Farm (Narrative, 18).

70 Ibid., 14–15. On critical treatments of this scene, see McDowell, "In the First Place," 201–4; Hartman, Scenes, 3.

71 Douglass, Narrative, 15, 16, 15.

72 On the slave's embodied subjectivity, see Sidonie Smith, Subjectivity, 5–17. See also Sánchez-Eppler, Touching, 1–10.

73 Douglass, Narrative, 15. On the economic implications of this "bloody transaction," see Wald, Constituting, 81; Baker, Blues, 39–55.

74 Wiegman, American, 67. On the passage's psychosexual overtones, see Albert Stone, "Identity," 69; Sundquist, To Wake, 99; Franchot, "Punishment"; Foreman, "Senti-

mental Abolition," 197–99. On the gendered implications of the abolitionist positioning of the former slave as slavery's eyewitness, see DeLombard, "Adding" and "Eye-Witness," 250–51.

75 See Hartman, *Scenes*, 21. See also Best, *Fugitive's Properties*, 1–98.

76 Attuned to this scene's juridical overtones, Wald notes, "Douglass . . . participates in the scene by witnessing it, in the active sense of testifying rather than the more passive observing," thereby "bring[ing] the scene before a public whom he hopes to turn into a jury" (*Constituting*, 81). Although Douglass's testimonial writing represents a narrative intervention that encourages us to read Frederick's involvement as "a witness and a participant" in his aunt's whipping as an act of resistance rather than complicity, in this scene Douglass stresses young Frederick's passivity as a witness in order to emphasize the bifurcation of the visual and the verbal in the South. See also Foreman, "Sentimental Abolition," 196–98.

77 See Hartman, *Scenes*, 7–8.

78 Douglass, *Narrative*, 23.

79 Ibid., 24.

80 As Wiegman notes, complicating Foucault, nineteenth- and twentieth-century U.S. technologies of race *combine* spectacle and surveillance in the sense that specularity reinforces panopticism (*American*, 37–42). See also Hartman, *Scenes*, 7–8.

81 Douglass, *Narrative*, 24.

82 Ibid.

83 Ibid.

84 Ibid.

85 Ibid., 25.

86 Ibid., 47.

87 Ibid., 50–51. See Suggs, *Whispered*, 61; Leverenz, *Manhood*, 108–34; Franchot, "Punishment," 154; Yarborough, "Race," 166–67.

88 Douglass, *Narrative*, 51, 29.

89 Ibid., 60.

90 Ibid.

91 See Harris, "Whiteness."

92 Douglass, *Narrative*, 60.

93 Ibid.

94 Ibid.

95 Ibid., 61.

96 Ibid., 63.

97 Ibid., 65.

98 Ibid., 62.

99 Ibid., 63.

100 Ibid.

101 Ibid.; Douglass critiques the kind of quietist sentimentalism discussed in Fisher, *Hard Facts*, 110.

102 Douglass, *Narrative*, 64.

103 Felman, *Juridical*, 81.

104 Ibid., 80.

105 Here, as in the defense for the O. J. Simpson criminal trial, "law is invoked as part and parcel" of the racial "trauma" (ibid., 91).

106 Douglass, Narrative, 62.

107 See Starling, Slave Narrative, 221–48; Andrews, To Tell, 97–166.

108 On vision and visuality in the witnessing scenes discussed here, see DeLombard, "Eye-Witness."

109 Douglass, Narrative, 74.

110 Ibid., 75.

111 Ibid.

112 Ibid.

113 PASS, Narrative, 15, 14.

114 Cannon, Case, 12.

115 On a similar dynamic in press coverage of the Christiana trials, see Slaughter, Bloody, 92–93, 97, 110.

116 On Douglass's self-presentation as former slave as against free black abolitionist Charles Lenox Remond, see Lampe, Frederick Douglass, 106–7.

117 For illustrations of the rhetorical challenges facing free African Americans in the 1840s who could lay claim to neither the testimonial posture of the slave nor the full citizenship of the white abolitionist advocate, see Ripley, Black Abolitionist Papers, 3:368–74, 428–29, 442–45. Perhaps the most striking example of this conundrum appears in Ward, Autobiography.

Chapter Four

1 Contemporary accounts of the Cambria incident vary as to the details. See Pettinger, "Send" and "At Sea," 160–62. For the Cambria's passenger list, see Daily Evening Transcript, 16 Aug. 1845. For contemporary coverage in the abolitionist press, including reprints from other periodicals, see British and Foreign Anti-Slavery Reporter, 12 Nov. 1845, 212; the Liberator, 26 Sept. 1845, 3 Oct. 1845, 10 Oct. 1845, 16 Jan. 1846; and the National Anti-Slavery Standard, 15 Jan. 1846. For antiabolitionist coverage, see New York Herald, 27 Sept. 1845, 6 Oct. 1845, and 1 Dec. 1845. For accounts of the incident in contemporary travelogues, see Warburton, Hochelaga, 2:358–62; Alexander James, L'Acadie, 2:258–62. Douglass recounted the incident repeatedly in his speeches and writing. See Douglass, My Bondage, 370–72, 380–81; Life and Times, 677–79; Frederick Douglass Papers, 1:61–66, 79–86, 90–92, 133, 139–42; Life and Writings, 5:12. For discussions of the Cambria and Captain Judkins in the context of maritime history, see Fry, History, 55–65, 105, 126; Bowen, Century, 33–52, 77; Babcock, Spanning, 15–35, 54–59, 74–77 (Cambria advertisement at 92).

2 This scene's ironic reversal of the Middle Passage has made it a set-piece of the Black Atlantic, as theorized in Gilroy, Black Atlantic. See Rice and Crawford, "Triumphant," 3. In his British speeches, Douglass himself cast the shipboard events in a juridical rather than a maritime register.

3 Douglass, "Heroic Slave," 520. In 1841, while being transported from Virginia to New Orleans, the slaves on the ship Creole staged an uprising, led by Madison Wash-

ington. Upon their arrival in the free port of Nassau, Bahamas, the British authorities determined they had no legal authority to return the former captives. See Cover, *Justice*, 109–16. See also Sundquist, *To Wake*, 115–34; Sale, *Slumbering*, 150–51, 173–97.

4   Abolitionist lecturers regularly encountered violence. A famous incident occurred in Pendleton, Indiana, on 16 Sept. 1843, when Douglass sustained a permanent injury to his right hand and was knocked unconscious. See Douglass, *Life and Times*, 675–76; McFeely, *Frederick Douglass*, 108–12. See also Leonard L. Richards, *Gentlemen*; Grimsted, *American Mobbing*.

5   For a contemporary nationalist account, see *New York Herald*, 27 Sept. 1845; contrast Douglass, "Letters."

6   Licensed in Maine on 3 July 1844, Allen soon afterward moved to Boston and was admitted to the bar in the first week of May 1845 (Contee, "Macon B. Allen," 67–68). See also *In Memoriam*, 31–32; Charles Sumner Brown, "Genesis," 148–49; Bloomfield, *American Lawyers*, 312; J. Clay Smith Jr., *Emancipation*, 93–96.

7   Mack, "Social History," 1412.

8   Jefferson, *Notes*, 177. For a parallel reading of the same cluster of texts that focus on Scottish Common Sense philosophy, see Lee, *Slavery*, 93–132.

9   Walker, *Appeal*, 8.

10   Edwin Garrison Walker, the fourth African American lawyer admitted to the Suffolk County bar and the first elected to the Massachusetts legislature, may well have been David Walker's son (Hinks, *Awaken*, 270–71). See also J. Clay Smith Jr., *Emancipation*, 100, where Walker is incorrectly identified as "Edward."

11   Pease and Pease, *They*, 156–70. For a sample California due-process petition, see Ripley, *Black Abolitionist Papers*, 4:104–207.

12   Charlotte Ray "became the nation's first black woman lawyer, and one of the first women of any race to join the profession, in 1872 when she was admitted in Washington, D.C." (Mack, "Social History," 1416).

13   Morris lost the 1848 school-desegregation case, *Roberts v. City of Boston*; *Roberts* was subsequently cited in *Plessy v. Ferguson* and is widely acknowledged as a precursor to *Brown v. Board of Education*. See J. Clay Smith Jr., *Emancipation*, 96–99; Collison, *Shadrach*, 83, 105, 116, 119, 122, 123, 130, 142, 147–48, 194–96; Von Frank, *Trials*, 42–46, 55, 116, 128, 239, 242, 295, 315; Horton and Horton, *Black Bostonians*.

14   Langston claimed that his 1855 election to town clerk in Brownhelm, Ohio, made him "the first colored man ever nominated in the United States to an office, and who was elected on a popular vote" (*Virginia Plantation*, 144–45). Langston held a number of public offices until, after a contested election, he briefly served in the House of Representatives (1890–91) as a Virginia Republican. See Cheek and Cheek, *John Mercer Langston*; Bloomfield, *American Lawyers*, 318–39; J. Clay Smith Jr., *Emancipation*, 43–45, 230–31, 407–9. On Hughes, see Andrews, Foster, and Harris, *Oxford Companion*, 368.

15   Langston, *Virginia Plantation*, 114.

16   Ibid., 104.

17   Ibid., 104–5.

18   *In Memoriam*, 11.

19   Ibid., 12.
20   Ibid., 21, 22.
21   Ibid., 33.
22   Ibid.
23   Langston, *Virginia Plantation*, 164.
24   Ibid.
25   Ibid., 164–65.
26   Ibid., 165.
27   Ibid.
28   Ibid., 165–66.
29   Ibid., 167.
30   For newspaper clippings, see "U.S. *vs. Morris*," folder 1062, Dana Papers, AAS.
31   *Report*, 23.
32   Ibid., 23, 24.
33   Ibid., 36–37.
34   Again, we might extend Mack's insight about gender in the courtroom back to the racialized context of antebellum America: "Issues of body, dress, and appearance that were obscured when the bar was composed of [white] men only, suddenly became visible and took on both symbolic and practical import when [African Americans] entered the profession" ("Social History," 1434).
35   For a particularly relevant contrast of fugitive slave testimony and blackface minstrelsy, see Fabian, *Unvarnished*, 108–11. For an alternative view of these two types of "performances," see Hartman, *Scenes*, 27. On rhetorical inscription of African American bodies, see Mailloux, "Re-Marking."
36   Douglass, *My Bondage*, 105.
37   Ibid.
38   Habermas, *Structural Transformation*, 171; Sundquist, *To Wake*, 97. On the new importance of personality to Jacksonian rhetorical performance, see Baxter, *Frederick Douglass's*, 59–83.
39   Douglass, *My Bondage*, 106.
40   Ibid.
41   Ibid.
42   Cobb, *Inquiry*, 42–43.
43   On the Scottish Common Sense philosophy concept of "apprehension" elsewhere in *My Bondage*, see Lee, *Slavery*, 126.
44   Gates, "Editor's Introduction: Writing 'Race,'" 11.
45   Jefferson, *Notes*, 175. See also Eze, *Race*, 29–33, 38–64.
46   See Jefferson, *Notes*, 169, 172, 175, 182.
47   Ibid., 179.
48   Ibid.
49   Ibid.
50   Ibid., 177.
51   Ibid.
52   Ibid., 100.

53 Ibid., 178.

54 Ibid.

55 See Habermas, *Structural Transformation*, 36. On Jefferson and nineteenth-century racial thought, see Fredrickson, *Black Image*, 1–3; Boulton, "American Paradox"; Gates, *Trials*, 40–49, 59–61.

56 In Query XIV's triadic grouping of law, race, and education, the mutual interdependence of (white) citizenship and education make blacks' imputed intellectual inferiority virtually synonymous with their civic exclusion. See Oakes, "Why Slaves," 191.

57 Boulton, "American Paradox," 485.

58 Douglass, *My Bondage*, 367.

59 On the appropriateness of Holocaust scholarship to the study of slavery and abolition, see Gilroy, *Black Atlantic*, 215. The purpose here is better to understand, in theoretical terms, the status of testimonial speech in the nexus of power relations from which it arises. For a similar approach, see Marcus Wood, *Slavery*, 20–53.

60 Young, *Writing*, 15, 9.

61 Ibid., 23.

62 Douglass, *Frederick Douglass Papers*, 1:3. See also Lampe, *Frederick Douglass*, 66–70.

63 Douglass, *Frederick Douglass Papers*, 1:3.

64 Ibid.

65 See Pease and Pease, *They*, 3–16.

66 Douglass, *Frederick Douglass Papers*, 1:29.

67 On poststructuralism and the countermovement of Holocaust testimony to "documentary realism," see Young, *Writing*, 17. On the critical pitfalls of reifying "experience," see Scott, "Evidence."

68 Young, *Writing*, 38. See also ibid., 15–39.

69 Foucault, *History of Sexuality*, 67.

70 *In Memoriam*, 18. This comment may also refer to changes in legal education more generally, as Morris's generation of attorneys trained in law-office apprenticeships was replaced by the products of professional law schools. On legal training, see J. Clay Smith Jr., *Emancipation*, 33–92; Bloomfield, *American Lawyers*, 302–39.

71 Blight, "Peculiar," xvii.

72 Bingham, *Columbian Orator*, 210.

73 Douglass, *Narrative*, 32. On Bingham in the eighteenth-century master-slave dialogue tradition, see Bruce, *Origins*, 22–24, 51–52, 67–70.

74 Douglass, *Narrative*, 32.

75 See Blassingame, introduction, xxii–xxiii; Blight, "Peculiar"; Fishkin and Peterson, "We Hold," 190–92; Levine, *Martin Delany*, 27; McFeely, *Frederick Douglass*, 34–36; Martin, *Mind*, 8–9, 274; Sundquist, *To Wake*, 104–5; Lampe, *Frederick Douglass*, 9–13, 101–2.

76 I am indebted to my former students Kristen Proehl and Briallen Hopper for first calling this discrepancy to my attention.

77 Blight, "Peculiar," xxiv.

78 Bingham, *Columbian Orator*, 210.

79 Newman, Rael, and Lapsansky, "Theme," 22.

80 Ibid.

81 Walker, *Appeal*, 76, 15.

82 For a critique of uplift ideology in McCune Smith's introduction and the work as a whole, see Levine, *Martin Delany*, 112–15.

83 On Douglass's use of a black-authored authenticating document, see Foster, *Witnessing*, 148, and Andrews, *To Tell*, 217.

84 Douglass, *My Bondage*, 125.

85 Ibid., 125, 132, 137. On Douglass's representative Americanness, see Sundquist, *To Wake*, 86, 92, 101.

86 Douglass, *My Bondage*, 126, 133. For a more direct critique of Jefferson's Query XIV, see McCune Smith, "Fourteenth." See also Gates, *Trials*, 64–65.

87 Douglass, *My Bondage*, 126.

88 Ibid., 134.

89 Ibid., 129.

90 Ibid.

91 Ibid., 133, 134.

92 Newmyer, "John Marshall," 523. For Marshall's ambiguous position on slavery, see ibid., 526. On Marshall in a literary context, see Ferguson, *Law and Letters*, 23.

93 Douglass, *My Bondage*, 125.

94 *Notes*'s structure, Ferguson has shown, rests on the inductive logic of empiricism and the common law: "Only slavery resists rational management in Jefferson's hands, . . . precisely because it defies legal terminology and solution within the framework of an eighteenth-century lawyer. Slavery exists, but against natural law; it becomes, in consequence, a structural incongruity in *Notes*, spilling between and among sections." The anomalous, extralegal status of the slave disrupts not only *Notes*'s structural coherence but its logical progression as well. In contrast to the inductive legal logic that provides *Notes* with its structure, Jefferson's discussion of blacks and law moves in the opposite direction: observed evidence of blacks' inferiority is marshaled to support the premise of their necessary civic exclusion (*Law and Letters*, 38, 46, 51). See also Waldstreicher, "Nature," 29–34. On the philosophical contexts for McCune Smith's emphasis on the superiority of induction, see Lee, *Slavery*, 108.

95 Bingham, *Columbian Orator*, 209. Conflating servitude and criminality, the word *villain* is especially charged here, given contemporary debates about the legal precedent for American slavery in the archaic English practice of villeinage. See Wiecek, "Origins," 1715–18; Higginbotham, *Matter*, 322–23, 338–44; Morris, *Southern Slavery*, 52–55.

96 Bingham, *Columbian Orator*, 210.

97 Ibid.

98 Douglass, *Narrative*, 33; compare Douglass, *My Bondage*, 227. See also Fishkin and Peterson, "We Hold," 195.

99 Douglass, *My Bondage*, 225–26.

100 Ibid., 226.

101 For an updated version of Bingham's "Dialogue," Douglass's own "Letter to His Old

Master," see Douglass, *My Bondage*, 412–18. On literary historical connections to Jefferson's *Notes*, see Bruce, *Origins*, 69, 246. The most suggestive synthesis of testimonial authority and civic assertion appears in a narrative published six years after *My Bondage and My Freedom*, in the first year of the Civil War. The title page proclamation of J. H. Banks's *Narrative*, "I am a witness against American slavery," prefaces an account that depicts Banks repeatedly engaging his enslavers in extended debates over the justice of slavery and, at one point, contracting with his fellow fugitives, who are "thus covenanted and leagued together as a band of liberty-hunting pilgrims" (Pennington, *Narrative*, 21–24, 42–45, 60–62, 72).

102 On Douglass's nuanced understanding of citizenship in *My Bondage* as well as African Americans' strategic embrace of normative citizenship, see Castronovo, *Necro*, 50–61, 206, 214.

103 Gewirtz, "Narrative," 5, 7.

104 See Clover, "Law," 103–4, 118.

105 Andrews, Foster, and Harris, *Oxford Companion*, 667.

106 Gates, *Classic*, ix.

107 Ibid.

108 Those scholars who, like Fabian, have acknowledged that abolitionists "employed the methods and metaphors of the courtroom" have not offered sustained analyses of the implications of such rhetoric as a means for structuring the antebellum debate over slavery (Fabian, *Unvarnished*, 95). Davis, for example, alludes in passing to the testifying black witness as "a defining trope in the slave narrative tradition" (Mary Kemp Davis, *Nat Turner*, 116). Marcus Wood offers a brief, brilliant discussion of legal rhetoric in antislavery materials (*Blind Memory*, 82–87).

109 Amrine et al., "Status," 24.

110 Ibid.

111 Ibid. See also Blassingame, "Using"; Yellin, introduction, xxxi–xxxv.

112 For a particularly insightful elaboration of the challenges facing the field, see McKay, "Naming." That such pressures have diminished rather than subsided is perhaps indicated by the extensive documentary apparatus attending the cloth, facsimile, and trade-paperback editions of *The Bondwoman's Narrative* (2002). See, for example, Crafts, *Bondwoman's*, xi–xciii, 303–58. Similarly, the ongoing scholarly debate over the Denmark Vesey conspiracy has rephrased persistent legal doubts about black testimony in historiographical terms (Michael P. Johnson, "Denmark Vesey," 942, 948, 949, 962–63). See also Michael P. Johnson, "Reading Evidence," 201–2.

113 Delgado, "Storytelling," 2414, 2415.

114 Ibid., 2414 (n. 16). Delgado's examples of storytelling in this article vary widely. For his own autobiographical storytelling, see Delgado, "Imperial." It should be noted that Delgado rejects his critics' emphasis on his use of personal narrative, stressing, quite rightly, his more frequent use of nonautobiographical narratives. See Delgado, "Coughlin's Complaint," his rebuttal to Coughlin, "Regulating."

115 Culp, "Autobigraphy," 541–42. For an alternative critique of Culp's use of Douglass, see Coughlin, "Regulating," 1263–68. See also Culp's rebuttal, "Telling," 81–89.

116 Delgado, "Storytelling," 2415, 2435. For a more general critique of the legal academy's celebration of narrative, see Weisberg, "Proclaiming."

117 For opposing views on Foucault's relevance to the storytelling debate, see West, "Feminism"; Coughlin, "Regulating," 1326.

My purpose here is not to reject the claims made by Delgado and others on behalf of legal storytelling; quite the contrary, Delgado's assertion that storytelling serves two basic purposes for members of oppressed groups, both as "a means of psychic preservation" and "as a means of lessening their own subordination," seems quite sound in both the nineteenth-century context and today ("Storytelling," 2428–29, 2411). Nevertheless, it is my contention that the potentially empowering aspect of storytelling is highly dependent upon the rhetorical framework in which it is presented and that, as the experience of Douglass and other nineteenth-century African American storytellers suggests, CRT's objectives could be better met by complicating the emphasis on the liberating aspects of testimonial speech.

118 Ross, "Rhetorical," 40.

119 Culp, "Autobiography," 547.

120 Ibid., 546. Delgado, for example, contrasts the drawbacks of civil rights litigation with the advantages of oppositional storytelling ("Storytelling," 2428–29).

121 Henderson, "Legality," 1596, 1603. See also Ross, "Rhetorical," 19–26.

122 The point here is not uncritically to reify "experience" but to acknowledge the place of testimonial personal narrative in argumentation, both legal and extralegal, on behalf of African American citizenship. For further elaboration of these ideas, see Scott, "Evidence"; Coughlin, "Regulating," 1234–51. As Coughlin demonstrates, however, the structures of various autobiographical forms (apology, confession, etc.) risk subsuming their authors' radical legal arguments in an overarching narrative of liberal individualism. Again, see Culp's rebuttal, "Telling," 74–81.

123 Culp, "Telling," 88. See also Culp, "Autobiography," 558–59.

124 Douglass, My Bondage, 380.

125 Douglass, Frederick Douglass Papers, 1:63–64. No transcript of the Cambria speech survives; an echo may be heard in a later speech Douglass composed for a nonabolitionist audience in Rochester, New York: "What, then, are the facts? Here I will not quote my own experience in slavery; for this you might call one sided testimony. I will not cite the declarations of abolitionists; for these you might pronounce exaggerations. I will not rely upon advertisements cut from newspapers; for these you might call isolated cases. But I will refer you to the laws adopted by the legislatures of the slave States. I give you such evidence, because it cannot be invalidated nor denied. I hold in my hand sundry extracts from the slave codes of our country, from which I will quote" (ibid., 2:265).

126 Douglass was traveling to England in part to promote his newly published Narrative; his fellow traveler, abolitionist-singer John Hutchinson, recalled that the "curious of both nationalities [British and American] were interested in him, and after reading his little 'Narrative,' which we took pains to circulate among the passengers, the desire to him hear him speak was expressed" (Story, 2:145).

127 Douglass, *My Bondage*, 368.

128 Douglass, *Frederick Douglass Papers*, 1:64 (n. 11).

129 Ibid., 60.

130 Ibid., 61.

131 Ibid.

132 Ibid. On slave literacy and the law, see Cornelius, *Title*.

133 Douglass, *Frederick Douglass Papers*, 1:61–62.

134 See Pease and Pease, *They*; Ripley, *Black Abolitionist Papers*, 3:20–57.

Chapter Five

1 George M. Stroud qtd. in Stowe, *Key*, 90.

2 Stowe, *Key*, 91.

3 Ibid.

4 Ibid.

5 Ibid.

6 Ibid.

7 George M. Stroud qtd. in ibid., 90.

8 Ibid., 88.

9 Whitney, "Shadow," 554. On the centrality of facts to the *Key*'s revised sentimental approach to slavery, see Weinstein, *Family*, 66–94.

10 Stowe, *Key*, 91.

11 As Marcus Wood observes in a discussion of repentant slave-ship captain turned abolitionist spiritual autobiographer John Newton, "The testimony of slavery opens up in those spaces, not where no one spoke but where someone else spoke for them. The crime here is not to silence the victims but to try to acquire their voices, to efface them through compulsive reinscription" (*Slavery*, 35). Accordingly, Robert Alexander's play, *I Ain't Yo' Uncle: The New Jack Revisionist Uncle Tom's Cabin* (1992), places Stowe herself on trial for misrepresenting African American characters and issues (Otter, "Stowe," 15–27, 22, 23).

12 Stowe, *Key*, 19, 254. Although outside the scope of this study, *Uncle Tom in England* (1852) merits brief mention here. Like Stowe's *Key*, this anonymous British "echo" places a revised "Uncle Tom" ("Thomas Brown") in a juridical context—but, when offered a lawyer, this Uncle Tom enacts an early model of black advocacy by representing himself in court. This, along with the civic agency displayed by both its male and female black characters and its imaginative mingling of scenes and characters from Stowe's novel and Douglass's *Narrative*, makes it a fascinating transatlantic manifestation of popular legal consciousness in the print debate over slavery.

13 Crane, "Dangerous," 181. The classic treatments of Stowe's sentimentalism are Douglas, *Feminization*; Tompkins, *Sensational*; Fisher, *Hard Facts*; Gillian Brown, *Domestic Individualism*; Samuels, *Culture*. For a reassessment, see Weinstein, *Family*. On Stowe and law, see Crane, "Stowe"; Crane, "Dangerous"; Crane, *Race*, 56–86; Rowe, "Stowe's Rainbow"; Whitney, "Shadow"; Clark, "Sacred"; Thomas, *Cross-Examinations*, 113–37; Grüner, "Stowe's Dred"; Best, *Fugitive's Properties*, 101–200; Tushnet, *Slave Law*; Loebel, *Letter*, 127–71. The most thorough examination of Stowe, senti-

ment, and antebellum law has been conducted by Alfred L. Brophy in a series of articles: "Over and Above," "Reason," and "Humanity."

14 Stowe, Uncle Tom's Cabin: Authoritative, xiii.

15 On Stowe's editing of the Confessions in Dred, see Levine, Martin Delany, 174.

16 Hedrick, Harriet Beecher Stowe, 190–92, 201–2.

17 Stowe, Uncle Tom's Cabin: Authoritative, 384.

18 Sand, "Review," reprinted in ibid., 463.

19 Brophy, "Over and Above," 479. Whereas Clark, "Sacred," joins Brophy in emphasizing the influence of Stowe's sentimental critique on subsequent legal reform, Thomas argues that Stowe's sentimental embrace of separate-spheres ideology compromises the political efficacy of her antislavery fiction. See Thomas, Cross-Examinations, 130–31.

20 Brophy, "Over and Above," 479. On legally oriented Southern responses to Stowe's work, see ibid., 479–93. See also Henry Field James, Abolitionism, 30.

21 Stowe, Key, 70.

22 Angelina Grimké qtd. in Barnes, Antislavery Impulse, 231 (n. 21).

23 Stowe, Key, 3. For challenges to the accuracy of Uncle Tom's Cabin's portrayal of slave law, see ibid., 67–70. On Stowe's response, see Whitney, "Shadow," 553–55. See also Rowe, "Stowe's Rainbow"; Grüner, "Stowe's Dred"; Judie S. Newman, introduction.

24 Judie S. Newman, introduction, 14.

25 See Sánchez-Eppler, Touching, 27–29; Whitney, "Shadow"; Crane, "Dangerous," 178–79.

26 Stowe, Key, 70.

27 See Judie S. Newman, introduction, 11–13. On "Bleeding Kansas" and Dred, see Boyd, "Violence." On Dred and the 1856 Republican presidential campaign, see Grant, "Stowe's Dred."

28 Von Frank, Trials, 13–14; Hedrick, Harriet Beecher Stowe, 256–57.

29 Whitney, "Shadow," 555.

30 Crane, "Dangerous," 179 (n. 7). Alternatively, Grüner associates Stowe's apparent inability to envision African American citizenship with that of Supreme Court Chief Justice Roger B. Taney ("Stowe's Dred," 11–12).

31 Judie S. Newman, introduction, 22. See also Levine, Martin Delany, 160–65; Davis, Nat Turner, 110–41; Cowan, Slave, 138–54.

32 On Dred's lawyers, judges, and legislators as representatives of antebellum legal approaches ranging from formalism to utilitarianism and instrumentalism, see Brophy, "Humanity."

33 See Levine, Martin Delany; Stepto, "Sharing."

34 Stepto and Levine focus largely on African American male activist authors' influence on and exchanges with Stowe, although Levine does devote considerable attention to Stowe's more problematic relations with women such as Harriet Jacobs, Sojourner Truth, and Milly Edmondson. On Mary Ann Shadd Cary's own struggles for representative identity as it was conducted across the borders of gender, class, and nation, see Rhodes, Mary Ann Shadd Cary, 51–134.

35　See Stepto, "Sharing," 137, 151–52; Levine, *Martin Delany*, 83–85. See also Grüner, "Stowe's *Dred*," 12; Judie S. Newman, introduction, 22.

36　Fishkin and Peterson, "We Hold," 199.

37　Ibid., 199–200. Alternatively, see Yarborough, "Race."

38　Levine, *Martin Delany*, 155; Stepto, "Sharing," 151. Two recent critics find Stowe reaching a similar impasse in *Dred*. In the context of antebellum philosophy, see Lee, *Slavery*, 52–54, 83–84. Approaching *Dred* as "an anti-anti-Tom" novel, Meer also notes "*Dred*'s self-contradicting stress on the importance of black voices," in a reading that emphasizes the novel's "dramatizing [of] the conflict between black and white (proslavery) utterances in the public arena" while at the same time demonstrating "the paradox of a white author's championing of black testimony, itself a variant on blackface's simultaneous attraction to and ventriloquizing [of] black speakers" (*Uncle Tom*, 237, 254, 225).

39　Andrews, *To Tell*, 72–77; Sundquist, *To Wake*, 36–56.

40　Gray qtd. in Stowe, *Dred*, 680.

41　Jacobs, *Incidents*, 2; Greenberg, *Confessions*, 40. Sundquist notes that the *Confessions*'s surrounding legal apparatus effectively reverses the slave narrative's authenticating documents in that "the legalistic materials further the imprisonment of Turner" by "assist[ing] in [his] execution . . . by corroborating the evidence brought against him" (*To Wake*, 45, 46). On the ironic designation, see ibid., 68. On similarities between proslavery Southern and abolitionist portrayals of Turner, see ibid., 53–54.

42　A fairly transparent roman á clef, *Dred* incorporates well-known court cases and political events into its plot and features characters closely resembling real-life figures in the slavery controversy. Judge Clayton (Edward's father) finds his counterpart in North Carolina Judge Thomas Ruffin. The brutal slaveowner Tom Gordon is based on the equally vicious slaveholder Simon Souther, the defendant in *Souther v. Commonwealth* (1851). See also Stowe, *Dred*, 691–95. The tragic infanticide Cora Gordon recalls the desperate fugitive slave mother Margaret Garner, as well as the emancipated and legally reenslaved wife of Mississippi planter Elisha Brazealle in the case *Hinds v. Brazealle* (1835). See Weisenburger, *Modern Medea*; Stowe, *Key*, 114–15; Davis, *Nat Turner*, 113. Whereas the prophet-rebel Dred is a composite of Denmark Vesey and Nat Turner, the evangelical Milly resembles Sojourner Truth, and the articulate biracial slave Harry, who knocks down his master and whom Dred proclaims "a witness and commander to the people," brings to mind Frederick Douglass (Judie S. Newman, introduction, 21–22). Edward Clayton suggests the Reverend William King, former slaveholder and founder of Ontario's Elgin Settlement. See Pease and Pease, "Uncle Tom" and *Black Utopia*, 84–108. An additional model for Clayton may have been abolitionist lawyer, governor of Ohio, and U.S. senator, Salmon P. Chase. See Brophy, "Humanity," 1153. Grüner sees in Anne Clayton and her exemplary plantation school an allusion to Connecticut schoolmistress Prudence Crandall, whose decision to run an interracial girls' school led to the celebrated 1834 court case *Crandall v. State* (Grüner, "Stowe's *Dred*," 27). See also Finkelman, *Slavery in the Courtroom*, 138–43. On Anne Clayton as an avatar of Catharine Beecher, see Lee, *Slavery*, 80.

43 Gray qtd. in Stowe, Dred, 680.

44 Stowe, Dred, 276, 277. See also Sundquist, To Wake, 79. On the similarities between Stowe's portrayal of Dred and early newspaper depictions of Turner, see Davis, Nat Turner, 126. For an alternative reading, see Meer, Uncle Tom, 227–28, 235.

45 Greenberg, Confessions, 8.

46 Gray qtd. in Stowe, Dred, 681.

47 On the antebellum antislavery bar's ideology, see Cover, Justice, 159–91.

48 Barney, Secessionist Impulse, 50, 51.

49 States with relevant (albeit widely varying) statutes were Virginia, North Carolina, Mississippi, Kentucky, Alabama, Tennessee, South Carolina, and Florida (Morris, Southern Slavery, 251–53). Slaves, of course, could not be plaintiffs in most lawsuits, whether civil or criminal.

50 Ibid., 253.

51 The judge's obiter dictum notwithstanding, the Georgia Supreme Court subsequently ruled against this policy in a separate case, Lingo v. Miller & Hill (1857). Jim (a slave) v. State (1854) qtd. in ibid., 252.

52 Although the requirement to provide counsel could lead to ironic results—Morris notes two cases in which slaveholders were assessed fees for refusing to arrange counsel for slaves who had attempted to murder them—Georgia Supreme Court Judge Henry L. Benning's observation that "every master has an interest to prevent his slave from being punished" makes it clear that such statutes served the interest of the slaveholding community primarily and that of the slave only incidentally (Benning qtd. in ibid.). See also Cobb, Inquiry, 268, 271. For reminders of the gap between statute law and everyday practice, however, see Gross, Double Character; Ely, Israel, 225–83.

53 This point is addressed by Brophy, "Humanity," 1157–58, 1159. On Clayton and Stowe, see Levine, Martin Delany, 167. On Stowe's feminization of law, see Grüner, "Stowe's Dred," 6–7.

54 Weld to Sarah Grimké and Angelina Grimké, 22 May 1837 (Barnes and Dumond, Letters, 1:389).

55 Ibid. Weld refers to Lydia Maria Child and Lucretia Chapman.

56 See Abzug, Passionate Liberator, 175–80; David A. J. Richards, "Abolitionist Feminism." The abolitionist movement would soon fracture over this among other issues. See Barnes, Antislavery Impulse, 153–60; Kraditor, Means, 39–77.

57 National Anti-Slavery Standard, 23 Feb. 1856, qtd. in Weisenburger, Modern Medea, 170.

58 Weisenburger, Modern Medea, 170.

59 Lucy Stone qtd. in ibid., 172.

60 Francis T. Chambers qtd. in Weisenburger, Modern Medea, 175.

61 Brophy, "Revolution," 47. See also Brophy, "Over and Above," 484–85, 488. On McCord, see Fought, Southern Womanhood. Another instructive example is antebellum women's sentimental antipolygamy fiction in the campaign for the legal protection of marriage, to which Stowe contributed. See Gordon, "Our National," 311.

62 Evans, Macaria, 185.

63 Hedrick, *Harriet Beecher Stowe*, 238. See also Newbury, *Figuring*, 96.

64 See Hedrick, *Harriet Beecher Stowe*, 223–24, 264. On the copyright case, *Stowe v. Thomas*, see Best, *Fugitive's Properties*, 115–19, 122–25; Homestead, *American*, 105–49.

65 Brophy, "Reason," 1212.

66 Stowe to Daniel R. Goodloe, 9 Feb. 1853, qtd. in Susan M. Ryan, *Grammar*, 154.

67 Brophy, "Revolution," 75.

68 Stowe, *Dred*, 383.

69 Ibid., 44.

70 Tushnet, *Slave Law*; Crane, "Dangerous," 194–204; Crane, *Race*, 70–77; Grüner, "Stowe's *Dred*," 21–24; Brophy, "Humanity"; Whitney, "Shadow"; Thomas, *Cross-Examinations*, 117–19, 133–35; Cover, *Justice*, 34–65; Wiethoff, *Peculiar*, 90–91, 128–29.

71 Stowe, *Dred*, 381.

72 Ibid.

73 Ibid., 381.

74 Ibid., 382.

75 Ibid.

76 Ibid., 389.

77 Ibid.

78 Ibid.

79 Ibid., 450. The colloquial expression derives from the description of Joseph's unjust enslavement and physical bondage in Psalms 105:17–18. On the image in another white sentimentalist depiction of slavery, that of Lawrence Sterne, see Marcus Wood, *Slavery*, 13–18.

80 Brophy, "Humanity," 1152, makes a similar observation. On Phillips and the Garrisonian concession to formalism, see Cover, *Justice*, 150–54. A contemporary memoir cites three examples of would-be lawyers (Charles C. Burleigh, George Thompson, and Wendell Phillips) relinquishing legal careers to become abolitionist advocates. See May, *Recollections*, 63–66, 113, 228–29. On James Gillespie Birney's disbarment from the Alabama Supreme Court for his abolitionism, see ibid., 207.

81 Stowe, *Dred*, 495.

82 Ibid., 493–94.

83 Ibid., 450.

84 Ibid., 453. See also Tushnet, *Slave Law*, 85, 95–96.

85 Stowe, *Dred*, 482.

86 Ibid., 549–50.

87 See DeLombard, "Adding."

88 Jacobs, *Incidents*, 1.

89 Ibid., 2; Stowe, *Dred*, 636.

90 Stowe, *Dred*, 550.

91 Writing "in behalf of" her "persecuted people," Jacobs presented Isaiah 32:9 as an epigraph to her narrative: "Rise up, ye women that are at ease! Hear my voice, ye careless daughters! Give ear unto my speech" (*Incidents*, xxxv). See Foster, "Resisting," 72; Garfield, "Earwitness," 110.

92 The parallel here with Stowe's notorious exchange with Jacobs over "ownership" of the slave's story is suggestive. See Hedrick, *Harriet Beecher Stowe*, 249. See also Yellin, *Harriet Jacobs*, 119–21. For a more generous reading, see Levine, *Martin Delany*, 151–52.

93 Stowe, *Dred*, 643.

94 Ibid., 490.

95 Ibid., 627. See also ibid., 691.

96 Ibid., 555–56.

97 Stowe, *Uncle Tom's Cabin: Authoritative*, 385.

98 Stepto, "Sharing," 137.

99 Levine, *Martin Delany*, 145.

100 Meer reminds us, however, of the similarity between Stowe's retrospective authentication of *Uncle Tom's Cabin* in *Key* and the "many blackface performers" who "claimed specific black sources for their acts, claims that were often both spurious and revealing about the exploitative processes the form involved" (*Uncle Tom*, 228).

101 Stowe, *Dred*, 568. An allusion to Genesis 31:46–54, "Jegar Sahadutha" refers to the pile of stones Jacob and Laban collect as a monument, or "heap of witness," to their reconciliation and brotherhood. See Young, *Writing*, 19–20. In *Dred*, the heap stands as "a witness of blood against tyrannous whites," the betrayal of interracial fraternity, the political brotherhood that is forged in this all-male gathering of slaves, and the reconciliation between the biracial collaborationist Harry and the "intensely black" rebel Dred (Stowe, *Dred*, 741, 566–67, 261).

102 Stowe, *Dred*, 568.

103 Ibid.

104 Ibid., 571.

105 One slave recounts the events recorded in the 1851 Virginia case, *Souther v. Commonwealth* as happening to his brother Sam, while Tom Gordon's murder of Hark recalls another 1851 Virginia case, *State v. Castleman* (ibid., 571–73). For documentation, see Stowe, *Key*, 79–82, 101–3; Stowe, *Dred*, 691–702.

106 Stowe, *Dred*, 571.

107 A less charitable reading of Stowe might see her, like Wood's Reverend John Newton, as "a spiritual dung beetle rolling an ever-growing ball of testimony before him, catastrophically but almost comically trying to speak for the slave" (*Slavery*, 36).

108 On this dilemma in Stowe's post-*Tom* engagement with the theory of moral sentiments, see Lee, *Slavery*, 68–78.

109 Stowe, *Dred*, 556. On Kemble's negotiation of the white abolitionist's conflicting tasks of listening, telling, and advocacy, especially in contrast to Stowe's authorial omnipresence, see Weinstein, *Family*, 70–76, 87.

110 Stowe, *Dred*, 632.

111 Ibid. Critics diverge widely in their readings of this frequently cited passage. See Levine, *Martin Delany*, 171; Rowe, "Stowe's Rainbow," 47–48. Neither account seems sufficiently to address Clayton's paternalism; in his revised discussion of *Dred*, Crane reaches conclusions very similar to my own (*Race*, 76).

112 Stowe, Dred, 639, 641.

113 Unlike some critics, I do not see the swamp as an inherently revolutionary site whose presence compensates for (or at least mitigates) the novel's paternalist conclusion. See Rowe, "Stowe's Rainbow"; Karafilis, "Spaces"; contrast Cowan, Slave.

114 Judie S. Newman, introduction, 24; Hedrick, Harriet Beecher Stowe, 259. On Milly and Dred's confrontation in the swamp and a parallel incident between Sojourner Truth and Frederick Douglass, see Judie S. Newman, introduction, 21–22; Levine, Martin Delany, 282–83 (n. 49). See also Stowe, "Sojourner Truth," 480.

115 Levine contends that "what prevents Dred from putting his desires into action, in addition to his apprehension of God's silence at this particular moment, is . . . the state's brutal legal and policing authority" (Martin Delany, 169–70). But this claim is only partially true, for, as Clayton's worries make clear, the slaves' planned rebellion does not end with Dred's death but, rather, as a result of Clayton's direct intervention. In her survey of British and American dramatizations of Dred, Judie S. Newman documents the extent to which the former carried through with the novel's threatened (or promised) insurrection, albeit at the cost of reaffirming the stereotype of black savagery ("Staging"). Noting similar rebellions in earlier stage adaptations of Uncle Tom's Cabin, Meer argues that Stowe's portrayal of Dred represents "not a rejection of black revolution but indecision," in that she "could not follow the British dramatizations of Uncle Tom so far as to paint a full-scale insurrection, but she was willing to raise the possibility" (Uncle Tom, 227).

116 Stowe, Dred, 642.

117 The last time Harry is represented through tagged direct discourse is at the death of Dred; after this point, he is merely described in third person by the narrator. On Stowe's ambivalent relationship to black speech, see Mary Kemp Davis, Nat Turner, 117; Meer, Uncle Tom, 225–51. Rowe contends that Dred's "other fugitive slaves literally find their own voices and testify to others regarding their brutalization under slavery and their commitment to freedom" but does not address Harry's disturbing silence at the novel's end ("Stowe's Rainbow," 50).

118 In one of the few studies to focus on this scene, Lee reaches similar conclusions regarding Stowe's efforts to negotiate the theory of moral sentiments and Calvinism. Although his reading does not focus on Edward Clayton, Lee finds in Dred signs of Stowe's growing "skepticism" about the project of literary abolitionism, noting in particular that "more than Uncle Tom's Cabin, Dred critically traces the uneven path toward correct affection. It dwells on the fear that achieving true sympathy is never a settled thing, for self-interest has a way of hiding behind seemingly benevolent motives" (Slavery, 78–84 [quotations at 54, 83]).

119 Stowe, Dred, 577.

120 Ibid., 582.

121 Ibid.

122 See William Lee Miller, Arguing; Zaeske, Signatures.

123 Meer, Uncle Tom, 225–51.

124 See Douglas, Feminization; Fisher, Hard Facts, 104–22; Thomas, Cross-Examinations, 113–37.

125 Stowe, Dred, 581.

126 Ibid., 582.

127 To make this observation is not necessarily to join the emerging critical consensus about the "pessimism" of Dred's ending. See Boyd, "Models," 28; Brophy, "Humanity," 1160. (Acknowledging such pessimism, Tushnet argues that Stowe's faith in individual salvation may point to a broader abolitionist commitment to reform through the informal institutions of civil society [Slave Law, 104, 123–37].) Quite the contrary, what finally makes Dred so disturbing is the way in which Clayton's paternalism seemingly offers the novel a hopeful conclusion, as indicated by Stowe's use of devices such as marriage, birth, and comedy (including minstrelsy) in the work's final pages. See Grüner, "Stowe's Dred," 24.

128 See Levine, Martin Delany.

129 See Robbins, "Gendering," 547–53.

130 Much like Clayton in his exchanges with Dred's black revolutionaries, Melville's Delano represents "the revolutionary mind at odds with itself, impassioned for freedom but fearful of continuing revolution, energized by the ideals of paternalistic humanitarianism but blind to the recriminating violence they hold in check" (Sundquist, To Wake, 154). On the benevolent humanitarianism of both the historical and the fictional Delano, see also Downes, "Melville's Benito Cereno"; Susan M. Ryan, Grammar, 69–77. On the novella's legal contexts, see Yellin, "Black Masks"; Rogin, Subversive, 211–14; Thomas, Cross-Examinations, 93–112; Sale, Slumbering; Ferguson, "Untold"; Susan Weiner, Law, 113–38.

131 For comparative readings of Melville and Douglass, see Sale, Slumbering, 146–97; Sundquist, To Wake, 177–78. On Stowe and Douglass, see Stepto, "Sharing," 137, 151–52; Levine, Martin Delany, 83–85.

132 See Fishkin and Peterson, "We Hold," 198–200; Castronovo, Necro, 183–86.

133 On Peter Poyas and Babo, see Yellin, "Black Masks," 687; Sundquist, To Wake, 182. For a parallel example from Gabriel's Rebellion, see Ferguson, "Untold." On speech, property, and criminal versus civic agency in the context of slavery, see Lee, Slavery, 144; Dayan, "Legal."

134 Melville, "Benito," 89.

135 Ibid., 102.

136 Ibid. On Babo's silence, see Yellin, "Black Masks," 687–89; Karcher, Shadow, 139–41; Rogin, Subversive, 217; Thomas, Cross-Examinations, 99, 111–12; Ferguson, "Untold"; Sale, Slumbering, 159–61, 170–72; Dana D. Nelson, Word, 127–30; Sundquist, To Wake, 181–82.

137 Melville, "Benito," 102.

Chapter Six

1 "Book Notices."

2 Ibid.

3 John Reuben Thompson, "Notices," 320. A 6 Nov. 1856 review in the Petersburg, Virginia, Daily Democrat did not survive to be microfilmed (personal correspondence with Mary Dessypris, reference librarian, Library of Virginia, 6 May 2005).

4 "Editorial," 447–48.

5 For attribution, see R. Glenn Wright, *Author Bibliography*, 328; Lyle H. Wright, *American Fiction*, 61.

6 Burwell, *Last Words*, 23–26.

7 Scholarly fascination with *Uncle Tom's Cabin* has revitalized interest in antebellum Southern and proslavery literature, until very recently the domain of regional literary criticism. See Castronovo, "Incidents"; Meer, *Uncle Tom*; Jordan-Lake, *Whitewashing* (brief discussion of *White Acre* at 10–11). For checklists of anti-Tom literature, see also Gossett, *Uncle Tom's Cabin*; Gardiner, "Proslavery Propaganda." On legally oriented responses to Stowe and abolitionist propaganda, see Brophy, "Over and Above" and "Revolution."

8 For an incisive contemporary Southern account of why Southern works—and specifically, those published by Burwell's comparatively prominent Richmond publisher, J. W. Randolph—failed to compete with those of a heavily capitalized, industrialized, and organized Northern firm like Harper and Brothers, see Simms, "Literary Prospects," 100–103.

9 The best discussion of these elements is Meer, *Uncle Tom*, 75–101 (*Graham's Magazine's* reference to "Cabin Literature" qtd. at 79).

10 On the agricultural address's influential form and idiom, see Faust, *Southern Stories*, 29–53. For an antebellum critique of agrarian provincialism as the primary impediment to Southern literary culture, see Simms, "Literary Prospects." On Southern honor rituals as alternatives to and in tandem with the adversarial process of law, see Ayers, *Vengeance*, 18, 23; Wyatt-Brown, *Southern Honor*, 366; Gross, *Double Character*, 53. On honor in interracial legal encounters, see Gross, *Double Character*, 54–57; Greenberg, *Honor*, 33–46. On proslavery sentimentalism, see Weinstein, *Family*, 66–94. For a contemporary example of agricultural and chivalric rhetoric, see H[eath], "Southern Literature."

11 Although its adversarial trial structure sets Burwell's novel apart, its adoption of the juridical metaphor is consistent with anti-Tom literature's more general dependence upon Northern cultural forms from minstrelsy to the slave narrative and the sentimental novel for its portrayals of Southern slavery. See Meer, *Uncle Tom*, 75–101; Castronovo, "Incidents."

12 The lawsuit in John Pendleton Kennedy's *Swallow Barn* (1832; rev. 1851)—a land dispute between two neighboring planters whose families (and thus property) are soon to be united by marriage—offers a representative example of a legal proceeding in Southern fiction. A property dispute that drags on for years, the lawsuit provides one of the litigants with a valued source of entertainment and both with ample opportunities for displays of honor. For an overview of these themes, see Brophy, "Revolution."

13 For a revealingly botched Southern attempt to respond to the North's juridical antislavery rhetoric in the South's language of honor, see chapter 10, "Our Best Witnesses and Masters in the Art of War," of Fitzhugh, *Cannibals*, 85–106. See also Hayne, *Speech*, 14–15. For the Southern tendency to protest or dismiss abolitionist

appeals to popular legal consciousness, see McCord, *Louisa S. McCord*, 247–48, 254–65, 274, 278, 342, 347–49, 431, 435–36.

14   On antebellum Southern periodical publishing, see Bassett, introduction; Richard J. Calhoun, "Literary Magazines." For contemporary accounts, see [Whitaker,] "Newspaper"; Simms, "Southern Literature"; a representative sample is reprinted in Bassett, *Defining*, 45–120.

15   White, "Publisher's Notice."

16   Emerson, *Selected*, 225.

17   Ibid., 234. For a contemporary discussion of Southern literary sectionalism in light of American literary nationalism, see Timrod, "Literature."

18   See Hammond, "'Mud-Sill,'" 122.

19   Qtd. in White, "Publisher's Notice."

20   Ibid.

21   Hammond, "'Mud-Sill,'" 122; Poe, "Georgia Scenes," 58.

22   See, for example, "An Inquiry"; Simms, "Literary Prospects," 103; Timrod, "Literature," 113. Of course, with origins roughly contemporaneous with the publication of David Walker's *Appeal* and the *Liberator*, as well as Nat Turner's uprising, Gray's *Confessions*, and the founding of the AASS, Southern literary sectionalism always had a defensive proslavery posture; it merely became more explicit in the 1850s. See Bassett, introduction; Werner, "Old South." See, for example, [Whitaker,] "Newspaper."

23   W. R. A., "Duty," 241.

24   Ibid., 243, 242.

25   Ibid., 243; Holcombe qtd. at 243. Calls for Southern literature frequently contrasted Southern success in politics, law, and oratory with the section's literary lack. See Legaré, "American," 47; "An Inquiry," 389–90.

26   Holcombe qtd. in W. R. A., "Duty," 243.

27   W. R. A., "Duty," 246.

28   Ibid., 243.

29   H[eath], "Southern Literature," 1. See also "Commercial," 2.

30   W. R. A., "Duty," 245–46.

31   Ibid., 245, 242, 247, 244.

32   Ibid., 244.

33   Ibid., 246.

34   [Burwell,] *White Acre*, 9.

35   Ibid., 19, 14.

36   Ibid., 39, 41.

37   Ibid., 42, 43.

38   Ibid., 52.

39   Ibid., 52. On "indebted servitude," see Hartman, *Scenes*, 125–63; Best, *Fugitive's Properties*, 80–83, 301–3 (n. 120).

40   [Burwell,] *White Acre*, 57.

41   Ibid., 82.

42 See Genovese, *Slaveholders' Dilemma*. See also Faust, *Southern Stories*, 15–28, 72–87. McCord outlined her own anti-Tom "novel of legal possibilities," a sentimental melodrama of wage labor's destruction of a poor urban family (*Louisa S. McCord*, 267–68). Similar plots appear in Eastman, *Aunt Phillis's Cabin*; Hentz, *Planter's*.

43 Grant's historical counterpart was doughface Bowery Boy politico Mike Walsh. See Wilentz, *Chants*, 326–35.

44 [Burwell,] *White Acre*, 216; similar subplots appear in Eastman, *Aunt Phillis's Cabin*; Hentz, *Planter's*.

45 On Herrenvolk democracy and the South, see Fredrickson, *Black Image*, 61–68, 90–94. On the lack of sectional cohesiveness arising from the conflicting politics of elite and egalitarian republicans, see Freehling, *Road*. On Fitzhugh, see Genovese, *World*, 118–244. On Southern views of material and moral "progress," see Genovese, *Slaveholders' Dilemma*. The attempt to negotiate elitism and egalitarianism in the name of Southern progress is also evident in Burwell, *Address*.

46 For contemporary examples, see [Whitaker,] "Newspaper," and McCord, *Louisa S. McCord*, 281–349. Meer identifies an entire subgenre of "anti-British anti-Tom" fiction (*Uncle Tom*, 133–222 [quotation at 197]). See also Leonard L. Richards, *Slave Power*, 143 (n. 15), and *Gentlemen*, 65–71.

47 [Burwell,] *White Acre*, 26.

48 Ibid., 66, 63.

49 Ibid., 24, 132, 136.

50 W. R. A., "Duty," 247.

51 On Hentz and proslavery sentimentalism more generally, see Moss, *Domestic*.

52 [Burwell,] *White Acre*, 86.

53 Ibid., 100.

54 Ibid., 96.

55 Ibid., 98.

56 Ibid., 104.

57 Ibid., 105, 104.

58 Ibid., 108.

59 On abolitionist fetishization of black suffering, see Sánchez-Eppler, *Touching*, 14–49; Hartman, *Scenes*, 17–23.

60 Douglass, *My Bondage*, 365. See Mailloux, "Re-Marking."

61 [Burwell,] *White Acre*, 118.

62 Ibid.

63 On abolitionism, commodification of the slave, and the rise of corporate law, see Best, *Fugitive's Properties*.

64 [Burwell,] *White Acre*, 118–19. As a child, Vulcan accidentally chopped off two of his own fingers with an axe (Hentz, *Planter's*, 530). On proslavery appropriations of the slave narrative genre, see Castronovo, "Incidents."

65 [Burwell,] *White Acre*, 119.

66 Ibid.

67 See Wyatt-Brown, *Lewis Tappan*, 145, 151–52. See, for example, the black mourning borders on *Fugitive Slave Bill*.

68 [Burwell,] *White Acre*, 119.

69 Ibid., 120.

70 Ibid.

71 Ibid., 101. Again, the parallels with Hentz bear noting; Brainerd begins his criminal career as a "felon boy" imprisoned for theft, growing into an "accomplished criminal" who successfully "eluded the punishment of his transgressions" prior to his arrest at the close of the novel as a bogus abolitionist lecturer (Hentz, *Planter's*, 460, 568).

72 [Burwell,] *White Acre*, 122.

73 Ibid.

74 Likewise, Vulcan's "terrible-looking scar" is "probably embellished by a few touches of reddish paint" (Hentz, *Planter's*, 561).

75 Genovese, *Slaveholders' Dilemma*, 61. See also ibid., 57–63.

76 [Burwell,] *White Acre*, 212.

77 See Macpherson, *Possessive Individualism*; Gilian Brown, *Domestic Individualism*, 13–60.

78 The scene recalls Dayan's discussion of the "taint" of race slavery ("Legal," 54–66).

79 [Burwell,] *White Acre*, 123.

80 Ibid.

81 On the confluence of slavery, capitalist speculation, law, and abolitionist print propaganda in the eighteenth-century British context, see Baucom, *Specters*.

82 In its "Black Acre" entry, the *Oxford English Dictionary* notes that a third parcel of land might be designated "green acre," speculating that "the choice of the words 'black,' 'white,' and 'green' was perhaps influenced by their use to indicate different kinds of crops," dating usage of the terms back to at least Sir Edward Coke's *Institutes of the Laws of England* (1628–44) (<http://www.dictionary.oed.com>). Thanks to Gregg Crane for alerting me to these terms' legal significance. A colloquial use of the terms appears in a homiletic item from a Petersburg, Virginia, contributor to the *Southern Literary Messenger*, which characterizes "Life" as "a tasseled pavement—dovetailed mosaic—here black acre and there white acre,—clouds to-day, sunshine to-morrow" (C. C[ampbell], "Ceremony").

83 [Burwell,] *White Acre*, 67.

84 Holthouse, *New Law Dictionary*, 139–40.

85 [Burwell,] *White Acre*, 154, 161.

86 Ibid., 154–55. As "a common-law action to recover personal property wrongfully taken by another," *detinue* can refer to a detained person as well as a chattel (Black, *Black's Law Dictionary*, 460).

87 Stroud, *Sketch*, 1827, 76–84.

88 Holthouse, *New Law Dictionary*, 139–40. Legal emancipation, Southerners emphasized, was first and foremost "the renunciation of a property right," one that by no means conferred to the emancipated civic status; this insistence on the property-law dimensions of emancipation could not, however, skirt the questions of public policy it inevitably raised (Morris, *Southern Slavery*, 371–73).

89 [Burwell,] *White Acre*, 59.

90 Ibid., 64.

91 Ibid., 66.

92 Ibid., 141.

93 Ibid., 139–40.

94 Wyatt-Brown, *Lewis Tappan*, 155.

95 See Gewirtz, "Aeschylus' Law."

96 [Burwell,] *White Acre*, 158.

97 Ibid., 141.

98 Ibid., 139.

99 Ibid., 69.

100 See Stroud, *Sketch*, 1827, 73–74.

101 [Burwell,] *White Acre*, 141. On the figure of the cavalier in Southern fiction, see Ritchie Devon Watson Jr., *Yeoman*.

102 [Burwell,] *White Acre*, 141–42.

103 Ibid., 160.

104 Ibid., 160–61.

105 Ibid., 166.

106 Ibid., 168.

107 Ibid., 184.

108 Ibid.

109 See ibid., 173, 146. On the view of lawyers as cultural conservators in conjunction with a Southern understanding of law that emphasized property rights over social reform, see Brophy, "Revolution."

110 [Burwell,] *White Acre*, 219.

111 Ibid.

112 Ibid.

113 On proslavery writers' target elite audiences, see Wyatt-Brown, "Proslavery," 323.

114 Black, *Black's Law Dictionary*, 144, 224, 965.

115 Holthouse, *New Law Dictionary*, 86.

116 [Burwell,] *White Acre*, 248–49.

Conclusion

1 Despite the slave insurrection panic of 1856, widespread fears about abolitionist-led uprisings were most intense following Harpers Ferry. See Barney, *Secessionist Impulse*, 163–88.

2 The Secret Six were Thomas Wentworth Higginson, Gerrit Smith, Theodore Parker, George Stearns, Samuel Gridley Howe, and Franklin Sanborn. See Renehan, *Secret*. On the relationships among Douglass, Brown, and Gerrit Smith, as well as James McCune Smith, see Stauffer, *Black Hearts*.

3 "The Way in Which Fred. Douglass."

4 On the charges, see Oates, *To Purge*, 314.

5 Douglass, *Life and Writings*, 2:461.

6 On the iconography of the runaway, including portrayals of Douglass, see Marcus Wood, *Blind Memory*, 78–142.

7 Douglass, *Narrative*, 29.

8   With the acquisition in 1858 of a high-speed press, *Frank Leslie's* typically had a lead time of one week. Accordingly, the paper was "advance-dated one week and the printed date marked the end of that issue's week, not its beginning" (Joshua Brown, *Beyond*, 254–55 [n. 2]). See also Gambee, *Frank Leslie*, 56.

9   See Littlefield, "Blacks"; Greenberg, *Honor*, 24–50.

10   Oates, *To Purge*, 310–12, 320–24, 353–56, 360–61. For the responses of specific constituencies, see Knupfer, "Crisis"; Finkelman, "Manufacturing"; Venet, "Cry"; Wallerstein, "Incendiaries"; Joyner, "Guilty."

11   Finkelman, "Manufacturing," 60, 61; Nudelman, "Blood."

12   See "Pictorial." *Frank Leslie's* "furnished a thorough, on-the-spot pictorial report of the whole tragic drama on a scale which appears not to have been surpassed—if indeed even attempted—by any other publication" (Gambee, *Frank Leslie*, 77). See also Tebbel and Zuckerman, *Magazine*, 19–20.

13   "Ossawattamie"; "Stephens"; "Prisoners"; "View in Charlestown"; "Cannon"; "Sleeping Room."

14   "View of the Courtroom"; "Portraits." See also "Pictorial." Each sheet typically measured 22 by 16 inches; pages in the supplement were more than twice that size, at approximately 44 by 36½ inches.

15   "The Way a Criminal Trial."

16   Ferguson, "Story," 44.

17   Ibid.; Finkelman, "Manufacturing," 43–44; Nudelman, "Blood."

18   Phillips, "Speech," 109.

19   Oates, *To Purge*, 307–58; Ferguson, "Story"; Finkelman, "Manufacturing"; Nudelman, "Blood"; Reynolds, *John Brown*, 334–479.

20   *Life*, 76. On the woman, C. C. Fouke, see Venet, "Cry," 111. See also Oates, *To Purge*, 296–97.

21   *Life*, 76.

22   See Ferguson, "Story," 64–65.

23   *Life*, 55.

24   Ibid. Brown's counsel was court-appointed members of the Virginia bar who either resigned or were dismissed when Northern lawyers appeared to represent him. As Ferguson notes, "During the six-day trial, Brown was represented by six lawyers in all, none of whom were formal defense counsel for more than half of the proceedings. . . . Each new lawyer asked for a delay in trial to prepare a proper defense, a request that the court consistently refused." These and other procedural irregularities, Ferguson suggests, "should have supplied grounds for delay, change of venue, and later, for prejudicial error" ("Story," 43 [n. 13], 63 [n. 64]). The injustice of the Virginia high court's summary refusal to grant a writ in error did not escape the notice of contemporary observers. See Drew, *John Brown*, 59, 110.

25   *Life*, 55.

26   Ibid.

27   Ibid.

28   See Ferguson, "Story," 55–56.

29   Griswold appeared as John Brown's defense counsel after Brown asked judges Dan-

iel R. Tilden and Thomas Russell to represent him: although Russell arrived only in time for sentencing, Tilden sent Griswold as his proxy. Apparently acknowledging the publicity value of a moderate lawyer, Brown had explicitly instructed Tilden and Russell, "do not send an ultra Abolitionist" (Villard, *John Brown*, 493).

30 *Life*, 84.
31 Ibid., 85.
32 Ibid.
33 Ibid.
34 Ibid.
35 Ibid., 75.
36 Ibid., 91.
37 Ferguson, "Story," 38. See also Knupfer, "Crisis," 147 (n. 71).
38 Redpath, *Public Life*.
39 See Reynolds, *John Brown*, 444–70.
40 See Venet, "Cry," 109; Karcher, *First Woman*, 416–27.
41 Reynolds, *John Brown*, 445–49, 61–62.
42 Oates, *To Purge*, 318–19; Finkelman, "Manufacturing," 46–50.
43 Drew, *John Brown*, 59.
44 Phillips, "Speech," 109.
45 Emerson, *Complete Works*, 11:270.
46 See Finkelman, "Manufacturing," 59–60; Reynolds, *John Brown*, 482–83.
47 Emerson, *Complete Works*, 11:270–71.
48 Ibid., 272. In their rejection of "forms" or "formalism," Phillips and Emerson drew on the conventional meaning of the term, as excessive adherence to established procedures or practices, rather than the legal sense of formalism as doctrinal analysis through analogical or deductive reasoning, although that secondary meaning may also pertain in fruitful ways. On slavery and antebellum legal formalism, see Cover, *Justice*. For a reassessment in light of literary abolitionism, see Brophy, "Humanity" and "Over and Above," 499–503.
49 Emerson, *Complete Works*, 11:271.
50 On the effects of the "impasse of resistance and containment" on late antebellum portrayals of slavery, see Sundquist, *To Wake*, 156.
51 Joshua Brown, *Beyond*, 44.
52 Ibid., 26–28, 45; Gambee, *Frank Leslie*, 69–72. On sensationalism, morality, and reform in nineteenth-century print culture, see Reynolds, *Beneath*.
53 Joshua Brown, *Beyond*, 243. Although Brown does not address this issue with respect to coverage of Harpers Ferry, he tracks it throughout the paper's history (ibid., 118, 179, 203, 211, 226).
54 "Chief-Justice."
55 "Visit."
56 On Frank Leslie's efforts to maintain a nonpartisan editorial tone, his likely Democratic political leanings, and his antiabolitionism, see Gambee, *Frank Leslie*, 19–20.
57 "Insurrection," 336, 343. For another example of the paper's strained neutrality (chastising both the "rabid," "fire-eating" Richmond *Enquirer* and the "abolition

fanatics" who applaud the speeches of antislavery lecturers like Wendell Phillips), see "Richmond." Despite its studied antiabolitionist editorial posture, the paper received criticism from Southern readers outraged by its Harpers Ferry coverage (Joshua Brown, *Beyond*, 30, 46–47). On Southern distribution bans on *Frank Leslie's* following Harpers Ferry, see Reynolds, *John Brown*, 417–18. On the debate over Brown's sanity, particularly its legal and political implications, see Oates, *To Purge*, 329–24; McGlone, "John Brown"; Reynolds, *John Brown*, 339–40, 350–51, 357–58.

58 "Expulsion." The first artist sent to cover the Harpers Ferry crisis was *Harper's Weekly's* Porte-Crayon (David Strother), who "gained unequal access to the trial"; his trial illustrations did not appear in the paper, however, due to editorial wariness "of the vituperation provoked by [*Harper's*] pictorial coverage" (Joshua Brown, *Beyond*, 30). For *Frank Leslie's*, Jewett was preceded by Albert Berghaus, whom he was sent to assist. Rumored to have sold one of his sketches to abolitionist Horace Greeley's *New York Tribune*, Jewett left Virginia in early November (Gambee, *Frank Leslie*, 78). Making no reference to any sale of a sketch, *Frank Leslie's* "distinctly and positively den[ied]" the rumor that Jewett "wrote letters to the New York Tribune"— "the only point" in the accusations that the paper claimed to "view seriously" (see "Expulsion"). Notwithstanding Jewett's departure, coverage of Harpers Ferry continued in subsequent issues.

59 "Expulsion." See Drescher, "Servile," 266.

60 "Expulsion."

61 Ibid.

62 Ibid.

63 "Retreat." Gambee tentatively attributes the cartoon to H. L. Stephens (*Frank Leslie*, 78).

64 "Retreat."

65 Ibid.

66 Ibid.

67 As accounts of the innovative engraving process at *Frank Leslie's* make clear, however much the paper publicized its "special artist" in the field, the images that filled the newspaper's pages resulted from the collaborative efforts of up to forty draftsmen in the New York office (who could include the returned special artist as well). The absence of signatures on engravings in antebellum issues of *Frank Leslie's* reflects this process (Joshua Brown, *Beyond*, 32–40; Gambee, *Frank Leslie*, 40–50). On contemporary identifications of illustrated news engravings with academic history painting, see Joshua Brown, *Beyond*, 14–15.

68 Joshua Brown, *Beyond*, 68.

69 "Carrying."

70 Ralph Waldo Emerson, "Courage," qtd. in Reynolds, *John Brown*, 366.

71 On the Southern honor code, see Greenberg, *Honor*.

72 "Irrepressible."

73 Forbes, Garibaldi insurgent turned professional fencing master and *New York Tribune* reporter and translator, was hired by Brown to serve as the raiders' military instructor and to edit his previous two-volume guide to military tactics down to a hand-

book, *Manual of the Patriotic Volunteer*. The disgruntled Forbes subsequently sought to expose Brown's conspiracy and, after Harpers Ferry, gave an exclusive interview to the *New York Herald* detailing his knowledge of Brown's plans (Oates, *Purge*, 200–201, 312). See also Villard, *John Brown*, 285–345, 396, 478, 531.

74 "Irrepressible."
75 Ibid.
76 Ibid.

BIBLIOGRAPHY

Archival Sources
Boston, Mass.
    Massachusetts Historical Society
        John A. Andrews Papers
        Henry I. Bowditch Papers
        Daniel Foster Papers
Worcester, Mass.
    American Antiquarian Society
        Richard Henry Dana Papers

Newspapers
British and Foreign Anti-Slavery Reporter (London)
Christian Register (Boston)
Commonwealth (Boston)
Courier (Boston)
Daily Evening Transcript (Boston)
Freedom's Journal (New York)
Genius of Universal Emancipation (Baltimore)
Liberator (Boston)
National Anti-Slavery Standard (New York)
National Philanthropist and Investigator (Boston)
New York Atlas
New York Evening Post
New York Herald

Published Sources
"The Abuses of the Law Courts." *United States Magazine and Democratic Review*, Oct. 1847,
    305–11.
Abzug, Robert H. *Cosmos Crumbling: American Reform and the Religious Imagination.* New
    York: Oxford University Press, 1994.
———. *Passionate Liberator: Theodore Dwight Weld and the Dilemma of Reform.* New York:
    Oxford University Press, 1980.

Accomando, Christina. *"The Regulations of Robbers": Legal Fictions of Slavery and Resistance.* Columbus: Ohio State University Press, 2001.

A[d]ventures of Jammie [sic] Parker, the Fugitive. Advertisement. *Daily Morning Commonwealth* (Boston), 25 Apr. 1851: n.p.

American and Foreign Anti-Slavery Society. *The Fugitive Slave Bill: Its History and Unconstitutionality; with an Account of the Seizure of James Hamlet, and His Subsequent Restoration to Liberty.* New York, 1850.

The American Heritage Dictionary of the English Language. 3rd ed. New York: Houghton Mifflin, 1992.

Amrine, Frederick, et al. "The Status of Evidence: A Roundtable." *PMLA* 111:1 (Jan. 1996): 21–31.

Anderson, Benedict. *Imagined Communities: Reflections on the Origin and Spread of Nationalism.* London: Verso, 1983.

Andrews, William L. *To Tell a Free Story: The First Century of Afro-American Autobiography, 1760–1865.* Urbana: University of Illinois Press, 1986.

———, ed. *Critical Essays on Frederick Douglass.* Boston: G. K. Hall, 1991.

———, ed. *Sisters of the Spirit: Three Black Women's Spiritual Autobiographies.* Bloomington: Indiana University Press, 1986.

Andrews, William L., Frances Smith Foster, and Trudier Harris, eds. *The Oxford Companion to African American Literature.* New York: Oxford University Press, 1997.

Anthony, David. "The Helen Jewett Panic: Tabloids, Men, and the Sensational Public Sphere in Antebellum New York." *American Literature* 69:3 (Sept. 1997): 487–514.

Appleby, Joyce. *Inheriting the Revolution: The First Generation of Americans.* Cambridge: Belknap–Harvard University Press, 2000.

———. *Liberalism and Republicanism in the Historical Imagination.* Cambridge: Harvard University Press, 1992.

Appleton, John. *The Rules of Evidence Stated and Discussed.* Philadelphia, 1860.

"Are Court Houses Jails?" *Commonwealth* (Boston), 7 Apr. 1851: n.p.

Arkin, Marc M. "The Federalist Trope: Power and Passion in Abolitionist Rhetoric." *Journal of American History* 88:1 (June 2001): 75–98.

Auerbach, Jerold S. *Justice without Law?* New York: Oxford University Press, 1983.

Ayers, Edward L. *Vengeance and Justice: Crime and Punishment in the Nineteenth-Century American South.* New York: Oxford University Press, 1984.

Babcock, Franklin Lawrence. *Spanning the Atlantic.* New York: Knopf, 1931.

Bailyn, Bernard. *The Ideological Origins of the American Revolution.* Enlarged ed. 1967. Reprint. Cambridge: Harvard University Press, 1992.

Baker, Houston A., Jr. *Blues, Ideology, and Afro-American Literature: A Vernacular Theory.* Chicago: University of Chicago Press, 1984.

Baldasty, Gerald J. *The Commercialization of the News in the Nineteenth Century.* Madison: University of Wisconsin Press, 1992.

Barber, John W. *A History of the Amistad Captives. . . .* New Haven, 1840.

Barnes, Gilbert Hobbs. *The Antislavery Impulse, 1830–1844.* 1933. Reprint. New York: Harcourt, Brace, and World–Harbinger, 1961.

Barnes, Gilbert H., and Dwight L. Dumond, eds. *Letters of Theodore Dwight Weld, Angelina Grimké Weld, and Sarah Grimké, 1822–1844*. 2 vols. New York: Da Capo, 1970.

Barney, William L. *The Secessionist Impulse: Alabama and Mississippi in 1860*. 1974. Reprint. Tuscaloosa: University of Alabama Press, 2004.

Bassett, John. Introduction. In *Defining Southern Literature: Perspectives and Assessments, 1831–1852*, edited by John Bassett, 15–39. Madison, N.J.: Fairleigh Dickinson University Press, 1977.

———, ed. *Defining Southern Literature: Perspectives and Assessments, 1831–1852*. Madison, N.J.: Fairleigh Dickinson University Press, 1997.

Baucom, Ian. *Specters of the Atlantic: Finance Capital, Slavery, and the Philosophy of History*. Durham: Duke University Press, 2005.

Baxter, Terry. *Frederick Douglass's Curious Audiences: Ethos in the Age of the Consumable Subject*. New York: Routledge, 2004.

Beecher, Edward. *Narrative of the Riots at Alton*. Edited by Robert Meredith. 1838. Reprint. New York: E. P. Dutton, 1965.

Benezet, Anthony. *A Caution and Warning to Great Britain and Her Colonies, in a Short Representation of the Calamitous State of the Enslaved Negroes in the British Dominions. . . . Submitted to the Serious Consideration of All, More Especially of Those in Power*. Philadelphia, 1766.

———. *Observations on the Inslaving, Importing, and Purchasing of Negroes. . . .* 2nd ed. Germantown, 1760.

———. *Some Historical Account of Guinea. . . .* Philadelphia, 1771.

Bentham, Jeremy. *Rationale of Judicial Evidence, Specially Applied to English Practice*. Vol. 1. London, 1827.

Bercovitch, Sacvan. *The American Jeremiad*. Madison: University of Wisconsin Press, 1978.

Best, Stephen M. *The Fugitive's Properties: Law and the Poetics of Possession*. Chicago: University of Chicago Press, 2004.

Bibb, Henry. *Narrative of the Life and Adventures of Henry Bibb, an American Slave, Written by Himself*. New York, 1849.

Bingham, Caleb. *The Columbian Orator: Containing a Variety of Original and Selected Pieces Together with Rules, Which Are Calculated to Improve Youth and Others in the Ornamental and Useful Art of Eloquence*. Edited by David W. Blight. 1797. Reprint. New York: New York University Press, 1998.

Black, Henry Campbell. *Black's Law Dictionary*. 6th ed. St. Paul: West Publishing, 1990.

Blassingame, John W. Introduction. In *The Frederick Douglass Papers*, series 1, *Speeches, Debates, and Interviews*, edited by John W. Blassingame et al., 1:xxi–lxix. New Haven: Yale University Press, 1979.

———. "Using the Testimony of Ex-Slaves: Approaches and Problems." In *The Slave's Narrative*, edited by Charles T. Davis and Henry Louis Gates Jr., 78–98. Oxford: Oxford University Press, 1985.

Blight, David W. "Editor's Introduction: The Peculiar Dialogue between Caleb Bingham and Frederick Douglass." In *The Columbian Orator: Containing a Variety of Original and Selected Pieces Together with Rules, Which Are Calculated to Improve Youth and Others in the*

Ornamental and Useful Art of Eloquence, edited by David W. Blight, xiii–xxix. 1797. Reprint. New York: New York University Press, 1998.

Bloomfield, Maxwell. *American Lawyers in a Changing Society, 1776–1876*. Cambridge: Harvard University Press, 1976.

Bolster, W. Jeffrey. *Black Jacks: African American Seamen in the Age of Sail*. Cambridge: Harvard University Press, 1997.

Bondage, Freedom, and the Constitution: The New Slavery Scholarship and Its Impact on Law and Legal Historiography. 2 vols. Special issue of *Cardozo Law Review* 17:6 (May 1996): 1685–2235; 18:2 (Nov. 1996): 263–902.

"Book Notices." *DeBow's Review*, Dec. 1856, 661–62.

Bosco, Ronald A. "Lectures at the Pillory: The Early American Execution Sermon." *American Quarterly* 30:2 (Summer 1978): 156–76.

Boulton, Alexander O. "The American Paradox: Jeffersonian Equality and Racial Science." *American Quarterly* 47:3 (Sept. 1995): 467–92.

Bowditch, Henry I. *Proceedings of the Citizens of the Borough of Norfolk, on the Boston Outrage, in the Case of the Runaway Slave George Latimer*. Boston, 1843.

Bowen, Frank C. *A Century of Atlantic Travel, 1830–1930*. London: Sampson, Low, Marston, 1932.

Boyd, Richard. "Models of Power in Harriet Beecher Stowe's *Dred*." *Studies in American Fiction* 19:1 (Spring 1991): 15–30.

———. "Violence and Sacrificial Displacement in Harriet Beecher Stowe's *Dred*." *Arizona Quarterly* 50:2 (Summer 1994): 51–72.

Breen, T. H., and Stephen Innis. *"Myne Owne Ground": Race and Freedom on Virginia's Eastern Shore, 1640–1676*. New York: Oxford University Press, 1980.

Brooks, Joanna, and John Saillant, eds. *"Face Zion Forward": First Writers of the Black Atlantic, 1785–1798*. Boston: Northeastern University Press, 2002.

Brooks, Peter, and Paul Gewirtz, eds. *Law's Stories: Narrative and Rhetoric in the Law*. New Haven: Yale University Press, 1996.

Brophy, Alfred L. "Humanity, Utility, and Logic in Southern Legal Thought: Harriet Beecher Stowe's Vision in *Dred: A Tale of the Great Dismal Swamp*." *Boston University Law Review* 78:4 (Oct. 1998): 1113–61.

———. "'Over and Above . . . There Broods a Portentous Shadow, the Shadow of Law': Harriet Beecher Stowe's Critique of Slave Law in *Uncle Tom's Cabin*." *Journal of Law and Religion* 12:2 (1995–1996): 457–506.

———. "Reason and Sentiment: The Moral Worlds and Modes of Reasoning of Antebellum Jurists." Rev. of *Heart versus Head: Judge-made Law in Nineteenth Century America*, by Peter Karsten. *Boston University Law Review* 79:5 (1999): 1161–213.

———. "'A Revolution Which Seeks to Abolish Law, Must End Necessarily in Despotism': Louisa McCord and Antebellum Southern Legal Thought." *Cardozo Women's Law Journal* 5:1 (1998): 33–77.

Brown, Charles Sumner. "The Genesis of the Negro Lawyer in New England. Part I." *Negro History Bulletin* 22:7 (Apr. 1959): 147–52.

Brown, Gilian. *Domestic Individualism: Imagining Self in Nineteenth-Century America*. Berkeley: University of California Press, 1990.

Brown, Joshua. *Beyond the Lines: Pictorial Reporting, Everyday Life, and the Crisis of Gilded Age America.* Berkeley: University of California Press, 2002.

Brown, William Wells. *Narrative of William Wells Brown, A Fugitive Slave, Written by Himself.* 2nd ed. In *From Fugitive Slave to Free Man: The Autobiographies of William Wells Brown,* by William Wells Brown, edited by William L. Andrews, 13–109. 1848. Reprint. New York: Mentor-Penguin, 1993.

Bruce, Dickson D., Jr. *The Origins of African American Literature, 1680–1865.* Charlottesville: University Press of Virginia, 2001.

Buell, Lawrence. *The Environmental Imagination: Thoreau, Nature Writing, and the Formation of American Culture.* Cambridge: Belknap–Harvard University Press, 1995.

Bunsen, Christian Charles Josias. *The Law of Slavery in the United States.* Boston, 1863.

Burwell, William MacCreary. *Address Delivered before the Society of Alumni of the University of Virginia at Their Annual Meeting.* Richmond, 1846.

———. *Last Words from the Pen of Hon. William M. Burwell, an Eminent Virginia Journalist, Who Died March 4th, 1888.* Richmond, 1888.

———. *White Acre vs. Black Acre: A Case at Law, Reported by J. G., Esq., A Retired Barrister, of Lincolnshire, England.* 1856. Reprint. Miami: Mnemosyne, 1969.

Cain, William E., ed. *William Lloyd Garrison and the Fight Against Slavery: Selections from the Liberator.* Boston: Bedford–St. Martin's, 1995.

Calhoun, Craig, ed. *Habermas and the Public Sphere.* Cambridge: MIT Press, 1992.

Calhoun, Richard J. "Literary Magazines in the Old South." In *The History of Southern Literature,* edited by Louis D. Rubin et al., 157–63. Baton Rouge: Louisiana State University Press, 1985.

C[ampbell], C. "Ceremony, Experience and Life." *Southern Literary Messenger,* Aug. 1839, 572.

Campbell, Stanley W. *The Slave Catchers: Enforcement of the Fugitive Slave Law, 1850–1860.* Chapel Hill: University of North Carolina Press, 1970.

Cannon, Arthur. *Case of Passmore Williamson.* Philadelphia, 1856.

"Cannon Planted Outside the Court-House during the Trial." *Frank Leslie's Illustrated Newspaper,* 12 Nov. 1859, 367.

"Carrying the Prisoners from the Armory to the Railroad Station, en Route to Charlestown, Va., for Trial." *Frank Leslie's Illustrated Newspaper,* 12 Nov. 1859, 379.

Castronovo, Russ. "Incidents in the Life of a White Woman: Economies of Race and Gender in the Antebellum Nation." *American Literary History* 10:2 (Summer 1998): 239–65.

———. *Necro Citizenship: Death, Eroticism, and the Public Sphere in the Nineteenth-Century United States.* Durham: Duke University Press, 2001.

Catterall, Helen Tunnicliff, ed. *Judicial Cases Concerning American Slavery and the Negro.* 5 vols. Washington, D.C.: Carnegie Institution of Washington, 1926–1937.

"Chains and Slavery." *Courier* (Boston), 7 Apr. 1851: n.p.

[Chandler, Peleg W.] "The Latimer Case." *Law Reporter* (1843): 493–95.

Cheek, William, and Aimee Lee Cheek. *John Mercer Langston and the Fight for Black Freedom, 1829–65.* Urbana: University of Illinois Press, 1989.

"Chief-Justice Taney." *Frank Leslie's Illustrated Newspaper,* 28 Mar. 1857, 256.

Child, Lydia Maria. *An Appeal in Favor of That Class of Americans Called Africans*. Edited by Carolyn L. Karcher. 1833. Reprint. Amherst: University of Massachusetts Press, 1996.

"The Chivalry on Hand." *Daily Commonwealth* (Boston), 31 May 1854, evening ed.: n.p. (2).

Clark, Elizabeth B. " 'The Sacred Rights of the Weak': Pain, Sympathy, and the Culture of Individual Rights in Antebellum America." *Journal of American History* 82:2 (Sept. 1995): 463–93.

[Clarkson, Thomas.] *Abstract of the Evidence Delivered before a Select Committee of the House of Commons, in the Years 1790 and 1791, on the Part of the Petitioners for the Abolition of the Slave Trade*. 1791. Reprint. Miami: Mnemosyne, 1969.

———. *Substance of the Evidence of Sundry Persons on the Slave Trade Collected in the Course of a Tour Made in the Autumn of the Year 1788*. London, 1789.

Clover, Carol J. "Law and the Order of Popular Culture." In *Law in the Domains of Culture*, edited by Austin Sarat and Thomas R. Kearns, 97–119. Ann Arbor: University of Michigan Press, 2000.

Cobb, Thomas R. R. *An Inquiry into the Law of Negro Slavery in the United States of America*. 1858. Reprint. Athens: University of Georgia Press, 1999.

Cohen, Daniel A. *Pillars of Salt, Monuments of Grace: New England Crime Literature and the Origins of American Popular Culture, 1674–1860*. New York: Oxford University Press, 1993.

———. "Social Injustice, Sexual Violence, Spiritual Transcendence: Constructions of Interracial Rape in Early American Crime Literature, 1767–1817." *William and Mary Quarterly* 56:3 (July 1999): 481–526.

Cohen, Patricia Cline. *The Murder of Helen Jewett: The Life and Death of a Prostitute in Nineteenth-Century New York*. New York: Vintage–Random House, 1998.

Collison, Gary. *Shadrach Minkins: From Fugitive Slave to Citizen*. Cambridge: Harvard University Press, 1997.

"The Commercial Review; Its Position in Relation to Southern and Western Periodical Literature, and Southern and Western Interests." *Commercial Review*, Jan. 1846, 2–6.

Contee, Clarence G. "Macon B. Allen: 'First' Black in the Legal Profession." *Crisis* 83 (Feb. 1976): 67–69.

Conway, Moncure Daniel. *Autobiography: Memories and Experiences of Moncure Daniel Conway*. Vol. 1. Boston: Houghton Mifflin, 1904.

Cooper, Thomas. *A Treatise on the Law of Libel and the Liberty of the Press. . . .* New York, 1830.

Cornelius, Janet Duitsman. *When I Can Read My Title Clear: Literacy, Slavery, and Religion in the Antebellum South*. Columbia: University of South Carolina Press, 1991.

Coughlin, Anne M. "Regulating the Self: Autobiographical Performances in Outsider Scholarship." *Virginia Law Review* 81:5 (Aug. 1995): 1229–1340.

"Court House in Chains." *Christian Register*, 12 Apr. 1851, 59.

"The Court in Session with Closed Doors." *Daily Evening Commonwealth* (Boston), 8 Apr. 1851, n.p.

Cover, Robert M. *Justice Accused: Antislavery and the Judicial Process*. New Haven: Yale University Press, 1975.

———. "Nomos and Narrative." In *Narrative, Violence, and the Law: The Essays of Robert Cover*, edited by Martha Minow, Michael Ryan, and Austin Sarat, 95–172. Ann Arbor: University of Michigan Press, 1995.

———. "Violence and the Word." In *Narrative, Violence, and the Law: The Essays of Robert Cover*, edited by Martha Minow, Michael Ryan, and Austin Sarat, 203–38. Ann Arbor: University of Michigan Press, 1995.

Cowan, William Tynes. *The Slave in the Swamp: Disrupting the Plantation Narrative*. New York: Routledge, 2005.

Crafts, Hannah. *The Bondwoman's Narrative: A Novel*. Edited by Henry Louis Gates Jr. New York: Warner Books, 2003.

Crane, Gregg D. "Dangerous Sentiments: Sympathy, Rights, and Revolution in Stowe's Anti-Slavery Novels." *Nineteenth-Century Literature* 51:2 (Sept. 1996): 176–204.

———. *Race, Citizenship, and Law in American Literature*. Cambridge: Cambridge University Press, 2002.

———. "Stowe and the Law." In *The Cambridge Companion to Harriet Beecher Stowe*, edited by Cindy Weinstein, 154–70. Cambridge: Cambridge University Press, 2004.

Crèvecoeur, J. Hector St. John de. *Letters from an American Farmer and Sketches of Eighteenth-Century America*. 1782. Reprint. New York: Penguin, 1986.

Crosby, David L. "Anthony Benezet's Transformation of Anti-Slavery Rhetoric." *Slavery and Abolition* 23:3 (Dec. 2002): 39–58.

Cugoano, Quobna Ottobah. *Thoughts and Sentiments on the Evil of Slavery*. Edited by Vincent Carretta. 1787. Reprint. New York: Penguin, 1999.

Culp, Jerome McCristal, Jr. "Autobiography and Legal Scholarship and Teaching: Finding the Me in the Legal Academy." *Virginia Law Review* 77:3 (Apr. 1991): 539–59.

———. "Telling a Black Legal Story: Privilege, Authenticity, 'Blunders,' and Transformation in Outsider Narratives." *Virginia Law Review* 82:1 (Feb. 1996): 69–93.

Curtis, Michael Kent. "The Curious History of Attempts to Suppress Antislavery Speech, Press, and Petition in 1835–37." *Northwestern University Law Review* 89:3 (1994–1995): 785–870.

———. *Free Speech, The People's Darling Privilege: Struggles for Freedom of Expression in American History*. Durham: Duke University Press, 2000.

Davis, David Brion. *The Slave Power Conspiracy and the Paranoid Style*. Baton Rouge: Louisiana State University Press, 1969.

Davis, Edward M. *Extracts from the American Slave Code*. Philadelphia, 1845.

Davis, Mary Kemp. *Nat Turner before the Bar of Judgment: Fictional Treatments of the Southampton Slave Insurrection*. Baton Rouge: Louisiana State University Press, 1999.

Dayan, Joan. "Legal Slaves and Civil Bodies." In *Materializing Democracy: Toward a Revitalized Cultural Politics*, edited by Russ Castronovo and Dana D. Nelson, 53–94. Durham: Duke University Press, 2002.

Dayton, Cornelia Hughes. *Women before the Bar: Gender, Law, and Society in Connecticut, 1639–1789*. Chapel Hill: University of North Carolina Press, 1995.

Dean, Bradley P., and Ronald Wesley Hoag. "Thoreau's Lectures before *Walden*: An Annotated Calendar." In *Studies in the American Renaissance, 1995*, edited by Joel Myerson, 127–228. Charlottesville: University Press of Virginia, 1995.

"The Decision." *Daily Commonwealth* (Boston), 2 June 1854, "Extra" evening ed.: n.p.

Delgado, Richard. "Coughlin's Complaint: How to Disparage Outsider Writing, One Year Later." *Virginia Law Review* 82:1 (Feb. 1996): 95–109.

———. "The Imperial Scholar: Reflections on a Review of Civil Rights Literature." *University of Pennsylvania Law Review* 132:3 (Mar. 1984): 561–78.

———. "Storytelling for Oppositionists and Others: A Plea for Narrative." *Michigan Law Review* 87:8 (Aug. 1989): 2411–41.

DeLombard, Jeannine. "Adding Her Testimony: Harriet Jacobs' *Incidents* as Testimonial Literature." In *Multiculturalism: Roots and Realities*, edited by C. James Trotman, 30–48. Bloomington: Indiana University Press, 2002.

———. " 'Eye-Witness to the Cruelty': Southern Violence and Northern Testimony in Frederick Douglass's 1845 *Narrative*." *American Literature* 73:2 (June 2001): 245–75.

Desai, Gaurav, Felipe Smith, and Supriya Nair. "Introduction: Law, Literature, and Ethnic Subjects." *MELUS* 28:1 (Spring 2003): 3–17.

DeWaard, Jeanne Elders. " 'Indelicate Exposure': Sentiment and Law in *Fall River: An Authentic Narrative*." *American Literature* 74:2 (June 2002): 373–401.

Dimock, Wai Chee. *Residues of Justice: Literature, Law, Philosophy*. Berkeley: University of California Press, 1996.

Dorsey, Peter A. "Becoming the Other: The Mimesis of Metaphor in Douglass' *My Bondage and My Freedom*." *PMLA* 111:3 (May 1996): 435–50.

Douglas, Ann. *The Feminization of American Culture*. New York: Anchor-Doubleday, 1977.

Douglass, Frederick. *The Frederick Douglass Papers. Series 1, Speeches, Debates, and Interviews*. Edited by John W. Blassingame et al. 5 vols. New Haven: Yale University Press, 1979–1992.

———. "The Heroic Slave." In *Uncle Tom's Cabin*, by Harriet Beecher Stowe, edited by Jean Fagan Yellin, 482–520. 1853. Reprint. Oxford: Oxford University Press, 1998.

———. "Letter from a Fugitive Slave." *Evening Journal* (Albany), reprinted in *Liberator*, 16 Jan. 1846.

———. "Letters from Frederick Douglass and James N. Buffum." *Liberator*, 26 Sept. 1845.

———. *Life and Times of Frederick Douglass. Written by Himself*. In *Autobiographies*, by Frederick Douglass, edited by Henry Louis Gates Jr., 453–1045. 1881. Reprint. New York: Library of America, 1994.

———. *Life and Writings of Frederick Douglass*. Edited by Philip S. Foner. 5 vols. New York: International Publishers, 1950–1955, 1975.

———. *My Bondage and My Freedom*. 1855. In *Autobiographies*, by Frederick Douglass, edited by Henry Louis Gates Jr., 103–452. New York: Library of America, 1994.

———. *Narrative of the Life of Frederick Douglass, an American Slave, Written by Himself: Authoritative Text, Contexts, and Criticism*. Edited by William L. Andrews. 1845. Reprint. New York: W. W. Norton, 1997.

Downes, Paul. "Melville's *Benito Cereno* and the Politics of Humanitarian Intervention." *South Atlantic Quarterly* 103:2/3 (Spring/Summer 2004): 465–88.

Drake, W. E. *The Prophet! A Full and Accurate Report of the Judicial Proceedings in the Extraordinary and Highly Interesting Case of Matthews, alias Matthias. . . .* New York, 1834.

Drescher, Seymour. "Servile Insurrection and John Brown's Body in Europe." In *His Soul Goes Marching On: Responses to John Brown and the Harpers Ferry Raid*, edited by Paul Finkelman, 253–95. Charlottesville: University Press of Virginia, 1995.

Drew, Thomas. *The John Brown Invasion. An Authentic History of the Harper's Ferry Tragedy with Full Details of the Capture, Trial, and Execution*. . . . Boston, 1860.

Dumond, Dwight Lowell. *Antislavery Origins of the Civil War in the United States*. 1939. Reprint. Ann Arbor: University of Michigan Press, 1969.

Eastman, Mary H. *Aunt Phillis's Cabin; or, Southern Life as It Is*. Philadelphia, 1852.

Eden, Kathy. *Poetic and Legal Fiction in the Aristotelian Tradition*. Princeton: Princeton University Press, 1986.

"Editorial, Book Notices, Etc." *DeBow's Review*, Oct. 1857, 444–48.

Ehrlich, Walter. *They Have No Rights: Dred Scott's Struggle for Freedom*. Westport, Conn.: Greenwood Press, 1979.

"Elective Judiciary." *United States Magazine and Democratic Review*, Mar. 1848, 199–206.

Ely, Marvin Patrick. *Israel on the Appomattox: A Southern Experiment in Black Freedom from the 1790s through the Civil War*. New York: Knopf, 2004.

Emerson, Ralph Waldo. *The Complete Works of Ralph Waldo Emerson*. Edited by Edward Waldo Emerson. 12 vols. 1876. Reprint. Boston: Houghton Mifflin, 1903–1921.

————. *Selected Writings*. New York: Signet-Penguin, 2003.

Ernest, John. *Resistance and Reformation in Nineteenth-Century African-American Literature: Brown, Wilson, Jacobs, Delany, Douglass, and Harper*. Jackson: University Press of Mississippi, 1995.

Evans, Augusta Jane. *Macaria; or, The Altars of Sacrifice*. Edited by Drew Gilpin Faust. 1864. Reprint. Baton Rouge: Louisiana State University Press, 1992.

Ewick, Patricia, and Susan S. Silbey. *The Common Place of Law: Studies from Everyday Life*. Chicago: University of Chicago Press, 1998.

"The Expulsion of Our Artist from Charlestown." *Frank Leslie's Illustrated Newspaper*, 26 Nov. 1859, 408.

Eze, Emmanuel Chukwudi, ed. *Race and the Enlightenment, A Reader*. Malden: Blackwell, 1997.

Fabian, Ann. *The Unvarnished Truth: Personal Narratives in Nineteenth-Century America*. Berkeley: University of California Press, 2000.

Fanuzzi, Robert A. *Abolition's Public Sphere*. Minneapolis: University of Minnesota Press, 2003.

————. "'The Organ of an Individual': William Lloyd Garrison and the *Liberator*." *Prospects* 23 (1998): 107–27.

Farber, Daniel A., and Suzanna Sherry. "Telling Stories Out of School: An Essay on Legal Narratives." *Stanford Law Review* 45:4 (Apr. 1993): 807–55.

"The Farce Ended!" *Genius of Universal Emancipation*, July 1830, 50.

Faust, Drew Gilpin. *Southern Stories: Slaveholders in Peace and War*. Columbia: University of Missouri Press, 1992.

Fehrenbacher, Don E. *The Dred Scott Case: Its Significance in American Law and Politics*. New York: Oxford University Press, 1978.

Felman, Shoshana. *The Juridical Unconscious: Trials and Traumas in the Twentieth Century.* Cambridge: Harvard University Press, 2002.

Ferguson, Robert A. *Law and Letters in American Culture.* Cambridge: Harvard University Press, 1984.

———. "Story and Transcription in the Trial of John Brown." *Yale Journal of Law and the Humanities* 6:1 (Winter 1994): 37–73.

———. "Untold Stories in the Law." In *Law's Stories: Narrative and Rhetoric in the Law*, edited Peter Brooks and Paul Gewirtz, 84–98. New Haven: Yale University Press, 1996.

Finkelman, Paul. "Legal Ethics and Fugitive Slaves: The Anthony Burns Case, Judge Loring, and Abolitionist Attorneys." *Cardozo Law Review* 17:6 (May 1996): 1793–1858.

———. "Manufacturing Martyrdom: The Antislavery Response to John Brown's Raid." In *His Soul Goes Marching On: Responses to John Brown and the Harpers Ferry Raid*, edited by Paul Finkelman, 41–66. Charlottesville: University Press of Virginia, 1995.

———. *Slavery in the Courtroom: An Annotated Bibliography of American Cases.* Washington, D.C.: Library of Congress, 1985.

———, comp. *Slavery, Race, and the American Legal System, 1700–1872.* 16 vols. New York: Garland, 1988.

———, ed. *His Soul Goes Marching On: Responses to John Brown and the Harpers Ferry Raid.* Charlottesville: University Press of Virginia, 1995.

———, ed. *Law, the Constitution, and Slavery.* New York: Garland, 1989.

———, ed. *Race, Law, and American History, 1700–1990.* 11 vols. New York: Garland, 1992.

———, ed. *Slavery and the Law.* Madison: Madison House, 1997.

Finney, Charles G. *The Memoirs of Charles G. Finney. The Complete Restored Text.* Edited by Garth M. Rosell and Richard A. G. Dupuis. Grand Rapids, Mich.: Academie, 1989.

Fisher, Philip. *Hard Facts: Setting and Form in the American Novel.* New York: Oxford University Press, 1985.

Fishkin, Shelley Fisher, and Carla L. Peterson. "'We Hold These Truths To Be Self-Evident': The Rhetoric of Frederick Douglass's Journalism." In *Frederick Douglass: New Literary and Historical Essays*, edited by Eric Sundquist, 189–204. New York: Cambridge University Press, 1990.

Fitzhugh, George. *Cannibals All! Or, Slaves without Masters.* Edited by C. Vann Woodward. 1856. Reprint. Cambridge: Belknap–Harvard University Press, 1960.

Fitzpatrick, Peter. *The Mythology of Modern Law.* New York: Routledge, 1992.

Fliegelman, Jay. *Declaring Independence: Jefferson, Natural Language, and the Culture of Performance.* Stanford: Stanford University Press, 1993.

Foner, Philip S. *Business and Slavery: The New York Merchants and the Irrepressible Conflict.* Chapel Hill: University of North Carolina Press, 1941.

Foreman, P. Gabrielle. "Sentimental Abolition in Douglass's Decade: Revision, Erotic Conversion, and the Politics of Witnessing in 'The Heroic Slave' and *My Bondage and My Freedom.*" In *Criticism and The Color Line: Desegregating American Literary Studies*, edited by Henry B. Wonham, 191–204. New Brunswick: Rutgers University Press, 1996.

Forten, Charlotte L. *The Journals of Charlotte Forten Grimké.* Edited by Brenda Stevenson. New York: Oxford University Press, 1988.

Foster, Frances Smith. "Resisting Incidents." In Harriet Jacobs and Incidents in the Life of a Slave Girl: New Critical Essays, edited by Deborah M. Garfield and Rafia Zafar, 57–75. Cambridge: Cambridge University Press, 1996.

——. Witnessing Slavery: The Development of Ante-bellum Slave Narratives. Westport, Conn.: Greenwood, 1979.

Foucault, Michel. The History of Sexuality. Vol. 1, An Introduction. Translated by Robert Hurley. New York: Vintage–Random House, 1990.

Fought, Leigh. Southern Womanhood and Slavery: A Biography of Louisa S. McCord, 1810–1879. Columbia: University of Missouri Press, 2003.

Fox, Richard Wightman. Trials of Intimacy: Love and Loss in the Beecher-Tilton Scandal. Chicago: University of Chicago Press, 1999.

Franchot, Jenny. "The Punishment of Esther: Frederick Douglass and the Construction of the Feminine." In Frederick Douglass: New Literary and Historical Essays, edited by Eric Sundquist, 141–65. New York: Cambridge University Press, 1990.

Fredrickson, George M. The Black Image in the White Mind: The Debate on Afro-American Character and Destiny, 1817–1914. Hanover, N.H.: Wesleyan University Press, 1971.

Freehling, William W. The Road to Disunion: Secessionists at Bay, 1776–1854. New York: Oxford University Press, 1990.

Friedman, Lawrence M. A History of American Law. 2nd ed. New York: Touchstone–Simon and Schuster, 1985.

Fry, Henry. The History of North Atlantic Steam Navigation. London, 1896.

The Fugitive Slave Bill: Its History and Unconstitutionality; with an Account of the Seizure of James Hamlet, and His Subsequent Restoration to Liberty. New York, 1850.

"Fugitive Slave Law—Hamlet in Chains." New York Atlas, 13 Oct. 1850.

"Fugitive Slave Law—Hamlet in Court." New York Atlas, 20 Oct. 1850.

Gambee, Budd Leslie. Frank Leslie and His Illustrated Newspaper, 1855–1860. Ann Arbor: University of Michigan Department of Library Science, 1964.

Gardiner, Jane. "Proslavery Propaganda in Fiction Written in Answer to Uncle Tom's Cabin, 1852–61: An Annotated Checklist." Resources for American Literary Study 7 (1977): 201–9.

Garfield, Deborah M. "Earwitness: Female Abolitionism, Sexuality, and Incidents in the Life of a Slave Girl." In Harriet Jacobs and Incidents in the Life of a Slave Girl: New Critical Essays, edited by Deborah M. Garfield and Rafia Zafar, 100–130. Cambridge: Cambridge University Press, 1996.

Garrison, Wendell P., and Francis Jackson Garrison. William Lloyd Garrison, 1805–1879: The Story of His Life, Told by His Children. Vol. 1. New York, 1885.

Garrison, William Lloyd. A Brief Sketch of the Trial of William Lloyd Garrison, for an Alleged Libel on Francis Todd, of Massachusetts. [Baltimore?], 1830.

——. A Brief Sketch of the Trial of William Lloyd Garrison, for an Alleged Libel on Francis Todd, of Newburyport, Mass. Boston, 1834.

——. "Dangers of the Nation: An Address." National Philanthropist and Investigator, 22 July 1829.

"Garrison's Second Trial." Genius of Universal Emancipation, Oct. 1830, 99.

Garvey, T. Gregory. "Frederick Douglass's Change of Opinion on the U.S. Constitution: Abolitionism and the 'Elements of Moral Power.'" *ATQ* 9:3 (Sept. 1995): 229–43.

Gates, Henry Louis, Jr. "Editor's Introduction: Writing 'Race' and the Difference It Makes." *Critical Inquiry* 12:1 (Autumn 1985): 1–20.

———. "From Wheatley to Douglass: The Politics of Displacement." In *Frederick Douglass: New Literary and Historical Essays*, edited by Eric Sundquist, 47–65. New York: Cambridge University Press, 1990.

———. "In Her Own Write." Foreword. In *The Collected Works of Phillis Wheatley*, by Phillis Wheatley, edited by John Shields, vii–xxii. New York: Oxford University Press, 1988.

———. *The Trials of Phillis Wheatley: America's First Black Poet and Her Encounters with the Founding Fathers*. New York: Perseus–Basic Civitas Books, 2003.

———, ed. *The Classic Slave Narratives*. New York: Penguin, 1987.

Genovese, Eugene D. *The Slaveholders' Dilemma: Freedom and Progress in Southern Conservative Thought, 1820–1860*. Columbia: University of South Carolina Press, 1992.

———. *The World the Slaveholders Made: Two Essays in Interpretation*. 1969. Reprint. Middletown: Wesleyan University Press, 1988.

Gewirtz, Paul. "Aeschylus' Law." *Harvard Law Review* 101:5 (Mar. 1988): 1043–55.

———. "Narrative and Rhetoric in the Law." In *Law's Stories: Narrative and Rhetoric in the Law*, edited by Peter Brooks and Paul Gewirtz, 2–13. New Haven: Yale University Press, 1996.

———. "Victims and Voyeurs: Two Narrative Problems at the Criminal Trial." In *Law's Stories: Narrative and Rhetoric in the Law*, edited by Peter Brooks and Paul Gewirtz, 135–61. New Haven: Yale University Press, 1996.

Gilfoyle, Timothy J. "'America's Greatest Criminal Barracks': The Tombs and the Experience of Criminal Justice in New York City, 1838–1897." *Journal of Urban History* 29:5 (July 2003): 525–54.

Gilman, Sander. "Black Bodies, White Bodies: Toward an Iconography of Female Sexuality in Late Nineteenth-Century Art, Medicine, and Literature." *Critical Inquiry* 12:1 (Autumn 1985): 204–42.

Gilman, Winthrop S. *Alton Trials. . . .* New York, 1838.

Gilroy, Paul. *The Black Atlantic: Modernity and Double Consciousness*. Cambridge: Harvard University Press, 1993.

Glaude, Eddie S., Jr. *Exodus! Religion, Race, and Nation in Early Nineteenth-Century Black America*. Chicago: University of Chicago Press, 2000.

Goddu, Teresa A. *Gothic America: Narrative, History, and Nation*. New York: Columbia University Press, 1997.

Goodell, Abner C., Jr. "John Saffin and His Slave Adam." In *Publications of the Colonial Society of Massachusetts: Transactions, 1892–1894*, 84–112. Boston, 1895.

Goodell, William. *The American Slave Code in Theory and Practice: Its Distinctive Features Shown by Its Statutes, Judicial Decisions, and Illustrative Facts*. 1853. Reprint. New York: Negro Universities Press–Greenwood, 1968.

Goodman, Nan. *Shifting the Blame: Literature, Law, and the Theory of Accidents in Nineteenth-Century America*. Princeton: Princeton University Press, 1998.

Gordon, Sarah Barringer. "Blasphemy and the Law of Religious Liberty in Nineteenth-Century America." *American Quarterly* 52:4 (Dec. 2000): 682–719.

———. "'Our National Hearthstone': Anti-Polygamy Fiction and the Sentimental Campaign against Moral Diversity in Antebellum America." *Yale Journal of Law and the Humanities* 8:2 (Summer 1996): 295–350.

Gossett, Thomas F. *Uncle Tom's Cabin and American Culture*. Dallas: Southern Methodist University Press, 1985.

Grant, David. "Stowe's *Dred* and the Narrative Logic of Slavery's Extension." *Studies in American Fiction* 28:2 (Autumn 2000): 151–78.

Greenberg, Kenneth S. *Honor and Slavery: Lies, Duels, Noses, Masks, Dressing as a Woman, Gifts, Strangers, Humanitarianism, Death, Slave Rebellions, the Proslavery Argument, Baseball, Hunting, and Gambling in the Old South*. Princeton: Princeton University Press, 1996.

———, ed. *The Confessions of Nat Turner and Related Documents*. Boston: Bedford–St. Martin's Press, 1996.

Grimsted, David. *American Mobbing, 1828–1861: Toward Civil War*. New York: Oxford University Press, 1998.

Gross, Ariela J. *Double Character: Slavery and Mastery in the Antebellum Southern Courtroom*. Princeton: Princeton University Press, 2000.

Grossberg, Michael. *A Judgment for Solomon: The D'Hauteville Case and Legal Experience in Antebellum America*. New York: Cambridge University Press, 1996.

Grüner, Mark Randall. "Stowe's *Dred*: Literary Domesticity and the Law of Slavery." *Prospects* 20 (1995): 1–37.

Habermas, Jürgen. *The Structural Transformation of the Public Sphere: An Inquiry into a Category of Bourgeois Society*. Translated by Thomas Burger and Frederick Lawrence. Cambridge: MIT Press, 1991.

Hall, David D. *Worlds of Wonder, Days of Judgment: Popular Religious Belief in Early New England*. Cambridge: Harvard University Press, 1989.

Hall, Kermit. *The Magic Mirror: Law in American History*. New York: Oxford University Press, 1989.

———, ed. *The Law of American Slavery: Major Historical Interpretations*. New York: Garland, 1987.

Halttunen, Karen. *Confidence Men and Painted Women: A Study of Middle-Class Culture in America, 1830–1870*. New Haven: Yale University Press, 1982.

———. *Murder Most Foul: The Killer and the American Gothic Imagination*. Cambridge: Harvard University Press, 1998.

Hambrick-Stowe, Charles E. *Charles G. Finney and the Spirit of American Evangelism*. Grand Rapids: Wm. B. Eerdmans, 1996.

Hammond, James Henry. "'Mud-Sill' Speech." In *Slavery Defended: The Views of the Old South*, edited by Eric L. McKitrick, 121–25. Englewood Cliffs: Spectrum–Prentice-Hall, 1963.

Harris, Cheryl I. "Finding Sojourner's Truth: Race, Gender, and the Institution of Property." *Cardozo Law Review* 18:2 (Nov. 1996): 309–409.

———. "Whiteness as Property." *Harvard Law Review* 106:8 (June 1993): 1707–91.

Hartman, Saidiya V. *Scenes of Subjection: Terror, Slavery, and Self-Making in Nineteenth-Century America*. New York: Oxford University Press, 1997.

Hartog, Hendrik. "The Constitution of Aspiration and 'The Rights that Belong to Us All.'" *The Constitution and American Life*. Special issue of *Journal of American History* 74:3 (Dec. 1987): 1013–34.

Hartz, Louis. *The Liberal Tradition in America: An Interpretation of American Political Thought since the Revolution*. New York: Harvest–Harcourt, Brace, and World, 1955.

Hayne, Robert Young. *Speech of Mr. Hayne of South Carolina, in the Senate of the United States, January 21, 1830*. Portland, 1830.

H[eath], [James Ewell]. "Southern Literature." *Southern Literary Messenger*, Aug. 1834, 1–3.

Hedrick, Joan D. *Harriet Beecher Stowe: A Life*. New York: Oxford University Press, 1995.

Henderson, Lynne N. "Legality and Empathy." *Michigan Law Review* 85:7 (June 1987): 1574–1653.

Hening, William Waller. *The Statutes at Large; Being a Collection of All the Laws of Virginia, from the First Session of the Legislature, in the Year 1619*. Vol. 4. Richmond, 1820.

Hentz, Caroline Lee. *The Planter's Northern Bride*. 1854. Reprint. Chapel Hill: University of North Carolina Press, 1970.

Higginbotham, A. Leon, Jr. *In the Matter of Color: Race and the American Legal Process, The Colonial Period*. New York: Oxford University Press, 1978.

Hinks, Peter P. *To Awaken My Afflicted Brethren: David Walker and the Problem of Antebellum Slave Resistance*. University Park: Pennsylvania State University Press, 1997.

Hoare, Prince. *Memoirs of Granville Sharp, Esq. . . .* London, 1820.

Hochschild, Adam. *Bury the Chains: Prophets and Rebels in the Fight to Free an Empire's Slaves*. New York: Houghton Mifflin, 2005.

Hoeflich, M. H. "John Livingston and the Business of Law in Nineteenth-Century America." *American Journal of Legal History* 44:4 (Oct. 2000): 347–68.

———. "Legal History and the History of the Book: Variations on a Theme." *University of Kansas Law Review* 46:3 (Apr. 1998): 415–31.

Holthouse, Henry James. *A New Law Dictionary*. Edited by Henry Pennington. Philadelphia, 1847.

Homestead, Melissa. *American Women Authors and Literary Property, 1822–1869*. New York: Cambridge University Press, 2005.

Horton, James Oliver, and Lois E. Horton. *Black Bostonians: Family Life and Community Struggle in the Antebellum North*. Rev. ed. New York: Holmes and Meier, 1999.

Horwitz, Morton J. *The Transformation of American Law, 1780–1860*. Cambridge: Harvard University Press, 1977.

Howard-Pitney, David. *The African-American Jeremiad: Appeals for Justice in America*. Rev. ed. Philadelphia: Temple University Press, 2005.

Howe, Mark DeWolfe. *The Garden and the Wilderness: Religion and Government in American Constitutional History*. Chicago: University of Chicago Press, 1965.

———. "Juries as Judges of Criminal Law." *Harvard Law Review* 52:4 (Feb. 1939): 582–616.

Hudson, Frederic. *Journalism in the United States from 1690 to 1872*. New York, 1873.

Humez, Jean. "Reading the *Narrative of Sojourner Truth* as a Collaborative Text." *Frontiers* 16:1 (Jan. 1996): 29–53.

Huntress, Keith. " 'Guinea' of *White-Jacket* and Chief Justice Shaw." *American Literature* 43:4 (Jan. 1972): 639–41.

Hurd, John Codman. *The Law of Freedom and Bondage in the United States.* 2 vols. Boston, 1858–62.

———. *Topics of Jurisprudence Connected with Conditions of Freedom and Bondage.* New York, 1856.

Hutchinson, John Wallace. *Story of the Hutchinsons (Tribe of Jesse).* Compiled and edited by Charles E. Mann. Vol. 2. 1896. Reprint. New York: Da Capo, 1977.

"In Chains." *Daily Morning Commonwealth* (Boston), 8 Apr. 1851: n.p.

In Memoriam. Robert Morris, Sr. Born June 8, 1823. Died December 12, 1882. [Boston: n.p., 1883?].

"An Inquiry into the Present State of Southern Literature." *Southern Literary Messenger,* Nov. 1856, 387–91.

"Insurrection at Harper's Ferry." *Frank Leslie's Illustrated Newspaper,* 29 Oct. 1859, 335–36, 343–44.

"Investigation before the Committee of the Senate." *Daily Morning Commonwealth* (Boston), 12 Apr. 1851.

"The Irrepressible Conflict." *Frank Leslie's Illustrated Newspaper,* 19 Nov. 1859, 398.

Jacob, Herbert. "The Elusive Shadow of the Law." *Law and Society Review* 26:3 (1992): 565–90.

Jacobs, Harriet A. *Incidents in the Life of a Slave Girl, Written by Herself.* Edited by Jean Fagan Yellin. 1861. Reprint. Cambridge: Harvard University Press, 1987.

James, Alexander. *L'Acadie; or, Seven Years' Exploration in British America.* Vol. 2. London, 1849.

James, Henry Field. *Abolitionism Unveiled; Or, Its Origin, Progress, and Pernicious Tendency Fully Developed.* Cincinnati, 1856.

Jay, William. *Inquiry into the Character and Tendency of the American Colonization and American Anti-Slavery Societies.* 1835. *Miscellaneous Writings on Slavery.* Boston, 1853.

Jefferson, Thomas. *Notes on the State of Virginia.* Edited by David Waldstreicher. 1787. Reprint. New York: Bedford–St. Martin's, 2002.

Jenkins, Philip. *Mystics and Messiahs: Cults and New Religions in American History.* New York: Oxford University Press, 2000.

John P. Jewett and Company. Advertisement. *American Slave Code, in Theory and Practice.* In *A Key to Uncle Tom's Cabin,* by Harriet Beecher Stowe, 263–64. London, 1853.

Johnson, Alex M., Jr. "Defending the Use of Narrative and Giving Content to the Voice of Color: Rejecting the Imposition of Process Theory in Legal Scholarship." *Iowa Law Review* 79:4 (May 1994): 803–52.

Johnson, Michael P. "Denmark Vesey and His Co-Conspirators." *William and Mary Quarterly* 3rd ser. 58:4 (Oct. 2001): 915–76.

———. "Reading Evidence." *William and Mary Quarterly* 3rd ser. 59:1 (Jan. 2002): 193–202.

Johnson, Paul E., and Sean Wilentz. *The Kingdom of Matthias: A Story of Sex and Salvation in Nineteenth-Century America*. New York: Oxford University Press, 1994.

[Jolliffe, John.] *Belle Scott; Or, Liberty Overthrown! A Tale for the Crisis*. Cincinnati, 1856.

———. *Chattanooga*. Cincinnati, 1858.

Jordan, Winthrop D. *White over Black: American Attitudes toward the Negro, 1550–1812*. Chapel Hill: University of North Carolina Press, 1968.

Jordan-Lake, Joy. *Whitewashing Uncle Tom's Cabin: Nineteenth-Century Women Novelists Respond to Stowe*. Nashville: Vanderbilt University Press, 2005.

Joyner, Charles. "'Guilty of Holiest Crime': The Passion of John Brown." In *His Soul Goes Marching On: Responses to John Brown and the Harpers Ferry Raid*, edited by Paul Finkelman, 296–334. Charlottesville: University Press of Virginia, 1995.

"Judge Wells Decision for Open Courts." *Daily Evening Commonwealth* (Boston), 8 Apr. 1851: n.p.

Kaplan, Carla. "Narrative Contracts and Emancipatory Readers: *Incidents in the Life of a Slave Girl*." *Yale Journal of Criticism* 6:1 (Spring 1993): 93–120.

Kaplan, Sidney. "Samuel Sewall and the Iniquity of Slavery." In *The Selling of Joseph: A Memorial*, by Samuel Sewall, edited by Sidney Kaplan, 27–67. Amherst: University of Massachusetts Press, 1969.

Karafilis, Maria. "Spaces of Democracy in Harriet Beecher Stowe's *Dred*." *Arizona Quarterly* 55:3 (Autumn 1999): 23–49.

Karcher, Carolyn L. *The First Woman in the Republic: A Cultural Biography of Lydia Maria Child*. Durham: Duke University Press, 1994.

———. *Shadow over the Promised Land: Slavery, Race, and Violence in Melville's America*. Baton Rouge: Louisiana State University Press, 1980.

Kennedy, John Pendleton. *Memoirs of the Life of William Wirt, Attorney-General of the United States*. Vol. 2. Rev. ed. Philadelphia, 1850.

"The Kidnapping of Sims." *Daily Morning Commonwealth* (Boston), 25 Apr. 1851: n.p.

Kimnach, Wilson H. "General Introduction to the Sermons: Jonathan Edwards' Art of Prophesying." In *Sermons and Discourses, 1720–1723*, edited by Wilson H. Kimnach, 3–179. Vol. 10 of *The Works of Jonathan Edwards*. New Haven: Yale University Press, 1992.

King James Bible. Nashville: Thomas Nelson, 1984.

Knupfer, Peter. "A Crisis in Conservatism: Northern Unionism and the Harpers Ferry Raid." In *His Soul Goes Marching On: Responses to John Brown and the Harpers Ferry Raid*, edited by Paul Finkelman, 119–48. Charlottesville: University Press of Virginia, 1995.

Kohl, Lawrence Frederick. *The Politics of Individualism: Parties and the American Character in the Jacksonian Era*. New York: Oxford University Press, 1989.

Korobkin, Laura Hanft. *Criminal Conversations: Sentimentality and Nineteenth-Century Legal Stories of Adultery*. New York: Columbia University Press, 1998.

Kraditor, Aileen S. *Means and Ends in American Abolitionism: Garrison and His Critics on Strategy and Tactics, 1834–1850*. 1967. Reprint. Chicago: Elephant–Ivan R. Dee, 1989.

Kramer, Larry D. *The People Themselves: Popular Constitutionalism and Judicial Review*. Oxford: Oxford University Press, 2004.

Kronman, Anthony. "Leontius' Tale." In *Law's Stories: Narrative and Rhetoric in the Law*, edited by Peter Brooks and Paul Gewirtz, 54–56. New Haven: Yale University Press, 1996.

Lakoff, George, and Mark Johnson. *Metaphors We Live By*. Chicago: University of Chicago Press, 2003.

Lambert, Frank. *Inventing the Great Awakening*. Princeton: Princeton University Press, 1999.

Lampe, Gregory P. *Frederick Douglass: Freedom's Voice, 1818–1845*. East Lansing: Michigan State University Press, [1998].

Langbein, John H. *The Origins of Adversary Criminal Trial*. Oxford: Oxford University Press, 2003.

———. *Prosecuting Crime in the Renaissance: England, Germany, France*. Cambridge: Harvard University Press, 1974.

———. "Response." *Journal of Legal History* 26:1 (Apr. 2005): 85–89.

Langston, John Mercer. *From the Virginia Plantation to the National Capitol[,] Or The First and Only Negro Representative in Congress from the Old Dominion*. Hartford, 1894.

Lee, Maurice. *Slavery, Philosophy, and American Literature, 1830–1860*. Cambridge: Cambridge University Press, 2005.

Legal Storytelling. Special issue of *Michigan Law Review* 87:8 (Aug. 1989): 2073–504.

Legaré, Hugh Swinton. "American Literature." In *Defining Southern Literature: Perspectives and Assessments, 1831–1852*, edited by John Bassett, 45–48. Madison, N.J.: Fairleigh Dickinson University Press, 1977.

Lemmings, David. "Criminal Trial Procedure in Eighteenth-Century England: The Impact of Lawyers." *Journal of Legal History* 26:1 (Apr. 2005): 63–70.

Leverenz, David. *Manhood and the American Renaissance*. Ithaca: Cornell University Press, 1989.

Levesque, George A. "Boston's Black Brahmin: Dr. John S. Rock." *Civil War History* 26:4 (Dec. 1980): 326–46.

Levine, Robert S. *Martin Delany, Frederick Douglass, and the Politics of Representative Identity*. Chapel Hill: University of North Carolina Press, 1997.

Levy, Leonard W. *The Law of the Commonwealth and Chief Justice Shaw*. Cambridge: Harvard University Press, 1957.

"The Libel Suit—Again." *Genius of Universal Emancipation*, June 1830, 33–36.

The Life, Trial and Execution of Captain John Brown. . . . New York, [c. 1859].

Linebaugh, Peter, and Marcus Rediker. *The Many-Headed Hydra: Sailors, Slaves, Commoners, and the Hidden History of the Revolutionary Atlantic*. Boston: Beacon Press, 2000.

Littlefield, Daniel C. "Blacks, John Brown, and a Theory of Manhood." In *His Soul Goes Marching On: Responses to John Brown and the Harpers Ferry Raid*, edited by Paul Finkelman, 41–66. Charlottesville: University Press of Virginia, 1995.

Loebel, Thomas. *The Letter and the Spirit of Nineteenth-Century American Literature: Justice, Politics, and Theology*. Montreal: McGill–Queen's University Press, 2005.

Looby, Christopher. *Voicing America: Language, Literary Form, and the Origins of the United States*. Chicago: University of Chicago Press, 1996.

Lovejoy, Joseph C., and Owen Lovejoy. *Memoir of the Rev. Elijah P. Lovejoy; Who Was*

Murdered in Defence of the Liberty of the Press, at Alton, Illinois, Nov. 7, 1837. 1838. Reprint. Freeport, N.Y.: Books for Libraries Press, 1970.

Mabee, Carleton, and Susan Mabee Newhouse. *Sojourner Truth: Slave, Prophet, Legend.* New York: New York University Press, 1993.

Mack, Kenneth Walter. "Social History of Everyday Practice: Sadie T. M. Alexander and the Incorporation of Black Women into the American Legal Profession, 1925–1960." *Cornell Law Review* 87:6 (Sept. 2002): 1405–74.

Macpherson, C. B. *The Political Theory of Possessive Individualism, Hobbes to Locke.* New York: Oxford University Press, 1962.

Madison, James, Alexander Hamilton, and John Jay. *The Federalist Papers.* 1788. Reprint. New York: Penguin, 1987.

Mailloux, Stephen. *Reception Histories: Rhetoric, Pragmatism, and American Cultural Politics.* Ithaca: Cornell University Press, 1998.

———. "Re-Marking Slave Bodies: Rhetoric as Production and Reception." *Philosophy and Rhetoric* 35:2 (2002): 96–119.

———. *Rhetorical Power.* Ithaca: Cornell University Press, 1989.

[Mann, Daniel.] *The Virginia Philosopher, or Few Lucky Slave-Catchers: A Poem.* Boston, 1843.

Martin, Waldo E., Jr. *The Mind of Frederick Douglass.* Chapel Hill: University of North Carolina Press, 1985.

Massachusetts Anti-Slavery Society. *A Full Statement of the Reasons . . . Showing Why There Should Be No Penal Laws Enacted, and No Condemnatory Resolutions Passed by the Legislature; Respecting Abolitioni[s]ts and Anti-Slavery Societies.* Boston, 1836.

Masur, Louis P. *Rites of Execution: Capital Punishment and the Transformation of American Culture, 1776–1865.* New York: Oxford University Press, 1989.

Mather, Cotton. *Tremenda. The Dreadful Sound with Which the Wicked Are to Be Thunderstruck. In a Sermon Delivered unto a Great Assembly, in Which Was Present, a Miserable African, Just Going to Be Executed for a Most Inhumane and Uncommon Murder.* Boston, 1721.

"Matthias and His Impostures." Rev. of *Matthias and His Impostures,* by William L. Stone. *North American Review,* Oct. 1835, 307–26.

May, Samuel J. *Some Recollections of the Antislavery Conflict.* 1869. Reprint. Miami: Mnemosyne, 1969.

Mayer, Henry. *All on Fire: William Lloyd Garrison and the Abolition of Slavery.* New York: Griffin–St. Martin's, 1998.

Mayo, Joseph. *A Guide to Magistrates: With Practical Forms for the Discharge of their Duties out of Court. . . .* 2nd ed. Richmond, 1860.

McBride, Dwight A. *Impossible Witnesses: Truth, Abolitionism, and Slave Testimony.* New York: New York University Press, 2001.

McCord, Louisa. *Louisa S. McCord: Political and Social Essays.* Edited by Richard C. Lounsbury. Charlottesville: University Press of Virginia, 1995.

McCune Smith, James. "On the Fourteenth Query of Thomas Jefferson's *Notes on Virginia.*" *Anglo-African Magazine,* Aug. 1859, 225–38.

McDade, Thomas M. *The Annals of Murder: A Bibliography of Books and Pamphlets on American Murders from Colonial Times to 1900.* Norman: University of Oklahoma Press, [1961].

————. "Matthias, Prophet without Honor." New York Historical Quarterly 62:4 (1978): 311–34.

McDowell, Deborah E. "In the First Place: Making Frederick Douglass and the Afro-American Narrative Tradition." In Critical Essays on Frederick Douglass, edited by William L. Andrews, 201–4. Boston: G. K. Hall, 1991.

McFeely, William S. Frederick Douglass. New York: Touchstone–Simon and Schuster, 1991.

McGlone, Robert E. "John Brown, Henry Wise, and the Politics of Insanity." In His Soul Goes Marching On: Responses to John Brown and the Harpers Ferry Raid, edited by Paul Finkelman, 213–52. Charlottesville: University Press of Virginia, 1995.

McHenry, Elizabeth. Forgotten Readers: Recovering the Lost History of African American Literary Societies. Durham: Duke University Press, 2002.

McKay, Nellie Y. "Naming the Problem That Led to the Question 'Who Shall Teach African-American Literature?' or, Are We Ready to Disband the Wheatley Court?" PMLA 113:3 (May 1998): 359–69.

McKivigan, John R. "The Frederick Douglass–Gerrit Smith Friendship and Political Abolitionism in the 1850s." In Frederick Douglass: New Literary and Historical Essays, edited by Eric Sundquist, 205–32. New York: Cambridge University Press, 1990.

McManus, Edgar J. Law and Liberty in Early New England: Criminal Justice and Due Process, 1620–1692. Amherst: University of Massachusetts Press, 1993.

Meer, Sarah. Uncle Tom Mania: Slavery, Minstrelsy, and Transatlantic Culture in the 1850s. Athens: University of Georgia Press, 2005.

Mellen, G. W. F. The Old "Habeas Corpus." A New Song Set to Old Music. N.p., n.d.

Melville, Herman. "Benito Cereno." In Melville's Short Novels: Authoritative Texts, Contexts, Criticism, by Herman Melville, edited by Dan McCall, 34–102. New York: W. W. Norton, 2002.

Memoirs of Matthais the Prophet, with a Full Exposure of His Atrocious Impositions, and of the Degrading Delusions of His Followers. New York, 1835.

Miller, Perry. The Life of the Mind in America from the Revolution to the Civil War. New York: Harcourt, Brace, and World, 1965.

Miller, William Lee. Arguing about Slavery: John Quincy Adams and the Great Battle in the United States Congress. New York: Vintage–Random House, 1995.

Mills, Charles W. "Whose Fourth of July? Frederick Douglass and 'Original Intent.'" In Frederick Douglass: A Critical Reader, edited by Bill E. Lawson and Frank M. Kirkland, 100–142. Malden: Blackwell, 1999.

M'Keehan, Hattia. Liberty or Death; Or, Heaven's Infraction of the Fugitive Slave Law. Cincinnati, 1858.

Mnookin, Robert H., and Lewis Kornhauser. "Bargaining in the Shadow of the Law: The Case of Divorce." Yale Law Journal 88:5 (Apr. 1979): 950–97.

Morris, Thomas D. Southern Slavery and the Law, 1619–1860. Chapel Hill: University North Carolina Press, 1996.

Morrison, Toni. Playing in the Dark: Whiteness and the Literary Imagination. Cambridge: Harvard University Press, 1992.

Moss, Elizabeth. Domestic Novelists in the Old South: Defenders of Southern Culture. Baton Rouge: Louisiana State University Press, 1992.

Mott, Frank Luther. *American Journalism, A History: 1690–1960.* 3rd ed. New York: Macmillan, 1962.

Nelson, Dana D. *The Word in Black and White: Reading "Race" in American Literature, 1638–1867.* New York: Oxford University Press, 1993.

Nelson, William E. *Americanization of the Common Law: The Impact of Legal Change on Massachusetts Society, 1760–1830.* Cambridge: Harvard University Press, 1975.

Nerone, John. "Newspapers, the Public Sphere, and the Changing Culture of Print." In *The Industrial Book, 1840–1880,* edited by Scott Casper, Jeffrey Groves, Stephen Nissenbaum, and Michael Winship. Vol. 3 of *The History of the Book in America.* Chapel Hill: University of North Carolina Press, forthcoming 2007.

Newbury, Michael. *Figuring Authorship in Antebellum America.* Stanford: Stanford University Press, 1997.

Newman, Judie S. Introduction. In *Dred: A Tale of the Great Dismal Swamp,* by Harriet Beecher Stowe, edited by Judie S. Newman, 9–25. 1856. Reprint. Exeter: Edinburgh University Press, 1999.

———. "Staging Black Insurrection: *Dred* on Stage." In *The Cambridge Companion to Harriet Beecher Stowe,* edited by Cindy Weinstein, 113–30. Cambridge: Cambridge University Press, 2004.

Newman, Richard S. *The Transformation of American Abolitionism: Fighting Slavery in the Early Republic.* Chapel Hill: University of North Carolina Press, 2002.

Newman, Richard, Patrick Rael, and Phillip Lapsansky. "Introduction: The Theme of Our Contemplation." In *Pamphlets of Protest: An Anthology of Early African American Protest Literature, 1790–1860,* edited by Richard Newman, Patrick Rael, and Phillip Lapsansky, 1–31. New York: Routledge, 2001.

Newmyer, R. Kent. "John Marshall." In *The Oxford Companion to the Supreme Court of the United States,* edited by Kermit L. Hall, 523–36. New York: Oxford University Press, 1992.

Northup, Solomon. *Twelve Years a Slave.* Edited by Sue Eakin and Joseph Logsdon. 1853. Reprint. Baton Rouge: Louisiana State University Press, 1968.

Nudelman, Franny. "'The Blood of Millions': John Brown's Body, Public Violence, and Political Community." *American Literary History* 13:4 (Winter 2001): 639–70.

Nwankwo, Ifeoma Kiddoe. *Black Cosmopolitanism: Racial Consciousness and Transnational Identity in the Nineteenth-Century Americas.* Philadelphia: University of Pennsylvania Press, 2005.

Nye, Russel B. *Fettered Freedom: Civil Liberties and the Slavery Controversy, 1830–1860.* 1948. Reprint. East Lansing: Michigan State University Press, 1963.

Oakes, James. "Why Slaves Can't Read: The Political Significance of Jefferson's Racism." In *Thomas Jefferson and the Education of a Citizen,* edited by James Gilreath, 177–92. Washington, D.C.: Library of Congress, 1999.

Oates, Stephen B. *To Purge This Land with Blood: A Biography of John Brown.* 2nd ed. Amherst: University of Massachusetts Press, 1984.

Oldfield, J. R. *Popular Politics and British Anti-Slavery: The Mobilization of Public Opinion against the Slave Trade, 1787–1807.* London: Frank Cass, 1998.

O'Neall, John Belton. *The Negro Law of South Carolina*. Columbia, 1848.

[Osborn, Laughton.] *The Vision of Rubeta, an Epic Story of the Island of Manhattan. With Illustrations, Done on Stone*. Boston, 1838.

"Ossawattamie Brown on His Way from the Court to His Prison, after Hearing Sentence of Death Pronounced upon Him." *Frank Leslie's Illustrated Newspaper*, 12 Nov. 1859, 367.

Otter, Samuel. "Stowe and Race." In *The Cambridge Companion to Harriet Beecher Stowe*, edited by Cindy Weinstein, 15–38. Cambridge: Cambridge University Press, 2004.

Oxford English Dictionary Online. <http://www.dictionary.oed.com>. 21 May 2006.

Painter, Nell Irvin. *Sojourner Truth: A Life, A Symbol*. New York: W. W. Norton, 1996.

Papke, David Ray. *Framing the Criminal: Crime, Cultural Work, and the Loss of Critical Perspective, 1830–1900*. Hamden: Archon, 1987.

Pease, Jane H., and William H. Pease. *Black Utopia: Negro Communal Experiments in America*. Madison: State Historical Society of Wisconsin, 1963.

———. *The Fugitive Slave Law and Anthony Burns: A Problem of Law Enforcement*. Philadelphia: J. B. Lippincott, 1975.

———. *They Who Would Be Free: Blacks' Search for Freedom, 1830–1861*. New York: Atheneum, 1974.

———. "Uncle Tom and Clayton: Fact, Fiction, and Mystery." *Ontario History* 50 (1958): 61–73.

Pennington, J[ames] W. C. *A Narrative of Events in the Life of J. H. Banks, an Escaped Slave, from the Cotton State, Alabama, in America*. Liverpool, 1861.

Pennsylvania Anti-Slavery Society. *Narrative of Facts in the Case of Passmore Williamson*. Philadelphia, 1855.

Peterson, Mark A. "*The Selling of Joseph*: Bostonians, Antislavery, and the Protestant International, 1689–1733." *Massachusetts Historical Review* 4 (2002): 1–22.

Petrulionis, Sandra Harbert. "Editorial Savoir Faire: Thoreau Turns his Journal into 'Slavery in Massachusetts.'" *Resources for American Literary Study* 25:2 (1999): 206–31.

Pettinger, Alasdair. "'At Sea—Coloured Passenger.'" In *Sea Changes: Historicizing the Ocean*, edited by Bernhard Klein and Gesa Mckenthum, 159–66. New York: Routledge, 2004.

———. "Send Back the Money: Douglass and the Free Church of Scotland." In *Liberating Sojourn: Frederick Douglass and Transatlantic Reform*, edited by Alan J. Rice and Martin Crawford, 31–55. Athens: University of Georgia Press, 1999.

Phillips, Wendell. "Speech of Wendell Phillips." In *The John Brown Invasion. An Authentic History of the Harper's Ferry Tragedy with Full Details of the Capture, Trial, and Execution*, by Thomas Drew. Boston, 1860.

"Pictorial History of the Harper's Ferry Insurrection. A Supplement to Frank Leslie's Illustrated Newspaper." *Frank Leslie's Illustrated Newspaper*, 19 Nov. 1859.

Pierpont, John. *A Discourse on the Covenant with Judas*. Boston, 1842.

Pierson, Emily Catharine. *Jamie Parker, the Fugitive*. Hartford, 1851.

Pocock, J. G. A. *The Machiavellian Moment: Florentine Political Thought and the Atlantic Republican Tradition*. 1979. Reprint. Princeton: Princeton University Press, 2003.

Poe, Edgar Allan. "Georgia Scenes." In *Defining Southern Literature: Perspectives and Assessments, 1831–1852*, edited by John Bassett, 57–59. Madison, N.J.: Fairleigh Dickinson University Press, 1977.

"Portraits of the Judge, Counsel, and Jurors." *Frank Leslie's Illustrated Newspaper*, 12 Nov. 1859, 378–79.

[Pray, Isaac.] *Memoirs of James Gordon Bennett and His Times*. New York, 1855.

"Precarious." *The American Heritage Dictionary of the English Language*. 3rd ed. 1992.

Prince, Mary. *The History of Mary Prince, a West Indian Slave, Related by Herself*. Edited by Sara Salih. 1831. Reprint. London: Penguin, 2004.

"The Prisoners Cook, Coppic, Greene, and Copeland Receiving Sentence of Death." *Frank Leslie's Illustrated Newspaper*, 26 Nov. 1859, 406.

Proceedings against William Lloyd Garrison, for a Libel. Baltimore, 1847.

Quarles, Benjamin. *Black Abolitionists*. New York: Oxford University Press, 1969.

———. *Frederick Douglass*. 1948. Reprint. New York: DaCapo, 1997.

Rael, Patrick. *Black Identity and Black Protest in the Antebellum North*. Chapel Hill: University of North Carolina Press, 2002.

Redpath, James. *The Public Life of Capt John Brown, with an Autobiography of His Childhood and Youth*. Boston, 1860.

Renehan, Edward J., Jr. *The Secret Six: The True Tale of the Men Who Conspired with John Brown*. Columbia: University of South Carolina Press, 1997.

Report of the Proceedings at the Examination of Charles G. Davis, Esq., on a Charge of Aiding and Abetting in the Rescue of a Fugitive Slave. Boston, 1851.

"The Retreat of Our Artist from Charlestown, Virginia." *Frank Leslie's Illustrated Newspaper*, 26 Nov. 1859, 414.

Reynolds, David S. *Beneath the American Renaissance: The Subversive Imagination in the Age of Emerson and Melville*. New York: Knopf, 1988.

———. *John Brown, Abolitionist: The Man Who Killed Slavery, Sparked the Civil War, and Seeded Civil Rights*. New York: Knopf, 2005.

———. *Walt Whitman's America: A Cultural Biography*. New York: Vintage–Random House, 1995.

Rhodes, Jane. *Mary Ann Shadd Cary: The Black Press and Protest in the Nineteenth Century*. Bloomington: Indiana University Press, 1998.

Rice, Alan J., and Martin Crawford. "Triumphant Exile: Frederick Douglass in Britain, 1845–1847." In *Liberating Sojourn: Frederick Douglass and Transatlantic Reform*, edited by Alan J. Rice and Martin Crawford, 1–12. Athens: University of Georgia Press, 1999.

Rice, James D. "The Criminal Trial before and after the Lawyers: Authority, Law, and Culture in Maryland Jury Trials, 1681–1837." *American Journal of Legal History* 40:4 (Oct. 1996): 455–75.

Richards, David A. J. "Abolitionist Feminism, Moral Slavery, and the Constitution: 'On the Same Platform of Human Rights.'" *Cardozo Law Review* 18:2 (Nov. 1996): 793–99.

Richards, Leonard L. *"Gentlemen of Property and Standing": Anti-Abolition Mobs in Jacksonian America*. London: Oxford University Press, 1970.

————. The Slave Power: The Free North and Southern Domination, 1780–1860. Baton Rouge: Louisiana State University Press, 2000.

"The Richmond Enquirer on Wendell Phillips." Frank Leslie's Illustrated Newspaper, 19 Nov. 1859, 392.

Rickford, John Russell, and Russell John Rickford. Spoken Soul: The Story of Black English. New York: John Wiley and Sons, 2000.

Ripley, C. Peter, ed. The Black Abolitionist Papers. 5 vols. Chapel Hill: University of North Carolina Press, 1985–1992.

Robbins, Sarah. "Gendering the History of the Antislavery Narrative: Juxtaposing Uncle Tom's Cabin and Benito Cereno, Beloved and Middle Passage." American Quarterly 49:3 (Sept. 1997): 531–73.

Roeber, A. G. Faithful Magistrates and Republican Lawyers: Creators of Virginia Legal Culture, 1680–1810. Chapel Hill: University of North Carolina Press, 1981.

Rogin, Michael Paul. Subversive Genealogy: The Politics and Art of Herman Melville. 1979. New York: Knopf, 1983.

Rohrbach, Augusta. Truth Stranger than Fiction: Race, Realism, and the U.S. Literary Marketplace. New York: Palgrave, 2002.

Ross, Thomas. "The Rhetorical Tapestry of Race: White Innocence and Black Abstraction." William and Mary Law Review 32:1 (Fall 1990): 1–40.

Rowe, John Carlos. "Between Politics and Poetics: Frederick Douglass and Postmodernity." In Reconstructing American Literary and Historical Studies, edited by Günter H. Lenz, Harmut Keil, and Sabine Bröck-Sallah, 192–210. New York: St. Martin's Press, 1990.

————. "Stowe's Rainbow Sign: Violence and Community in Dred: A Tale of the Great Dismal Swamp (1856)." Arizona Quarterly 58:1 (Spring 2002): 37–55.

Russell, Thomas D. "Slave Auctions on the Courthouse Steps: Court Sales of Slaves in Antebellum South Carolina." In Slavery in the Courtroom: An Annotated Bibliography of American Cases, edited by Paul Finkelman, 329–64. Washington, D.C.: Library of Congress, 1985.

Ruttenburg, Nancy. Democratic Personality: Popular Voice and the Trial of American Authorship. Stanford: Stanford University Press, 1998.

Ryan, Mary P. "Gender and Public Access: Women's Politics in Nineteenth-Century America." In Habermas and the Public Sphere, edited by Craig Calhoun, 259–88. Cambridge: MIT Press, 1992.

Ryan, Susan M. The Grammar of Good Intentions: Race and the Antebellum Culture of Benevolence. Ithaca: Cornell University Press, 2003.

Sacks, Sheldon, ed. On Metaphor. Chicago: University of Chicago Press, 1979.

Saffin, John. A Brief and Candid Answer to a Late Printed Sheet, Entituled, The Selling of Joseph. In "John Saffin and His Slave Adam," by Abner C. Goodell Jr., Publications of the Colonial Society of Massachusetts: Transactions, 1892–1894, 103–12. Boston, 1895.

Sale, Maggie Montesinos. The Slumbering Volcano: American Slave Ship Revolts and the Production of Rebellious Masculinity. Durham: Duke University Press, 1997.

Salih, Sara. Introduction. In The History of Mary Prince, a West Indian Slave, Related by

Herself, by Mary Prince, edited by Sara Salih, vii–xxxiv. 1831. Reprint. London: Penguin, 2004.

Salvatore, Nick. *We All Got History: The Memory Books of Amos Webber*. New York: Times–Random House, 1996.

Samuels, Shirley, ed. *The Culture of Sentiment: Race, Gender and Sentimentality in Nineteenth-Century America*. New York: Oxford University Press, 1992.

Sánchez-Eppler, Karen. *Touching Liberty: Abolition, Feminism, and the Politics of the Body*. Berkeley: University of California Press, 1997.

Sand, George. Rev. of *Uncle Tom's Cabin*. In *Uncle Tom's Cabin: Authoritative Text, Backgrounds and Contexts, Criticism*, by Harriet Beecher Stowe, edited by Elizabeth Ammons, 459–63. 1852. Reprint. New York: W. W. Norton, 1994.

Sarat, Austin, and Thomas R. Kearns, eds. *Law in Everyday Life*. Ann Arbor: University of Michigan Press, 1993.

———, eds. *Law in the Domains of Culture*. Ann Arbor: University of Michigan Press, 2000.

Savage, W. Sherman. *The Controversy over the Distribution of Abolition Literature, 1830–1860*. Washington, D.C.: Association for the Study of Negro Life and History, 1938.

Schiller, Dan. *Objectivity and the News: The Public and the Rise of Commercial Journalism*. Philadelphia: University of Pennsylvania Press, 1981.

Schrader, David E. "Natural Law in the Constitutional Thought of Frederick Douglass." In *Frederick Douglass: A Critical Reader*, edited by Bill E. Lawson and Frank M. Kirkland, 85–99. Malden: Blackwell, 1999.

Schudson, Michael. "Was There Ever a Public Sphere? If So, When? Reflections on the American Case." In *Habermas and the Public Sphere*, edited by Craig Calhoun, 143–63. Cambridge: MIT Press, 1992.

Scott, Joan W. "The Evidence of Experience." *Critical Inquiry* 17:4 (Summer 1991): 773–97.

Sekora, John. "Black Message/White Envelope: Genre, Authenticity, and Authority in the Antebellum Slave Narrative." *Callaloo* 10:3 (Summer 1987): 482–515.

———. "'Mr. Editor, If You Please': Frederick Douglass, *My Bondage and My Freedom*, and the End of the Abolitionist Imprint." *Callaloo* 17:2 (Summer 1994): 608–26.

Sensbach, Jon F. *Rebecca's Revival: Creating Black Christianity in the Atlantic World*. Cambridge: Harvard University Press, 2005.

Sewall, Samuel. *The Selling of Joseph: A Memorial*. Edited by Sidney Kaplan. 1700. Reprint. Amherst: University of Massachusetts Press, 1969.

Sharp, Granville. *An Appendix to the Representation. . . .* London, 1772.

———. *A Representation of the Injustice and Dangerous Tendency of Tolerating Slavery; or of Admitting the Least Claim of Private Property in the Persons of Men, in England*. London, 1769.

[Sheppard, Furman.] *Passmore Williamson vs. John K. Kane: Argument for Defendant*. [Philadelphia, 1856?].

Sherwin, Richard K. *When Law Goes Pop: The Vanishing Line between Law and Popular Culture*. Chicago: University of Chicago Press, 2000.

Shields, John C. "Phillis Wheatley's Struggle for Freedom in Her Poetry and Prose." In

The Collected Works of Phillis Wheatley, by Phillis Wheatley, edited by John Shields, 229–70. New York: Oxford University Press, 1988.

Simms, William Gilmore. "Literary Prospects of the South." In Defining Southern Literature: Perspectives and Assessments, 1831–1852, edited by John Bassett, 92–107. Madison, N.J.: Fairleigh Dickinson University Press, 1977.

———. "Southern Literature." In Defining Southern Literature: Perspectives and Assessments, 1831–1852, edited by John Bassett, 60–72. Madison, N.J.: Fairleigh Dickinson University Press, 1977.

Slaughter, Thomas P. Bloody Dawn: The Christiana Riot and Racial Violence in the Antebellum North. New York: Oxford University Press, 1991.

"Slavery." Rev. of Appeal in Favor of that Class of Americans Called Africans, by Lydia Maria Child. North American Review, July 1835, 170–93.

"Sleeping Room of the Jury at Gibson's Hotel, Belmount." Frank Leslie's Illustrated Newspaper, 19 Nov. 1859, 394.

Slotkin, Richard. "Narratives of Negro Crime in New England, 1675–1800." American Quarterly 25:1 (Mar. 1973): 3–31.

Smith, J. Clay, Jr. Emancipation: The Making of the Black Lawyer, 1844–1944. Philadelphia: University of Pennsylvania Press, 1993.

Smith, Rogers M. Civic Ideals: Conflicting Visions of Citizenship in U.S. History. New Haven: Yale University Press, 1997.

Smith, Sidonie. Subjectivity, Identity, and the Body: Women's Autobiographical Practices in the Twentieth Century. Bloomington: Indiana University Press, 1995.

"Southern Court-House." Daily Evening Commonwealth. 8 Apr. 1851: n.p.

Srebnick, Amy Gilman. The Mysterious Death of Mary Rogers: Sex and Culture in Nineteenth-Century New York. New York: Oxford University Press, 1995.

Starling, Marion Wilson. The Slave Narrative: Its Place in American History. Washington, D.C.: Howard University Press, 1988.

Stauffer, John. The Black Hearts of Men: Radical Abolitionists and the Transformation of Race. Cambridge: Harvard University Press, 2002.

"Stephens, as He Appeared in Court." Frank Leslie's Illustrated Newspaper, 19 Nov. 1859, 394.

Stephenson, Mason W., and D. Grier Stephenson Jr. " 'To Protect and Defend': Joseph Henry Lumpkin, the Supreme Court of Georgia, and Slavery." In The Law of American Slavery: Major Historical Interpretations, edited by Kermit Hall, 522–51. New York: Garland, 1987.

Stepto, Robert B. "I Rose and Found My Voice: Narration, Authentication, and Authorial Control in Four Slave Narratives." In The Slave's Narrative, edited by Charles T. Davis and Henry Louis Gates Jr., 225–41. Oxford: Oxford University Press, 1985.

———. "Sharing the Thunder: The Literary Exchanges of Harriet Beecher Stowe, Henry Bibb, and Frederick Douglass." In Frederick Douglass: New Literary and Historical Essays, edited by Eric Sundquist, 135–53. New York: Cambridge University Press, 1990.

Stetson, Erlene, and Linda David. *Glorying in Tribulation: The Lifework of Sojourner Truth.* East Lansing: Michigan State University Press, 1994.

Stevens, Charles Emory. *Anthony Burns: A History.* 1856. Reprint. Williamstown: Corner House, 1973.

Stewart, James Brewer. *Holy Warriors: The Abolitionists and American Slavery.* Rev. ed. New York: Hill and Wang, 1996.

Stone, Albert. "Identity and Art in Frederick Douglass's *Narrative.*" In *Critical Essays on Frederick Douglass,* edited by William L. Andrews, 62–78. Boston: G. K. Hall, 1991.

Stone, William L. *Matthias and His Impostures: or, the Progress of Fanaticism. . . .* New York, 1835.

Stowe, Harriet Beecher. *Dred: A Tale of the Great Dismal Swamp.* Edited by Judie Newman. 1856. Reprint. Exeter: Edinburgh University Press, 1999.

———. *A Key to Uncle Tom's Cabin; Presenting the Original Facts and Documents upon Which the Story is Founded. Together with Corroborative Statements Verifying the Truth of the Work.* 1853. Reprint. Port Washington, N.Y.: Kennikat Press, 1968.

———. "Sojourner Truth, The Libyan Sybil." *Atlantic Monthly,* Apr. 1863, 473–81.

———. *Uncle Tom's Cabin: Authoritative Text, Backgrounds and Contexts, Criticism.* Edited by Elizabeth Ammons. 1852. Reprint. New York: W. W. Norton, 1994.

———. *Uncle Tom's Cabin. With Twenty-Seven Illustrations on Wood by George Cruikshank.* London, 1852.

Stroud, George M. *Ein Abriss der Gesetze betreffend die Sklaverei: in verschiedenen Staaten der Vereinigten Staaten von America.* Philadelphia, 1856.

———. *A Sketch of the Laws Relating to Slavery in the Several States of the United States of America.* Philadelphia, 1827.

———. *A Sketch of the Laws Relating to Slavery in the Several States of the United States of America.* 2nd ed. Philadelphia, 1856.

———. *Southern Slavery and the Christian Religion: To the Editor of North American and U.S. Gazette. . . .* Philadelphia, 1863.

Suggs, Jon-Christian. *Whispered Consolations: Law and Narrative in African-American Life.* Ann Arbor: University of Michigan Press, 2000.

Sundquist, Eric J. *To Wake the Nations: Race in the Making of American Literature.* Cambridge: Belknap–Harvard University Press, 1993.

———, ed. *Frederick Douglass: New Literary and Historical Essays.* New York: Cambridge University Press, 1990.

"The Supreme Court of the United States: Its Judges and Jurisdiction." *United States Magazine and Democratic Review,* Jan. 1838, 143–72.

Surrency, Edwin C. "The Beginnings of American Law Literature." *American Journal of Legal History* 31:3 (July 1987): 207–20.

———. "Law Reports in the United States." *American Journal of Legal History* 25:1 (Jan. 1981): 48–66.

Tebbel, John, and Mary Ellen Zuckerman. *The Magazine in America, 1741–1990.* New York: Oxford University Press, 1991.

Thomas, Brook. *American Literary Realism and the Failed Promise of Contract.* Berkeley: University of California Press, 1997.

————. *Cross-Examinations of Law and Literature: Cooper, Hawthorne, Stowe, and Melville.* Cambridge: Cambridge University Press, 1987.

Thompson, A. C. C. "From the Albany Patriot: Narrative of Frederick Douglass." *Liberator*, 20 Feb. 1846, 29.

————. "From the Delaware Republican. To the Public. Falsehood Refuted." *Liberator*, 12 Dec. 1845, 197.

Thompson, John Reuben. "Notices of New Works." *Southern Literary Messenger*, Oct. 1856, 314–20.

Thoreau, Henry David. "Slavery in Massachusetts." In *Reform Papers*, edited by Wendell Glick, 91–109. Princeton: Princeton University Press, 1973.

Timrod, Henry. "Literature in the South." In *Defining Southern Literature: Perspectives and Assessments, 1831–1852*, edited by John Bassett, 108–20. Madison, N.J.: Fairleigh Dickinson University Press, 1977.

Tocqueville, Alexis de. *Democracy in America.* Translated by Henry Reeve. 1835. Reprint. New York: Bantam-Random House, 2000.

Tompkins, Jane. *Sensational Designs: The Cultural Work of American Fiction, 1790–1860.* New York: Oxford University Press, 1985.

"To Our Patrons." *Freedom's Journal*, 16 Mar. 1827, 1.

Towner, Lawrence W. "The Sewall-Saffin Dialogue on Slavery." *William and Mary Quarterly* 3rd ser. 21:1 (Jan. 1964): 40–52.

————. "True Confessions and Dying Warnings in Colonial New England." In *Sibley's Heir: A Volume in Memory of Clifford Kenyon Shipton*, 523–39. Boston: Colonial Society of Massachusetts, 1982.

Tragle, Henry Irving, ed. *Southampton Slave Revolt of 1831: A Compilation of Source Material.* Amherst: University of Massachusetts Press, 1971.

"Trial by Jury." Rev. of *A Treatise on the Law and Practice of Juries*, by James Kennedy. *American Jurist* 2 (1829): 274–97.

Truth, Sojourner. "Letter from Sojourner Truth." *Commonwealth* (Boston), 3 July 1863.

————. *Narrative of Sojourner Truth; a Bondswoman of Olden Time, Emancipated by the New York Legislature in the Early Part of the Present Century; with a History of Her Labors and Correspondence Drawn from her "Book of Life."* Edited by Jeffrey C. Stewart. 1878. Reprint. New York: Oxford University Press, 1991.

————. *Narrative of Sojourner Truth, a Northern Slave, Emancipated from Bodily Servitude by the State of New York, in 1828. With a Portrait.* Boston, 1850.

Tucher, Andie. *Froth and Scum: Truth, Beauty, Goodness, and the Ax Murder in America's First Mass Medium.* Chapel Hill: University of North Carolina Press, 1994.

Tushnet, Mark V. *Slave Law in the American South: State v. Mann in History and Literature.* Lawrence: University Press of Kansas, 2003.

Uncle Tom in England; or, A Proof that Black is White. An Echo to the American "Uncle Tom." London, 1852.

U.S. Congress. *Biographical Dictionary of the American Congress, 1774–1961.* Washington, D.C.: Government Printing Office, 1961.

Vale, G[ilbert] *Fanaticism; Its Source and Influence, Illustrated by the Simple Narrative of Isabella in the Case of Matthias, Mr. and Mrs. B. Folger, Mr. Pierson, Mr. Mills, Catherine, Isabella, &C.*

&C. A Reply to W. L. Stone, with Descriptive Portraits of All the Parties, While at Sing-Sing and at Third Street.—Containing the Whole Truth—and Nothing but the Truth. 2 vols. in 1. New York, 1835.

Venet, Wendy Hamand. "'Cry Aloud and Spare Not': Northern Antislavery Women and John Brown's Raid." In His Soul Goes Marching On: Responses to John Brown and the Harpers Ferry Raid, edited by Paul Finkelman, 98–115. Charlottesville: University Press of Virginia, 1995.

"View in Charlestown, Virginia, Showing the Prison, Guard-House, and Court-House Where the Prisoners Were Tried." Frank Leslie's Illustrated Newspaper, 19 Nov. 1859, 390.

"View of the Courtroom during the Trial, with Accurate Portraits of the Presiding Judge, the Twelve Jurymen, the Counsel for the Prisoner and Prosecution, and Brown, as He Reclined on his Couch." Frank Leslie's Illustrated Newspaper, 12 Nov. 1859, 374–75.

Villard, Oswald Garrison. John Brown, 1800–1859. A Biography Fifty Years After. New York: Houghton Mifflin, 1910.

"Visit to Dred Scott." Frank Leslie's Illustrated Newspaper, 27 June 1857, 49–50.

Von Frank, Albert J. The Trials of Anthony Burns: Freedom and Slavery in Emerson's Boston. Cambridge: Harvard University Press, 1998.

W. R. A. "The Duty of Southern Authors." Southern Literary Messenger, Oct. 1856, 241–47.

Wald, Priscilla. Constituting Americans: Cultural Anxiety and Narrative Form. Durham: Duke University Press, 1995.

Waldstreicher, David. "Introduction: Nature, Race, and Revolution in Jefferson's America." In Notes on the State of Virginia, by Thomas Jefferson, edited by David Waldstreicher, 1–38. 1787. New York: Bedford–St. Martin's, 2002.

Walker, David. David Walker's Appeal, in Four Articles; Together with a Preamble, to the Coloured Citizens of the World, But in Particular, and Very Expressly, to Those of the United States of America. Edited by Sean Wilentz. 1829. Reprint. New York: Hill and Wang, 1995.

Wallerstein, Peter. "Incendiaries All: Southern Politics and the Harpers Ferry Raid." In His Soul Goes Marching On: Responses to John Brown and the Harpers Ferry Raid, edited by Paul Finkelman, 149–73. Charlottesville: University Press of Virginia, 1995.

Warburton, George D. Hochelaga; or, England in the New World. Vol. 2. London, 1847.

Ward, Samuel Ringgold. Autobiography of a Fugitive Negro: His Anti-Slavery Labors in the United States, Canada, and England. 1855. Reprint. Chicago: Johnson, 1970.

Warner, Michael. The Letters of the Republic: Publication and the Public Sphere in Eighteenth-Century America. Cambridge: Harvard University Press, 1990.

Warner, Samuel. Authentic and Impartial Narrative of the Tragical Scene Which Was Witnessed in Southampton County. . . . New York, 1831.

Washington, Margaret. "Introduction: The Enduring Legacy of Sojourner Truth." In Narrative of Sojourner Truth, edited by Margaret Washington, ix–xxxiii. New York: Vintage–Random House, 1993.

Watson, Henry. Narrative of Henry Watson, a Fugitive Slave. Written by Himself. Boston, 1848.

Watson, Ritchie Devon, Jr. Yeoman versus Cavalier: The Old Southwest's Fictional Road to Rebellion. Baton Rouge: Louisiana State University Press, 1993.

"The Way a Criminal Trial Is Conducted." *Frank Leslie's Illustrated Newspaper*, 16 May 1857, 365–66.

"The Way in Which Fred. Douglass Fights Wise of Virginia." *Frank Leslie's Illustrated Newspaper*, 12 Nov. 1859, 382.

Wechsler, Herbert. "Toward Neutral Principles of Constitutional Law." *Harvard Law Review* 73:1 (Nov. 1959): 1–35.

Weiner, Mark S. *Black Trials: Citizenship from the Beginnings of Slavery to the End of Caste.* New York: Knopf, 2004.

Weiner, Susan. *Law in Art: Melville's Major Fiction and Nineteenth-Century American Law.* New York: Peter Lang, 1992.

Weinstein, Cindy. *Family, Kinship, and Sympathy in Nineteenth-Century American Literature.* Cambridge: Cambridge University Press, 2004.

Weisberg, Robert. "Proclaiming Trials as Narratives: Premises and Pretenses." In *Law's Stories: Narrative and Rhetoric in the Law,* edited by Peter Brooks and Paul Gewirtz, 61–83. New Haven: Yale University Press, 1996.

Weisenburger, Steven. *Modern Medea: A Family Story of Slavery and Child-Murder from the Old South.* New York: Hill and Wang–Farrar, Straus, and Giroux, 1998.

Weld, [Theodore] Dwight. *American Slavery as It Is: Testimony of a Thousand Witnesses.* 1839. Reprint. New York: Arno–New York Times, 1969.

Werner, Craig. "The Old South, 1815–1840." In *The History of Southern Literature,* edited by Louis D. Rubin et al., 81–91. Baton Rouge: Louisiana State University Press, 1985.

West, Robin. "Feminism, Critical Social Theory, and Law." *University of Chicago Legal Forum* (1989): 59–97.

Wheatley, Phillis. *The Collected Works of Phillis Wheatley.* Edited by John Shields. New York: Oxford University Press, 1988.

Wheeler, Jacob D. *A Practical Treatise on the Law of Slavery.* New York, 1837.

Whipple, Charles K. *The Family Relation as Affected by Slavery.* Cincinnati, 1858.

[Whitaker, Daniel.] "The Newspaper and Periodical Press." *Southern Quarterly Review,* Jan. 1842, 5–66.

White, T. W. "Publisher's Notice." *Southern Literary Messenger,* Aug. 1834, 1.

Whitman, Walt. *Leaves of Grass.* 1855. Reprint. New York: Penguin, 1986.

Whitney, Lisa. "In the Shadow of Uncle Tom's Cabin: Stowe's Vision of Slavery from the Great Dismal Swamp." *New England Quarterly* 66:4 (Dec. 1993): 552–69.

Whittier, John Greenleaf. *Narrative of James Williams: An American Slave.* New York, 1838.

Wiecek, William M. "Latimer: Lawyers, Abolitionists, and the Problem of Unjust Laws." In *Antislavery Reconsidered: New Perspectives on the Abolitionists,* edited by Lewis Perry and Michael Fellman, 219–37. Baton Rouge: Louisiana State University Press, 1979.

———. "The Origins of the Law of Slavery in British North America." *Cardozo Law Review* 17:6 (May 1996): 1711–92.

———. *The Sources of Antislavery Constitutionalism in America, 1760–1848.* Ithaca: Cornell University Press, 1977.

Wiegman, Robyn. *American Anatomies: Theorizing Race and Gender.* Durham: Duke University Press, 1995.

Wiethoff, William E. *A Peculiar Humanism: The Judicial Advocacy of Slavery in High Courts of the Old South, 1820–1850.* Athens: University of Georgia Press, 1996.

Wilentz, Sean. *Chants Democratic: New York City and the Rise of the American Working Class, 1788–1850.* New York: Oxford University Press, 1984.

Williams, Daniel E., comp. *Pillars of Salt: An Anthology of Early American Criminal Narratives.* Madison: Madison House, 1993.

Williams, Patricia J. *The Alchemy of Race and Rights: Diary of a Law Professor.* Cambridge: Harvard University Press, 1991.

Wilmer, Lambert A. *Our Press Gang; or, a Complete Exposition of the Corruptions and Crimes of the American Newspapers.* Philadelphia, 1859.

Wilson, James. *The Works of James Wilson.* Edited by Robert Green McCloskey. Vol. 1. Cambridge: Belknap–Harvard University Press, 1967.

Winter, Steven L. *A Clearing in the Forest: Law, Life, and Mind.* Chicago: University of Chicago Press, 2001.

Wise, Steven M. *Though the Heavens May Fall: The Landmark Trial That Led to the End of Human Slavery.* Cambridge, Mass.: Merloyd Lawrence–Da Capo, 2005.

Wood, Gordon S. *The Creation of the American Republic, 1776–1787.* 1969. Reprint. Chapel Hill: University of North Carolina Press, 1998.

Wood, Marcus. *Blind Memory: Visual Representations of Slavery in England and America, 1780–1865.* New York: Routledge, 2000.

———. *Slavery, Empathy, and Pornography.* Oxford: Oxford University Press, 2002.

Woolman, John. *Some Considerations on the Keeping of Negroes and Considerations on the Keeping of Negroes.* 1754 and 1762. Reprint. Northampton, Mass.: Gehanna Press, 1970.

Wright, Lyle H. *American Fiction, 1851–1875: A Contribution toward a Bibliography.* San Marino: Huntington Library, 1957.

Wright, R. Glenn. *Author Bibliography of English Language Fiction in the Library of Congress through 1950.* Vol. 4. Boston: G. K. Hall, 1973.

Wyatt-Brown, Bertram. *Lewis Tappan and the Evangelical War against Slavery.* 1969. Reprint. Baton Rouge: Louisiana State University Press, 1997.

———. "Proslavery and Antislavery Intellectuals: Class Concepts and Polemical Struggle." In *Antislavery Reconsidered: New Perspectives on the Abolitionists,* edited by Lewis Perry and Michael Fellman, 308–36. Baton Rouge: Louisiana State University Press, 1979.

———. *Southern Honor: Ethics and Behavior in the Old South.* New York: Oxford University Press, 1982.

Yarborough, Richard. "Race, Violence, and Manhood: The Masculine Ideal in Frederick Douglass's 'The Heroic Slave.'" In *Frederick Douglass: New Literary and Historical Essays,* edited by Eric Sundquist, 166–88. New York: Cambridge University Press, 1990.

Yellin, Jean Fagan. "Black Masks: Melville's 'Benito Cereno.'" *American Quarterly* 22:3 (Autumn 1970): 678–89.

———. *Harriet Jacobs: A Life.* Cambridge, Mass.: Basic Civitas–Perseus Books, 2004.

———. Introduction. In *Incidents in the Life of a Slave Girl, Written by Herself*, by Harriet A. Jacobs, edited by Jean Fagan Yellin, xv–xli. 1861. Reprint. Cambridge: Harvard University Press, 1987.

Young, James E. *Writing and Rewriting the Holocaust: Narrative and the Consequences of Interpretation.* Bloomington, Indiana University Press, 1988.

Zaeske, Susan. *Signatures of Citizenship: Petitioning, Antislavery, and Women's Political Identity.* Chapel Hill: University of North Carolina Press, 2004.

Zafar, Rafia. "Franklinian Douglass: The Afro-American as Representative Man." In *Frederick Douglass: New Literary and Historical Essays*, edited by Eric Sundquist, 99–117. New York: Cambridge University Press, 1990.

Zeigler, Mary B. "Something to Shout About: AAVE as a Linguistic and Cultural Treasure." In *Sociocultural and Historical Contexts of African American English*, edited by Sonja L. Lanehart, 169–85. Amsterdam: John Benjamins, 2001.

Ziff, Larzer. *Writing in the New Nation: Prose, Print, and Politics in the Early United States.* New Haven: Yale University Press, 1991.

INDEX

Abolitionism: and African Americans, 3, 6, 25, 26, 59, 72, 101, 102, 105, 107–9, 111, 120, 126, 131, 141, 142, 149, 157, 170; antebellum, 3, 6–15, 24, 25, 27, 28, 38, 42, 68–69, 77, 95, 201; and antijudicialism, 21–22, 37, 41, 58, 60–61, 63, 102; black advocates, 26, 27, 102, 103–4, 111, 122, 125, 132–39, 141, 142–43, 170, 221; black versus white roles in, 26, 126; British, 4–5, 16, 18–19, 35–36, 38, 184, 197, 201, 218–19, 229 (n. 111), 260 (n. 12); and capitalism, 182, 183, 184, 185, 187, 189–90, 197; colonial, 3–4; and colonization, 25, 134; as conspiracy, 42, 199, 200–201, 219; as criminal, 7, 40, 41, 49, 50–52, 57, 196, 199, 219, 220, 237 (n. 84); early national, 6; and emigration, 25; and evangelicalism, 13–14, 15, 72, 79; and extradition, 51; and feminism, 160, 161; and free speech, 40, 41, 58; Garrisonian, 19, 101, 102, 135–36, 138, 139, 140, 192–93, 224 (n. 29); gradual, 6, 162; and Harpers Ferry, 28, 199–200, 208, 211–12, 220; immediatist, 6–7, 21, 25; interracial, 25–26, 154, 157, 163, 200, 222; juridical metaphor of, 1–2, 3, 12–15, 16, 27, 30, 43, 105, 120, 121, 123, 132–33, 142, 152, 160, 161, 165, 174, 178, 190, 193, 208, 220–22; and law, 1–12 passim, 16, 17, 27, 29, 40, 42, 49, 51, 58, 59, 163, 208, 220; lecture circuit, 25, 101, 102, 103, 199; and legal reform benchmarks, 24; literary, 2, 7, 25, 64–66, 68, 88, 95, 154–59, 170–71, 172, 174–75, 180, 197; material culture of, 192; mob violence against, 41, 49, 50, 56–57, 74, 87; and penny press, 3, 7, 51, 55–56, 238 (n. 112); portrayals of, 42; and postal campaign of 1835, 49–50, 74; and print/propaganda, 1–17 passim, 27, 35–69, 185, 209, 212; proslavery and Southern views of, 42, 57, 178–79, 184, 185–98; public perception of, 42, 50; public reversal of opinion on, 50, 57; and religion/morality, 13–15, 17, 18; and representative identity, 157; and rhetoric, 14, 16–17, 22–27, 43, 145, 208; rhetorical decriminalization of, 29, 40, 49, 110; and scientific racism, 135; tactics and strategies of, 1–2, 6–31 passim, 38, 40, 41, 44, 49–50, 55–56, 65, 66, 98, 138, 139, 152, 155, 156, 162, 163, 165, 173–75, 177, 178, 185, 186, 190, 192, 201, 208, 212, 224–25 (n. 29); and white advocacy, 25–26, 98, 139, 157–60, 171, 196, 220; and white paternalism, 153, 163, 164, 172, 173, 242 (n. 8); and women, 160–61, 185–86, 197

Adam Negro, 3–4, 223 (n. 9)

Adam Negro's Tryall, 3–4, 223 (n. 9)

Adams, F. C.: *Manuel Pereira* (1853), 7

Adultery, 13, 232 (n. 157)

Advertisements, 11, 48, 64

Advocates: black, 26, 27, 103–5, 111, 122, 125–49, 153, 170, 219, 220, 221, 222; for slavery, 165, 181–82; white female, 160, 161; white male, 26, 151–70, 174, 190, 196, 220

African Americans: and abolitionism, 3, 6, 25–27, 38, 59, 72, 101–5, 102, 109–23, 141, 149, 178; as advocates, 26, 27, 103–5, 111, 122, 125–49, 153, 170, 219, 220, 221, 222; and authorship, 6, 96, 133, 134; and citizenship, 2, 27, 29–30, 104, 105, 123, 201, 220, 261 (n. 30); and civic agency, 77, 78, 103, 108, 122–23, 127, 173, 219, 260 (n. 12); and civic equality, 134, 222; and civic exclusion, 25, 41, 77–78, 104, 125, 126, 134–35, 170, 193, 195, 208, 257 (n. 94); and civic identity, 24, 30, 97, 115; and civic participation, 2, 24, 28, 30, 111, 149, 222; commodification of, 190; and confessional discourse, 77, 78, 97; corporeality of, 111, 114, 118, 131, 186–90; credibility of, 133; and criminality, 5, 6, 7, 40, 56, 73, 77, 78, 84, 85, 86, 87, 89, 91, 92, 97, 123, 134, 141, 220; and education, 127, 134–35, 148, 262 (n. 42); and evangelicalism, 79; humanity of, 143; intellectual capacity of, 126, 128, 133, 134, 138–42, 148; and law, 4, 5, 6, 15–16, 30, 42, 65, 75–78, 107–9, 112, 170; and lecture circuit, 25, 103–4; and legal profession, 26, 27, 126–31, 145; legal status of, 10, 25, 27, 72, 75, 118, 120, 170, 220; as litigants, 72, 214; mendacity of, 77, 92; natural rights of, 14, 15, 52, 178; and political office, 126, 127; and political speech, 137; and print culture, 5, 6, 41, 85–86; procedural rights of, 24; rhetorical decriminalization of, 27, 29, 69, 97, 110, 153, 158; rhetorical dehumanization of, 145; sexualization of, 13, 80, 81, 82, 83, 85, 86–87, 88, 89, 97, 186; as testifying witnesses, 27, 69, 71, 74–75, 97, 109, 110, 111, 143–44; veracity of, 96, 121; violence against, 49, 57, 111–14, 118–20. See also Fugitive slaves; Slaves

African American studies, 126, 232–33 (n. 157); evidentiary pressures on, 143–44; testimonial rhetoric of, 126

Afro-Britons, 260 (n. 12)

Aikin, John, 137; "Dialogue between a Master and a Slave," 137–38, 139, 141

Alabama, 51

Alcott, Louisa May, 234 (n. 6)

Alexander, Robert: I Ain't Yo' Uncle (1992), 260 (n. 11)

Allegory, 177, 178, 179, 184, 191, 194, 197, 221

Allen, Macon Bolling, 126

Allen, Richard, 6

Althusser, Louis, 120

Alton (Ill.) Tragedy, 56–57, 58, 63

American Anti-Slavery Society, 6, 12, 16, 49–50, 57, 103, 211; founding of, 79, 269 (n. 22)

American Colonization Society, 140

Americanism: ascriptive, 29

American Jurist, 20, 21

American Revolution, 4, 5, 198

American Slavery as It Is, 16–17, 19, 155

Amistad cases, 7, 8

Anthony, Aaron, 113

Antiabolitionism: and mob violence, 41, 49, 50, 51, 56–58, 63, 74, 87; and Southern literature, 177, 179–82, 221

Antijudicialism, 21–22, 37, 41, 58, 60–61, 63, 102

Antipolygamy fiction, 263 (n. 61)

Antislavery movement. See Abolitionism

Anti-Slavery Record, 187

Anti-Slavery Standard, 67

Auld, Hugh, 119–20, 121, 163

Auld, Sophia, 119, 163

Commonwealth (newspaper), 62, 64, 67–68, 69

Commonwealth v. Anthes (1855), 240 (n. 134)

Commonwealth v. Aves (1836), 8

Compromise of 1850, 7, 9, 58, 65, 194, 208, 234 (n. 15)

Confession, 72–73, 77, 97, 168; criminal, 80; testimony replacing, 78, 97

Conformity, 55

Congress. See U.S. Congress

Conscience Whigs, 21

Constitution, British, 4

Constitution, U.S.; Garrison's burning of, 66; and judicial supremacy, 19; and slave status, 8, 15, 66, 67, 102, 103, 104, 234 (n. 116); and treason definition, 51. See also First Amendment

Constitutionalism: antislavery, 7, 22; popular, 19, 21, 54, 57, 58, 231 (n. 152). See also Due process

Constitutional law, 8, 22, 29, 141

Consumer culture, 53, 190

Conway, Moncure Daniel, 71, 72

Cook, John E., 201

Cooper, James Fenimore, 20–21, 179; The Ways of the Hour (1850), 21

Cooper, Thomas, 47–48, 53; Treatise on the Law of Libel (1830), 46, 47–48, 55

Copeland, John, 201, 209

Coppoc, Edwin, 210

Cornell, Sarah, 7

Cornish, Samuel, 6, 104

Corporeality, 111, 114, 118, 186–90, 248–49 (n. 150)

Cosby, William, 46

Counternarrative, 144

Courier, 62, 69

Courier and Enquirer, 87

Court Day: and slave sales, 64–66

Courthouses: iconography of, 41, 65; as jails, 9, 59–64; and slave sales, 64–66; Southern, 64–65

Court of public opinion. See Public opinion, court of

Courts. See Judges/judiciary; Trials

Court Square. See Boston courthouse

Couverture, 161

Cover, Robert M., 8, 10, 22, 232 (n. 157); Justice Accused, 8; "Nomos and Narrative," 22

Covey, Edward, 101, 116–17, 118

Cradle of Liberty, 238 (n. 112)

Crafts, Hannah: Bondwoman's Narrative (2002), 258 (n. 112)

Crandall, Prudence, 8, 51, 262 (n. 42)

Crandall, Reuben, 51

Crandall v. State (1834), 262 (n. 42)

Crane, Gregg D., 156, 271 (n. 82)

Creole, 102; and Douglass's "Heroic Slave," 125, 157; slave uprising on, 8

Creswell, John T., 244 (n. 37)

Creswell's Executors v. Walker (1861), 77

Crime: abolitionism as, 7, 40, 41, 49, 50–52, 57, 196, 199, 219, 220, 237 (n. 84); and African Americans, 5, 6, 7, 40, 56, 73, 77, 78, 84, 85, 86, 87, 89, 91, 92, 97, 123, 134, 141, 220; antislavery violence as, 57; changing views of, 13; civil injury versus, 15; confessions of, 80; literature of, 5, 80, 81, 85–86, 232 (n. 157), 247 (n. 83); and morality, 13–14; penny-press coverage of, 41, 53–54, 56, 80, 85–86; and property, 13, 15; and sexuality, 13, 86; as sin, 13, 14, 15, 228 (n. 86); and slaveholders, 1, 12, 14, 15–18, 52, 78, 112, 120, 142, 159, 222; slavery as, 1, 7, 12–18, 24, 30, 52, 69, 112, 178–79, 190, 222. See also Criminal law and litigation; Murder

Criminal law and litigation, 222; and abolitionist suits, 190, 191, 195, 196, 197; and abolitionist trial trope, 1–2, 3, 12–15, 16, 22, 24–27, 29, 30, 40, 105, 121, 123, 133, 152, 161, 165, 174, 178, 190, 193, 208, 220–22, 231 (n. 151); as adversarial procedure paradigm, 2, 16, 17, 22, 23, 26, 30, 53, 81, 142–43, 182, 190, 198, 208, 213, 221, 228 (n. 86); civil law versus, 15; crime definition under, 15; cultural focus on, 29; "lawyer-ization" of, 16, 18, 229 (n. 111); lay involvement in, 18; and libel, 43–44, 45, 47, 51, 235–36 (nn. 32, 39); Puritan influence on, 13, 15; and slave plaintiff, 229 (n. 96). See also Due process; Judges/judiciary; Jury; Trials

Critical Race Theory, 107, 144–45

Cruikshank, George, 38

Cugoano, Quobna Ottobah, 5, 6

Culp, Jerome McCristal, Jr., 144, 145

Cultural historians, 132 (n. 157), 232–33 (n. 157)

Cultural legal studies, 28–31

Curtis, Benjamin R., 66

Curtis, Michael Kent, 47

Custis, William, 107

Dana, Richard Henry, Jr., 59, 130–31

Davis, Charles G., 130

Day of Judgment, 18

Death sentence. See Execution

DeBow, James D. B., 177

DeBow's Review, 28, 177, 196, 199

Declaration of Independence, 169

Delano, Amasa, 104; Narrative of Voyages and Travels (1817), 176

Delany, Martin R., 157

Delgado, Richard, 107, 144–45

Demby (slave), 115, 116, 119, 120

Democratic Party, 21, 234 (n. 6), 274 (n. 56)

Dew, Thomas Roderick, 180; Review of the Debate (1832), 226 (n. 44)

D'Hauteville case, 7

Dialect, 242 (n. 8)

Disestablishment, 13

Disunionism, 101, 103

Documentary, 136–37

Domesticity, 80, 81, 82, 83, 84, 153, 155, 173. See also Separate-spheres ideology

Double character, 77, 106–7, 117

Double standard (legal), 52, 134

Douglass, Frederick, 31, 98, 101–5, 109–43 passim, 152, 171, 178, 197; "American Prejudice against Color" (1845), 145–49; as antislavery witness, 1–2, 23–24, 27, 102, 103, 109–22, 136, 138, 174, 190; and black advocacy, 26, 27, 104–5, 122, 125, 126, 127, 131–39, 142–43, 145–49, 153, 170, 220, 231 (n. 151); British lecture tours of, 101, 103, 125, 146–49, 199–200, 201; and Cambria riot, 125, 126, 145, 146–49; and constitutional law, 22; debate over early career of, 101–2; and Dred Scott case, 102, 103; "The Dred Scott Decision" (1857), 102; and Garrisonian abolitionism, 102, 135–36, 138–39, 140; and Harpers Ferry, 199–200, 201, 209; "The Heroic Slave" (1853), 7, 125, 157, 175; intellectual abilities of, 139, 141; and Latimer case, 102–3; and legal rhetoric, 27, 104–5, 149; Life and Times (1881), 132; My Bondage and My Freedom (1855), 17, 101, 102, 103, 105, 122, 126, 132–45 passim, 175; Narrative (1845), 2, 24, 27, 101, 103, 105, 109–22, 125, 131, 137, 142, 145, 157, 170, 190, 220; portrayals of, 102, 199–200, 217–20; print self-fashioning of, 2, 101, 102–5; and Southern violence, 111–14, 118–19, 121, 163; speeches of, 12, 102–3, 105, 109–10, 122, 125, 136–37, 146–49; and Stowe, 157, 262 (n. 42); and white advocacy, 157

Dred Scott v. Sandford (1857), 9, 19, 103, 156, 195, 201, 208, 214, 220

Dresser, Amos, 51

Drew, Thomas: The John Brown Invasion (1860), 211, 212

Due process: and African Americans, 24, 134, 149; and antislavery principles, 41, 44, 52, 57, 58, 77, 192, 208; as civil liberty, 220; and Compromise of 1850, 58; and Fugitive Slave Law, 40, 62, 63, 208; public's familiarity with, 10, 24;

and slavery, 58, 62, 134, 173, 214, 220; and South, 192–93, 209–11, 212, 217, 218

Eastman, Mary: *Aunt Phillis's Cabin* (1852), 28, 178
Edmondson, Milly, 170, 261 (n. 34)
Education: and African Americans, 127, 134–35, 148, 262 (n. 42); and law, 254 (n. 13); legal, 256 (n. 70); and literacy, 147–48
Elgin Settlement, 262 (n. 42)
Emancipation, 72, 104, 105, 138, 149, 162, 191
Emancipator, 51, 185
Emerson, Ralph Waldo, 68, 179–80, 181, 211–13, 217, 220
Empiricism, 15, 257 (n. 94)
England. *See* Britain
English law, 4–5, 13, 15, 271 (n. 82); and common law, 4, 13, 46; and criminal trials, 16; and jury, 20; and popular constitutionalism, 19
Engravings, 38, 41, 64, 69, 203, 209, 216–17
Enlightenment, 14, 29, 134, 135, 137
Equiano, Olaudah, 5, 6
Equity, 4
Evangelicalism: and abolitionism, 13–14, 15, 72, 79, 154, 185, 187, 225 (n. 29); and testifying, 14, 72
Evans, Augusta Jane, 161
Everett, Edward, 237 (n. 84)
Evidence: definition of, 17; hearsay, 4; and jury's role, 20; newly discovered, 17; precarious, 77; rejection of, 76; rules of, 13, 16, 77, 105–6; slave narratives as, 109–23, 143–44, 188; and testimony, 143–44, 147; white versus black, 91, 96, 98, 109. *See also* Confession; Testimony; Witnesses
Ewick, Patricia, 23
Execution, 5, 13; execution sermons, 77; of Harpers Ferry conspirators, 200, 208, 210, 212, 217; privatized, 80; of Turner, 1. *See also* Gallows literature
Exegetical authority, 137, 147
Exodus, 15
Extradition, 51
Eyewitness account. *See* Witnesses

Fair trial. *See* Due process
Falconbridge, Alexander: *Account of the Slave Trade* (1788), 5
Fanuzzi, Robert A., 235–36 (n. 39), 236 (n. 54), 238 (n. 96)
Farnsworth, Amos, 237 (n. 84)
Farnum, Executor of Tuttle Hubbards v. Brooks (1829), 42
Federal commissioners, 37
Felman, Shoshana, 17, 120
Feminism, 160, 161
Ferguson, Robert A., 5, 203, 208, 211, 257 (n. 94)
Fiction. *See* Literature
Finney, Charles Grandison, 13, 14
First Amendment, 13, 45; extension to states, 47. *See also* Freedom of speech/press
Fishkin, Shelley Fisher, 157
Fitzhugh, George, 28, 184; *Cannibals All!* (1857), 177, 178
Folger, Ann, 72, 74, 79, 81–84, 87–93, 95, 96
Folger, Benjamin, 72, 74, 79–95 passim; libel suit, 72, 90, 95
Folktales, 144
Follen, Charles, 51
A Forensic Dispute on the Legality of Enslaving Africans (1773), 4
Forbes, Hugh, 218, 219–20, 275–76 (n. 73)
Forten, James, 6
Foster, Frances Smith, 78, 233 (n. 157)
Foster, George, 135
Foucault, Michel, 137, 144
Fourth of July speeches, 42, 66
Framingham Grove meeting, 66, 68, 71

Habeas corpus, 107, 108, 122; and Fugitive Slave Law, 10–11, 37
Habermas, Jürgen, 53, 55, 132, 230 (n. 114)
Hall, Kermit, 20
Hall, Prince, 6
Halttunen, Karen, 80, 81, 82, 85
Hamilton, Alexander, 46
Hamlet, James, 30, 38, 58
Hammond, James Henry, 28
Hanging. See Execution; Gallows literature
Hanno, Joseph, 5
Harper and Brothers, 81, 268 (n. 8)
Harpers Ferry raid, 26, 199–220, 221; abolitionist responses to, 208, 211; graphic portrayals of, 201–7, 209; literary portrayals of, 211–12; Northern responses to, 211–13; periodical portrayals of, 199–200, 208, 213–14, 216; Southern responses to, 209, 215, 216, 217; treason trials for, 1, 2, 28, 200, 201–8, 209
Harper's Weekly, 214, 275 (n. 58)
Harris, George Washington, 234 (n. 6)
Hartman, Saidiya V., 97
Hathaway, J. C., 14
Henson, Josiah, 170
Hentz, Caroline Lee: Planter's Northern Bride (1854), 28, 185, 187, 271 (n. 71)
Hermeneutics, 137, 144, 147, 233 (n. 158)
Herrenvolk democracy, 184
Herrick, Anson, 234 (n. 6)
Higginson, Thomas Wentworth, 272 (n. 2)
Higher law, 13–14, 15, 66–67, 68, 154, 178
Hildreth, Richard: Atrocious Judges (1856), 21, 107
Hill, Daniel M., 63
Hinds v. Brazealle (1838), 262 (n. 42)
Hitchcock, H., 11
Hogarth, William, 86
Holcombe, James, 180
Holocaust literature, 136, 256 (nn. 59, 67)

Honor, 178, 181, 184, 185, 217, 268 (nn. 12, 13)
House of Commons, 4, 5
Howard University Law School, 127
Howe, Mark DeWolfe, 13
Howe, Samuel Gridley, 272 (n. 2)
Hughes, Langston, 127
Hume, David, 134
Hunter, Andrew, 211
Hurd, John Codman, 11, 12; Law of Freedom and Bondage (1858–62), 12; Topics of Jurisprudence (1856), 12
Hutchinson, John, 259 (n. 126)

Illinois mob violence, 56, 57, 58
Illustrations, 213; abolitionist, 38, 41, 187; of Harpers Ferry case, 201–7, 209. See also Cartoons; Engravings
Incendiary publications legislation, 42, 47. See also Sedition
Independence Hall, 10
Individual rights. See Civil liberties
Insurrection, 9, 162, 169, 171–72; incitement charges, 51, 199, 200, 201; insurrection trials, 156; maritime, 7, 8, 125, 126, 157, 175; Turner's, 1, 8, 51, 158–59. See also Violence

Jackson, Andrew, 49
Jackson, Francis, 237 (n. 84)
Jacksonian era, 18, 21, 36–37, 41, 47, 55, 56, 74, 221
Jacobs, Harriet A., 261 (n. 34), 265 (n. 92); as antislavery witness, 10–12; Incidents in the Life of a Slave Girl (1861), 95–96, 109, 144, 168, 264 (n. 91)
Jails. See Prisons
Jay, William, 41, 49, 53, 69; Inquiry into the Character and Tendency of the American Colonization and American Anti-Slavery Societies (1835), 49–50
Jefferson, Thomas, 139, 140, 141, 142, 177; Notes on the State of Virginia (1787), 1, 25, 126, 137, 138, 147, 148

Jeremiads, 18
Jerry Rescue, 9
Jewett, Helen, 7, 54, 97
Jewett, John P., 21
Jewett, William S. L., 214–18
Johnson, Jane, 107, 108, 109, 122, 123
Johnson, Mark, 22
Johnson, Paul E., 79, 85
Jolliffe, John, 9, 158; *Belle Scott* (1858), 7, 226 (n. 56); *Chattanooga* (1860), 7, 226 (n. 56)
Jones, Absalom, 6
Journalism. *See* Press; Print culture
Judges/judiciary: and adversarial process, 143, 213; and antijudicialism, 21–22, 37, 41, 58, 60–61, 63, 102; common-law power of, 230 (n. 119); debate over, 18–22, 60; failures of, 28, 208, 213, 221; and Fugitive Slave Law of 1850, 37–38, 41, 58, 60, 208, 213; and fundamental law, 19, 20; and judicial supremacy, 19, 208; and jury, 20, 21, 46, 47; and press, 40, 41, 45, 47, 49, 69, 221; proslavery, 41, 56, 57, 58, 66, 68, 208, 213; and slave sales, 43–44, 64–66. *See also* Courthouses; Trials
Judgment Day, 18
Judiciary. *See* Judges/judiciary
Juridical rhetoric/metaphor, 1–3, 15–18, 19, 43, 105, 120, 121, 123, 132–33, 142, 143, 152, 160, 161, 165, 174, 178, 190, 193, 208, 220, 221, 222, 228 (n. 86), 231 (n. 151); and civil liberties, 213; in proslavery novel, 177–79, 182–98, 221
Jurisprudence, 10, 18, 20, 76; and print culture, 47, 48; of sentiment, 154, 156, 162; Southern, 75, 152
Jury, 16; and adversarial process, 143; African American inclusion in, 30; autonomy of, 46, 47; and Fugitive Slave Law of 1850, 21, 37; and ideological blinders, 120; and libel trials, 46, 47; limitations on, 18, 20; readers as, 22;

as representing the people, 18, 19, 20, 21; rights and powers of, 20, 47; selection of, 193, 230 (n. 126). *See also* Due process
Jury of the Nation, 55
Justice, 28, 48, 105; as blind, 36, 120; denial to slaves, 62; iconography of, 36, 65; and judicial procedure, 213; and penny press, 54; and South, 45, 48, 64, 65, 75, 208, 209, 212, 217. *See also* Due process

Kane, John K., 107, 108, 122
Kansas, 155, 201
Kansas-Nebraska Act of 1854, 7, 155, 234 (n. 15)
Kant, Immanuel, 134
Kemble, Fanny, 171
Kennedy, John Pendleton: *Swallow Barn* (1832), 268 (n. 12)
Kent, James, 55
King, Rodney, 120
King, William, 262 (n. 42)
Kingdom of Matthias. *See* Matthias scandal
Knapp, Isaac, 51
Kramer, Larry D., 19

Laisdell, Isabella, 80
Lakoff, George, 22–23
Lane, Lunsford, 170
Langbein, John H., 16
Langston, John Mercer, 126–30, 131, 145; *From the Virginia Plantation to the National Capitol* (1894), 127–28
Lapsansky, Phillip, 138
Lassell, William, 63
Latimer, George, 8–9, 59, 102–3
Latimer case, 8–9, 59, 102–3
Latimer Journal and North Star, 9
Latimer Law, 59
Law: abuses of, 54; changing views of, 45, 54; commercial influences on, 46;

cultural meaning of, 22, 28–31; Democratic views of, 21; double standard in, 52, 134; and equity, 4; fundamental, 19, 20; higher law versus, 154; iconography of, 36, 65; and landmark cases, 8–9; legal reform, 24, 156; literacy in, 10, 11, 196; and literature, 145; literature of, 8, 10, 11–12; and metaphor, 22–24, 26–27; natural, 133, 195, 257 (n. 94); and personal liberty, 9; popular consciousness of, 23, 28–29, 54, 187, 201, 208, 212, 220, 232 (n. 156), 260 (n. 12); positive versus fundamental, 19; precedents in, 8; property, 13, 15–16, 29, 185, 190, 195, 197, 268 (n. 12); Puritan, 13–14; Whig views of, 21. *See also* Civil law and litigation; Criminal law and litigation; Higher law; Judges/judiciary; Jurisprudence; Justice; Legal history; Slave law; State law; Trials

Law Reporter, 9

Lawyers: abolitionists as, 26, 166, 264 (n. 80); adversarial role of, 143; African American, 27, 126–31, 145; changing role of, 16, 18, 20, 30; power of, 26; professionalization of, 13, 16, 26, 46; slaveholders as, 158–59, 195; social role of, 131; in South, 157–59; training of, 256 (n. 70); women as, 127, 161. *See also* Bar

Lecture circuit, 25, 101, 102, 103, 199

Legal history, 2–12, 64–65, 127, 232–33 (n. 157); and criminal procedure, 16, 54; and judicial power, 19; and libel trial, 46; and religion, 12–15

Legal literacy, 10, 11, 196

Legal profession. *See* Judges/judiciary; Lawyers

Legal reform, 24, 156

Legal spectatorship. *See* Spectatorship, legal

Legal storytelling, 145

Legal treatises: on slavery, 8, 10, 11–12

Leslie, Frank, 274 (n. 56)

"Letter from Wendell Phillips, Esq.," 111

Levine, Robert S., 170, 261 (n. 34), 266 (n. 115)

Lewis, Thomas, 229 (n. 96)

Libel/libel cases: and abolitionists, 1, 8, 40–51 passim, 56, 69, 72, 208; civil, 42, 45, 48, 235–36 (nn. 32, 39); criminal, 43–44, 45, 47, 51, 235–36 (nn. 32, 39); group, 51

Liberator, 8, 44, 51, 55, 67–68, 69, 238 (n. 112), 269 (n. 22)

Life, Trial, and Execution of Capt. John Brown (1859), 211

Lingo v. Miller & Hill (1857), 263 (n. 51)

Literacy: and African Americans, 134, 149, 200; and law, 147–48, 149; legal, 10, 11, 196; and slaves, 147–48. *See also* Print culture

Literature: adaptability of forms of, 221; African American, 6, 94, 127–28, 133, 134, 144, 243 (nn. 20, 22), 261 (n. 34); antislavery, 2, 7, 9, 14, 25, 26–28, 64, 65–66, 69, 138, 151, 152, 154–76, 180, 197; cabin, 178; crime, 5, 80, 81, 85–86, 232 (n. 157), 247 (n. 83); documentary, 136–37; gallows, 5, 74, 78, 97, 232 (n. 157), 248 (n. 150); Holocaust, 136, 256 (nn. 59, 67); multiethnic, 232 (n. 157); nationalist, 68, 179; proslavery, 2, 28, 161, 176–99 passim, 221; as seditious, 42; sentimental fiction, 22, 41, 163, 165, 174–75, 221, 232 (n. 157), 263 (n. 61); Southern, 22, 77, 154, 157–59, 177, 179–82, 218, 221; temperance, 228 (n. 84); testimonial, 136; travel, 228 (n. 83), 229 (n. 100). *See also* Authorship; Readers/reading public; *specific authors*

Litigation: as antislavery vehicle, 6, 7; print as alternative to, 47. *See also* Civil law and litigation; Criminal law and litigation; Trials

Moral sentiments, theory of, 266 (n. 118)

Moral suasion, 18, 130, 153, 169, 173, 201, 212, 249 (n. 13)

Morris, Robert, 126–27, 128–29, 130–31, 137

Morris, Thomas D., 159

Morrison, Toni: *Beloved* (1987), 9, 226 (n. 56)

Morton, Perez, 54

Mott, Frank Luther, 53–54

Mott, Lucretia, 160

Moyamensing Prison, 7

Murder, 222; by antiabolitionist mob, 56–57, 58; of antislavery editor, 41; executions for, 80; and Matthias scandal, 74, 78–98 passim; penny-press coverage of, 54, 85; sensational trials for, 7, 72, 80–81, 240 (n. 134); of slaves, 115–16, 119, 120. *See also* Lynching

Nantucket speech (Douglass), 122

Narratives, 3, 22–24, 105, 134; and advocacy, 149; in Critical Race Theory, 107, 144–45; and interpretation, 147; and law, 145; personal, 137–38. *See also* Slave narratives

National Anti-Slavery Standard, 60, 109, 160, 161

Nationalism, literary, 68, 179

National Police Gazette, 54

Native Americans, 188

Natural law, 133, 195, 257 (n. 94)

Natural rights, 14, 15, 52, 178

Nell, William C., 157

New Jersey, 80

Newman, Judie S., 155, 266 (n. 115)

Newman, Richard S., 5, 138

New Orleans Delta, 177

Newspapers. *See* Press

Newton, John, 5, 265 (n. 107); *Thoughts upon the African Slave Trade* (1788), 260 (n. 11)

New York: antiabolitionist riots, 74, 87; and fugitive slaves, 35, 37, 234 (n. 6); and Matthias scandal, 74, 79–84, 96; and penny-press crime coverage, 53–54; and private executions, 80; and seditious libel case, 46; and slave emancipation, 72, 97–98

New York Atlas, 35, 36–37, 38, 40, 41, 58, 69, 234 (nn. 6, 7)

New York Aurora, 234 (n. 6)

New York Evening Post, 21

New York Halls of Justice, 233 (n. 3)

New York Herald, 54, 148–49, 276 (n. 73)

New York Independent, 155–56

New York Journal, 47

New York Legal Rights Association, 126

New York Manumission Society, 6

New York Star, 11–12

New York Sun, 53, 81, 84, 86, 94

New York Sunday Morning News, 50

New York Transcript, 53

New York Tribune, 66, 67, 218, 219, 275 (n. 58)

New-York Weekly Journal, 46

North: and capitalism, 36, 85, 182–92 passim, 197; and civil liberties, 59, 62, 63, 64, 208, 209, 214, 220; and freedom concept, 189; and free speech rights, 47; and Harpers Ferry case, 201, 211–13; industrialization of, 181, 187, 190; in proslavery and Southern literature, 177–98; and public opinion, 38, 40, 120; and slavery, 8–9, 58, 64, 72, 97–98, 218–20, 234 (n. 16); and unionism, 201. *See also* Abolitionism; Fugitive slaves

North American, 10

North American Review, 81, 88

North Carolina, 51, 155, 156, 163

Northern Star and Freeman's Advocate, 6

North Star, 104

Northup, Solomon: *Twelve Years a Slave* (1853), 17, 144, 170

Novels. *See* Literature

Oberlin College, 127, 128
Oberlin-Wellington Rescue, 9
Observer, 56, 57
O'Connor, William: *Harrington* (1860), 7
Ohio: fugitive slave case in, 160–61; legal community in, 127, 128, 129–30
The Old *"Habeas Corpus"* (song sheet), 10–11
Orality, 30, 31
Oxford Companion to African American Literature, 143

Pamphlets, 22, 69; and African Americans, 5, 6, 138, 139; on Garrison libel case, 44, 45, 46, 47–49; and John Brown case, 211; and law, 4, 8, 9, 11; sensational accounts in, 14, 81; as trial coverage, 5, 8
Parker, Andrew, 217
Parker, Theodore, 272 (n. 2)
Park Street Church, 42–43
Parliament, 4, 5
Partridge, Alden, 7
Paternalism: of Matthias cult, 79, 83; of slaveholders, 119, 159, 162–72 passim, 178, 183, 184, 187, 189, 197, 221; of white abolitionists, 153, 163, 164, 172, 173, 242 (n. 8)
Paulding, James Kirke, 179
Pennington, James W. C., 141
Pennsylvania: first public execution in, 80; slave cases in, 107–9, 122; slave uprising in, 9, 10
Pennsylvania Abolition Society, 6
Pennsylvania Anti-Slavery Society, 108
Penny press/cheap press, 53–56; and abolitionism, 3, 7, 51, 55–56, 238 (n. 112); artisanal republicanism of, 54, 55; and courts, 5, 53–54; and crime coverage, 41, 53–54, 56, 80, 85–86; mass readership of, 81; and private executions, 80; and scandal, 27, 53–54, 72, 80–82, 85–86, 94; and sensationalism, 7, 54–55, 81, 88, 94
Perfectionism, 79

Perjury, 76
Personal liberty laws, 9
Personal testimony. *See* Testimony
Perspectivism, 144
Peterson, Carla L., 157
Petitions, 4, 6, 19, 102, 156, 173; Gag Rule and, 7, 51
Philanthropist, 57
Philip, John, 75
Phillips, Wendell, 66, 112, 140, 145, 160, 166, 181, 208, 212, 220, 264 (n. 80), 275 (n. 57)
Pierpont, John, 9
Pierson, Elijah, 79, 80, 82, 84, 87, 95
Pierson, Emily Catharine, 68; *Jamie Parker, the Fugitive* (1851), 64, 65–66
Plantation novel, 178, 193, 221
Plessy v. Ferguson (1896), 254 (n. 13)
Poe, Edgar Allan, 177, 180; "Mystery of Marie Rôget" (1842–43), 7
Poetry. *See* Literature
Police court, 5, 53–54
Political activism, 173
Popular constitutionalism, 19, 21, 54, 58, 231 (n. 152); and mob violence, 57
Popular legal consciousness, 23, 28–29, 54, 187, 201, 208, 212, 220, 232 (n. 156), 260 (n. 12)
Popular sovereignty, 18–19
Popular tribunal. *See* Public opinion, court of
Porte-Crayon (David Strother), 275 (n. 58)
Positive law: fundamental law versus, 19
Possessive individualism, 14, 189
Postal campaign of 1835, 49–50, 74
Poyas, Peter, 175
Press: African American, 6, 26, 101, 104; as alternative to court of law, 1–3, 46–48, 49, 68–69; antislavery, 2, 8, 9, 41, 42, 55–56, 68, 69, 101; fugitive slave coverage by, 35, 62, 68, 69; judicial hostility to, 45, 48; and legal cases, 5, 7, 10, 28, 30, 45–46, 53–54, 69, 81,

208, 211; mass-circulation, 211; prior
to penny press, 81; republican views
of, 41, 44–48, 54, 55, 56, 138; supervisory function of, 48. *See also* Penny
press/cheap press; Print culture
Press freedom. *See* Freedom of speech/
press
Prigg v. Pennsylvania (1842), 8, 9
Print culture, 1–7, 30, 35–69, 218; and
abolitionism, 1–2, 6, 7, 16–31 passim,
40, 41, 49, 50, 138, 152, 177, 178, 185,
186, 208; and African American eye-
witness accounts, 78, 115, 137; as
alternative tribunal on slavery, 1, 2, 6,
10–12, 22–25, 30–31, 41, 68, 142, 198,
221; Anglo-American, 2–3, 6; changes
in, 27, 41; and civil liberties, 40; and
crime, 80, 81, 85–86; and Harpers
Ferry trial, 199–200, 208, 213–14, 216;
industrialization of, 181, 190, 211, 221;
juridical rhetoric in, 19, 221; and law,
45, 47, 110; and legal literacy, 196; and
legal spectatorship, 5, 7, 9–10, 12, 28,
29, 54, 55, 56, 58, 62, 82, 193, 220;
and legal treatises on slavery, 11–12;
and nonwhite confessions, 77; and oral
texts, 31; and popular legal consciousness, 201; power of, 221–22; proslavery
responses in, 177–78, 182, 218–19,
221, 226 (n. 44). *See also* Freedom of
speech/press; Libel/libel cases; Literature; Pamphlets; Penny press/cheap
press; Press; Readers/reading public
Printing-House Square, 234 (n. 6)
Prisons, 18; courthouses as, 9, 59–64;
executions in, 80
Private sphere. *See* Domesticity; Separate-
spheres ideology
Privy Council's Committee on Trade and
Plantations, 4
Procedural rights, 24. *See also* Due process
Proceedings against William Lloyd Garrison
(1847), 45
Property: "black acre"/"white acre"

designations, 190; property law, 13, 15–
16, 29, 185, 190, 195, 197, 268 (n. 12);
slaves as, 6, 15–16, 28, 64–66, 76–77,
106–7, 111, 112, 114, 117, 134, 143, 154,
159, 178, 189, 221
Prophet Matthias. *See* Matthews, Robert
Proslavery movement: and Constitution,
103, 104; and courtroom imagery, 133;
and judiciary, 41, 56, 57, 58, 66, 68,
208, 213; and law, 11, 42, 47–48, 76,
179; and print propaganda, 218–19, 226
(n. 44); proslavery ideologues, 28, 46,
47, 161, 179; proslavery literature, 2, 28,
161, 176, 177–98, 199, 221; proslavery
rhetoric, 25, 52, 178; proslavery sentimentalism, 185. *See also* Slaveholders;
South
Protestantism. *See* Evangelicalism
Public opinion, court of, 1, 2, 7, 12, 221;
and abolitionists, 18–20, 27, 28, 40,
41, 44, 49, 50, 190, 208, 220; and
black advocates, 122, 131, 138; court
of law superseded by, 41, 81; courts as
alternative to, 19; and due process, 10,
24; extralegal appeals to, 57, 115; and
fugitive slave cases, 60; literary influence on, 174–75; as menace to law and
order, 55; and North, 38, 40, 120; and
penny press, 55; and press freedom,
46, 47–48; and proslavery argument,
196–98; and slaveholders, 17–18, 181–
82, 190, 197; and slavery, 133, 161;
and slave testimony, 73, 109, 112,
120, 166, 220. *See also* Readers/reading
public
Public sphere, 25, 45–46, 53, 221, 243
(n. 20); and popular constitutionalism,
230 (n. 114). *See also* Separate-spheres
ideology
Publishing. *See* Press; Print culture
Punishment; legal, 15; religious, 18. *See
also* Execution
Puritans, 5, 13, 15, 18
Putnam's Monthly Magazine, 175

Sanborn, Franklin, 272 (n. 2)

Sánchez-Eppler, Karen, 88, 111

Sancho, Ignatius: *Letters* (1782), 135

Sand, George, 154

Satire: counternarrative, 144; proslavery, 28, 186–90, 192, 196

Scandals, 97; of legal origin, 53, 72; press coverage of, 27, 53–54, 72, 80–82, 85–86, 94. *See also* Matthias scandal

Scapegoating, 84, 85, 92

Schiller, Dan, 54

Scientific racism, 135

Scott, Dred, 9, 156, 214. See also *Dred Scott v. Sandford*

Scottish Common Sense philosophy, 14, 255 (n. 43)

Scripture. *See* Bible

Searle, George W., 137

Secession, 201

Secret Six, 199. *See also* Brown, John; Harpers Ferry raid

Sectionalism, 181, 215–16, 217, 221, 269 (n. 22)

Sedition, 42, 46, 51, 237 (n. 83)

Sedition Act of 1798, 47

Segregation, 126, 145

Sekora, John, 110

Sensationalism, 213; and abolitionism, 14, 56, 102–3, 138, 186–89; and penny press, 7, 53–55, 72, 81, 88, 94

Sentimentalism: antislavery, 2, 15, 22, 38, 41, 65, 155, 156, 162, 163, 165, 173–75, 192, 201; critical reevaluation of, 153; and fiction genre, 22, 41, 163, 165, 174–75, 221, 232 (n. 157), 263 (n. 61); legal rhetoric as alternative to, 154–56; proslavery, 185

Separate-spheres ideology, 11, 160, 161–62, 261 (n. 19)

Sewall, Samuel (seventeenth century), 15, 25; *The Selling of Joseph* (1700), 3

Sewall, Samuel E. (nineteenth century), 51

Seward, William H., 218, 225 (n. 29)

Sexuality, 13, 80, 81, 82, 83, 85, 86–89, 97, 186

Shadow of law, 23

Sharp, Granville, 6, 229 (n. 96); *A Representation of the Injustice and Dangerous Tendency of Tolerating Slavery* (1769), 4

Shaw, Lemuel, 8, 59–60, 102

Sheriffs, 64–65

Silbey, Susan S., 23

Simms, William Gilmore: *Woodcraft* (1854), 178

Simpson, Orenthal James (O. J.), 120

Sims, Thomas, 9, 59, 60, 62, 63, 64

Sin: blackness associated with, 77; crime as, 13, 14, 15, 228 (n. 86); slavery as, 13, 14, 15, 18, 155

Slander, 72

Slave cases, 107–9, 160

Slave code. *See* Slave law

Slaveholders: as criminals, 1, 12, 14, 15–18, 52, 78, 112, 120, 142, 222; as defendants, 2, 27, 178–79; and group libel, 51; iconography of, 217; as innocent, 195–96; and justice, 120, 209; and law, 3–4, 8–12, 15–16, 151–52, 159; as leisure elite, 180; and natural rights, 14; and paternalism, 119, 159–72 passim, 178, 183, 184, 187, 189, 197, 221; and public opinion, 17–18, 181–82, 190, 197; self-justification by, 165, 197; slave fictional dialogue with, 137–38, 141; testimony against, 78, 97, 109. *See also* Insurrection; Proslavery movement

Slave law, 15, 58, 75, 76, 112, 117, 151–52, 167, 193, 208; Douglass's *Cambria* reading of, 125, 146–49; Stowe's trilogy on, 154, 155, 162, 166

Slave narratives, 12, 14, 25, 78, 97, 109–23, 138, 139, 221; authenticating documents in, 95, 98, 139, 144, 157–58; and black advocacy, 138–39; and crime literature, 78; and forensic images, 110; reader response to, 110, 163; as testimony, 2, 74, 78, 98, 105, 107, 109–10,

143-44, 168, 170, 188; white corroboration of, 91, 94-95, 96, 98, 145, 153, 157, 158, 163. *See also specific narratives*

Slave Power, 40, 41, 48, 57, 58, 62, 64, 68, 210, 214, 218-19, 234-35 (n. 16)

Slavery: abolitionist definition of, 190; and antijudicial sentiment, 21-22; and capitalism, 182; as civil/property matter, 6, 15, 190, 191, 195, 196-97, 221; congressional debates over, 50, 51, 155, 156, 173; as crime, 1, 7, 12-18, 24, 30, 69, 178-79, 190, 222; and due process, 58, 220; and English law, 4; and federal law, 6-2, 208; and Gag Rule, 51; iconography of, 35-36, 38, 41, 187; idealization of, 183; juridical metaphor of, 1-2, 3, 12-15, 16, 17, 22, 24-25, 26, 27, 29, 30, 40, 105, 121, 123, 133, 152, 161, 165, 174, 178, 190, 193, 208, 220-22, 231 (n. 151); legal crises of, 7-12, 156; legal status of, 68; literary portrayals of, 26-27, 65-66, 153-76, 181, 183-84; as man-stealing, 12-15; master-slave dialogue over, 137-38; metaphors for, 65, 228 (n. 86); and paternalism, 119, 159-72 passim, 178, 183, 184, 189, 197; print debates over, 22-24, 68-69; and public opinion, 133; revisionist history of, 182; as sin, 13, 14, 15, 18, 155; and state law, 6, 8, 9, 11-12, 15, 40, 50, 58, 134, 151-52, 154-55, 156, 159, 163; and U.S. law, 1, 7, 22, 24, 57, 107-9, 172, 174, 232 (n. 157); and wage labor, 181, 182, 183, 184, 189, 192, 197, 270 (n. 42). *See also* Abolitionism; Fugitive Slave Law of 1793; Fugitive Slave Law of 1850; Slaveholders; Slave trade; South

Slaves: as chattel/property, 6, 15-16, 28, 64-66, 76-77, 106-7, 111, 112, 114, 117, 134, 143, 154, 159, 178, 189, 221; confessional speech of, 72-73; corporeality of, 111, 114, 118, 186-90, 248-49

(n. 150); court's role in sale of, 64-66; as criminals, 56, 73, 74, 77, 133, 134, 141, 159; dehumanization of, 8, 145; double character of, 77, 106-7, 117; emancipation of, 72, 104, 105, 138, 149, 162, 191; humanity of, 165; interstate transit of, 8, 107; invisibility of, 94, 120; and literacy, 147-48; presumed inferiority of, 133, 165; sale of, 41, 65; sexualized brutality against, 88; silence of, 111-20; as spectacles, 187-88; stereotypes of, 106, 133, 138, 155, 165; veracity of, 96, 121; as victims, 1, 88, 91, 92, 97-98, 110-22 passim, 136, 153, 186-87, 194; Wedgwood image of, 35-36; and white advocacy, 151-76, 196; as witnesses, 1-2, 4-5, 14, 17, 23-24, 27, 69, 72, 74, 75-77, 78, 97, 102, 103, 105, 106, 110-18, 120-22, 126, 134, 136, 138, 139, 143, 153, 154, 170-71, 174, 176, 187-88, 220. *See also* Fugitive slaves; Slave narratives

Slave trade: and Britain, 184; domestic, 41-42, 43, 64-66; and Middle Passage, 4, 253 (n. 2); witnessed accounts of, 4, 14, 18

Slave uprisings. *See* Insurrection

Smith, Gerrit, 160, 218, 219, 272 (n. 2)

Smith, James McCune, 26, 140, 141, 272 (n. 2); and *My Bondage and My Freedom*, 126, 139

Smith, Rogers M., 29

Social contract, 15, 195

Society for the Abolition of the Slave Trade: London Committee, 4; Wedgwood seal, 35-36

Somerset v. Stewart (1772), 4, 9

Songs, slave, 144

South: and abolitionism, 13-14, 49, 50, 51, 52, 162, 177, 184; in abolitionist literature, 64; and agrarianism, 178, 179, 181; authors in, 179-82; and civil liberties, 210, 215; and economic interests,

36, 189; and elitism, 180, 184, 222; and Harpers Ferry raid, 201, 210–11, 214–15, 217, 220; and honor, 178, 181, 184, 185, 217, 268 (nn. 12, 13); and justice, 45, 48, 64, 65, 75, 208, 209, 212, 217; and law, 11–12, 15, 50, 64, 112, 117, 125, 146–48, 152, 154, 163, 166–67; legal profession in, 11, 158–59, 195; literature of, 77, 154, 157–59, 177, 179–82, 218, 221; and Northern economic interests, 36, 184; and popular legal consciousness, 23, 28–29, 54, 187, 201, 208, 212, 220, 232 (n. 156), 260 (n. 12); and print culture, 48, 49, 218; and racism, 146; and repression, 216, 218; and secession, 201; and segregation, 126, 145; and silence, 112–13, 115–16, 117, 119; views of British in, 184; and violence, 49, 74, 111–21 passim, 162, 209, 215, 216, 217, 218, 220. *See also* Proslavery movement; Slaveholders; Slavery; Slaves

Southampton rebellion, 8

South Carolina, 74, 151; Charleston riot, 49, 64; slave antiliteracy law, 147–48

Souther, Simon, 262 (n. 42)

Southern Literary Messenger, 177, 179–82, 185, 271 (n. 82)

Souther v. Commonwealth (1851), 156, 265 (n. 105)

Southwick, Joseph, 237 (n. 84)

Sparf and Hansen v. United States (1895), 20, 262 (n. 42)

Spectatorship, legal, 5, 7, 9–10, 12, 28, 29, 54–56, 58, 193, 220; abolitionist appeal to, 185, 197, 209, 212; denial of, 61–62; and press reports, 5, 7, 9–10, 12, 28, 29, 54, 55, 56, 62, 82, 220

Speech, freedom of. *See* Freedom of speech/press

Spooner, Lysander, 225 (n. 29); *Essay on the Trial by Jury* (1852), 21

State law, 6, 8, 9, 11–12, 40, 58, 134, 151–52, 154–55, 156, 159, 163; against abolitionist print materials, 50; against seditious literature, 42; slavery's protection under, 15. *See also* Slave law

States' rights, 8, 36

State v. Castleman (1851), 156, 265 (n. 105)

State v. Mann (1829), 155, 163

Stearns, George, 272 (n. 2)

Stepto, Robert B., 170, 261 (n. 34)

Sterne, Lawrence, 264 (n. 79)

Stevens, Aaron, 201, 209, 217

Stewart, Maria, 6

Still, William, 107, 122

Stone, Lucy, 66, 161

Stone, William Leete, 74, 79, 89, 91, 92; *Commercial Advertiser*, 81, 87–88; *Matthias and His Impostures* (1835), 74, 81, 82–83, 84, 88, 89–90, 91, 92

Story, Joseph, 140, 141

Storytelling. *See* Critical Race Theory; Narratives

Stowe, Calvin, 161–62

Stowe, Charley, 154

Stowe, Harriet Beecher, 68, 90, 97, 152–75, 176, 180, 197, 225 (n. 29); and advertisements, 11; as advocate for slaves, 65–66, 155–56, 157, 169–70, 220–21; and anti-Tom literature, 28, 268 (nn. 7, 11), 270 (nn. 42, 46); "An Appeal to the Women of the Free States" (1854), 155–56; criticism of works of, 161, 173, 177–78, 260 (n. 11); *Dred* (1856), 7, 12, 21, 27–28, 152–78 passim, 183; German translation of works of, 161–62; illustrations in works of, 38, 41; *Key to Uncle Tom's Cabin* (1853), 11, 12, 17, 75, 151–52, 153, 155, 156, 157, 162–63, 165, 170; and law, 12, 27, 154, 155, 160, 162, 172–73; proslavery and Southern responses to, 161, 177, 180, 185; and sentimental fiction, 2, 155, 156, 162, 163, 165, 173, 174–75; and separate-spheres ideology, 161–62, 261 (n. 19)

"Sojourner Truth, the Libyan Sybil"
(1863), 72, 97–98; *Uncle Tom's Cabin*
(1852), 7, 17, 21, 27, 38, 65, 151, 153,
154–56, 157, 169, 170, 172, 173, 174–75,
234 (n. 15); worldwide success of, 180

Strother, David, 275 (n. 58)

Stroud, George M., 11, 12; *Sketch of the
Laws*, 11, 75, 147–48, 155, 156; *Sketch of
the Laws* (German translation), 11

Suffrage, 30, 55, 127, 149

Sumner, Charles, 155

Sundquist, Eric J., 132

Supreme Court. *See* U.S. Supreme Court

Taney, Roger B., 214, 261 (n. 30)

Tappan, Arthur, 51, 79, 185, 192, 225
(n. 29), 235 (n. 32)

Tappan, Lewis, 51, 79, 87, 185, 192, 225
(n. 29)

Taylor, Robert, 63

Temperance movement, 228 (n. 84)

Testimonial literature, 136

Testimony, 71–98; abolitionist, 18–19,
160; admissibility of, 37, 75, 92, 105–
12, 120, 121, 152, 163, 166; and African
American corporeality, 111, 112, 121–
22; and African American experience,
145–49, 170; of African American
eyewitnesses, 10, 74–75, 77–78, 110,
122, 126, 137, 145; and African American vernacular, 72; and authority, 97;
black advocacy versus, 105, 143; and
confession, 72, 77, 78, 168; corroborative, 17, 94–95, 97, 98; credibility of,
78, 107, 109; evangelical, 14, 72; and
Judeo-Christian oath, 75; legal, 24, 75;
nonwhite, 75–76, 77, 91, 92, 94–95,
97, 98, 102, 112; and racial ideology,
92; as rhetorical strategy, 14, 16–17, 41,
71, 110, 137, 143; slave, 1, 4–5, 12, 14,
75–76, 109–23, 126, 131, 134, 143, 144,
152–53, 154, 162, 163, 166, 167, 172,
196, 220; witnesses' gap with, 116, 119.
See also Confession; Witnesses

Thompson, George, 264 (n. 80)

Thompson, William, 209, 217

Thoreau, Henry David, 66–68, 71, 211–12,
225 (n. 29); "Slavery in Massachusetts"
(1854), 41, 66–68

Tilden, Daniel R., 273–74 (n. 29)

Titus, Frances, 242 (n. 8)

Tocqueville, Alexis de, 23, 26

Todd, Francis, 41, 42; libel suits of, 43,
44, 48, 235–36 (nn. 32, 39)

Tombs, 233 (n. 3)

Townsend, Joseph B., 108

Transcendentalism, 179–80

Treason: antislavery activity construed as,
50–51, 199; and Christiana uprising, 9,
10; and Harpers Ferry raid, 1, 28, 200,
201–3, 209. *See also* Sedition

Treatise on the Law and Practice of Juries
(1826), 20

Trial by jury. *See* Due process; Jury

Trials: of abolitionists, 1, 2, 7–10, 28, 69,
156, 200, 201–8, 209; and invisibility,
120; and legal spectatorship, 28, 81,
197, 209, 212; literary portrayals of, 5;
and mass culture, 53, 81; as metaphors,
24, 26, 177–79, 182–98; pamphlet reports of, 5, 8; personae of, 16, 25; press
coverage of, 5, 7, 10, 28, 30, 45–46,
53–54, 69, 81, 208, 211; procedures of,
193; proslavery allegorical parody of,
177–79, 182–98, 208, 221; sensational,
7, 53–54, 72, 81, 208, 212, 220; transcripts of, 30. *See also* Criminal law and
litigation; Due process; Juridical rhe-
toric/metaphor; Jury; Libel/libel cases;
Litigation

True womanhood, 161–62

Truth, Sojourner, 27, 31, 71, 72, 74, 78–
98, 261 (n. 34), 262 (n. 42); alternate
names of, 72, 98; as criminal, 74, 89,
90; *Fanaticism* (1835), 81–82, 83, 84, 91–
97, 98; and Gilbert Vale, 74, 78, 79,
81–82, 90–91, 96–97, 101; and law, 72,
75, 90, 242–43 (n. 15); libel suit by,

72; and Matthias scandal, 74, 78–98
passim; and Moncure Daniel Conway,
71, 72; *Narrative* (1850), 98, 242 (n. 8);
and Olive Gilbert, 72, 97–98; portrayals
of, 71, 92–93, 97–98; as slave, 71; and
"Sojourner Truth, the Libyan Sybil," 71,
97–98; speeches of, 66, 71; and Stowe,
72; and testimony, 90, 94–95; trial of, 2

Tukey, Francis, 61

Turner, Nat, 162, 262 (n. 42), 263 (n. 44);
Confessions (1831), 8, 77, 157–59; execution of, 1; trial of, 8, 156; uprising of,
51, 269 (n. 22)

Twain, Mark: *The Adventures of Huckleberry
Finn* (1884), 187

Uncle Tom in England (1852), 260 (n. 12)

Unionism, 201, 215, 216, 217

Unionist, 8

University of Virginia, 177, 180

U.S. Congress, 50, 155, 156, 173; first
African American members of, 127, 254
(n. 13); and Gag Rule, 51

U.S. Constitution. *See* Constitution, U.S.

U.S. Supreme Court, 8, 20, 103, 156, 214

Utica (N.Y.) riot, 237 (n. 83)

Vale, Gilbert, 74, 78, 79, 81–82, 96, 98;
Fanaticism (1835), 74, 81–82, 83, 84, 89,
90–98, 101

Van Evrie, John H.: *Negroes and Negro
"Slavery"* (1853), 177

Van Wagenen, Isabella. *See* Truth, Sojourner

Vesey, Denmark, 156, 162, 175, 258
(n. 112), 262 (n. 42)

Violence: antiabolitionist, 41, 49, 51,
56–58, 209; Southern, 49, 74, 111–14,
117–21, 162, 209, 215–18, 220; witnessing of, 111–14. *See also* Insurrection;
Lynching; Mobs; Murder; Riots

Virginia: and due process, 210–11, 212;
Guide to Magistrates, 50; and nonwhite
testimony, 75–76, 77; and racialized
traits, 134; and slave antiliteracy law,
148; and slave law, 156; slavery debate
in, 7. *See also* Harpers Ferry raid

Virginia Patriot, 177

Voting rights. *See* Suffrage

Voyeurism. *See* Spectatorship, legal

Wage labor, 181, 182, 183, 184, 189, 192,
197, 270 (n. 42)

Wager House Hotel, 209

Walker, David, 6, 18, 126, 254 (n. 10);
Appeal (1829), 42, 51, 138, 269 (n. 22)

Walker, Edwin Garrison, 129

War, 197–98, 228 (n. 86)

Ward, Samuel Ringgold, 141

Warner, Michael, 46

War of 1812, 184, 198

Washington (D.C.) seditious libel trial, 51

Washingtonian temperance narrative, 228
(n. 84)

Watson, Esquire, 119–20, 121, 145

Watson, Henry: *Narrative* (1848), 109

Webb, James Watson, 87

Webster, Daniel, 42, 43, 194

Webster-Parkman murder case, 240
(n. 134)

Wedgwood, Josiah: antislavery seal,
35–36

Weekly Advocate, 6

Weisenburger, Steven, 161

Weld, Theodore Dwight, 2, 160, 161, 171,
174, 225 (n. 29); *American Slavery as It Is*
(1839), 14

Wells, Daniel, 60, 61

Western, Henry B., 90, 98

Wheatley, Phillis: *Poems* (1773), 95

Wheeler, Jacob D.: *Practical Treatise* (1837),
11–12

Wheeler, John H., 107, 108, 122

Whig Party, 21

White, Joseph, 238 (n. 103)

White acre, 190

Whitman, Walt, 212

Whitney, Lisa, 156